CHARLES COUNTY GENTRY

Colonel James Noble Edelin, U.S.M.C.
1790-1869

Four times Commandant of Marine Barracks, Washington

CHARLES COUNTY GENTRY

A Genealogical History of Six
Emigrants — Thomas Dent, John
Dent, Richard Edelen, John Hanson, George Newman, Humphrey
Warren. All Scions of Armorial
Families of Old England who settled in Charles County, Maryland,
and their descendants showing mi-
grations to the South and West

by

HARRY WRIGHT NEWMAN

CLEARFIELD

Originally Published
Washington, 1940

Reprinted
Genealogical Publishing Company
Baltimore, 1971

Reprinted for
Clearfield Company, Inc. by
Genealogical Publishing Co., Inc.
Baltimore, Maryland
1990, 1997, 2002

Library of Congress Catalog Card Number 75-88098
International Standard Book Number 0-8063-0486-3

FOREWORD

A HOBBY is always an indulgence. But it is hoped that the interest which I have found in the genealogy of the early Maryland families, especially those of my own ancestry, and their ultimate publication have not proved too great an indulgence upon the public. Each successive publication has brought its disappointments, but also a few invisible compensations. Much has been learned since the publication of my first adventure in 1933, yet a genealogist is never infallible or invulnerable, and while it has been the desire to make these chronicles as perfect as possible, yet there are always the limitations of the human mind.

HARRY WRIGHT NEWMAN,
1701 H Street Northwest,
Washington, D. C.

TABLE OF CONTENTS

Dent

DENT FAMILY

PERHAPS no family of Southern Maryland is better known than the Dent which in the formative days of the Province produced some of the most prominent and outstanding colonial subjects of Lord Baltimore and the Crown. Like many old families of St. Mary's and Charles Counties, the descendants are residents of Southern Maryland today and are for the most part carrying on the tradition and culture of the earlier generations. Many, however, have migrated—some to the more southern States while others early in the nineteenth century felt the impulse of the westward movement and as a consequence their progeny are now scattered over a number of the near and far western States. Frederick Dent, of Missouri, the father of Mrs. U. S. Grant, was the son of a Maryland landed proprietor who laid out the town of Cumberland on the upper Potomac.

The early members were conspicuous for their public services, many holding high rank in the military forces of the Province. Several have been Members of Congress, but it has perhaps been in civil and judicial rôles that they have excelled most. During the colonial days the magisterial offices of Southern Maryland were continuously held by members of this family.

These chronicles deal with Thomas Dent and John Dent, presumably kinsmen, but many bearing that name emigrated early to Maryland as well as other British Colonies in America. It can be said, however, that the descendants of Thomas and John eclipsed all branches and with few exceptions they were the only ones who left behind tradition and a recorded history of their activities in war and peace.

In Overwharton Parish of Stafford County, Virginia, one finds an Arthur Dent marrying Elizabeth Manuel on December 11, 1742, and a list of their children's births. Contemporary with Arthur was Anne Dent who married William Black on October 17, 1745. To date these Dents have not been proved as descendants of Thomas or John Dent of Maryland.

In 1658 William Poll received 50 acres of land for the transportation of Edward Dent,[1] and in the same year Thomas Bradley assigned his land rights to Daniel Jenifer by virtue of bringing-in Charles Dent.[2] In 1674 John Pawson, merchant, of Anne Arundel County, proved his rights to land for "bringing into the Province to inhabit" Rachel Dent and William Dent.[3] In 1676 Edward Dawson, of Calvert County, assigned his rights to 50 acres of land to Captain Philemon Lloyd for transporting another William Dent.[4] Then there was also Abigail Dent who by 1677 had been transported by John Harris, mariner.[5]

The subsequent history of these Dent transportees except one William Dent or Dant fades into obscurity and thus fails to record whether they died without issue or removed to other parts.

William Dant of St. Mary's County in 1659 patented "Hopewell". It was either he or his son who married Mary Shirtcliffe, daughter of John and Anne (Spinke) Shirtcliffe, of St. Mary's, and who has been claimed erroneously to be the wife and then widow of Captain John Dent of Chaptico. The tract "Hopewell" was later held by John Dant as his dwelling-plantation who in 1763 willed it to his son John Baptist Dant (sometimes spelled Dent). Other heirs were his daughter Anne Spalding, son-in-law Edward Spalding, daughter Mary Anne Dant, daughter Mary Mills, wife Eleanor Dant, and sons Charles and Joseph who received equalled portions of "West Filled", and son Francis.[6] Prior to this date there is a will of William Dantt proved in 1715 at St. Mary's, naming cousins John Dant and William Mills who received "Popular Neck" and "Annstroder"; brother Peter Mills; and cousin Eleanor Nevet.[7]

From circumstances it is concluded that this family was of the Roman Catholic faith, while Thomas and John Dent were staunch supporters of the Church of England. The spelling of Dant later became Dent and at times has added to some confusion in the history of the two families. Several lines after the Revolution which have difficulty in connecting with those of Thomas and John are perchance of this Dant family.

On March 26, 1663, "Thomas Dent, Gent., enters his rights *viz*. John Dent, John Winne, Constant Stephenson, George Athley, John Venable, and Thomas Dent, himself . . ." for land due him, therefore the Surveyor General issued a warrant "to lay out for Thomas Dent 300 acres return 30 September next".[8]

On May 26, 1673, he appeared at the Land Office in St. Mary's City and proved rights to additional land. "Came Thomas Dent of St. Marie's County, Gent., and proved his rights to 600 acres, it being due to him for transporting Jerman Shyn, John Moderman, John Akers, John James, William Rutter, Charles Wheeler, Edward Crouch, Mary Evans, Sarah Case, Ann Ffetherston, Elizabeth Danset, and John Dent into the Province to inhabit".[9]

It is noted that he twice proved headrights for a John Dent. It seems reasonable to believe that both were for the one and the same man. Settlers returning to England for a temporary period were not infrequent. Anyhow one was certainly the Captain John Dent who later appeared as an important personage in St. Mary's County.

It is claimed that Thomas Dent and John Dent were brothers, yet no facts in the archives of Maryland have been unearthed to indicate blood relationship. The two lived separate lives in the Province and were not connected in business nor were there any early matrimonial alliances between the two families—marrying of cousins frequently occurred in Maryland.

Much has been written regarding the English background, most of which seems to bear some credence. There is a market town on the banks of the River Dee in West Riding of Yorkshire called Dent, and it is generally believed that the family derived its name from this town. About 1318 Willielmus filius Roberti de Dent deeded land in the village of Wertherny for the use of the Knight Templars. It later reverted to the Dent family and according to the Historical and Archaeological Journal of Yorkshire (1889) was still held by descendants. A list of freemen of Yorkshire in 1365 records the name of Willielmus de Dente, parchemener.[10]

The fact that Judge Thomas Dent came from Gisborough in Yorkshire is authenticated. One of his land patents was given the name of "Gisborough", it being characteristic of the Maryland gentry to name their plantations after the ancestral estates in Old England. Gisborough is a town and parish situated in North Riding about six miles northwest of Ormsby, the more ancient estates of the forbears of Thomas Dent.

The proving of the English parentage of American settlers is most difficult, and through the unscrupulousness of early as well as some modern genealogists, many flagrant errors have been made. It can be stated, however, that the parents of Thomas Dent have been proved with absolute certainty. The following was recorded in 1684 by Peter Dent, naturalist and professor of Cambridge University, and is in the Herald's College, London, under Cambridgeshire pedigrees:

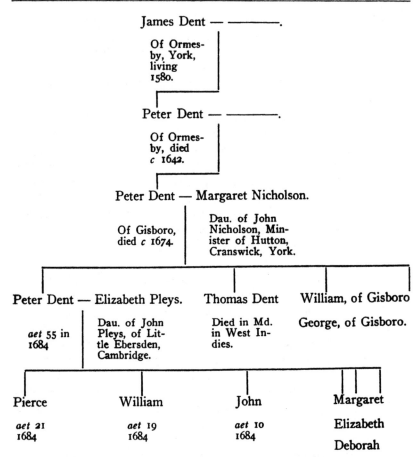

In the above pedigree one sees unmistakably names common to the early generations of the Dents in Maryland. It is noted that Thomas Dent "Died in Maryland in the West Indies". The popular conception of geography in seventeenth century England was somewhat distorted. Humphry Warren was recorded in the private papers of his illustrious family as having died in the West Indies, when it is known that he was a prominent subject of the Calverts and died in Maryland. When Cabot discovered the North American continent, he named it Virginia and for sometime, even after the settlement of the individual colonies, the country was referred to in English records as Virginia. There are notations in several visitations where a member of the family "went to Virginia", when it has been proved that he settled in New England.

James Dent, the last known ancestor of the American emigrant, was closely related to Roger Dente, of Newcastell, who used the same coat-of-arms as the Dents of Ormesby. Roger Dente was born *circa* 1500 and could possibly be the grandfather of James of Ormesby. Roger Dente married Anne, daughter of Sir Roger Fenwycke, of Wallyington and Mydelton, an old family of Northumberland whose escapades with and against the Dukes of Northumberland made very thrilling history when the Percys and other border families were opposing the English kings.

Roger Dente and Anne Fenwyck his wife had — George, Rawfe, Thomas, William, George II, Robert, Richard, and Katherine. It was William Dent, the fourth son, who had his pedigree recorded at the Visitation of Yorkshire in 1561. He was Sheriff of Newcastell and Mayor in 1562, and by 1548 he had purchased considerable monastic possessions in Newcastell, Bourbe, and other places. In 1582 he and his son William conveyed the priory of St. Michael de Wall Knoll to trustees for the corporation of that town.

The following shows the maternal descent from Sir John Fenwick, Knt., Lord of Wallington, a contemporary of Henry VIII:

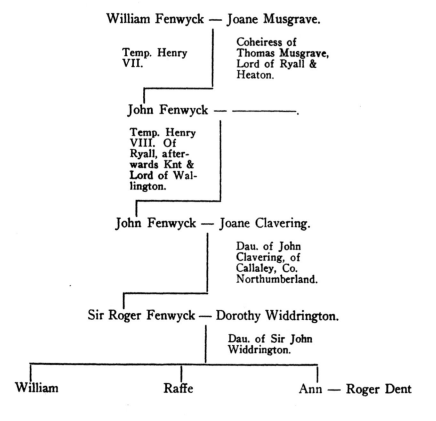

William Fenwyck — Joane Musgrave.

Temp. Henry VII.

Coheiress of Thomas Musgrave, Lord of Ryall & Heaton.

John Fenwyck — ——————.

Temp. Henry VIII. Of Ryall, afterwards Knt & Lord of Wallington.

John Fenwyck — Joane Clavering.

Dau. of John Clavering, of Callaley, Co. Northumberland.

Sir Roger Fenwyck — Dorothy Widdrington.

Dau. of Sir John Widdrington.

William   Raffe   Ann — Roger Dent

The arms used by the Maryland Dents is the same as used by Roger Dent, of New Castell, described as "Or on a blend, sable three lozenges erminois". This arms with certain quarterings is used by the present Dents of Ribston Hall, Yorkshire, and Winterton, Lincolnshire. In the past as well as the present the family is connected through marriage with some of the older houses of nobility. Henry Dent, of Middlethrope Manor, Yorkshire, married in 1881 Marion Lascelles, the granddaughter of the Third Earl of Harewood.

Colonel William Dent, son of Thomas the Emigrant, willed a silver bowl with "the family coat-of-arms thereon" to his eldest son Thomas. It is therefore proved conclusively that the Dents of Maryland were an armorial family and that their rights to bear arms are unquestionable.

---

[1] Liber Q no. 2, folio 69, Land Office, Annapolis.
[2] Liber 7, folio 464.
[3] Liber 18, folio 331.
[4] Liber 15, folios 363, 443.
[5] *Ibid.*, folio 430.
[6] Wills, Liber 31, folio 1048.
[7] *Ibid.*, folio 221.
[8] Liber 5, folio 245.
[9] Liber 17, folio 448.
[10] Surtees Society, vol. 96, p. 99.

THOMAS DENT, GENT.[1]

(1630-1676)

Thomas Dent was born about 1630 in the Parish of Guisborough, Yorkshire, making him slightly less than thirty years of age upon his arrival in America. It was not so very long after his landing in Maryland that he wedded Rebecca, the Virginia born daughter of the Rev. William Wilkinson and Naomi his wife.

The Rev. Mr. Wilkinson is distinguished for being the first Anglican clergyman in Maryland, although services of the Church of England had been read by laymen from the beginning. He was the son of the Rev. Gabriel Wilkinson, born 1576, in Yorkshire, a graduate of Merton College, Oxford, and vicar of Wooburn, Buckinghamshire, until his death on December 17, 1658. William, the son, was born 1612, entered Magdalen College at fourteen, and received his master of arts in 1632. Within three years he had married and settled in the New World.

On November 20, 1635, William Wilkinson, Minister, received 700 acres of land at "Linhaven, commonly known Chisopeian river, west on Thomas Keeling and Georg Downes, south unto the woods, eastwardly along the creek being opposite to Captain Adam Thorrogoods plantation in Lynhaven and north upon Chisopeian bay". Two hundred acres were due by assignment, 50 acres for his own personal adventure, 150 acres for the transportation of three servants, 100 acres for his own personal adventure of himself and wife Naomy Wilkinson, and 400 acres for the transportation of 8 persons.[1]

On June 21, 1644, "William Wilkinson, Minister of the word of God", received by grant 100 acres in Elizabeth City County, in or near Buckerowe, by assignment of headrights from Henry Herrick and Anne his wife in 1643. It is probable that he later lived on this tract which adjoined a plantation of 700 acres held by Madame Elizabeth Claiborne "wife of William Claiborne, His Majesty's Treasurer of this colony of Virginia".[2]

After a residence of some 15 years in Virginia during which time he buried his wife Naomi and married the Widow Budden with a daughter Elizabeth, he settled in Maryland. On October 10, 1650, he applied to his Lordship's Land Office at St. Mary's for 900 acres of land, his rights for his own personal adventure and for the transportation of his three daughters Mary, Rebecca, and Elizabeth, his wife and her daughter, and three servants—William Warren, Robert Cornish, and Anne Stevens.

He died testate in 1663 and bequeathed property to his step-daughter Elizabeth Budden and his grandsons William Dent and William Hatton. The residue of the estate was to be divided equally between his sons-in-law, Thomas Dent and William Hatton.[3]

On February 4, 1673, Thomas Dent, Gent., appeared before the Prerogative Court and showed that William Wilkinson, Clerke, executed his will before his death and named him and William Hatton as the executors. He furthermore proved to the satisfaction of the court that they had cared for Elizabeth Budden for several years who recently died intestate, and thus requested letters of administration upon her estate.[4]

Children of Thomas and Rebecca (Wilkinson) Dent

1. William Dent married Elizabeth Fowke. *q.v.*
2. Thomas Dent married Anne Bayne. *q.v.*
3. Peter Dent married Jane Pittman Gray. *q.v.*
4. George Dent, *d.s.p.* before 1702.
5. Margaret married May 26, 1681, Edmund Howard. Issue: Rebecca born and died 1683; William Stevens born Nov. 3, 1684; George born Mar. 18, 1686; Thomas born Sept. 5, 1690; Edmund born Aug. 30, 1695; John; and Elizabeth.
6. Barbara Dent married Thomas, son of Thomas and Eleanor (Hatton) Brooke. Issue: Nathaniel; John; Benjamin; Baker; Thomas; Jane; Rebecca; Mary; Elizabeth; Lucy.

Thomas Dent established his residence in St. Mary's County, where most of his children were born and spent their childhood. He became one of the first aldermen of St. Mary's City, and an acre of land was patented to him by the name of "The Lawyer's Lodging", which is indicative of his profession, although he was also engaged in mercantile pursuits, and the cultivation of the soil. The record shows that prior to the patent of this lot which was on Aldermansbury Street, of which not a vestige now remains, Thomas Dent had built upon it and was a next door neighbor to Governor Thomas Notley.

On September 4, 1663, Thomas Dent was issued a warrant for 850 acres of land patented under the name of "Gisborough", lying on the east side of the Anacostia River in a branch of the said river called Eastern Branch in Charles County standing by a little bay called Gisborough Bay.

On September 27, 1666, a commission was issued to Thomas Dent by the Prerogative Court to swear Sarah Frissell, the relict and administratrix of Alexander Frissell, late of Herring Creek, St. Mary's County, and also to swear Robert Cager and Stamp Roberts, the appraisers of the estate. At the same court he was ordered to swear William Cote and Thomas Griffin as the appraisers of the estate of

Joseph Edloe. He also swore John Waghop and William Watts, the appraisers of the estate of Robert Cager in 1666, and Richard Bankers, the appraiser of John Lawson's estate.

On April 13, 1675, Thomas Dent appeared in court and stated that William Ditton, Merchant, on his voyage from England fell sick and shortly after his arrival in the Patuxent River died at the home of Richard Keene of the Patuxent "that afore he died he declared his will in these words or to this effect that Captain Leonard Webber the commissioner of the ship Golden Lyon that the said Ditton came from England and that his clothes, goods, and bills of lading should be put into the hands of Thomas Dent in St. Mary's County and he to give amount thereof to Mr. Edward Lassells, of London, Merchant". Letters of administration upon the estate were subsequently granted to Thomas Dent.

By virtue of a warrant dated March 20, 1671, from the Secretary Office, Richard Edelen, Deputy Surveyor, stated that he had laid out for William Hatton and Thomas Dent a tract of land called "Brothers' Joint Interest" lying in Charles County in the woods above Piscataway.

Thomas Dent was appointed in 1664 High Sheriff of St. Mary's and a justice of the county court. On August 19, 1668, he as Thomas Dent, Gent., of the Quorum, was appointed a Commissioner of the Peace. He represented his county at the General Assembly in 1669, 1674, 1675, and perhaps other years.

He felt keenly his duty as an able-bodied subject of His Lordship to protect the Province and his property, and became engaged in the early conflicts with the Indians. The Council on February 8, 1667, commissioned him and Robert Slye to "secure 28 barrels of corn and 4,000 weight of meat out of St. Marie's County", as subsistence for the colonial forces which were to embark upon an Indian campaign.[5]

The Council on September 6, 1676, entrusted Thomas Dent with a letter to Colonel John Washington and Isaac Allerton of Virginia, advising the Virginia Colony that Maryland would raise five troops of men with sufficient horses, arms, and ammunition to aid in an expedition against the Susquehanna Indians. He returned within a short time from his diplomatic mission to Virginia and in November 1676, he was appointed by the Council on the commission to equip and organize the militia of St. Mary's County in anticipation of the expedition.[6]

Thomas Dent died at his seat in St. Mary's County. His will, dated March 28, 1676, was admitted to probate on April 21, 1676, by William Hatton and William Harper. He named his wife Rebecca as executrix and devised her land at Port Tobacco Clifts in Charles County. William received "Westbury Manor" and a portion of the land on the Nanjemoy in Charles County. Thomas was devised the residue of the land at Nanjemoy, while Peter and George were willed equally "Gisborough" and "Brother's Joint Interest". Margaret received one acre of land in St. Mary's County.[7]

No mention was made of an unborn child in his will, however, sometime after his death his widow gave birth to a daughter who was given the name of Barbara.

Rebecca Dent, the widow and executrix, exhibited his will at the Prerogative Court on September 9, 1676, thereupon the Deputy Commissary ordered William Hatton and William Harper to appraise the estate in St. Mary's County, and Nicholas Proddy and John Ward to appraise the estate in Charles County. She also requested the commissary to take the oath of Captain Leonard Webber regarding the estate of Ditton. At the same court William Hatton stated that Thomas Dent was supposed to have sworn the appraisers of the estate of Richard Hatton but he died before the oaths were administered. The estate of Thomas Dent was appraised at 44,019 pounds of tobacco.

By May 21, 1677, the widow had married Colonel John Addison of Charles County, and as the "relict and executrix of Thomas Dent" who was the executor of Henry Hull, Gent., deceased, exhibited the inventory of the latter's estate. On October 19, 1677, she requested the commissary to allow her more time before filing an account upon her deceased husband's estate "time for her husband John Addison to return to the Province".

Sometime after 1694 Colonel John Addison returned to England and there he died presumably intestate, leaving a widow and son in America.

It is concluded that the marriage of the Widow Dent to the Bachelor Addison, then nearly fifty, alienated the Dent children, save Barbara, from their mother. It is known that John Addison profited materially by this marriage and obtained a great deal of the estate of Thomas Dent. Furthermore, Rebecca Dent-Addison mentioned none of her Dent children except Barbara in her will, and it is also noted that none of the Dent children ever referred to their half-brother Thomas Addison.

Rebecca Dent-Addison signed her will on November 4, 1724, the latter being probated in Prince Georges County on August 20, 1726. She bequeathed her son, Colonel Thomas Addison, £20, and her grandchildren Lucy, Baker, and Thomas, the children of her daughter Barbara, the wife of Thomas Brooke, each £200. In the event that they died then to her grandson Benjamin Brooke. She named her daughter Barbara, the executrix, and devised her the residue of the estate. The witnesses were Alexander Contee, John Howard, and Mary Delihunt.[8]

[1] Patent Book no. 1, pt. 1, pp. 315, 405, Richmond.
[2] Patent Book no. 2. p. 82.
[3] Wills, Liber 1, folio 190.
[4] Test. Pro., Liber 6, folio 79.
[5] Archives, vol. 5, pp. 22, 23.
[6] *Ibid.*, vol. 15, pp. 49, 59.
[7] Wills, Liber 5, folio 19.
[8] Wills, Liber 19, folio 520.

COLONEL WILLIAM DENT, GENT.[2]

(1660-1705)

The public service cut short by the death of Thomas Dent in 1676 was amply carried on by his eldest son and heir William. He was born in St. Mary's County about 1660, according to his deposition in 1697 at the age of 37. By the will of his father he came into possession of large tracts of land bordering the Nanjemoy in Charles County, and there his private life centered until his death. On May 8, 1681, he was granted 70 acres of land near the head of Nanjemoy Creek, known as "Baltimore's Gift".

On February 8, 1684, by the Rev. John Turling he was married to Elizabeth, daughter of Anne (Thorowgood) Chandler-Fowke and the deceased Colonel Gerard Fowke, late of Virginia and Maryland. Both the Thorowgood and Fowke families were armorial English houses.

Children of William and Elizabeth (Fowke) Dent

1. Thomas Dent.
2. William Dent, born Dec. 13, 1687, died Nov. 18, 1695.
3. Gerard Dent, bap. Feb. 3, 1688/9, buried Durham churchyard.
4. Elizabeth Dent, born 1688, died 1699.
5. George Dent married Anne Harbert. *q.v.*
6. Anne Dent, born Mar. 1692, died unmarried and buried Durham churchyard.
7. Peter Dent married Mary Brooke. *q.v.*
8. Philip Dent, *d.s.p.*
9. Elizabeth Dent married Richard Tarwin. Issue: George; Richard; William; Thomas; John; Martha; Elizabeth; Anne; and Rebecca.

In 1694 William Dent patented "Friendship", a tract of 1,571 acres in the Piscataway District of Prince Georges County. He entered first into public life about the winter of 1693, for in that year he was granted the power of an attorney and the privilege to administer oaths. In

February of the same year, he was appointed a judge to officiate at Battle Towne, Calvert County.

That same year he was elected to the General Assembly, the beginning of a career in the law-making body of the Province which continued until his death. He was the author of the rules for the Provincial Court, thereupon the Assembly in 1693 ordered that William Dent be allowed 1,000 pounds of tobacco out of the next public levy as his compensation. On October 18, 1695, he delivered an opinion on the jurisdiction of a court of delegates.[1]

William Dent was none the less active in the military life of the Province and was styled captain in 1693, but before his death he had been commissioned a lieutenant colonel. Besides his work in the General Assembly he held from time to time many other positions of various grades and rank. On July 30, 1694, he, as Captain William Dent, succeeded John Stone as coroner of Charles County. In the same year he represented William Anderson of Accomac County at court.

In 1693 William Dent petitioned the Assembly to engage in commercial intercourse with the Indians. Later he was appointed by the Governor to negotiate a treaty with the Indians who were, by raids and other outlawry, causing considerable distress among the frontiersmen.

His greatest endeavor, however, lay at the bench. On November 13, 1694, he was made assistant to the Attorney General of the Province. By the next year he appeared as His Majesty's Solictor General.

On December 12, 1696, William Dent petitioned the Council that since November 13, 1694, he had "assisted the Attorney General as Solicitor General in all His Majesty's places of the Crown both Criminal and Civil and had refused to take any fees of any person where His Majesty's interest has been concerned save only what I was engaged in when your Excellence laid commends on me. That I have not as yet received any salary for service although I can demonstrate that the same has been out of my pocket about 10,000 pounds of tobacco a year in my private practice by several persons that I have been sued and prosecuted in His Majesty's name whose Attorney I should have been had I not been sworned to His Majesty's service."

On November 17, 1694, Captain William Dent was made a Naval Officer for Upper Charles County, his jurisdiction beginning at Port Tobacco. On May 28, 1695, he delivered bond of £1,000 lawful money of England for the performance of such duty. The next year he was ordered to issue writs of process upon all forfeited navigation bonds. On October 12, 1696, he was appointed Naval Officer of the entire Potomac District, a position formerly held by Philip Clark. At a council meeting during the same month he was promoted from the Assistant Attorney General of the Province to that of Attorney General. In that year he was styled major.[2]

True to the tradition of the house of Dent, he was a member of the Established Church, though he followed the school of low churchmanship. At St. Mary's City in 1694, he signed with other members of the General Assembly the following: "There is not any transubstantiation in the Sacrement of the Lord Supper or in the elements of bread and wine at or after the consecration thereof by any person whatsoever".

In 1694 William Dent contributed 2,000 pounds of tobacco towards the building of free public schools in the Province. In recognition of his ability and interest in public education in July 1696, he was appointed one of the trustees for the free schools of the Province. In that same year he was a trustee of King William's College, the first institution of learning in the Province and one of the first in the Colonies, now known as St. John's College, Annapolis.

Among his miscellaneous commissions was the serving on the committee in 1695 to determine the boundaries of St. Mary's, Charles, and Calvert Counties. During 1701 and 1702 he served on the committee for the public tax levy.

He was elected the Speaker of the Lower House of the General Assembly during the illness of Philemon Lloyd, taking the oath on October 3, 1704.[3]

He was named the executor of the will of Christopher Gregory in 1699, and besides being the sole executor, he was bequeathed certain property as well as his wife, son Thomas, and mother-in-law Anne Fowke.

By 1704 he had reached one of the highest honors of his career when as Lieutenant Colonel William Dent, he was appointed a member of the Privy Council. His service on the Council, however, was brief, for he died early in the year 1704/5. On May 18, 1705, John Contee was appointed to his seat.

At the time Colonel William Dent made his will on October 2, 1702, he was one of the largest land owners in Charles County. His will mentions realty far in excess of 4,000 acres.[4]

Elizabeth, his wife, was willed a life interest in the homestead at Nanjemoy which at her death would revert to their son Thomas. She also received a life interest in the mill and the following tracts—"St. Barbay's", "Wheelers' Palm", and "Thomkinson's Long Look For", all of which were to revert to their youngest son Philip.

Thomas, besides the dwelling-plantation at the decease of his mother, was given "Whitehaven" of 894 acres, and the lodge which was tenanted by Thomas Perry. He also with his brother,George, received the residue of "Lawrell Branch" at Mattawoman. George was devised the plantation at Port Tobacco which was tenanted by Richard Edgar and the adjoining lands of 300 acres—also "Harrison's Gift" of 118 acres, three unnamed tracts and the residue of "Harrison's Gift" at Pope's Creek.

Peter was devised 523 acres of "Friendship", and 400 acres of "Gisborough" which was inherited by the testator on the death of his brother George. Elizabeth was willed the plantation at Mattawoman and 500 acres adjoining.

Jonathan Matthews was named to collect all money due the estate, and to dispose of ships, cargoes, and other assets. The proceeds were to be divided equally among his widow and children. The sons were to have their estate in Maryland at 17 years and the money in England at 21 years—the daughters at marriage or majority.

By a codicil on March 1, 1703/4, he devised the land purchased from Peter Anhilles to his son Thomas, and that at Pope's Creek to his son George. Anne Fowke, his mother-in-law, was given several bequests. Thomas was willed the silver bowl, engraved with the *Dent coat-of-arms*, which had been given the testator by Governor Blackistone.

After the writing of the will his wife died, and Colonel Dent married shortly afterwards Sarah, the daughter of Thomas and Anne Brooke. The will was admitted to probate in Charles County on February 17, 1704/5, and proved by John Beale, Gerard Fowke, Samuel Peele, and Thomas Evans. His widow married shortly afterwards Philip Lee, of Prince Georges County, and had issue.

The rent roll of Pickawaxon Hundred *circa* 1707 showed that "Whitton Ditch", of 150 acres was surveyed May 3, 1672, for Thomas Warner and was possessed by "Captain Philip Lee of Prince Georges County in right of his wife the relict of Coll William Dent".[5]

---

[1] Archives, vol. 20, pp. 45, 66, 314.
[2] Archives, vol. 20, p. 186.
[3] *Ibid.*, vol. 24, p. 327; vol. 25, p. 177.
[4] Wills, Liber 3, folio 475.
[5] Rent Roll, p. 89, Md. Hist. Soc.

CAPTAIN THOMAS DENT, GENT.[2]

(16— - 17—)

Thomas Dent, son of Thomas and Rebecca (Wilkinson) Dent, was born in St. Mary's County. He married Anne, the daughter of John and Anne Bayne, of Westwood Manor, one-time Captain of the Horse, Justice of the Peace, and High Sheriff of St. Mary's County.[1]

Children of Thomas and Anne (Bayne) Dent

1. Thomas Dent married Elizabeth Cave. *q.v.*
2. William Dent married Anne Warren. *q.v.*

At the spring session of the General Assembly in 1715 as Captain Thomas Dent, he took his seat as a delegate from Charles County. He was reelected for the next session in 1716, but was not a delegate in 1717.

In November 1722, Thomas Dent and Anne his wife petitioned the court for permission to sell a portion of "Locust Thickett", lying in Prince Georges County, which had been entailed on Anne Dent and her heirs by her father John Bayne instead of the land on which they then resided, inasmuch as Thomas Dent had sustained financial losses and had no other means to meet his obligations unless by the selling of his realty.[2]

Further references to him are meager. He probably died intestate and inasmuch as his estate was negligible, it was settled privately among his heirs. It has sometimes been suggested that he left Maryland after his financial reverses and settled in the Northern Neck of Virginia.

---

[1] Archives, vol. 20, pp. 73, 77, 106, 543.
[2] *Ibid.*, vol. 38, p. 315.

CAPTAIN PETER DENT[2]

(1665 - 1711)

Peter Dent, son of Thomas and Rebecca (Wilkinson) Dent, was born about 1665 in St. Mary's County. As early as 1686 he had migrated to the Eastern Shore and settled in Somerset County. In that year he patented 200 acres of a tract called "New Wood Hall", which later became a part of Sussex County, Delaware.

His widow was Jane Pittman, daughter of Joseph and Elizabeth Gray, of Somerset County. The Rev. Mr. Torrence in "Old Somerset", however, states that Peter Dent became the third husband of Elizabeth Bullard, the widow of Thomas Wilson and John King.

In 1689 as a resident of Somerset County, Peter Dent signed the protestant petition to Their Majestys William and Mary. In 1692 he served as clerk to the committee of the Assembly on elections to inspect the elections in Calvert County, and for his services he received 3,000 pounds of tobacco. In 1696 he was one of the military officers of Somerset County.[1] At one time he was Deputy Collector of "his Majesty's Customs in the County of Somersett".

On February 28, 1695, he and Edmond Howard were appointed to appraise the estate of Henry Dingley, late of Somerset County. In 1697 he purchased from his brother-in-law, Edmond Howard, a tract of land called "Beckford" which was situated on the crest of the slope rising from the eastern bank of the Nanokin, beyond the outskirts of the present town of Princess Anne. Here Peter Dent established his seat and resided until his death. Beckford is now one of the show places of Somerset County, but the original mansion is not standing. The present dwelling dates from about 1776.

He died in 1711. His will, dated November 23, 1710, named his wife Jane Pitman and a daughter Rebecca. He spoke of a possible unborn child, and if so, then it were to receive "Tanton" at St. Martin. Certain personalty was bequeathed his daughter in memory of Thomas Wilson, and his daughter after his death was to make her home with Joseph Gray.[2]

His widow married subsequently John Scott. On April 8, 1712, "John Scott and Jane Pittman Scott his wife the relict and executrix of Peter Dent late of Somerset County deceased" rendered an account on the estate.

---

[1] Archives, vol. 20, p. 544.
[2] Wills, Liber 13, folio 207.

COLONEL GEORGE DENT[3]

(1690 - 1754)

George Dent, son of William and Elizabeth (Fowke) Dent, was born September 27, 1690, near Nanjemoy in Charles County. Before 1715 he married Anne, daughter of William Harbert, Gent., and Mary his wife, of Pickawaxon Hundred.

Children of George and Anne (Harbert) Dent

1. Rebecca Dent, born 1715, married Thomas Hanson, son of Thomas and Elizabeth Marshall. Issue: Thomas; Mary; Elizabeth; Anne.*
2. Elizabeth Dent married William Penn and Richard Harrison.**
3. Mary Dent married ——— Alexander.

---

*Tomb at Marshall Hall: "Rebecca Marshall daughter of Colonel George Dent and Ann his wife who departed 5 December 1770 in the 55 year . . . erected by her loving husband Thomas Hanson Marshall".

** Estate of William Penn settled Chas. Co. 1758 by Col. Richard Harrison and his wife Elizabeth and distributed to the widow Elizabeth Harrison and her sons Jezreal Penn and William Penn. (Balance Book No. 2, p. 98.)

4. Anne Dent married Gilbert Ireland and Major Sweeney.*** Issue: (first) John; William Herbert; Gilbert; Anne; Mary.
5. George Dent married Eleanor Hawkins. *q.v.*
6. Eleanor Dent married John Blackistone, son of John and Anne (Guibert) Blackistone; Alexander McParling; and —— Bayard. Issue: (first) Nehemiah Herbert; George; John.
7. Margaret Dent married Kenelm Truman Greenfield.
8. John Dent married Sarah Marshall. *q.v.*
9. Sarah Dent.
10. Letty Dent married Kenelm Truman Stoddert and Peter Dejean. Issue: (first) Kenelm Truman; Nancy; Maryanne; Elizabeth.

In 1715 by the will of her father, Mrs. Dent came into possession of 500 acres of "Clarke's Purchase" during life, then to her daughter Rebecca Dent and an unborn child. Accordingly on March 20, 1751, George Dent and Anne his wife conveyed to their son John for natural love and affections portions of "Clarke's Inheritance" and "Clarke's Purchase".[1]

In 1725 George Dent patented "Dent's Level", consisting of 480 acres in Prince Georges County and lying on the north side of "Clarke's Inheritance" which lay in Charles County. In 1727 as Captain George Dent he was named the overseer of the estate of Thomas Skinner, of Charles County. For three years he was High Sheriff of Charles County, one-time member of the General Assembly—1720, 1724, 1725, 1726, and perhaps other years—and at the time of his death Chief Justice of the Provincial Court.

On April 22, 1728, he deeded "Dent's Level" to John Edgar, of Prince Georges County. Anne Dent his wife waived dower rights.[2] A short time before his death in 1754 he bequeathed for love and natural affections a number of negroes to his daughter Margaret, the wife of Kenelm Truman Greenfield, of St. Mary's County.[3]

Colonel Dent lived until his sixty-fifth year, dying in Charles County on May 12, 1754. He devised his wife during widowhood the dwelling-plantation and one-half of the landed estate. The title was confirmed to the plantation where his son George was then living. The latter also received a number of slaves. John was devised lands on Mattawoman Creek, that is, "Clarke's Inheritance", "Clarke's Purchase", and "Dent's Level".

Elizabeth was willed slaves and the land which her father purchased from Norman Tomkins, where Captain Bates was then living. After her death the bequests were to revert to the heirs of the testator. Four

---

*** Dec. 23, 1772, Major Sweeney and Anne his wife of St. M. Co. conveyed to Mary Ireland for love and affections land on Mattawoman Swamp after the death of Anne Sweeney "given to the said Anne by her father George Dent". (Deeds, Liber S No. 3, p. 435.)

daughters, Anne Ireland, Sarah Dent, Rebecca Dent, and Lotty Dent were given equalled portions of land on Mattawoman Creek. His other three daughters, Mary, Eleanor, and Margaret, having already been provided for with dowries at their marriage, were given each one gold ring valued at £0/30 with the inscription "In memory of George Dent".[4]

The Maryland Gazette of Annapolis for May 16, 1754, carried the following notice of his death: "Sunday last (May 12) died, at his Plantation in Charles County in an advanced age, Colonel George Dent, who was in his younger years one of the Representatives of that County, one of their Magistrates, and for three years sheriff. In the year 1729 he was appointed one of the Justices of the Provincial Court and at the time of his death was Chief Justice of the Province. His conduct in public office, gained him applause; and in his private character as husband, parent, master or neighbour, he was truly exemplary".

The inventory of his personal estate was made on July 10, 1754, with his daughter Rebecca Dent and his son-in-law Richard Harrison signing as the kinsmen. His sons, George and John, were the executors.

It was probably his daughter, Elizabeth, who was visiting in Virginia when Colonel Fairfax dispatched a letter to George Washington upon his return to Mount Vernon from Braddock's Defeat in western Pennsylvania. Three maidens—Sally Fairfax, Ann Spearing, and Elizabeth Dent—added an amusing postscript to the letter, as follows:

> Dear Sir:
>
> After thanking Heaven for your safe return, I must accuse you of great unkindness in refusing us the pleasure of seeing you this night. I do assure you nothing but our being satisfied that our Company would be disagreeable should prevent us from trying if our legs would not carry us to Mount Vernon this night; but if you will not come to us, tomorrow morning, very early, we shall be at Mount Vernon.
>
> (signed) S. Fairfax   Ann Spearing   Eliz'th Dent

His widow lived until 1764. By her will she bequeathed her possessions which consisted of slaves and other personalty to her ten children—Elizabeth Harrison, Maryh Alexander, Ann Ireland, George Dent, Eleanor McPharling, Margaret Greenfield, John Dent, Sarah Dent, Rebecca Marshall, and Letty Stoddert; and to the following grandchildren—Herbert Blackiston, Ann Herbert Dent, William Herbert Ireland, Ann Dent, Ann Alexander, Ann Marshall, and Ann Stodert.[5]

---

[1] Deeds, Liber Z No. 2, folio 465, La Plata.
[2] Deeds, Liber M, folio 311, Marlborough.
[3] Deeds, Liber A No. 3, folio 183, La Plata.
[4] Wills, Liber 29, folio 193.
[5] Wills, Liber 32, folio 159.

Peter Dent, Gent.[3]

(1693 - 1757)

Peter Dent, son of William and Elizabeth (Fowke) Dent, was born 1693 in Charles County, but later established his seat in Prince Georges County. In 1726 he married his kinswoman Mary, born October 8, 1709, daughter of Thomas and Lucy (Smith) Brooke and the granddaughter of Barbara (Dent) Brooke. Thus, his wife was a direct descendant of Robert Brooke, Gent., one-time Acting Governor of the Province and Lord of Brooke Place and Delabrooke Manors.

Children of Peter and Mary (Brooke) Dent

1. Elizabeth Dent, born Apr. 23, 1727, spinster.
2. Peter Dent married twice. *q.v.*
3. William Dent married Verlinda Beall. *q.v.*
4. Mary Dent married John Beall.
5. Lucy Dent married Feb. 11, 1753, George Hardy jr.
6. Anne Dent.
7. Thomas Dent married Elizabeth Edelen. *q.v.*
8. Eleanor Dent married Alexander Burrell. *q.v.*
9. Barbara Dent.
10. Walter Dent married Elizabeth Montgomery. *q.v.*
11. Richard Dent, born 1748, *d.s.p.*

Peter Dent was a magistrate of Prince Georges County as early as 1729 and served in that office until his death in 1757, fourteen years of which were in the capacity of presiding justice. In 1734 "Whitehaven" which lay partly in Prince Georges and Charles Counties was resurveyed for him and was followed by warrants for additions to the same tract.

He died in Prince Georges County during November 1757. By his will he bequeathed his wife numerous slaves and the dwelling-plantation "Whitehaven" during life. To his unmarried daughter Elizabeth he willed slaves and other personalty, also the privilege of living at the mansion house until marriage. Peter received slaves and thirty shillings in consideration of what his father had already deeded him. William was devised all lands in Frederick County, while Richard was devised the remainder of "Whitehaven". The three unmarried daughters, Anne, Eleanor, and Barbara, were bequeathed slaves and other personalty. The two married daughters, Mary and Lucy, were each left fifty shillings.[1]

The following item appeared in the Maryland Gazette of Annapolis, as of October 20, 1757: "Sunday last died in Prince Georges County, Mr. Peter Dent, who had been Deputy Commissary of that County upward of 20 years and for many years and at the time of his death Chief

Justice of that County". Another obituary stated that he was commissioned a Deputy Surveyor for Prince Georges County on September 16, 1735, and recommissioned on August 30, 1742.

The inventory of the personal effects was taken on March 11, 1758, with his son Thomas as the executor and Peter Dent, Jr., and William Dent as the nearest of kin.

His son Richard Dent was the head of the family at the census of St. John's Parish in 1776, with the following comprising his household: Mary Dent (mother), Elizabeth Dent (sister), Elizabeth Hardy aged 13 years, Elizabeth Welch aged 16 years, and 15 slaves.

The will of the widow, Mary Dent, was dated January 10, 1779, and proved in Prince Georges County on December 11, 1781, by Jonathan Turner, James Adams, and Charles Cox. She named only two children —Richard and Elizabeth.

The will of Richard Dent was dated 1808 and proved in Prince Georges County. He devised all realty to his nephew William Dent Beall, son of his sister Mary Beall, and named him executor. Other heirs were his nephew Walter Dent, son of his brother Walter; nephew Samuel B. Dent, son of his brother Peter; Martha Tubman; and Polly Magruder, daughter of Colonel John H. Beanes.[2]

---

[1] Wills, Liber 30, folio 386.
[2] Wills, Liber T T No. 1, folio 24, Marlborough.

THOMAS DENT[3]

(17— - 1751)

Thomas Dent, son of Thomas and Anne (Bayne) Dent, was born in Charles County. He settled first in Overwharton Parish, Stafford County, Virginia, where in 1740 he leased a tract of land from Stephen de Lisle, of Hamilton Parish, Prince William County. In Overwharton Parish, he was married to Anne Cave, widow, on December 3, 1747.

His will refers to him as of Truro Parish, Fairfax County, Virginia, and was dated December 7, 1750, and proved on March 26, 1751, by John Minor, Richard Sanford, Robert Sanford, and William Henry Terret. He willed his wife Anne slaves and his daughter-in-law (stepdaughter) Elizabeth Withers also slaves which were to be the full part of the estate due her and on condition that her husband and heirs would not bring claim to any of the estate of her deceased father William Cave. After the decease of his widow, the estate was to revert to his brother William Dent and his heirs. He appointed his wife and brother William Dent executors.

WILLIAM DENT³

(17— - 1757)

William Dent, son of Thomas and Anne (Bayne) Dent, was born in Charles County. He married Anne, the daughter of John and Judith (Townley) Warren, of that county. In 1751 his wife shared in the estate of Townley Bruce, her half brother.

Children of William and Anne (Warren) Dent

1. Warren Dent, born 1744, *d.s.p.* 1794.
2. George Dent married twice. *q.v.*
3. Eleanor Dent married John Jordon.
4. Judith Dent married Jeremiah Chase.
5. Mary Dent married Rev. William Dowie. Issue: Judith; Eleanor.
6. Anne Dent married Samuel Briscoe. (died testate 1786.) Issue: William Dent; Anne Warren; Grace Dent; Mary Hanson; Eleanor Buchanan; Judith Chase.
7. Rebecca Dent married William, son of Richard and Dorothy (Hanson) Harrison. Issue: William Dent; Anne Warren; Rebecca.
8. Grace Dent married Robert, son of Richard and Dorothy (Hanson) Harrison.

The will of William Dent was negotiated during 1756, and proved in Charles County on February 21, 1756/7.[1] He bequeathed his wife a considerable number of slaves which, upon her decease, were to be divided among his five minor children—Mary, Warren, Anne, Rebecca, and Grace. The widow was also to enjoy the use of the homestead during life.

George, a minor, was granted land in Stafford County, Virginia, and all other lands belonging to the testator's brother Thomas Dent then in the possession of Mr. Cox who had married the widow of Thomas Dent. Warren was devised the homestead and all lands within the Province, but in the event of his death without issue then to his brother George. Judith Chase was left £20 with which to purchase plate for her home. Bequests were made to his grandchildren—William and Anne Jordon.

His personal estate was appraised on March 30, 1757, with his daughters Eleanor Jordon and Judith Chase, signing the inventory as the kinswomen. His widow, Anne Dent, signed as executrix. The latter died intestate during 1771.

The will of the bachelor son, Judge Warren Dent, was probated· in Charles County on December 3, 1794. He named his nieces Eleanor Dowie, Jannett Dent, and Mrs. Anne Harrison. All property from the estate of his late sister, Grace Harrison, he left to his nephew William

Dent Harrison, and nieces Anne Warren Harrison and Rebecca Harrison. He devised "Blue Plains" which he purchased from John Maddox to his nephew Robert Hanson Harrison, and the plantation where Samuel Ratcliffe lived to his niece Mrs. Anne Harrison. The residue was devised to his brother George whom he named as executor.[2]

---

[1] Wills, Liber 30, folio 272.
[2] Wills, Liber A K No. 11, folio 245, LaPlata.

CAPTAIN GEORGE DENT[4]

(17— - 1785)

George Dent, son of George and Anne (Herbert) Dent, was born in Charles County. He married Eleanor, daughter of Henry Holland Hawkins and Jane his wife, sometime after 1746, the year in which as a maiden she was named in the will of her father. At its probation George Dent, Jr., was one of the bondsmen for the executors, Jane Hawkins and Henry Hawkins. George Dent with his wife shared in the distribution of the estate of his bachelor brother-in-law Henry Hawkins, of Charles County, in 1772.

Children of George and Eleanor (Hawkins) Dent

1. Eleanor Dent, died spinster 1819.
2. Johannah Greenfield Dent.
3. Jane Dent, died spinster 1827.
4. Henry Dent. *q.v.*
5. George Dent married Elizabeth Yates. *q.v.*
6. Anne Dent married ——— Parnham.
7. Mary Dent married May 25, 1778, Henry Alexander Ashton and secondly ——— Storke. Note: Eleanor Ashton; Jane Ashton; Henry Ashton; George Dent Ashton; and Mary Ashton were named as nieces and nephews in will of their maternal aunt Susannah Hawkins, Oct. 29, 1800, Chas. Co.

He represented his county in the General Assembly, taking his seat for the first time, it is believed, at the session of 1757-58. He was styled captain, but it is believed that his military service occurred during the colonial period, inasmuch as his age in 1776 was rather against any vigorous participation. He was appointed a justice of the peace in 1778 and in this capacity as magistrate he took the oaths of allegiance and fidelity in his district.[1] He was also justice of the Orphan's Court of Charles County in 1778 and again in 1779.

Records show that "the elegant seat of George Dent, Esq., was plundered and reduced to ashes by the British in 1781". In 1783 he was assessed for 250 acres of "Harrison's Gift" and 150 acres of "High Clifts", both tracts bordering the Potomac. He was also seized of "Huckleberry" of 190 acres, comprising chiefly of woods. The latter tract he had purchased from Benjamin Philpott in 1782 for £24, but it was then designated as "Huckleberry Swamp". The transaction was witnessed by Walter Hanson and J. Parnham.

His will was dated September 12, 1785, and proved in Charles County on December 31, 1785. He willed his three single daughters Eleanor, Jane, and Johanna "Huckleberry Swamp", of 300 acres, but after their marriage or death it was to revert to his sons Henry and George. Negroes were bequeathed to two unnamed married daughters. He referred to his wife Eleanor.[2]

The will of his spinster daughter, Eleanor, was dated November 14, 1818, and proved in Charles County on March 24, 1819. She named her niece Elizabeth Dent Payton; nephew Joannes Greenfield Storke; sister Jane Dent; children of her brother and sister Ann Parnham; and children of her brothers Henry and George Dent.[3]

The will of the other spinster daughter, Jane, was dated January 25, 1825, and proved in Charles County on July 10, 1827. She devised to her brother George Dent "Jarbo of High Clifts" on the Potomac, many slaves providing that he "gives to my nephew Joannes Storke" his slave Aaron. A morning ring each was willed to her sister Ann Parnham, nieces Eleanor H. D. and Susan A. Parnham, and her nephew George D. Parnham. Other heirs were her niece Elizabeth Dent Payton, and nephews Henry Ashton; Henry D. Storke; George D. Storke.[4]

---

[1] Unpub. Md. Records, vol. 5, DAR; Archives, vol. 21.
[2] Wills, Liber A H No. 9, folio 165.
[3] Wills, Liber H B No. 14, folio 60.
[4] Wills, Liber W D M No. 15, folio 235.

GENERAL JOHN DENT, GENT.[4]

(1733 - 1809)

John Dent, son of George and Anne (Harbert) Dent, was born about 1733 at "Clarke's Inheritance-Clarke's Purchase", in Charles County, Maryland. On February 20, 1753/4, he received certain gifts from his parents in consideration of a marriage contract about to be negotiated between him and Sarah Marshall. The ceremony occurred seven days later, no doubt at the manorial estate "Marshall Hall", the seat of the bride's father. She was born 1735 and was the daughter of Thomas Marshall, Gent., and Elizabeth his wife.

Children of John and Sarah (Marshall) Dent

1. John Dent. *q.v.*
2. Anne Herbert Dent, born Oct. 30, 1756, died July 15, 1813, Adams Co., Miss., married Feb. 24, 1774, William Mackall Wilkinson, born Feb. 12, 1752, died Mar. 12, 1799, son of William and Barbara (Mackall) Wilkinson. Issue: Jane; William, Barbara, Sarah, and others.
3. George Dent married Anne Magruder Truman. *q.v.*
4. Thomas Marshall Dent. *q.v.*
5. Elizabeth Dent, died young.

In 1775 John Dent was a delegate from Charles County to the General Assembly. He signed the celebrated document of the Association of Freemen of Maryland, the original of which now hangs in the Maryland Historical Society. He also served on the Council of Safety.

On January 6, 1776, the Maryland Convention by ballot elected him Brigadier General commanding all militia of the Lower District on the Western Shore. As chairman of the Committee of Observation for Charles County, he recommended that George Dent, Jr., and Henry Dent be commissioned first lieutenants of the County militia.

He was appointed by the Council of Safety to cooperate with the Commissioners of Virginia in erecting beacon lights on the shores of the Potomac. By April 30, 1776, thirteen had been erected in Maryland—1 in Prince Georges County, 9 in Charles County, and 3 in St. Mary's County, averaging about five miles apart. On June 11, 1776, £50 were appropriated for the purpose.[1]

In July 1776, Brigadier General Dent reported to the Council that the fleet under Lord Dunmore had appeared at the mouth of the Potomac and it was feared that it would make a landing on some portion of the river in the Lower Counties.

A despatch to the Council July 19, 1776, Charles River Headquarters, Brigadier General Dent reported an engagement with the British and the wounding of Captain Rezin Beall. He also reported that four deserters came over from the British ship, and that about 150 Tories and 100 negroes all under the 14th Regiment were at the mouth of St. Mary's River opposite St. George's Island.

On August 1, 1776, John Dent tendered his resignation as Brigadier General of the Flying Camp and recommended that Major Price take command of St. George's Island. The Council replied in accepting his resignation:[2]

> "We tell you candidly that we have no reason to believe that you were not equal to the task, or that you were deficient either in military knowledge, assiduity, or personal courage, and   that we are

surprised you should entertain any such idea . . . we were actuated
by no other views than those of service to the public, and taking
effectual measures to repel the common enemy".

After his resignation from the Army, he was elected a deputy from
Charles County to the State Legislature. On November 8, 1776, he
addressed the Council and recommended Hugh Gardner of Charles as
captain.

In 1778 he was appointed a justice of the peace, and as magistrate he
took the oaths of allegiance and fidelity in his district.

On February 15, 1785, John Dent, Gent., conveyed to his son George
Dent, Gent., for natural love and affections "Clarke's Inheritance", lying
on the east side of the road leading from Port Tobacco to Pomonkey and
adjoining the tract "Dent's Level".[3]

According to the tax list of 1783, General Dent was a resident of
Pomonkey Hundred in possession of the following tracts: "Clarke's
Purchase" of 500 acres, "Clarke's Inheritance" of 300 acres, and "Dent's
Level", of 280 acres.

His wife died April 9, 1795, aged 59 years, 6 months, and was buried
on her father's estate now known as Marshall Hall. Her tomb reads
"This tribute due to the Memory of an Excellent Mother and good
woman, is made by George Dent".

The will of General Dent was dated March 10, 1803, and proved in
Charles County on August 24, 1809. He devised his son John the
dwelling-plantation "Clarke's Purchase", and devised slaves to his three
children—Anne H. Wilkinson, George Dent, and Thomas M. Dent. The
residue of the estate was to be divided equally among the three latter
children.[4]

---

[1] Archives, vol. 21.
[2] *Ibid.*, vol. 12.
[3] Deeds, Liber Z No. 3, folio 126.
[4] Wills, Liber H B No. 12, folio 44.

PETER DENT[4]
(1728 - 1785)

Peter Dent, son of Peter and Mary (Brooke) Dent, was born
January 10, 1728, in Prince Georges County. His birth is registered in
both Rock Creek and Piscataway Parishes. Some time before 1757 he
married Mary Eleanor ————.

Children of Peter and Mary Eleanor Dent

1. William Dent, born Mar. 4, 1756/7, parents proved by parish register.
2. George Dent married Susannah Dawson. *q.v.*

On December 12, 1760, Peter Dent, of Charles County, conveyed to Ninian Beall, of Frederick County, for £60 "Grubby Street", lying on Rocky Branch of Middle Seneca Creek in Frederick County. Anne Dent, his wife, waived all dower rights.[1] By that date, therefore, Peter Dent had become a widower and had remarried—to Anne whose family has not been established. The maternity of the following children is proved by the parish register:

Children of Peter and Anne Dent

3. Theodore Dent married Eleanor Sheid. *q.v.*
4. Mary Eleanor Dent, bap. Feb. 27, 1763, married George Hatton, July 2, 1786, per St. John's register.
5. Joseph Dent, bap. Dec. 16, 1764, removed from Md.
6. Martha Dent, bap. Sept. 28, 1766, married Samuel Tubman.
7. William Dent, born Feb. 4, 1773, *d.s.p.*

Inasmuch as the birth records of the following children have not been preserved, the maternal parent has not been placed:

8. Thomas Dent, *d.s.p.*
9. Henrietta Dent married ———— Dyer. Issue: Francis; George; Polly.
10. Frances A. Dent married Hawkins Tubman.
11. Samuel B. Dent, heir in will of uncle Richard Dent 1808; drafted in Rev. War 1781 (Archives vol. 18, pp. 377, 407); prvt in Capt. Clarkson's Co., Chas. Co. Militia. (Unpub. Md. Records, vol. 2, p. 263).

Peter Dent served as a private during the Revolution in the militia company of Captain Thomas Hanson Marshall, 26th Battalion of Charles County.[2]

It seems as if Peter Dent established his dwelling on that part of "Whitehaven" which lay in Charles County. In 1783 he was taxed for 160 acres of "Whitehaven", lying in Pomonkey Hundred, and 20 acres of "Snap", lying partly in Portobacco West Hundred and Pomonkey Hundred.

The will of Peter Dent was dated June 21, 1784, and proved in Charles County on March 26, 1785, by Walter McPherson, William Brawner, and Elizabeth King. He bequeathed his entire estate to his wife Anne during widowhood, then the personalty was to be divided among his unnamed daughters. He mentioned his sons—George, Theodore, Thomas, William, and "his wandering son Joseph".[3]

Inasmuch as the landed estate of Peter Dent lay in both counties, the inventory of his personal effects was filed at both Marlborough and LaPlata. It was appraised at £175/18/11, and signed by Anne Dent and Theodore Dent as the executors and Elizabeth Dent and Richard Dent as the kinsmen on September 17, 1785.[4]

Thomas Dent, the bachelor son, died intestate early in 1800. The inventory of his personal estate was appraised at $84.75 on March 20, 1800, with Theodore Dent as the administrator, and Fanny Dent and Martha Tubman signing as the next of kin.[5] The final account was rendered on December 3, 1808, when an overpayment of £5/6/2½ was noted.

Thomas Dent was indebted at the time of his death to Nicholas Surgan, George Lee, and Henry Marbury, merchants, of Pomonkey, Charles County. His brother, Theodore, administered on his estate, but failed to satisfy the above-named creditors. In 1810 they brought action against the heirs of Thomas Dent, the proceedings which gave a very interesting account of his heirs.

His sister, Henrietta Dyer, was deceased at that date and had left Francis Dyer, George Dyer, and Polly Magruder. Mary Eleanor Hatton was also deceased and had left Henrietta who married Collin Hunter of Alexandria, Virginia, and the following minor children of Prince Georges County: Nathaniel, Peter Dent, Anne M., and George. The other heirs were George Dent of Alleghany County, Theodore Dent of Charles County, Samuel Tubman and Hawkins Tubman, both of Charles County.[6]

---

[1] Deeds, Liber 7, folio 1206, Frederick.
[2] Unpub. Md. Records, DAR Library, vol. 2, p. 374.
[3] Liber A H No. 8, folio 21, LaPlata.
[4] Inventory, Liber A R No. 9, Marlborough; A H No. 8, folio 115, LaPlata.
[5] Inventory 1798-1802, folio 260, LaPlata.
[6] Chancery Papers no. 4492.

CAPTAIN WILLIAM DENT, GENT.[4]

(1730 - 1805)

William Dent, son of Peter and Mary (Brooke) Dent, was born August 8, 1730, according to the registers of both St. John and Rock Creek Parishes. By the will of his father he was devised all realty of his parent lying in Frederick County—a section of the Province where he later established his seat. About 1758 he married Verlinda, the daughter of Samuel and Eleanor Beall. She was named in the will of her father, Samuel Beall, Jr., which was dated October 15, 1774, and admitted to probate in Washington County, Maryland, on January 10, 1778.

Children of William and Verlinda (Beall) Dent

1. Mollie Dent married ———— Campbell and Smyth Moore.
2. William Dent. *q.v.*
3. Peter Dent, born Mar. 16, 1761.
4. Anne Dent, born Dec. 10, 1767, died St. Clair Co., Ill., married Dec. 5, 1790, Guilford Co., N. C. (license), Risdon Moore, born Dela. Nov. 20, 1760, died St. Clair Co., Ill. Issue (according to family records): Mary; William; Mary; Betsy; Annie; Jonathan; Verlinda Bell; Sarah Cooper; Charles Smyth; James Russell.

On January 4, 1749, William Dent., Gent., then a resident of Prince Georges County, received from Lucy Brooke, Gentlewoman, of Prince Georges County, for a consideration of £37/10 — the tract "Dann", lying on Rock Creek near the land of Thomas Clealands.[1] Later, in 1759 William Dent, then a resident of Frederick County, leased a portion of this tract to Nathan Smith and another to Philip Club, Jr.[2]

William Dent, of Frederick County, purchased in 1758 from George Beckwith "Resurvey on Charles' Choice", lying on Rock Creek. Anne Beckwith as wife waived dower rights.[3] About 1760 he bought from William Beckwith, of Frederick County, "Locust Thickett", lying on the north branch of Rock Creek called Crabb Branch, which was granted originally to John Wofford in 1732.[4] On April 11, 1763, he purchased from John Cooke, of Frederick County, "Need Wood", adjoining "Locust Thickett". Rachel Cooke, wife of John, waived all dower.[5] On October 30, 1765, William Dent conveyed "Resurvey on Needwood" to William Williams, son of Thomas, of Frederick County. Verlinda Dent, his wife, relinquished her third.[6]

Before this date, William Dent and Thomas Addison, Jr., had patented jointly a large tract of land called "Friendship", lying in Frederick County, when on June 17, 1766, they petitioned the court for an adjustment of the boundaries. Inasmuch as there were some questions regarding the landmarks, the case brought out several interesting depositions.

Colonel George Beall, aged 70 years, certified that about 50 years past he was riding with his brother Charles Long and came to a rock, and that his brother said it was the boundary of either Captain Dent or Major Dent. He also remembered hearing Butler Evans, son of Peter, state that the white oak was the landmark. Samuel Magruder, aged 58 years, asserted that about 38 years ago he with John Stoddert, Charles Beall, and Ninian Magruder was discussing the boundaries.[7]

On August 15, 1768, William Dent deeded to Benjamin Gittings and William Ridgeway certain portions of "Dann". Verlinda his wife waived dower rights.[8]

On October 17, 1772, William Dent, of Frederick County, conveyed to John Kennedy, of the same county, 82 acres of "Resurvey on Locust Thickett", and on November 19, 1772, he sold to Ambrose Cooke the tract "Granby". His wife Verlinda on both occasions waived her third.[9]

On February 2, 1773, William Dent purchased a 320-acre tract of land on Reedy Ford Creek in Orange County, North Carolina, later to become a part of Guilford County. There he settled and became a leading citizen of western North Carolina.

He was a delegate from Guilford County to the Provincial Congress of North Carolina held at Hillsborough on August 20, 1775. The same year he served as a member of the Committee of Safety for the District of Salisbury. When the Provincial Congress met at Halifax the next year, he was again a delegate. On December 11, 1776, he was commissioned a captain in the Revolutionary forces and was Commissary Officer of the 9th Battalion of North Carolina troops.[10]

On October 3, 1778, William Dent, of Guilford County, North Carolina, gave power of attorney to Brooke Beall, of Montgomery County, Maryland, to convey 188 acres of "Resurvey on Locust Thickett", also for one undivided moiety or half part of land and mill, and mill seat containing 169 acres.[11] On January 13, 1780, Brooke Beall sold to Elisha Owens, a portion of the deed reading "whereas William Dent then of Frederick County but now of Guilford County, North Carolina, did on October 29, 1765, convey to William Williams, of Thomas, a portion of Resurvey on Norwood".[12]

On July 22, 1811, a lawsuit developed in Maryland between James Gittings, Jr., Kinsey Gittings, and Leonard H. Johns vs. Lucy Brooke and William Dent over the tract "Dann" which had been conveyed on January 4, 1749, to William Dent by Lucy Brooke.[13]

After the Revolutionary War William Dent served as magistrate of his county, an office which he resigned on November 9, 1790, the resignation being presented to the House of Commons by John Hamilton.

He removed from North Carolina during 1792 and established his domicile near Sparta, Hancock County, Georgia. On February 16, 1795, Smyth Moore, attorney for William Dent, disposed of the latter's property in Guilford County. Captain Dent died in Georgia during 1805. Some of his children left Georgia shortly afterwards and settled in Shiloh Valley, St. Clair County, Illinois, where some of his descendants

are still living. It is said that his widow, Verlinda Dent, migrated about
1812 to St. Clair County with her son-in-law Risdon Moore and his
wife Anne.

Through the Moores who were Quakers, many of his descendants
became affiliated with that sect and adopted the Puritanic dogma of the
Quakers—quite foreign to the broad and gentry views of the Dents.

[1] Deeds, Liber B, folio 156, Frederick.
[2] Deeds, Liber F, folio 637, Frederick.
[3] *Ibid.*, folio 445.
[4] Deeds, Liber G, folio 393.
[5] Deeds, Liber H, folio 362.
[6] Deeds, Liber K, folio 124.
[7] Deeds, Liber K, folio 897.
[8] Deeds, Liber L, folio 508.
[9] Deeds, Liber P, folio 406, 462.
[10] Archives of North Carolina, vols. 10, 14.
[11] Deeds, Liber A, folio 210, Rockville.
[12] Deeds, Liber A, folio 421.
[13] Deeds, Liber W R No. 40, folio 650, Fred.

CAPTAIN THOMAS DENT[4]

(1735 - 1789)

Thomas Dent, son of Peter and Mary (Brooke) Dent, was born
1735 in St. John's Parish, Prince Georges County. On December 18,
1771, he and George Hardy, Jr., purchased from Charles Beatty, of
Frederick County, and George Frazier Hawkins, of Prince Georges
County, lots in Georgetown, being portions of "Knave's Disappointment". Susanna Trueman Hawkins and Martha Beatty, wives, acknowl-
eged the transaction.[1]

He was devised through the will of his brother-in-law, George
Hardy, Jr., in 1773 a lot at Piscataway, being a portion of "Pittsburg".
At that time it was shown that Thomas Dent and his brother-in-law
were occupying the same dwelling, inasmuch as George Hardy devised
to his son Thomas Dent Hardy "the stone house now occupied by
Thomas Dent and myself".

At the census of St. John and Prince George Parishes, taken by
Thomas Dent about 1776, he had in his immediate household John
Clarke aged 40, George Hardy aged 2, Judah Murray aged 35, and
19 slaves. At that date it is obvious that Thomas Dent was then a
bachelor of past 40 years. He, however, married shortly afterwards
Elizabeth, daughter to James and Salome (Noble) Edelen.

Children of Thomas and Elizabeth (Edelen) Dent

1. George Fairfax Dent, *d.s.p.*
2. George Washington Dent married twice. *q.v.*

3. Lewis Dent married Anne B. ————. *q.v.*
4. Horatio Dent, *d.s.p.*
5. Patrick Dent married Susannah G. Wood. *q.v.*

On May 2, 1777, Thomas Dent deeded to Richard Carnes "Little-worth", lying in Piscataway. Elizabeth Dent his wife waived all dower.[2]

Thomas Dent was present at a meeting of the Committee of Observation of Prince Georges County on August 4, 1775, held in the home of Richard Carnes at Piscataway. On May 15, 1776, Thomas Dent was recommended by Jonathan Beall to the Council of Safety as an officer in any regular force that may be raised in the Province either continental or provincial.[3] On September 1, 1777, he was commissioned a captain of the Lower Battalion of Prince Georges County Militia.[4] In 1778 he took the oath of fidelity and support to the State of Maryland.

His nephew, Thomas Dent Hardy, served in the naval service of his country and was captured by the British in 1780, taken a prisoner to New York where he died in the spring of 1781. By his will, dated February 25, 1780, he devised his uncle, Thomas Dent, "Traver's Industry", then called "Pittsburg", lying on the north fork of Piscataway Creek adjoining the land of the said Thomas Dent.

In 1802 legal action was instituted in the Court of Chancery regarding a house and lot at Piscataway sold by Thomas Dent as attorney for his nephew, Thomas Dent Hardy, to John Bayne, but the deed was never fully executed. The case furthermore showed that Thomas Dent had died intestate in 1788 or 1789 and had left a widow, Elizabeth Dent, and five minor children—two of whom in 1802 were deceased.[5]

In 1804 his widow Elizabeth Dent deeded negroes to her grandson John Walter Stoddert Dent of George.[6]

Her will was dated December 21, 1814, and proved May 21, 1816, in Prince Georges County by William Marshall, Joseph Edelen, and Richard Gregory.[7] She named her son George W. Dent, his wife Anne Dent, his minor children John W. S. Dent and Eleanor Matilda Dent, and two unnamed children by his second wife—also her son Lewis W. Dent, his wife Anne Dent; and the following grandchildren: George F. Dent, Elizabeth W. Dent, Thomas R. Dent, Mary Anne Dent, William W. Dent, and Patrick Dent. Other heirs were her sisters—Mary N. Stonestreet, Sarah Pye, and Catherine A. Edelen "the wife of my brother Joseph". The residue of her estate was to be divided among the children of George W. Dent, except the two oldest, and the children of Lewis W. Dent, except the eldest daughter. Her nephew Joseph N. Stonestreet was named executor.

The inventory of the personal estate was filed on October 11, 1816, and showed an appraisement of $2,080.

¹ Deeds, Liber O, folio 693, Fred.
² Deeds, Liber C C no. 2, folio 351.
³ Archives, vol. 11.
⁴ *Ibid.*, vol. 16.
⁵ Chancery papers no. 3291.
⁶ Deeds, Liber J R M no. 10, folio 396, Marlb.
⁷ Wills, Liber T T no. 1, folio 179.

WALTER DENT[4]

(1744 - ——)

Walter Dent, son of Peter and Mary (Brooke) Dent, was born 1744 in Piscataway Parish, Prince Georges County. About 1764, according to family records, he married Elizabeth Montgomery.

Children of Walter and Elizabeth (Montgomery) Dent

1. Walter Dent, born Jan. 7, 1765. Drafted 1781 in Major Higgins' battalion for service at Yorktown.
2. Chloe Hanson Dent,* bap. May 25, 1766, married Thomas James John, son of William Truman and Elizabeth Stoddert. License Sept. 21, 1790, Pr. Geo. Co.
3. Jane Dent, born 1771, apparently died young.
4. Anne Dent, born 1774.
5. Mark Winnett Dent married twice. *q.v.*
6. Absolam Dent, removed to Mo.
7. John Dent, born May 5, 1786, *d.s.p.* in Mo. 1859.
8. Jane Dent, born Sept. 9, 1790, died spinster in Mo. 1867.

On September 14, 1771, Walter Dent and Thomas Dent granted their share of "Whitehaven", lying on the Mattawoman, willed by their father, Peter Dent, to their brother Richard.[1]

At the census of St. John and Prince Georges Parishes in 1776, the household of Walter Dent comprised, besides his wife and children, Margaret Montgomery, aged 29, and two slaves. During the Revolution he served as a private in Captain Clarkson's Company of the militia.[2]

The first Federal Census showed him a resident of Prince Georges County. During the same year he granted power of attorney to Richard Dent and Thomas Mundell.

Inasmuch as no record exists in Maryland of the administration of his estate after his decease, it is not unlikely that he migrated to western

*Buried at Southampton, Charles Co. Headstone reads "Died Sept. 17, 1804, aged 38 years".

Virginia, where his younger children lived for a time before their ultimate settlement in Missouri.

_____
[1] Deeds, Liber A A no. 2, folio 292, Marlb.
[2] Unpub. Md. Records, DAR, vol. 2, p. 263.

CAPTAIN GEORGE DENT[4]

(17— - 1802)

George Dent, son of William and Anne (Warren) Dent, was born in Charles County, Maryland. On May 9, 1778, he was appointed captain of the 26th Battalion of Charles County Militia.[1] In March of the same year he took the oath of Fidelity and Allegiance to the State of Maryland in Charles County.[2]

He married twice, both wives being widows. His first adventure was Rose Townsend Knox, the widow of Captain Robert Knox and the daughter of Elizabeth Mastin.[3] On April 19, 1771, she shared in the estate of her sister Elizabeth Dade as Mrs. Knox.[4]

The will of Captain Robert Knox was dated September 1, 1781, and proved in Charles County on October 30, 1782, by G. B. Brown, Virlinda Mastin, Andrew Baillie, and William Miller.[5] He devised his son John "Summer Duck" in Virginia containing 5,000 acres, and his son Robert Dade all land in the State of Maryland. To his daughter Elizabeth Knox he willed "Beulah" in Virginia of 500 acres and negroes, and to his daughter Janet Knox "Fields", adjoining "Summer Duck" in Virginia, and certain negroes. The partnership of Knox & Baille was to be settled, and he mentioned his brothers John and William Knox. His wife Rose Townsend Knox was to receive one-third of the personal estate. The executors, so appointed, were his wife, Colonel Robert Hooe, of Alexandria, Andrew Baillee, and Alexander Beall Mastin.

By a codicil dated February 15, 1782, "whereas wife Rose Townsend is now with child therefore to the unborn child" he left £800, and also a legacy to William Allason, of Fauquier County, Virginia, whom he also named as an additional executor.

On December 3, 1782, his widow Rose Townsend Knox appeared in court, renounced the will, and demanded her third. The estate of her first husband was not settled until several years thereafter, when on April 27, 1792, as the wife of George Dent she filed an account.[6]

His second wife was Elizabeth, the widow of John Knox and the daughter of Richard Hanson Harrison. The will of Robert Townsend Hooe, late of Alexandria, Virginia, but formerly of Charles County, Maryland, one of the executors of the estate of Captain Robert Knox, died without issue and after several bequests he devised the residue of his estate which included extensive tracts of land to his cousin Richard H. Harrison "late partner in trade" and upon his death the devise was to revert to the children of the said Richard except Joseph W. Harrison, Walter H. Harrison and "Elizabeth Knox alias Dent lately intermarried with George Dent". The will was dated January 21, 1796, but was not proved until July 10, 1811.[7]

The estate of John Knox, late husband to Elizabeth (Harrison) Knox-Dent, was distributed in Fauquier County, Virginia, when his widow received £272/15; R. Knox £185/12/6; Elizabeth Knox £181/10; and Janett Dent £182/0.[8]

Children of George Dent

1. William Dent married Janet Knox. _q.v._
2. Anne Dent married ———— Thomas and Samuel Hanson.
3. Elizabeth Dent married Robert Knox and Elijah Brown.*
4. Janet Dent married John Shumate.
5. Rebecca Dent, born Mar. 9, 1789, married Jesse G. Scott. License Oct. 5, 1816, Fau. Co., Va.
6. Grace Harrison Dent, born Oct. 7, 1791, married Burgess Field. License Jan. 4, 1815, Fau. Co., Va.

On October 14, 1782, George Dent was granted letters of administration on the estate of Elizabeth Harrison, late of Charles County, with Thomas Hanson Marshall and Dr. John Parnham as his bondsmen.

On November 28, 1794, George Dent of Charles County conveyed land to Thomas Dotey, of Fauquier County, Virginia. On November 30, 1796, George Dent and Elizabeth his wife and William Dent and Jenet his wife, all of Fauquier County, Virginia, conveyed 84 acres of land to Alexander McConchie, of Fauquier County.

Consequently sometime before 1794 George Dent settled in Fauquier County, Virginia. On March 24, 1797, he conveyed "Chosen" and "Huckleberry Plains Enlarged" to John Colby, of Charles County, Maryland. No wife waived dower.[9] On January 7, 1798, he deeded "Warren's Discovery" to Robert Crain of Charles County. No wife waived dower. A few months later he conveyed "Hatton's Point" to John Maddox, and on November 10, 1801, he transferred another portion of "Warren's Discovery" to William Thomas, of St. Mary's County.[9]

---

*In 1806 the land of Robert Knox, deceased, of Fauquier Co. was divided among his representatives—Robert Knox; Elizabeth D. Brown; Jennet Dent formerly Jennet Knox; at the same time negroes were divided among William Dent, Robert Knox, and Elizabeth Brown. Ref: Liber 5, folio 37, Warrenton.

George Dent died shortly after this conveyance, inasmuch as on March 25, 1802, "Elizabeth Dent widow of George Dent of William late of Fauquier County, Virginia, deceased" deeded to William Thomas, of St. Mary's County, land in William and Mary Parish, Charles County, that had been granted to Bridget Legate on May 1, 1676.[10]

The inventory of the personal estate of George Dent in Charles County was filed at court on August 10, 1802, by his administrator, William Dent, and displayed a value of $4,648.50.

The distribution of his estate in Charles County was made on May 31, 1803, and divided among the following representatives: William Dent, Anne Thomas, Elizabeth Knox, John Shumate and Janet his wife, Rebecca Dent, and Grace Dent.[11]

The inventory of his personal estate was not taken in Fauquier County until July 2, 1803, and was appraised at £982/2/6. It was signed by John Hooe and Stanton Slaughter. His widow on October 19, 1804, married Enoch J. Brown, according to license issued in Fauquier County.

On August 12, 1816, William Dent, Janet Dent, Rebecca Dent, and Samuel Hanson and Anne his wife, all of Charles County, and described as the heirs of George Dent, deceased, deeded "Brawner's Chance" to Catherine Norris, Henry Speake, and Leo Speake — all of Charles County.[12]

---

[1] Archives, vol. 21.
[2] Durham Parish Register, p. 11.
[3] Wills, Liber A B no. 9, folio 59.
[4] Adm. Accts., Liber 10, folio 41, La Plata.
[5] Wills, Liber B no. L, folio 72.
[6] Adm. Accts., Liber 1791-1798, folio 77.
[7] Chancery papers no. 4954.
[8] Liber 3, folio 479, Warrenton.
[9] Deeds, Liber I B no. 2, folios 251, 326, 401, La Plata.
[10] Deeds, Liber I B no. 5, folio 151.
[11] Liber 1803, folio 45, La Plata.
[12] Deeds, Liber I B no. 11, folio 424.

LIEUTENANT HENRY DENT[5]

(17— - 1803)

Henry Dent, son of George and Eleanor (Hawkins) Dent, was born in Charles County, Maryland. On February 26, 1776, his uncle, General John Dent, recommended him for a first lieutenancy in the Revolutionary Army.[1] In 1778 he took the Oath of Fidelity and Allegiance to the State of Maryland under his father, Magistrate George Dent.[2] He died intestate. The inventory of his personal estate, specially stated as

"Henry Dent of George", was filed at court on August 9, 1803, by George Dent as the administrator. Eleanor Dent and Jane Dent signed as the kinsmen. The final account was rendered on August 9, 1815, showing a balance of £340/19/1 "to be distributed according to law", but no heirs were recorded.[3] Eleanor Dent, sister, bequeathed property in 1819 to children (unnamed) of her brother Henry.

[1] Archives, vol. 11.
[2] Unpub. Md. Rec., vol. 2, D.A.R.
[3] Inv. & Accts., Liber 1815, folio 486, La Plata.

GEORGE DENT[5]

(1773 - 1833)

George Dent, son of George and Eleanor (Hawkins) Dent, was born in or about 1773 in Charles County. On September 4, 1807, he purchased from Robert Yates for a consideration of $1000 the tract called "Manchester" of 180 acres in William and Mary Parish and here he established his seat to be known later as Prospect Hill.[1]

He married Elizabeth, the eldest daughter of Charles Yates, III. granddaughter of Charles Yates, II, great-granddaughter of Charles Yates, I, and Jane Bryan his wife, and great-great-granddaughter of Robert Yates, the Emigrant, a prominent planter and merchant of the Wicomico, and his first wife Rebecca Young.

Charles Yates, father to Elizabeth, dated his will January 14, 1794, it being proved in Charles County on March 1, 1794. He named six minor children among whom was Elizabeth.[2] At the final settlement of the estate on December 31, 1807, by John Bruce and Alexander Crain, Mrs. Elizabeth Dent received her portion of the balance, that is, $392.[3] Charles Yates, II, the grandfather, died intestate, but before his mother Jane (Bryan) Yates. His three children, Robert, Charles, and Henry Dade, however, shared in the estate of their grandmother, Jane Yates, in 1779.[4]

Children of George and Elizabeth (Yates) Dent

1. Eleanor Jane Dent, died spinster, June 11, 1838.
2. Anne Mary Dent, died spinster, Nov. 2, 1836.
3. Mary Eleanor Dent, married John Philip Stewart,* removed to Miss. Issue: Elizabeth Yates; Mary Bayne; Philip E.; George Dent; Frances Adaline; Ellen Anna; Agnes Floretta; and Jane Almira.
4. Elizabeth Yates Dent.
5. George Dent married Sophia Anne Ashton.
6. Charles M. P. H. Dent.

*Mary E. Dent married 4 September 1832 to J. Philip Stuart at Prospect Hill, Charles County, Maryland. (Natl. Intelligence, 16 Oct. 1832.)

The National Intelligence of April 4, 1833, stated that "George Dent, died 27 March 1833, aged 60, late of Prospect Hill, Charles County".

His will was dated December 20, 1832, and proved in Charles County on April 23, 1833. He bequeathed slaves to the following children: Eleanor Jane Dent, Anne Mary Dent, Mary Eleanor Stewart, Elizabeth Yates Dent, George Dent, and Charles M. P. H. Dent. The residue of the estate was directed to be divided equally among the children. In the event that he died before his son Charles (named as executor) attained 18 years or be incapable of acting by the law, then he appointed his friend and relative, George D. Parnham, the executor.[5]

The will of the spinster daughter, Elizabeth Y. Dent, was dated November 7, 1848, and proved in Charles County on December 5, 1848, by F. Stone, Margaret M. Sheirburn, and Bettie Edelen. She bequeathed silverware to her nephew, George, son of her brother George Dent, and various personalty to her sister Mary E. Stuart and brother George Dent. Certain articles were bequeathed to her sister "Mary E. Stuart during the lifetime of her husband John P. Stuart".[6]

---

[1] Deeds, Liber I B no. 7, folio 448.
[2] Wills, Liber A K no. 11, folio 206.
[3] Inv. & Accts. 1802-1808, folio 484.
[4] Wills, Liber A F no. 7, folios 100, 315.
[5] Wills, Liber W D M no. 15, folios 100, 315.
[6] Wills, Liber D J no. 16, folio 468.

JOHN DENT[5]

John Dent, son of General John Dent and Sarah Marshall his wife, was born at the parental plantation in Pomonkey Hundred, of Charles County. According to the will of his father, he was devised the dwelling-plantation, but soon afterwards he left the ancestral estate and settled with his brothers in Georgia. On July 4, 1816, "John Dent, of Augusta, Georgia", conveyed the plantation described as lying on the Mattawoman in Charles County, Maryland, to Sarah Marshall Briscoe, the adminis-tratrix of Dr. Edward Briscoe, of Charles County. Richard Tubman, of Augusta, Georgia, witnessed the document.[1]

---

[1] Deeds, Liber I B no. 11, folio 360, La Plata.

CAPTAIN GEORGE DENT, GENT.[5]
(1756 - 1813)

George Dent, son of John and Sarah (Marshall) Dent, was born 1756 at "Windsor Castle", the English name given to "Clarke's Inheritance", on the Mattawoman. He married Anne Magruder, the daughter of James and Elizabeth Truman, of Prince Georges County. On March 19, 1784, James Truman deeded for natural love and affections negroes to his grandchildren John Herbert Dent and Sarah Marshall Dent. He and his granddaughter, Elizabeth Truman Dent, died the same day and were interred in one grave in the old burying grounds at "Clarke's Inheritance". The headstone, still standing, states "Together are interred the remains of James Trueman and his granddaughter Elizabeth T. Dent. He died December 22, 1789, aged 47 years. She departed December 22, 1789, in her third year". He was a distinguished officer of the Revolutionary Army.

Children of George and Anne (Truman) Dent

1. John Herbert Dent, born 1782, died 1823.
2. Sarah Marshall Dent, born 1784, married Edward Briscoe.
3. Elizabeth Truman Dent, born 1786, died 1789.
4. Maria Dent, born 1788, married John Neilson.
5. George Columbus Dent, born Feb. 23, 1793.
6. Dennis Dent married Martha Beall. *q.v.*

At the outbreak of the Revolution George Dent served as First Lieutenant of the Third Battalion of the Flying Camp and saw active service in the early campaign around New York. After the disbandment of the Flying Camp in December 1776, he returned to his home in Charles County and there was commissioned a first lieutenant of Captain Thomas H. Marshall's Company of Militia. On May 9, 1778, he was promoted to the rank of captain and assigned to the Twenty-sixth Battalion. In 1778 he took the oath of allegiance and fidelity under his father John Dent.[1]

In 1789 George Dent, of John, and Horatio Middleton purchased from Sarah Ward, widow, her dwelling-plantation. In 1802 he conveyed to Thomas Marshall Dent "Clarke's Inheritance", lying on the north side of Mattawoman Swamp. Anne Dent, his wife, acknowledged the transaction.[2]

From 1782 to 1790 George Dent served as a member of the Maryland State Legislature, being speaker pro-tempore in 1788 and speaker in 1789, and unanimously reelected speaker in 1790. The next year he was elected to the State Senate and served as president of the latter in 1792, in which year he resigned his seat. He entered the United States House of Representatives in March 4, 1793, and served until March 3, 1801. At various times he was speaker pro-tempore. On April 4, 1801, he was appointed by Thomas Jefferson marshal of the District of Columbia, and it is said that for his staunch support of Thomas Jefferson against Aaron Burr he expected a more lucrative appointment than marshal. He held it only for a brief period and then removed to Georgia about 1802 with his brother Thomas Marshall Dent. He settled about twelve miles from the town of Augusta.

On August 18, 1806, Elizabeth Gordon Truman, widow of James Truman late of Prince Georges County, Anne Magruder Dent daughter of the said James Truman, and George Dent in his own right and in the right of his wife the said Anne Magruder Dent, all of Columbia County, Georgia, appointed Captain James Somerville, of Prince Georges County, their attorney to convey unto John Moran "Buttenton" of about 243 acres of land, lying partly in Charles and Prince Georges Counties, adjoining the land of Joshua Naylor. The northern portion was the property of the late James Truman, aforesaid deceased, and had been surveyed for Henry Truman on January 27, 1736. Thomas M. Dent was a witness to the instrument.

George Dent was thrown from his horse, the injuries of which caused his death on December 2, 1813. He was interred upon his plantation.

His eldest son, John Herbert Dent, rose in rank and distinction in the United States Navy and died July 31, 1823, at his plantation in St. Bartholomew's, South Carolina. On March 16, 1798, he became a midshipman under Truxton in the frigate "Constellation" and was on board when she captured the French frigate "Insurgente" on February 1, 1799. He was appointed a lieutenant on July 11, 1799, and was in the same ship when she took the French frigate "La Vengeance" on February 1, 1800. He was in the command of the schooners "Nautilus" and "Scourage" in Preble's squadron during the Tripolitan War, and took part in the attacks on the city of Tripoli in 1804. He was commissioned a master commander September 5, 1804, and a captain December 29, 1811.[3]

The second son, George Columbus Dent, was killed in a duel at Hamburg, South Carolina, across the Georgia line. It was this duel and his death which inspired Augusta Evans to write her well known novel _St. Elmo_.

[1] Archives, vols. 18, 21; Unpub. Md. Records, DAR.
[2] Deeds, Liber I B no. 5, folio 219.
[3] National Intelligence, Aug. 30, 1823.

THOMAS MARSHALL DENT[5]

(1761 - 1823)

Thomas Marshall Dent, son of John and Sarah (Marshall) Dent, was born at "Clarke's Purchase-Clarke's Inheritance" on October 22, 1761, according to the register of St. John's Piscataway Parish. He married Anne, the only daughter of Alexander Howard Magruder and Jane his wife. The births of the two children are registered in St. John's Parish.

Children of Thomas Marshall and Anne (Magruder) Dent

1. John Dent, born Feb. 15, 1792.
2. Mary Anne Dent, born Mar. 13, 1793, married 1813 James Longstreet (died 1830), son of William and Hannah (FitzRandolph) Longstreet. Issue: Gen. James Longstreet, C.S.A., etc. . . .

Marshall Dent, as he was better known, removed to Georgia with his brother George. He died at Augusta, Georgia, during August 1823.

GEORGE DENT[5]

(1755 - 1812)

George Dent, son of Peter, was born about 1755 perhaps in Charles County. It is practically proved that he was a child of the first marriage, and therefore the son of Mary Eleanor ————. At the census of Pomonkey Hundred in 1775, "George Dent of Peter" was of age and was subject to taxation, the only child of Peter Dent to be so listed in that year. Furthermore, in all legal proceedings regarding the heirs of Peter Dent, the name of George appears first, it being usually customary in such matters to enumerate the heirs according to seniority.

During the Revolutionary War, he served as a private in the militia of Charles County under Captain Thomas Hanson Marshall.[1]

Before 1785 George Dent left his native surroundings and settled in Washington County which in 1777 had been organized from the Upper District of Frederick. On April 20, 1785, at Frederick Town he secured license to marry Susannah Cromwell who was then the widow of Joseph Cromwell.* She was of distinguished ancestry and was born in Prince Georges County, the daughter of John Dawson and Martha Anne his wife. George Dent and his wife closed the estate of Joseph Cromwell in Frederick County.

---

*For Cromwell family, see Newman's "Anne Arundel Gentry".

Of several children born to George Dent and Susannah his wife, Frederick who married Ellen Bray Wrenshall (*q.v.*) became the most prominent.

George Dent was the official surveyor for the town of Cumberland and one of the early and distinguished citizens of the town. He and his young family lived first in a loghouse, still standing, and known as the Dent House. Later he erected a more pretentious brick dwelling which is also preserved.

On November 2, 1785, George Dent of Washington County mortgaged to Abraham Faw of Frederick County lots in Washington Town formerly called Cumberland. On September 10, 1785, he purchased from Thomas Beall of Samuel, of Washington County, lots in Cumberland. Verlinda Beall, wife of Thomas, waived dower rights.

On January 9, 1788, the Chancellor of Maryland appointed Daniel Stull of Washington County, trustee for the creditors of George Dent, an insolent debtor. Consequently, for $1.00 George Dent sold to Daniel Stull his realty and all household goods except the necessary wearing apparel of himself and family.

On December 8, 1795, George Dent purchased realty from Samuel Duval, of Frederick County, which Samuel Duval had purchased in 1785 from Thomas Beall of Samuel. Priscilla Anne Duval, wife of Samuel, acknowledged the conveyance. On December 5, 1796, George Dent and his wife Susannah conveyed a lot in Cumberland to Charles Frederick Broadhag.

On October 9, 1805, George Dent of Alleghany County, conveyed to Theodore Dent of Charles County a portion of "Whitehaven", being that which was claimed by George Dent as heir of his brother Thomas Dent. On October 22, 1810, George Dent of Alleghany County and Theodore Dent of Charles County testified that they saw George Dent give bond to Abraham Faw of Frederick County for £1,000 on October 15, 1787, for the conveyance of a portion of "Whitehaven", devised by his father Peter, to his son, William, and held by the said George Dent as heir to his brother William.

The remains of George Dent and his wife lie in the cemetery in the town of Cumberland.

---

[1] Unpub. Md. Records, vol. 2, p. 374, DAR.

THEODORE DENT[5]

(1761 - 1815)

Theodore Dent, son of Peter Dent and Anne his wife, was born in 1761, according to the register of Piscataway Parish. He married

Eleanor, the daughter of Martha Sheid, widow. The 1790 census for Prince Georges County records her as Patsey Shade with herself, another woman, and four slaves comprising the immediate household. On May 8, 1798, according to license in Prince Georges County, she as Martha Shield married Benjamin Cawood.

Children of Theodore and Eleanor (Sheid) Dent

1. Peter Dent married Mary Brown Rogerson. *q.v.*
2. William M. Dent married Henrietta H. ————.
3. Martha Ann Dent married Francis L. Rogerson.

On June 7, 1805, Theodore Dent purchased from his brother George Dent, of Alleghany County, Maryland, "Whitehaven" in Charles County, being all that portion of the said tract that George Dent claimed as one of the heirs of his brother Thomas Dent.

The brother of Mrs. Dent, Francis H. Sheid, died in 1810 and named as his executor his "friend" Theodore Dent. His will, dated November 3, 1810, proved in Charles County on December 8, same year, devised to his son Francis James the dwelling-plantation "Lee" which had been purchased from Samuel Chapman, except for four acres which included the mill. The latter he devised to his daughter Ann Gray Sheid. In the event that the two children died before majority, the land was to revert to Peter Dent, son of Theodore. A codicil stated that his son Francis James was to remain with his grandmother, Elizabeth Franklin, until he attained age, and that the daughter "to be brought up by my mother and sister Eleanor Dent". The instrument was proved by Edward Briscoe, George Power, and Samuel Hanson.[1]

On February 4, 1814, Samuel Chapman filed suit in the court of chancery against Theodore Dent for $800 which had been owed to William McConchie by Francis Sheid. McConchie had died intestate and letters of administration had been issued to Samuel Chapman. In the reply of Theodore Dent to the court he stated that "Francis H. Sheid in his lifetime lived in a dissipated state, did gamble and play at cards with a certain William McConchie late of Charles County, deceased, and lost $800 at one sitting. . . ."[2]

On May 29, 1818, Martha Cawood, of Charles County, conveyed to her daughter Eleanor Dent certain negro slaves.[3] And on June 9, 1818, Eleanor Dent, of Charles County, conveyed to John Marbury, of the District of Columbia, and Henry Brawner, of Charles County, certain negroes that had been conveyed to her "whereas judgement was obtained against Martha Cawood mother of Eleanor Dent and administrator of Benjamin Cawood in favor of Nicholas Blacklock".[4]

Theodore Dent maintained his plantation on that portion of "White-haven" which lay in Charles County, and there he died intestate during 1815. On September 2, of that year, his widow, Eleanor Dent, filed the inventory of his personal estate, appraised at $1683.92.[5]

On January 1, 1834, Francis L. Rogerson and Martha Anne his wife, of Charles County, conveyed to Walter W. Hanson, Jr., all their undivided interest in one-third of the tracts "Independency", "Cow Penns", and "Snap", containing in all 237 acres, which were formerly the property of Theodore Dent, deceased, and which descended to the said Martha Anne, wife of Francis L. Rogerson, from Theodore Dent her father, and then in the possession of Francis L. Rogerson and his wife, and Peter Dent who was also a descendant of the said Theodore Dent.

On December 19, 1836, Peter Dent and Mary his wife, and William M. Dent and Henrietta H. his wife, conveyed also portions of the above-named tracts under the same provisions and rights of ownership to Walter W. Hanson, Jr., as well as portions of "White Haven".[6]

On December 27, 1836, Peter Dent and Mary B. his wife, and Francis L. Rogerson and Martha A. his wife deeded to Joseph White lot no. 61 in Port Tobacco Town which on May 8, 1794, had been conveyed to Eleazer Davis by John Gwinn and afterwards sold to the Commissioners of the Court in the division of the estate of Eleazer Davis to Thomas Rogerson father of the said Francis L. Rogerson and Mary B. Dent.[7]

[1] Liber H B no. 13, folio 89, La Plata.
[2] Chancery Papers no. 1554.
[3] Deeds, Liber I B no. 12, folio 359.
[4] _Ibid.,_ folio 377.
[5] Inventory & Accounts 1815, folio 513.
[6] Deeds, I B no. 22, folio 366.
[7] _Ibid.,_ folio 376.

WILLIAM DENT[5]

William Dent, son of William and Verlinda (Beall) Dent, was born in Prince Georges County, Maryland. He migrated to western North Carolina with his parents in 1772, where within a few years he was actively engaged like his father in the American Revolution. Early in the war he accompanied Colonel Nicholas Long in his battalion of Minute Men and Volunteers from the District of Halifax to Norfolk, Virginia, as well as to Wilmington and Moore's Creek.[1] In 1790 he was the head of a family in Guilford County, North Carolina, with five males under the ages of 16 years, and three females.

[1] Public Accts., North Carolina, Book 1-6, folio 363, Raleigh.

GEORGE WASHINGTON DENT[5]

(177- - 18—)

George Washington Dent, son of Thomas and Elizabeth (Edelen) Dent, was born at Piscataway, Prince Georges County. Prior to 1802 he married Matilda, the daughter of John Bayne. In the latter year he and his wife figured in the law suit of Richard Marshall and Margaret his wife vs. Joseph Noble Bayne and other heirs of John Bayne, deceased.[1]

Children of George and Matilda (Bayne) Dent

1. John Walter Stoddert Dent.
2. Eleanor Matilda Bayne Dent, spinster.

George Washington Dent figured in the partition of his father's estate with his brother Lewis Dent in 1800. On October 6, 1804, he deeded negroes to his daughter Eleanor Matilda Bayne Dent.[2]

His first wife died young, after which he settled in Columbia County, Georgia, where he married Anne Hutchinson. The following appeared in Frederick Herald of September 6, 1806: "On August 21, 1806, at Columbia Court House, Georgia, George Dent married Miss Anne Hutcheson, both parties being of Charles County, Maryland."

Children of George and Anne (Hutchinson) Dent

4. Hutchinson Dent.
5. Mary Dent married ———— Collier.

In Columbia County, Georgia, on September 27, 1811, George Dent conveyed to John Tipplett, of Prince Georges County, Maryland, lots in Piscataway. At the same time he deeded to William Weems Clagett additional lots in Piscataway which had descended to the heirs of John Bayne and which George W. Dent purchased from James H. Bayne, and Philip Steuart and Mary F. his wife.

His spinster daughter, Eleanor Matilda, spent the latter years of her life in Prince William County, Virginia, where her will was proved on January 22, 1831.[3] She named as heirs her cousin Mary Francis Adeline Thornton (whose mother was named Ellen Matilda), the wife of Stuart G. Thornton; cousins Mary E. Thornton, Martha Stuart Thornton, and Francis Haws Thornton; brother Hutchison Dent; sister Mary Collier; cousins Mary Anne Dent and Lucinda Dent, daughters of Lewis Dent, deceased; and friends Maria Anne Booth and Anne Hebb. Her personal estate was appraised on August 11, 1831, at $1,720.

---

[1] Chancery papers no. 38291.
[2] Deeds, Liber I R M no. 10, folio 395, Marlb.
[3] Liber N, folio 344, Pr. Wm. Co., Va.

LEWIS WILLIAM DENT[5]

(17— - 1819)

Lewis William Dent, son of Thomas and Elizabeth (Edelen) Dent, was born at Piscataway, Prince Georges County. His wife was Anne Brook ————.

Children of Lewis and Anne Dent

1. George Fairfax Dent.
2. Lucinda Brooke Dent.
3. William Washington Dent.
4. Patrick Dent, *d.s.p.*
5. Elizabeth Margaret Dent.
6. Thomas Richard Dent.
7. Mary Anne Dent.
8. Matilda E. Dent.

During the War of 1812, Lewis William Dent served as a sergeant in the 43rd Maryland Regiment.[*]

By an indenture bearing date of November 22, 1800, Lewis William Dent, of Prince Georges County, and his brother George Washington Dent, of the same county, agreed to a partition of the realty. It was stated that the father of the above parties had died without a will and had also left a young son Patrick Dent. The land involved lay on Mattawoman Swamp as per deed from their father's brother, Peter Dent, of April 16, 1770, and willed to their father by his father Peter Dent, containing 330 acres, also land in Frederick County, Virginia, but then in Berkeley County, of 420 acres patented by their father in 1764. Anne Dent, the wife of Lewis, was a party to the deed.[1]

The will of Lewis W. Dent was dated November 30, 1817, and proved in Prince Georges County, on April 13, 1819, by George Boswell, Kenneln Boswell, Horatio Boswell, and George Edelen, with his widow Anne B. Dent as executrix.[2] He devised his son George F. Dent at the age of 21 years all lands in Frederick County, Virginia, which had been inherited from his father Thomas Dent. Other heirs were children— Lucinda, William W., Elizabeth M., Thomas R., Mary Anne, and Matilda E. Dent.

An account of November 23, 1827, showed that money had been paid to Anne B. Dent for the education and support of her children, for clothing of William W. Dent, and to Thomas Latimer, Jr., for tuition of Lucinda Dent.[3]

The will of the widow, Ann Brook Dent, of Prince Georges County, was dated May 6, 1826, and proved in Charles County on June 14, 1832.

---

[*] Marine's' *British Invasion of Maryland.*

She named her sons, George Farefax Dent, Thomas Richard Dent, and Patrick Dent, and daughter Elizabeth Margaret Dent. The dwelling-plantation she devised to her two daughters, Mary Ann Dent and Lucinda Brook Dent, and $50 to her son William Washington Dent at the age of 21 years. Her son George Farefax Dent was appointed executor, and the witnesses were Thomas D. Clagett, Robert Brawner, and Theodore Willet.[4]

[1] Deeds, Liber I R M no. 8, folio 514, Marlb.
[2] Wills, Liber T T no. 1, folio 240.
[3] Adm. Accts., Liber T T no. 4, folio 99.
[4] Wills, Liber W D M no. 15, folio 458, La Plata.

PATRICK DENT[5]

(17— - 1813)

Patrick Dent, son of Thomas and Elizabeth (Edelen) Dent, was born at Piscataway, Prince Georges County, Maryland. On July 22, 1809, he obtained license in Prince Georges County to marry Susannah Gerard Wood. He died intestate in Charles County, when the inventory of his personal estate was appraised at $601.44 and filed at court on April 5, 1813, by his administrator John T. Wood.[1]

[1] Inv. & Accts., 1813, folio 83, La Plata.

MARK WINNETT DENT[5]

(1777 - 1837)

Mark Winnett Dent, son of Walter and Elizabeth Dent, was born May 25, 1777, according to his Bible in his handwriting. All evidence points to the fact that it occurred at his parent's plantation near Piscataway, Maryland. In 1803 he made an exploratory trip to the then Territory of Missouri, but returned shortly afterwards to Rocky Mount in Southwestern Virginia. There he wedded his first wife Elizabeth Ferguson.

Children of Mark and Elizabeth (Ferguson) Dent

1. Joab Dent, born Sept. 5, 1806, in Va., died young.
2. Lewis Dent married Eliza Anne Simms. *q.v.*
3. Anne Dent, born Dec. 2, 1811, in Va., married Lorenzo Westover.
   Issue: James; Frances.

In 1811 Lewis Dent returned to St. Francois County, Missouri, and settled on land which he had negotiated a claim during his first trip.

With him were his wife and children, Joab and Nancy, leaving his youngest son Lewis at Rocky Mount with his uncle Jerry Ferguson. His first wife died in Missouri and after a few years he married Nancy Garrett, born January 3, 1790, in Virginia, but at that time the widow of Joseph Cooley with children.

Children of Mark and Nancy (Garrett) Dent

4. William Dent married Sarah Anne Sherrill. *q.v.*
5. Samuel Dent, born Sept. 30, 1822, married Lucy Haynes, went to California during the gold rush.
6. Cyprus Dent, born Apr. 23, 1825, married Mahala Jane Sherrill and Sallie Jones Johnson, widow. Issue: Henry; Samuel; Mary Ann; Sarah Jane; Sterling Price; Charles Cyrus; William John; John Sherrill; Lucy Ellen.
7. Elizabeth Dent, born Sept. 14, 1829, spinster.

After his settlement in Missouri, Mark Dent became prominent in civil affairs and was chairman of the committee to select the site for the county seat. During the War of 1812 he served under Colonel McNair who commanded a mounted regiment of militia composed of men from Illinois and Missouri. He was later sheriff for St. Francois County. His death occurred on December 3, 1837, and he was buried in the private graveyard near his home. His widow died on February 24, 1863.

WILLIAM DENT[5]

William Dent, son of George, was born in Charles County, Maryland, but it seems as if he lived at various times in Fauquier County, Virginia, as well as his native county. He married Janet S. Knox, daughter of Robert Knox, of Maryland and Virginia. This marriage would indicate that Robert Knox, Sr., was twice married and that Rose Townsend his wife was not the mother of his daughter Janet. William Dent is undoubtedly an issue of his father's marriage with Rose Townsend, no prior marriage has been found for him, inasmuch as it does not seem probable that William Dent would marry a half sister.

In 1806 the landed estate of Robert Knox was divided among Robert Knox, II, Elizabeth D. Brown (formerly Elizabeth D. Knox), Janet Dent (formerly Janet Knox), while the personal estate was distributed among William Dent, Robert Knox, II, and Elizabeth Brown.

Proved Children of William and Janet (Knox) Dent

1. Robert A. Dent.
2. William Dent.
3. George Dent.

On April 9, 1796, William Dent and Janet his wife of Maryland conveyed land to James Emmons, of Fauquier County, Virginia.

About February 1813, Robert D. Knox instituted action in the court of chancery against William Dent. The latter replied that he administered upon the estate of his deceased father George Dent who was the guardian to Robert D. Knox, then of Charles County. He furthermore stated that said Knox was a "near relative", was then insolvent, and had been persuaded to sue him, the administrator of his guardian's estate, by William Morris. Knox had married the ward and step-daughter of Morris.[1]

On June 14, 1815, William Dent in order to cover a judgement conveyed to Philip Stuart, of Charles County, land lying on the west side of Nanjemoy Creek, containing 900 acres known as "Friendship". The tract had been surveyed for Nicholas Gwyther in 1657 and was then the dwelling-plantations of William Dent and George Robertson. The tract, according to the deed, belonged formerly to William Dent, grandfather of the said grantor, and after his death to Warren Dent, uncle of the grantor, and after the latter's death to George Dent, father of the grantor. On April 18, of the same year, he transferred another portion of "Friendship" to Joseph Gray, Sr., and John F. Gray, at which time his wife Janet Dent waived all dower rights.[2]

On March 2, 1824, William Dent and Janet his wife, of Charles County, deeded to their sons — George Dent, Robert A. Dent, and William Dent—land in Fauquier County on the Rappahannock River called "Summerduck". The transfer was witnessed by Francis Adams and John F. Dunnington.[3] On December 28, of the same year, he sold to James T. Cropp, of Fauquier County, for $283.32 all interest and claim in land formerly owned by Thomas Dent, late of Prince William County, who derived title from Stephen Delite, being portions of "Berryman", lying in Prince William.[4]

A descendant of this branch of the Dent family, John Knox Dent by name, died testate in Baltimore City. His will, dated October 4, 1857, was proved on February 18, 1858. He referred to himself as millright, and requested that he be buried according to the rites of the Episcopal Church. To his sister, Jane Townsend Ransdale, he devised land in Fauquier County, Virginia, called "Summer Duck" during life, then to her children.

---

[1] Chancery papers no. 1550.
[2] Deeds, Liber T B no. 1, folios 101, 393, La Plata.
[3] Deeds, Liber 27, folio 428, Warrenton.
[4] Deeds, Liber 11, folio 17, Manassas.

GEORGE DENT[6]

(1808 - 1885)

George Dent, son of George and Elizabeth (Yates) Dent, was born February 29, 1808, at Prospect Hill, Charles County. He married Sophia Anne, born about 1817, daughter of Henry Ashton, of the same county. The license was obtained on October 21, 1833, in the District of Columbia. The births of the following children were taken from the 1850 census, at which time George Dent was domiciled in Allen's Fresh District, of Charles County, with realty assessed at $10,000. According to the family Bible his wife died in 1860, he died on June 30, 1885.

Children of George and Sophia (Ashton) Dent

1. Celcia E. Dent, born 1836.
2. Sophia Anne Dent, born 1838.
3. Sarah A. Dent, born 1840.
4. George Dent married Laura Maddox.
5. Eleanor Hawkins Dent, born 1844.
6. Mary A. Dent, born 1846.

DENNIS DENT[6]

(1796 - 1863)

Dennis Dent, son of George and Anne (Truman) Dent, was born in or about the year 1796 at "Clarke's Inheritance", Charles County, Maryland. He removed to Georgia with his parents, and there in 1815 he married Martha Tennison Beall. During the War of 1812, he served as sergeant in the 1st Georgia Militia Regiment under Colonel Harris. On September 14, 1818, he witnessed the will of Leroy Wilkins in Wilkes County, Georgia.

He later moved to Mobile, Alabama, where he became a commission merchant. The 1850 census shows him a resident of the Second Ward of Mobile, aged 64, and in his household were Frances Dent, aged 32, born in North Carolina; Mary Dent, aged 19, born in Alabama; and George W. Dent, aged 18, born in Alabama. According to DAR papers, he had a son John Herbert Dent, born 1822, died 1896, who married Charlotte McConley Travis.

The wife of Dennis died in 1853, he died in 1863.

FREDERICK FAYETTE DENT[6]

(1787 - 1873)

Frederick Fayette Dent, son of George and Susannah (Dawson) Dent, was born October 8, 1787, at Cumberland, Maryland. After leaving the parental dwelling, he lived for a time at Pittsburgh, from which place about 1812 he sailed down the Ohio River to the Mississippi and ultimately settled in St. Louis County, Missouri. To his estate he gave the name of "Whitehaven" after the ancestral home of his grandfather in Maryland. On December 22, 1814, he married Ellen Bray Wrenshall.

Children of Frederick and Ellen (Wrenshall) Dent

1. John Cromwell Dent married Ellen Dean and Anna Amanda Shurlds.
2. George Wrenshall Dent married Mary Shurlds.
3. Frederick Tracy Dent married Helen Lynd.
4. Lewis Dent married Elizabeth Baine.
5. Julia Boggs Dent, born Jan. 26, 1826, died Dec. 14, 1902, married Aug. 22, 1848, Ulysses Simpson Grant. Issue: Frederick Dent, born May 30, 1850; Ulysses S., born July 22, 1852; Ellen Wrenshall, born July 4, 1855; Jesse Root, born Feb. 6, 1858.
6. Ellen Wrenshall Dent, born 1828, married Alexander Sharp.
7. Mary Dent.
8. Emily Marbury Dent, married James Finnie Casey. *q.v.*

During the presidency of his son-in-law, U. S. Grant, he spent more time at the White House than at his plantation "Whitehaven" in Missouri. And at the White House he died on December 15, 1873.

PETER DENT[6]

(1798 - 18—)

Peter Dent, son to Theodore and Eleanor his wife, was born October 7, 1798, in Charles County, Maryland. About 1828 he married Mary Brown Rogerson, daughter of Thomas and Anstis (Olney) Rogerson.

Thomas Rogerson, the parent of Mrs. Dent, was born about 1759 in England and came to America with his father George Rogerson who settled in Providence, Rhode Island. About 1785 Thomas Rogerson removed to Alexandria, Virginia, where he was engaged in business until 1804 during which year he settled at Port Tobacco in Charles County. He married first in Rhode Island Anstis Olney, who became the mother of Mrs. Peter Dent, and secondly a widow Taney of Charles County by whom he had a son Francis Louis Rogerson. The latter married Martha

Ann, daughter of Theodore and Eleanor (Sheid) Dent. From 1818 to 1830 Thomas Rogerson served in the Maryland State Legislature and died at White Haven, the residence of his son-in-law in 1834, aged 75 years.[1]

Children of Peter and Mary (Rogerson) Dent

1. Theodore Dent married Elizabeth Catherine Dement. Issue: Mary Elizabeth; William Bell; Robert Lee; Frank Magruder; Ella Marbury; Ida Virginia; Rose Connington; Theodore Anstis; Edward Augustus.
2. Mary Anstis Dent married Peter Everett and Marcus Luckett.*
3. Thomas Dent.
4. Augustus Sheid Dent, died 1889, married first Rosina V. Connington (license D.C. July 15, 1858), and secondly Annie R. Sibley. Issue: (first) Peter R.; Edwin A.; Francis D.; Edwin H.
5. Simon Magruder Dent married twice. *q.v.*

Peter Dent died sometime prior to 1850, inasmuch as the census for that year, Mary B. Dent, aged 44 years, was the head of a family in Middletown District of Charles County, with the following children comprising her immediate household: Theodore, aged 21; Thomas, aged 18; Shade, aged 15; and Simon, aged 10.

---

[1] History of Alexandria-Washington Lodge, by Brockett, pub. 1876.

LEWIS DENT[6]

(1808 - 1880)

Lewis Dent, son of Mark Winnett and Elizabeth (Ferguson) Dent, was born December 11, 1808, in Virginia. He was raised by his maternal uncle, Jerry Ferguson, of Franklin County, Virginia, and did not join his father in Missouri until nearly manhood. He lived for a time in Tennessee but later returned to Missouri.

About 1840 he settled further into the interior of the State, traveling by wagon over primitive trails until he came to the headwaters of the Meramac River. There he established claims to a huge tract of land then included in Crawford County which is still in possession of his descendants. By the early fifties the population was sufficient to petition the State Legislature to organize a new county. It was established and named Dent in honor of Lewis Dent who was one of the civil leaders and pioneer settlers. He was elected the first representative to the State

---

*For the history and genealogy of the Luckett family, *see*, "The Lucketts of Portobacco," by Newman.

Legislature and throughout his life he remained one of the county's leading citizens. He died at the age of 72 and was buried in the family burial plot on his plantation.

About 1834 he married Eliza Anne Simms, born 1814, of St. Francois County, Missouri. The births of the following children are taken from the family Bible:

Children of Lewis and Eliza Anne (Simms) Dent

1. James Monroe Dent, born Dec. 21, 1835, died Feb. 3, 1873, married Sarah Springer. Issue: Louis Lee, born Sept. 21, 1871; Winnett.
2. Marshall Dent, born Jan. 29, 1838, killed in action while serving in the Confederate Army.
3. Mark Winnett Dent, born Jan. 27, 1840, died May 4, 1895, married Mary Rieser. Issue: James; Bertha; George; William Love.
4. Ferguson Dent married Rhoda Rosine Cook. *q.v.*
5. Lewis Henry Dent, born Feb. 14, 1846, married Amanda Dixon. Issue: Lewis; Mary; Fannie; Marshall.
6. Edwin Harrison Dent, born Feb. 19, 1848, married Julia Hite. Issue: Charles; John.
7. Frederick Fayette Dent, born Apr. 29, 1850, married Savannah McSpadden. Issue: Edwin; Herbert; Delphine.
8. Olivia Dent, born 1853, died 1856.
9. Elizabeth Dent, born Dec. 19, 1855, died Oct. 27, 1938, married Lewis Cass McSpadden. Issue: Pearl; Louis.
10. Samuel Jefferson Dent, born June 1, 1861, died 1939, married Martha Freeman. Issue: Alphus; Agnes; Landie; Emmett; Winnett; Farma.

WILLIAM DENT[6]

(1820 - 1875)

William Dent, son of Mark and Nancy (Garrett) Dent, was born July 2, 1820, in Missouri. In 1847 he married Sarah Anne Sherrill, born November 18, 1828. He died on April 9, 1875, while his widow died a few days later on April 17.

Children of William and Sarah Anne (Sherrill) Dent

1. Mary Ellen Dent, born Nov. 11, 1849, died 1916 in Mont., married Dallas Watkins and Samuel Barnes. Issue: (first) Marcus; Rooney; Judson Dent; Grace; Alice; (second) Asa; Coleman.
2. Laura Francis Dent, born Oct. 14, 1851, married John Hughes. Issue: James; Will; Minnie; Frank.
3. Henry Ferdiman Dent, born Nov. 23, 1854, died Sept. 2, 1936, in Calif., married Lucy Sherlock. Issue: Elmer; Leslie.

4. Walter Scott Dent, born Nov. 19, 1856, married Kate Eberhardt. Issue: Gertrude; Paul.
5. Tom Preston Dent, born Sept. 12, 1858, married Theresa Rieser. Issue: Tom Arthur, 129 Machine Gun Bn., died 1917, World War; Theresa Alice.
6. Nancy Alice Dent, born Sept. 14, 1860, married Milton Watkins. Issue: Lynn; Ray; Clyde.
7. John Albert Dent, died young.
8. William Edward Dent, born 1865, died bachelor 1939.
9, 10. Martin and Marcus Dent, twins, died young.
11. Anne Maude Dent, born Sept. 16, 1868, died spinster 1937.

CAPTAIN SIMON MAGRUDER DENT, C.S.A.[7]

(1841 - 1893)

Simon Magruder Dent, son of Peter and Mary Brown (Rogerson) Dent, was born in or about 1841, at Pomonkey, Charles County, Maryland. At the beginning of the War Between the States, he enlisted as a private in a cavalry regiment organized in northern Virginia. He was later promoted to First Lieutenant of Co. B, 5th Virginia Cavalry, under Captain Frederick R. Windsor, and was captured at Yellow Tavern in Alexandria.[1] A memorial article stated that he enlisted as a private in the 5th Virginia Cavalry, General Thomas L. Rosser's Regiment, and rose by gallant and meritorious services on the field of battle to the rank of captain. He was severely wounded but soon recovered. Later he was taken prisoner during a raid on the Union Lines and was one of the officers who was placed in front of Charleston, S. C., by the Union Army, to prevent the Confederate soldiers firing on the workmen.

After the war he returned home and within a few years he married Florence, daughter of Joseph Messenger and Olivia (Edelen) Parker. The ceremony was performed on July 27, 1870, at Washington, D. C.

Children of Simon and Florence (Parker) Dent

1. Ollie Dent, born Mar. 23, 1872, Piscataway, married June 8, 1892, Frederick, son of Ann Dorman and John Alexander Coe, at Brandywine, Md. He (Frederick) died Nov. 23, 1903. Issue: Magruder Dent, born Oct. 19, 1893; Anne Ursula, born Feb. 2, 1896; Frederick, born Aug. 17, 1901; Florence Angelia, born Apr. 26, 1899; John Alexander, born Feb. 2, 1904.
2. John Florence Dent, born Nov. 20, 1874, died Oct. 1935, in Chas. Co., married Feb. 5, 1907, Kate Hawkins, daughter of John Thomas and Julia (Hawkins) Clagett, at Accokee, Md. Issue: Julia Hawkins; John Florence; Henry Clagett; Katherine Ophelia; and Simon Magruder.

At Alexandria, Virginia, on July 5, 1884, Simon Magruder Dent married as his second wife Laura Virginia, the daughter of Bennett and Eleanor (Edelin) Gwynn.

Children of Simon and Laura (Gwynn) Dent

3. Bennett Gwynn Dent, born Oct. 8, 1885, at Alexandria, married Feb. 24, 1912, Opie Tuggle.
4. Eva Gwynn Dent, born Nov. 20, 1886, died Jan. 12, 1912, without issue, married Oct. 27, 1911, James Randall Caton, Jr.
5. Mary Anstis Dent, born May 8, 1888, at Alexandria, died May 6, 1911, without issue, married Nov. 27, 1910, Roy, son of Edelin and Ella Gwynn Parker.
6. Magruder Dent married Edith Baily. *q.v.*

Simon Magruder Dent died at Alexandria on January 31, 1893; his widow survived until March 19, 1899.

---

[1] Va. State Libr., vol. 8, folio 455; AGO, War Dept.

FERGUSON DENT, C.S.A.[7]

(1842 - 1921)

Ferguson Dent, son of Lewis and Eliza Ann (Simms) Dent, was born March 5, 1842, in Dent County, Missouri. Being a scion of an early landed proprietor of the State with its social and economic interests with the South, his sympathies were strongly in the Confederate Cause, and near the beginning of the war he enlisted as a private at Short Bend, a town about 10 miles from his home. He was assigned to Co. C, First Missouri Infantry and shared the many vicissitudes of that regiment throughout the conflict.[1] After the war he returned to his home and began rehabilitation necessary for a youth whose ideals had been defeated during four years of bitter struggle.

About 1873 he married Rhoda Rosine Cook who was born on July 1, 1851. She became the mother of his four children.

1. Everett Frank Dent, born May 1874, married Cora Clark.
2. William Ferguson Dent, born Dec. 21, 1875, *d.s.p.* 1928.
3. Clara Lee Dent, born May 25, 1878, married George D. Addison. Issue: George Ferguson, born June 20, 1905; Clara Barbara, born Aug. 2, 1907.
4. Louis Dent, born Jan. 15, 1884, married Feb. 24, 1909, Elizabeth Bell Dye, born Nov. 8, 1889. Issue: Elizabeth Rosine, born Nov.

5, 1909; Louis Linton, born May 30, 1911, married Nov. 10, 1938, Lorena Rice; James Ferguson, born June 6, 1914; Robert Vincent, born Apr. 13, 1916.

In 1894 Ferguson Dent organized the Dent County Bank of Salem whose management and ownership have since been retained by members of the family. His wife died on September 10, 1897; he died on August 12, 1921.

_____

[1] War Dept., Washington.

EMILY MARBURY DENT[7]

(1836 - 19—)

Emily Marbury Dent, the youngest and last surviving child of Colonel Frederick Dent, was born on June 6, 1836, at Whitehaven, Missouri. She married James Finnie Casey who was born on March 22, 1830, the son of Nicholas Wagner and Susan Gibson (Finnie) Casey, of Caseyville, Kentucky. Mrs. Casey spent her mature years in the nation's capital and died after the World War.

Children of James and Emily (Dent) Casey

1. Frederick Dent Casey, born Dec. 2, 1861.
2. Susan Gibson Casey, died young.
3. Louis Dent Casey, died young.
4. Jules Grant Casey, born July 8, 1869.
5. James Finnie Casey, married Antonia Harvey. q.v.
6. Emma Dent Casey, born Nov. 16, 1877.

James Finnie Casey, the youngest son, was born on January 16, 1872, at New Orleans, Louisiana. On February 1, 1900, at Washington, D. C., he married Antonia Lynch, daughter of Edward J. and Margaret (Lynch) Harvey, of New York. She was born November 16, 1876, and died December 14, 1939.

Children of James and Margaret (Harvey) Casey

1. James Finnie Casey, born Dec. 12, 1900, married June 8, 1940, Ruth, daughter of Christian E. and Catherine E. (Hildebrand) Young, of Baltimore, Md.
2. Margaret Shippen Casey, married Jan. 7, 1933, Robert Franklin, son of Albert Oscar Yates, of Vermont, and his wife Edna Asman, of Detroit.

MAGRUDER DENT[8]

Magruder Dent, son of Simon Magruder and Laura Virginia (Gwynn) Dent, was born June 1, 1889, at Alexandria, Virginia. On July 27, 1918, at Ardmore, Pennsylvania, he was married to Edith Houston Baily. She was born at Ardmore, Montgomery County, Pennsylvania, on November 15, 1895, the daughter of Frederick Lang and Caroline (Corliss) Baily. Mr. Dent maintains a residence at Greenwich, Connecticut, as well as a town house in New York City.

Children of Magruder and Edith (Baily) Dent

1. Magruder Dent, born May 8, 1919, at Augusta, Ga. A.B. Yale Univ., '40.
2. Frederick Baily Dent, born Aug. 17, 1922, at Cape May, N. J. Student (1940) St. Paul's Schl., Concord, N. H.
3. Edith Baily Dent, born June 8, 1924, at Ardmore, Pa. Student (1940) at Foxcroft Schl., Middleburg, Va.
4. Diana Gwynn Dent, born Oct. 1, 1928, at Phila. Attended (1940) Brearley Schl., N. Y. C.

CAPTAIN JOHN DENT, GENT.[1]
(16— - 1712)

It has been pointed out that Thomas Dent claimed headrights in 1663 and 1676, respectively, for the transportation of one John Dent. The question arises whether these John Dents are the one and the same. Most likely they are. It is possible and quite probable that John Dent settled in Maryland about 1658, returned to England, and again entered the Province about 1676. And there are definite circumstances which indicate that he probably married in England and left a wife or orphaned children in England.

Nothing has been unearthed to prove the degree of relationship which existed between Thomas and John, but it was popularly stated to be that of brothers. Modern research, however, has now proved the fallibility of that assumption. John could have been a nephew of Thomas, and thus a son of the elder brother William (see pedigree on page 4). John was too old to be the son of Peter Dent, of Cambridge, and likewise to be a son of the younger brother George. It is noted, however, that the name of Peter appears among the children of both Thomas and John, thus strengthening the belief that they were the descendants of Peter Dent, of Gisborough.

It was stated by a great-grandson of Captain John Dent that his forbears came from Yorkshire, a statement which could reasonably have been handed down with authenticity from father to son and which appears in a memorial to the Rev. Hatch Dent. Yet some discrepancies occur.

> "Rev. Hatch Dent, son of Hatch and grandson of John Dent of Yorkshire, England. One of the early settlers of the Province of Maryland, was born May 1757, died December 30, 1799. An honored officer in the Army of the Revolution of 1776, and an Eminent Teacher and Minister of the Church. Ordained by Bishop Seabury in 1785".

The inscription appears at the Dent Memorial Chapel at Charlotte Hall Military Academy, St. Mary's County. It is known that Hatch Dent was the great-grandson instead of the grandson of John Dent, and furthermore, the parish register gives his birth as 1751 instead of 1757.

While there is no record of this branch of the Dent family using a coat-of-arms during the early generations in Maryland, a silver pitcher which belonged to Captain Hezekiah Dent of the Revolution has come down in the family with the identical arms used by Judge Thomas Dent, and is now in the possession (1940) of Mrs. Lettie Gough Hayden, of Maddox, Maryland.

It has been stated that John Dent came into the Province as an indentured servant. While the latter was not always a stigma, John Dent was certainly not an indenture. His warrant for "Promise" is given as the basis for the statement. The following is an exact copy from the Land Office, Liber 18, folio 193:

> "Cecilius Absolute Lord & proprietary of the Province of Maryland and Avalon, Lord Baron of Baltemore & c. To all persons to whom these presents shall come Greetings in our Lord God Everlasting. Know ye that we for and in consideration that John Dent of Charles County in our said Province of Maryland hath due unto him one hundred and forty acres of land within our said Province, forty acres thereof due unto him for remainder of a warrant for two hundred acres to him formerly Granted and one hundred acres by assignment from Giles Wilson and Nicholas Clemens due to them for their times of Service performed within our said Province as appear upon Record . . . 1674 Wittness Dear Son Charles Calvert Esq. our Capt. Generall & Cheif Governour of our said Province of Maryland".

A careful reading of the above instrument will show definitely and intelligently that Giles Wilson and Nicholas Clemens had been the indentured servants and that they assigned their land rights to John Dent for a valuable consideration.

The tract "Promise" was surveyed by Richard Edelen on September 26, 1673, and was adjacent to "Baker's Rest" and the lands of Edward Swann and William Marshall.

Returning to the belief that John Dent married in England, it is significant that at the time of his death he had a son living outside of the Province. In his will he mentioned a son Peter who was bequeathed property on the condition "if he comes into this Province to inhabit". Thus it looks as if Peter had never been in Maryland which substantiates the supposition that John Dent married before his final departure for Maryland and left a child or children in England. It is also significant that in 1677 John Harris proved rights for 50 acres of land for the transportation of Abigail Dent who could have been a daughter left in Yorkshire.[1] And John Dent in his will provided for a spinster daughter Abigail.

Whether John Dent was a bachelor or widower at the time of his settlement in Maryland is consequently a debatable question, but it is known that sometime before 1678 he had married Mary, the daughter of John Hatch, an interesting character in early Maryland history.

Children of John Dent

1. Peter Dent.
2. Michael Dent, *d.s.p.*
3. John Dent married Catherine ————. *q.v.*
4. George Dent married twice. *q.v.*
5. Mary Dent.*
6. Lydia Dent married Samuel, son of Edward Turner. Issue: Edward; John; Samuel; Ruth; Micha.
7. Anne Dent married John Cadle. Issue: Robert; Mary; Elizabeth; Abigail; Edward.
8. Abigail Dent.
9. Christian Dent married Thomas Suite.**

Unlike Judge Thomas Dent who is believed to have been a conservative in Maryland affairs and thus popular with the Proprietary party, John Dent seems to have championed the liberal cause. While he escaped impeachment during the Fendall Rebellion, circumstances would tend to indicate that he was somewhat involved. He married a daughter of John Hatch, a well-known liberal and opportunist who rose to importance during the Commonwealth. From 1654 to 1658 John Hatch was a member of the commission or governing body of the Province which under the chairmanship of Richard Preston ruled the colony for four years or so. After the Puritan downfall Hatch regained his good favor with the Calverts only by the payment of a heavy fine.

During the sessions of the Council regarding the investigations emanating from Fendall's Rebellion, Thomas Perry, of St. Mary's County, under oath on October 12, 1682, made several references to John Dent which prove absolutely his marriage to a daughter of John Hatch. Perry thus states, ". . . if he (Dent) had declared all that he knew against Ffendall and which he (Dent) heard Ffendall say at his ffather in law Hatch's funeral he (Dent) could have hang'd him . . ."***

John Dent ultimately became one of the leading planters in Maryland and held many offices of trust under the Lord Proprietary. In 1670 he and James Walker were appointed by the court to appraise the estate

---

*Received "Ashman Freehold" in 1712 by father's will. May 1, 1714, William Maria Farthing conveyed this tract of 150 acres to William Heard. (Rent Rolls, St. M. & Chas. Cos. Liber 1 & 2, folio 33.)

**At a subsequent date Thomas Suite held 130 acres and Thomas Suite, Jr., 100 acres of "Cold Wells", originally a tract of 347 acres. Furthermore, Thomas Suite held 84 acres of "Trent Fork"—both tracts having been willed Christian by her father. Furthermore, there is the given name of Dent in this family.

***Archives, vol. 17, p. 119. Francis P. Culver, genealogist, whose claims to infallibility are well known stated in Md. Hist. Mag., vol. 19, p. 195, that John Dent married Mary Shirtcliffe. The latter intermarried with the Dant family of Catholic faith, of no connection with John Dent.

of Walter Beane. On November 9, 1673, he patented "Promise" for 140 acres of land, and the next year he patented "Barnaby", of 60 acres in Chaptico Hundred of St. Mary's County which seems to have become his dwelling-plantation. He negotiated no further land patents, but before his death he was the proprietor through purchase or inheritance of a landed estate exceeding 3000 acres.

On August 13, 1678, he and Mary his wife appointed Richard Edelen their attorney to "allow the right and title of the tract Promise to Richard Ashman of Charles County". The instrument was witnessed by Sarah X Gwin and Mary Alderne.[2]

He was a Commissioner and Justice of Peace for St. Mary's County in 1679, 1680, 1684, 1685, and perhaps in other years. He served during 1681 against the Susquehanna Indians, and at a session of the General Assembly in 1689, he was commissioned to raise a troop of horse for Chaptico Hundred, and made captain of the company.[3] In 1693 he was referred to as Captain of the Proprietary Forces and designated to regulate military affairs in Chaptico Hundred.[4]

In November 1683, he was commissioned to purchase and lay out towns in St. Mary's County for the advancement of trade. In 1689 he signed a petition to Their Majestys William and Mary as "a dutiful and Loyall Protestant Subject".

In 1690 John Harrison, of Charles County, negotiated his will and made John Dent the executor and principal heir, devising him tracts "Harrison's Adventure" and "Providence". The instrument was not probated until 1705, at which time "Captain Dent" in the administration of the estate showed that John Harrison had moved to Virginia and had left no personal property in Maryland.

At the organization of the parishes in 1692 by William and Mary, Chaptico Hundred bordering the eastern bank of the Wicomico was incorporated into King and Queen Parish, and John Dent became one of the first vestrymen. At various times he was spoken of as Justice of the Quorum. On November 24, 1698, the vestry of All Faith's Parish ordered the parish to purchase for £25 from Captain John Dent 50 acres of land "near a fountain of healing waters". This land is now the site of Charlotte Hall Military Academy.

Captain John Dent was the executor of William Husculah, late of St. Mary's County, and stated before Kenelm Cheseldine, Gent., Commissary, that the said Husculah left land but no personal estate.

Michael Dent, his son, died intestate sometime before June 23, 1697, and was apparently unmarried. The father refused to administer upon the estate as is evident from the proceedings of the Prerogative Court:

"for I will not be made Rich by my Son, neither shall my estate pay my son the bill my son have past to pay you is for Giles Hill, and Giles Hill saith he is willing to pay bill to you". The statement was made to Robert Mason, so likewise letters of administration were issued to Mason, of St. Mary's County. Philip Clarke and George Mushamp offered bond.[5]

The will of Captain John Dent was dated September 25, 1711, but it was not admitted to probate in St. Mary's County until May 5, 1712. Samuel Williamson, James Keech, and Henry Davis were present at the signing and proved it before the Prerogative Court.[6]

He named his wife, the executrix jointly with their son John, and bequeathed her personal property. John was devised the house and lot in Newportowne and the following tracts: "Cumberson" of 200 acres, "Barnaby" of 60 acres, "Reading" of 300 acres, "Evan's Addition" of 100 acres, 215-acre portion of "Providence", "Harrison's Adventure" of 250 acres, and all the land granted the testator by the will of John Harrison except 50 acres of "Haphazard".

George was granted the residue of "Haphazard" and 324 acres of "Freestone Point". "In the event son Peter coming into the Province to settle he is to have portions of lands devised to son John, also part of 'Horse Range' and one-half of 'Freestone Point' ".

From the tone of the will it looked as if all five daughters were unmarried. Mary received "Ashman's Freehold". Anne was devised "St. Stephen", 200 acres of "Coldman", and 100 acres of "Evans' Reserve". Abigail was granted 136 acres of "Love Adventure". Christian received 331 acres of "Coldwell's", 25 acres of "Trentforke", and 200 acres of "Horse Range". In the event that his daughters die without issue, the realty was to revert to the living heirs of their deceased father.

The inventory of his personal estate was made on May 5, 1712, with George Dent and Samuel Turner signing as the nearest of kin. His widow and son John rendered an account to the court on April 5, 1713, when all children were declared of age.

His widow, Mary Dent, died intestate during 1726, no doubt at an advanced age. The inventory of her personal estate was taken on June 2, 1726, with George Dent and Samuel Turner signing as the kinsmen.

[1] Warrants, Liber B B, folio 260.
[2] Deeds, Liber H no. 1, folio 2, La Plata.
[3] Archives, vol. 20, p. 106.
[4] Archives, vol. 13.
[5] Test. Proc., Liber 17, folio 13.
[6] Wills, Liber 13, folio 442.

John Dent[2]

(1674 - 1733)

John Dent, son of John and Mary (Hatch) Dent, was born in or about 1674 in Chaptico Hundred, St. Mary's County, inasmuch as in 1727 he declared himself to be 53 years of age. His widow was Catherine ————, and as no other wife has been found, it is assumed that she was the mother of his four proved sons. It is highly probable that several daughters were born, but one is unable to establish them through court records.

Children of John and Catherine Dent

1. John Dent. *q.v.*
2. Hatch Dent. *q.v.*
3. Michael Dent. *q.v.*
4. Benjamin Dent. *q.v.*

The landed estate of John Dent prior to 1720 consisted of the following tracts: "Cumberson" of 200 acres, originally granted in 1668 to Francis Pope; "Reading" of 300 acres, originally granted in 1671 to Abraham Rhodes; "Evans' Addition" of 100 acres, granted to Edward Evans in 1671; and "Barnaby" of 60 acres, granted to his father on July 29, 1674. These tracts were adjacent and lay west of Zachaiah Swamp in the vicinity of Newport. By a warrant from His Lordship's Land Office of March 13, 1720, they were resurveyed and adding contiguous lands of 509 acres, the patent was issued in the name of "Dent's Inheritance", containing in all 1169 acres "to be held of Calverton Manor".

John Dent died intestate during the late spring of 1733. The inventory of his personal effects was taken on June 8, 1733, when his brother George Dent and kinsman Edward Turner signed the papers. Catherine Dent was the administratrix and her bondsmen were Thomas Matthews and Samuel Turner, Jr.

It seems as if the patent to "Dent's Inheritance", though the warrant was issued in 1720, had not been delivered at the time of John Dent's decease. Accordingly on June 11, 1734, his eldest son and heir John Dent, III, petitioned the court with the following statement: "humbly sheweth that his father John Dent in his lifetime had resurveyed for him a certain tract of land called Dent's Inheritance containing 1,169 acres . . . but before his Lordship's grant to him given did issue, he the said John Dent died".

In the course of time John Dent, III, was granted "Dent's Inheritance" which he partitioned among his four brothers. This tract became the traditional seat of this branch of the Dent family, parts of it still being held by descendants.

GEORGE DENT[2]

(16— - 1750)

George Dent, son of John and Mary (Hatch) Dent, was born sometime after 1676 in Chaptico Hundred, of St. Mary's County. He married twice. His first wife was Elizabeth, daughter to George Short who died testate in Charles County. By his will dated October 17, 1718, and proved March 4, 1719/20, he devised "Simpson's Supply" to his daughter Elizabeth Dent and a half interest in the dwelling-plantation (unnamed) at the decease of his widow Anne.[1] The second wife of George Dent was Mary ————.

Children of George Dent

1. John Dent married Mary ————. *q.v.*
2. George Dent.
3. Mary Dent married James Armstrong.
4. Lydia Dent.
5. Charity Dent.
6. Peter Dent. *q.v.*
7. Thomas Dent married Elizabeth Edwards. *q.v.*
8. William Dent.

The will of George Dent, Sr., was dated April 5, 1746, and witnessed by John Hilton, Margaret Hilton, and Mary Hilton, but was not presented for probation in St. Mary's County until June 7, 1750. His son John was devised 100 acres of the plantation whereon he was then living, while son George was devised 50 acres of the plantation whereon he was residing. The residue of his landed estate was to be divided among his three youngest sons—Peter, Thomas, and William. The latter was to have that portion on which he was then domiciled. Various articles of personal property and negroes were bequeathed to his daughters Mary Armstrong, Lidia Dent, and Charity Dent. His wife Mary was bequeathed the personal estate during life, then it was to be divided among Peter, William, Thomas, and Charity.[2]

The will came before the Prerogative Court during October 1750, but no inventory or accounts were recorded. His widow was probably the Mary Dent who on October 26, 1751, married Justinian Mills, according to St. Andrew's Parish register.

It is believed that their son George settled in Fairfax County, Virginia, where he died intestate in 1757. The inventory of the estate was

taken on August 30, 1757, appraised at £39/11/6, and signed by John
Summers, Sr., John Ratcliff, and William Ashford.[3]

[1] Wills, Liber 15, folio 315.
[2] Wills, Liber 27, folio 395.
[3] Liber B, folio 177, Fairfax.

John Dent[3]

(17— - 1791)

John Dent, son of John, was born in the vicinity of Newport. Upon
the death of his father, he inherited as the eldest son "Dent's Inheritance" which on March 10, 1732/3, for the consideration of natural
love he conveyed 144 acres to his brother Hatch.[1] After several conveyances to other brothers and various sales, he retained 250 acres which
became his dwelling-plantation. His wife was Mary ————, who was
probably of some connection with the Blackman family. At least three
of her grandchildren carried this family name.

Children of John and Mary Dent

1. John Dent. *q.v.*
2. Mary Dent.
3. Hatch Dent married twice. *q.v.*
4. Sarah Dent* married ———— Clark.
5. Tabitha Dent married Walter Moreland.
6. Anne Dent married Charles Davis. Issue: Eleanor, born Apr. 7,
   1777; Benjamin, born Sept. 9, 1778; Thomas Blackman, born
   Aug. 23, 1782; Peter, born Aug. 13, 1786.
7. Bennett Dent, *d.s.p.* 1779.

On December 3, 1757, John Dent conveyed to Benjamin Dent a
portion of "Dent's Inheritance", lying on the north side of Pile's Fresh.[2]
On June 11, 1766, he conveyed to Hatch Dent "Dent's Place", lying on
the north side of a branch of Pile's Fresh. On August 11, 1777, he
deeded portions of "Dent's Inheritance" to Michael Dent and Thomas
Dent. At all three conveyances his wife Mary waived dower rights.[3]

In 1778 as John Dent of John he took the oath of allegiance and
fidelity to the State of Maryland in Charles County under magistrate
John Parnham.[4]

His will was dated December 21, 1788, and proved in Charles County
on August 22, 1791. John was devised 200 acres of "Dent's Inheritance"

*It is said that she married John Clarke and had William Dent, born 1788;
Nancy born 1791; Hatch born 1795; John born 1798; Thomas Blackman born
1801; and Anne born 1805.

and a portion of "Dent's Addition" to be laid off the dwelling-plantation. May Dent, his daughter, was devised 100 acres of "Dent's Inheritance", negroes, also the water and hand mill. Hatch was willed the residue of the realty. Sarah Clark, Tabitha Moreland, and Anne Davis, daughters, were bequeathed negroes.[5]

---

[1] Deeds, Liber M no. 2, folio 322.
[2] *Ibid.*, Liber G no. 3, folio 146.
[3] *Ibid.*, Liber V no. 3, folio 201.
[4] Unp. Md. Rec., vol. 5, DAR Library.
[5] Wills, Liber A K no. 11, folio 28, La Plata.

HATCH DENT[3]

(1707 - 1781)

Hatch Dent, son of John, was born about 1707, according to a deposition made in 1768, when he declared himself to be 61 years of age and the son of John Dent, deceased. About 1730 he married Anne ————, whose family has not been proved. Like his father he maintained his seat in Trinity Parish of Charles County, and there in the parish register may be found the births of his children.

Children of Hatch and Anne Dent

1. John Dent married Margaret Dyson. *q.v.*
2. Mary Dent, born Apr. 13, 1732.
3. Catherine Dent, born Nov. 4, 1734.
4. Anne Dent, born May 7, 1737, married Jan. 11, 1757/8, Thomas Swann. Issue: Martha, born Feb. 26, 1758/9; Zedakiah, born Apr. 16, 1760; Hatch, born Feb. 1, 1762/3; Asa, born July 2, 1764; Anne Chapman, born May 21, 1767; Esther, born Apr. 2, 1772; Ezra, born June 3, 1774.
5. Lydia Dent, born Dec. 22, 1739, married John Dyson.
6. Esther Dent, born May 10, 1742, married Feb. 17, 1760, Thomas Dyson. Issue: Amelia, born Jan. 29, 1761; John, born Feb. 10, 1763; Anne, born Oct. 6, 1765; William, born Mar. 17, 1768.
7. Rhoda Dent, born Nov. 4, 1744, married July 1, 1764, William Turner. Issue: John, born Apr. 12, 1765.
8. Hezekiah Dent married twice. *q.v.*
9. Hatch Dent married Judith Poston. *q.v.*

In 1749 Hatch Dent patented "Dent's Gore" of 34 acres and in 1754 "Dent's Palace" of 209 acres, both tracts lying in Charles County. He and John Dent were bondsmen for their sister Lydia Dyson, when in 1760 she was issued letters of administration for the estate of her deceased husband John Dyson.

In 1778 Hatch Dent took the oath of allegiance and fidelity to the State of Maryland in Charles County, his name appearing under the returns of magistrate John Parnham.[1]

The will of Hatch Dent was proved in Charles County during 1781. To his son Hezekiah, he devised the dwelling-plantation known as "Dent's Palace", providing that he allowed his mother the use of it during her lifetime. He mentioned his son Hatch, daughter Rhody Turner, the heirs of his son John, and other unnamed children, also his grandchildren Anne Dyson and Margaret Dyson.[2]

The inventory of his personal estate was taken on October 22, 1781, and appraised at £286/7/9, with Hezekiah Dent as the executor. Hatch Dent and Peter Dent signed as the kinsmen, while Thomas Dent and Michael Dent were the bondsmen.[3]

---

[1] Unpub. Md. Records, vol. 5, DAR Library.
[2] Wills, Liber A F no. 7, folio 665.
[3] Liber A F no. 7, folios 671, 681.

MICHAEL DENT[3]

(171- - 1795)

Michael Dent, son of John Dent and Catherine his wife, was born in what is now Trinity Parish, Charles County, Maryland. On September 3, 1735, he and Thomas Skinner were bondsmen for Mary Manning, the widow and executrix of John Manning, late of Charles County. At that time he had necessarily attained the then legal age of 18 years, so consequently his birth occurred before 1717. His share of the parental estate consisted of about 140 acres of "Dent's Inheritance", which became his dwelling-plantation.

Neither the family nor given name of his wife has been established, but Manning and Turner are found among the given names of his descendants. She was probably a daughter of John and Mary Manning, upon whose estate he was a bondsman in 1735.

Children of Michael Dent

1. Joseph Manning Dent married Mary ————. *q.v.*
2. Victory Dent, spinster.
3. John Dent. *q.v.*
4. Michael Dent. *q.v.*
5. Catherine Dent.
6. Mary Dent married Benjamin Edwards.
7. Elizabeth Dent married Joseph Watson.

In 1778 Michael Dent took the oath of allegiance and fidelity to the State of Maryland in Charles County under Magistrate John Parnham.[1]

At the tax list of 1783, Michael Dent was assessed for 154 acres of land lying in Newport West Hundred, with two in family. He was a communicant of Trinity Parish and at various times served as warden or vestryman of the parish.

His will was dated February 1, 1786, and proved in Charles County on October 12, 1795, by Elizabeth Dent, John Cooksey, and Peter Dent. He devised his son, Joseph Manning Dent, the dwelling-plantation "Dent's Inheritance", providing that he allowed his sister, Victory, the use of it during lifetime. John and Michael received £50 each. The residue of the estate was to be divided among Joseph, Catherine, and Victory providing that they pay their sisters, Mary and Elizabeth, 5 shillings each. He appointed his son Joseph Manning Dent and daughter Victory Dent the executors.[2]

The will of his spinster daughter Victory was proved in Charles County in 1802. She named Elizabeth and John Turner Dent, the children of her brother Joseph Manning Dent, and the following of no stated relationship: Sarah Dent, Pricy Dent, Lawson Dent, and Hezekiah Dent. She appointed Elizabeth Dent the executrix who later became Mrs. Joseph Watson.[3]

The inventory of the personalty was appraised at $892 and filed at court on December 13, 1802, by Elizabeth Dent. Prisy Dent and Mary X Dent signed as kinsmen, while Hatch Dent and Thomas Dent of William signed as the greatest creditors.

The first and only account was rendered in 1805 by Joseph Watson and Elizabeth his wife, with Thomas Dent of William and Joseph Watson as the bondsmen. Disbursements were made to the following: Trinity Parish, Eleazer Dent Higdon, Levi Higdon, Peter Dent, Thomas Turner, Josiah Dent, Henry Dent, Thomas Wathen, Joseph Watson, Thomas Dent, Martha Dent, Mary M. Dent, George Dyson, Jesse Jameston, William Turner, and Alexander McPherson.[4]

The degree of relationship of the heirs to the deceased is not known, probably some were nephews while others were husbands of nieces.

---

[1] Unpub. Md. Rec., vol. 5, DAR.
[2] Wills, Liber A K no. 11, folio 284.
[3] *Ibid.*, Liber A L no. 8, folio 61.
[4] Liber 1805, folio 306, La Plata.

BENJAMIN DENT[3]
(17— - 1778)

Benjamin Dent, son of John and Catherine Dent, was born at "Dent's Inheritance", Charles County. Before 1750 he married, but research fails to identify definitely the name of his wife. It is noted, however, that at his death he was seized of "St. Stephen" and "Coleman"—two tracts which his grandfather had willed to the latter's daughter who later became Mrs. John Cadle. In the absence of deeds showing the purchase of these tracts by him, it is not unlikely that he married one of his Cadle kinswomen who brought him these plantations.

Children of Benjamin Dent

1. Gibeon Dent married Mary ————. *q.v.*
2. John Brewer Dent married Priscilla Dent. *q.v.*
3. Benjamin Dent married Anne ————. *q.v.*
4. Shadrick Dent. Took Patriot's Oath 1778.
5. Zachariah Dent married Elizabeth ————. *q.v.*
6. Titus Dent married Mary ————. *q.v.*
7. Chloe Dent married Feb. 17, 1767, Joseph, son of James and Susannah Waters. Issue: Benjamin; Dent; Eva; Joseph; Kezia; Phebe; Susannah.
8. Kezia Dent married ———— Burroughs.
9. Johannah Dent married ———— Higdon.
10. Susannah Dent.

During March 1778, Benjamin X Dent subscribed to the Oath of Allegiance and Fidelity to the State of Maryland in Charles County before Magistrate Joshua Sanders.[1]

His will was dated July 5, 1778, and admitted to probate in Charles County on August 15, 1778. He devised to his unnamed wife the dwelling-plantation, consisting of 143 acres of "Dent's Inheritance" and 4 acres of "Turner's Forest" during life, then to his son. In the event of the death of Gideon without issue, then to the testator's son John Brewer. Benjamin, Jr., received realty, but in the event that he died without heirs of his body then to Shadrick. Zachariah was willed 96 acres of "Turner's Forest" and a portion of "Church Over". Titus was devised "St. Stephen" and "Coleman". Chloe Waters, Johannah Higdon, Kezia Burroughs, and Susannah Dent, all daughters, received slaves and other personalty.[2]

The records of Charles County fail to show any administration on the estate. His widow was probably Margaret Dent who, according to the 1783 tax list, was living upon 69 acres of unnamed land, with three in the immediate household.

[1] Unpub. Md. Records, vol. 5, DAR.
[2] Wills, Liber A F no. 7, folio 207.

JOHN DENT[3]

(17—- 1779)

John Dent, son of George and Elizabeth (Short) Dent, was born perhaps in St. Mary's County. On July 23, 1748, he conveyed to William Cooksey, of Charles County, "Simpson's Supply". This tract had belonged to his maternal grandfather, George Short, and had been willed to his mother in 1720. Inasmuch as no wife waived dower at the sale of this land, it is probable that John Dent married after this date.[1] His widow was Mary ————.

Children of John and Mary Dent

1. Judith Dent married ———— Wood.
2. Elizabeth Dent married James Chappelear. Issue: Nathan; Henry; Richard; Elizabeth; Rebecca; Mary; Cassandra; Ann; George; John; Benjamin.
3. John Dent married Verlinda Beall. *q.v.*
4. Rebecca Dent.
5. Susan Dent married William Burroughs, Feb. 9, 1783, All Faith's Par., St. M. Co.
6. Tabitha Dent.
7. Sarah Dent married George Harrison, Dec. 16, 1777, All Faith's Par.

The will of John Dent was dated October 13, 1778, and proved in St. Mary's County on August 12, 1779, by Dorcus Macklon, Mary Macklon, and Samuel Amory. He devised his wife Mary the dwelling-plantation "Freestone Point" during life then to his only son John. Other heirs were his daughters, Judith Wood, Elizabeth Chappelear, Rebecca Dent, Susan Dent, Tabithy Dent, and Sarah Harrison.[2]

[1] Deeds, Liber Z no. 2, folio 282.
[2] Wills, Liber J J no. 1, folio 104, Leonardtown.

PETER DENT[3]

Peter Dent, son of George, was born in Newport Hundred, Charles County. In 1778 he took the oath of allegiance and fidelity to the State of Maryland in Charles County under Magistrate Joshua Sanders.[1] According to the tax list of 1783, he was seized of 150 acres of "Dent's Inheritance" and 10 acres of "Cooksey's Hard Bargain", both tracts lying in Newport Hundred. He had six in family. On January 11, 1806, he purchased from John Edwards, of St. Mary's County, the following tracts: "Edward's Back Land" of 162 acres, "Wednesday's Project" of 98 acres, and "Higgs His Purchase" of 49 acres. The latter had been granted to Benjamin Edwards of Joseph, and the said Benjamin Edwards (whose wife was Sarah) were the parents of John Edwards who conveyed to Peter Dent.[2]

---

[1] Unpub. Md. Records, vol. 5, DAR.
[2] Deed Digests, Liber 1, folio 496.

THOMAS DENT[3]

Thomas Dent, son of George, was born about 1730 presumably in St. Mary's County. According to family tradition, he married Elizabeth Edwards, of St. Mary's, and who was probably the mother of all his children. On December 18, 1781, by the Rev. John McPherson, of William and Mary Parish, Charles County, he was married to Mary Ann Hancock, born in 1734. The following list of children may or may not be complete:

Children of Thomas and Elizabeth (Edwards) Dent

1. George Dent married Elizabeth Mills. *q.v.*
2. William Dent married Margaret Rettea Smoot. *q.v.*
3. Henry Dent married Charity Cox. *q.v.*
4. Thomas Dent married Rebecca Chappelear. *q.v.*

On August 11, 1777, Thomas Dent purchased from his kinsman, John Dent, a portion of "Dent's Inheritance". He died intestate prior to 1790. In the latter year, his widow Mary Dent was the head of a family in St. Mary's County, with two males over 16 years of age, and five females including herself in the immediate household. The records of St. Andrew's Parish show that Mary Anne Dent, "wife" of Thomas Dent, died May 30, 1823, aged 89 years.

JOHN DENT[4]
(17— - 1799)

John Dent, son of John and Mary Dent, was born at "Dent's Inheritance", Charles County. The name of his wife has not been established, but she is believed to be the mythical Violetta Winnett from whom many members of the Daughters of the American Revolution have claimed descent.*

Children of John Dent

1. John Shelton Dent. *q.v.*
2. Priscilla Dent married John Brewer Dent. *q.v.*

In March 1778, he took the oath of fidelity and allegiance to the State of Maryland in Charles County under Magistrate Joshua Sanders.[1]

The will of John Dent was dated January 16, 1799, and proved in Charles County on November 4, 1799. He devised his entire estate to his son John Shelton Dent, inasmuch as he had already provided for his daughter Priscilla. He named his brother Hatch Dent as executor and the guardian of his son John.[2]

The inventory of his estate was filed on December 10, 1799, by his executor, Hatch Dent. Mary X Newbury, John Chappelear, and Charles X Gill signed the papers. The estate was appraised at £779/20/–.[3]

The first account of "John Dent of John" was rendered on October 11, 1800, by Hatch Dent. The final account and distribution were made in 1806. Zephaniah Waters and James G. Watson were the bondsmen.[4]

[1] Unpub. Md. Records, vol. 7.
[2] Wills, Liber A K no. 11, folio 536.
[3] Inventories, Liber 1798-1802, folio 214.
[4] Adm. Accts., Liber 1798-1808, folio 158.

HATCH DENT[4]

(17— - 1816)

Hatch Dent, son of John and Mary Dent, was born at "Dent's Inheritance", Charles County, Maryland. An undocumented source (DAR papers) states that he married Susannah Edwards, and while it is possible, no proof during this research has been found. His widow, however, was Elizabeth.

Children of Hatch Dent

1. Elizabeth Anne Dent married ———— Turner.
2. Sophia Dent married Jesse C. Cook.
3. John Blackman Edwards Dent married Maria Turner. *q.v.*
4. Theodore Dent, *d.s.p.* 1816.
5. Hatch Dent.

*Many claim descent from a John Dent, born 1735, died 1830, and who was a member of the Maryland Convention during the Revolution. No such member of the Dent family ever existed. The correct lineage of more than ten members of the DAR who claim right of membership from this John Dent is given elsewhere in this book.

6. Susan Juliet Dent.
7. Llewellyn Marshall Dent.
8. Stoughton Warren Dent married twice. *q.v.*
9. Mary Emeline Dent.

During the Revolutionary War Hatch Dent served as a private in
Captain Clarkson's Company of Charles County Militia.[1] In 1801 he
purchased 141 acres of "Diamond's Venture" from Thomas Edwards
of St. Mary's County.[2]

The will of Hatch Dent was negotiated on January 19, 1816, and
admitted to probate in Charles County on February 26, 1816. His wife
Elizabeth received one-third of the dwelling-plantation "Dent's Inheritance" during life. Elizabeth Anne Turner and Sophia Cook, daughters,
were devised $1.00 each as well as Theodore Dent, Hatch Dent, and
Mary Emelia Dent. Llewellyn Marshall and Stoughton Warren were
devised the remaining portion of the dwelling-plantation consisting of
"Dent's Inheritance" and "Dent's Addition". John Blackman Edwards
Dent was devised the residue of the realty.[3]

The inventory was taken on May 14, 1816, while the final account
was rendered to the court on November 14, 1817, by his son and executor
John B. E. Dent, showing a balance of $1,694.65.

Theodore Dent, the bachelor son, dated his will January 23, 1816, it
being proved on February 24, 1816, by Alexander Dent and William
Good. He devised his brother Hatch all property in the State of Georgia.
Besides naming other brothers and sisters, he bequeathed personalty to
Jesse C. Cook, the named executor.[4]

---

[1] Unpub. Md. Records, vol. 2, p. 261, DAR.
[2] Digest of Deeds, Liber 1, folio 272.
[3] Wills, Liber H B no. 13, folio 449.
[4] Wills, Liber H B no. 13, folio 452.

JOHN DENT[4]
(1729 - 1778)

John Dent, son of Hatch and Anne Dent, was born December 2,
1729, in Trinity Parish, Charles County, Maryland. According to the
parish register, he married on February 3, 1757/8, Margaret Dyson.
She was the daughter of Thomas and Margaret Dyson, and was made
an heir in the will of her grandfather John Dyson whose estate was
distributed in 1760.

Children of John and Margaret (Dyson) Dent

1. Thomas Hatch Dent married Anne Trott. *q.v.*
2. Anne Dent, born Sept. 2, 1762, died in N. C.

3. Rebecca Dent, born Dec. 2, 1764.
4. James Dent, born Jan. 15, 1767.
5. Catherine Dent, born Mar. 15, 1769.
6. John Baptist Dent, born June 1, 1771. *q.v.*
7. Providence Trinity Dent, born 1772, died young.
8. Esther Dent, born Nov. 6, 1773.
9. Townsend Dent, born Jan. 25, 1776, married Mary Hightower. *q.v.*
10. Aaron Dent, born Mar. 1, 1778.

During the year of his death John Dent was magistrate of Charles County and in that capacity he took the oaths of allegiance and fidelity in his district.[1]

He died intestate. Letters of administration upon his estate were issued to his widow, Margot Dent, and Hezekiah Dent, with Oliver Burch and Peter Dent of Newport as the sureties. The inventory was taken on August 24, 1778, with an appraisement of £1080/11/1. Thomas Hatch Dent and Anne Dent signed as the kinsmen.[2] The final distribution was rendered on May 29, 1779, by the administrators, when the balance of £483/8/3 was distributed among the widow and the nine named representatives.

At the tax list of Charles County in 1783, Margaret Dent was seized of 153 acres of land lying in Bryan Town Hundred, with eight in her immediate family.

---

[1] Unpub. Md. Rec., vol. 7.
[2] Liber A F no. 7, folios 198, 251, 351.

Captain Hezekiah Dent[4]

(1747 - 1792)

Hezekiah Dent, son of Hatch and Anne Dent, was born August 2, 1747, in Trinity Parish, Charles County, Maryland. He married first on November 9, 1769, Catherine, born June 24, 1755, daughter of William and Priscilla Poston. The only issue from this union is believed to be Alexander Poston Dent, born March 22, 1773, who died shortly afterwards and whose birth was responsible for the death of the young mother. She died on April 6, following.[1]

On February 13, 1774, Hezekiah Dent married secondly Martha, daughter of John and Mary Ann Burch. On July 18, 1770, Martha Burch shared in the distribution of her father's estate.[2] On May 8, 1800, the mother deeded to her daughter Martha Dent for natural love and affections certain negro slaves.[3]

Children of Hezekiah and Martha (Burch) Dent

1. Hatch Dent, born Feb. 6, 1775, married Jeannette Meullion.*
2. Hezekiah Dent married Lareno Milburn. *q.v.*
3. John Chapman Dent, born Feb. 20, 1790. Served priv. 1 Md. Regt. War of 1812.
4. Orpah Burch, born and died 1782.
5. Martha Dent.
6. Wilfred Dent.
7. Anne Dent married Thomas O. Bean.*

On October 22, 1777, Hezekiah Dent was commissioned a first lieutenant of Captain Isaac McPherson's Company of the Lower Battalion of Charles County Militia.[4] On May 28, 1779, he was promoted to captain and assigned to the 12th Battalion in Charles County.

The dwelling-plantation of Hezekiah Dent lay in Newport Hundred of Charles County, where in 1783 he was seized of 50 acres of "Cooksey's Duckpond", 90 acres of "Simkin's Crow Back", and 209 acres of "Dent's Palace" on which his dwelling stood. In that year he had seven in his immediate family.

His will was dated May 10, 1792, and proved in Charles County on December 31, 1792. His realty, including "Dent's Palace", "Simpkin's Crow Back", and "Cooksey's Duckpond", was left to his wife Martha during life or widowhood. In the event of her remarriage, then she was to inherit one-third only, and the remaining portion was to be sold and divided equally among all his children. Negroes were bequeathed to the following children: Hatch, Hezekiah, John Chapman, Martha, Wilfred, and Anne. His wife and son Hatch were named executors.[5]

The inventory of the personal estate was made on March 18, 1793, and appraised at £1,020/13/0. The papers were signed by Thomas Hatch Dent, M. Blair, Samuel Dyson, and the Rev. Hatch Dent. The latter and James Russell were sureties.[6] At the subsequent account by the widow, disbursements were made to Trinity Parish and earmarked the "deceased subscription to the Ministry".[7]

The will of his widow was dated July 4, 1816, but it was not proved in Charles County until August 10, 1824, at which time it was noted that the son Wilfred was absent from the State. She bequeathed property to her son Wilfred, daughter Anne, and granddaughters Lucinda E. Dent and Emily Matthews.[8]

---

*Early DAR papers only source for these marriages.

Wilfred Dent and Lucinda E. Dent gave their receipts to the court for their share of the estate in 1826.[9]

---

[1] Trinity Parish Register, Cathedral, Washington.
[2] Balance Book, Liber 3, folio 51.
[3] Deeds, Liber J B no. 3, folio 196, La Plata.
[4] Archives, vol. 16.
[5] Wills, Liber A K no. 11, folio 131.
[6] Liber 1793, folio 133, La Plata.
[7] Liber A F no. 7, folio 171, La Plata.
[8] Wills, Liber H B no. 14, folio 324.
[9] Liber 1826, folio 234, La Plata.

CAPTAIN HATCH DENT[4]

(1751 - 1799)

Hatch Dent, son of Hatch and Anne Dent, was born May 20, 1751. He married on December 17, 1778, Judith, born January 10, 1758, the daughter of William and Priscilla Poston, of Charles County. As Judith Poston she was named in the will of her father in 1777 and as Judith Dent in the will of her mother in 1797.[1] According to the latter's will, she shared with her brothers and sisters in the landed estate.

Children of Hatch and Judith (Poston) Dent

1. Lucinda Dent, born Jan. 22, 1780, married ———— Dyson.
2. Mary Dent, born 1782, died spinster testate 1811, devising mother use of land in N. C., and naming children of sister Lucinda Dyson.
3. Priscilla Anne Dent married William Good.
4. William Hatch Dent married Katherine Brawner.
5. Catherine Amelia Judith Dent.
6. Julianna Chapman Dent married Nathan Smoot Dent. *q.v.*
7. Priscilla Anne Dent, born and died 1781.

On July 9, 1776, Hatch Dent was commissioned a second lieutenant of the Flying Camp, Smallwood's Battalion.[2] He saw active service in the campaign to capture New York from the British and at the disastrous battle of Long Island during August of that year, in which about 400 Marylanders were killed, he was taken prisoner with General Sullivan. He later was commissioned an officer of the First Maryland Regiment, and on April 20, 1778, he was exchanged by the British. At the close of the war he was elected one of the original members of the hereditary society of the Cincinnati.

After the Revolution as a layman he read services of the Episcopal Church and occasionally preached a sermon at the request of the vestry of Trinity Parish. He was a delegate to the Convention of the Episcopal

Church of Maryland held at Chestertown in 1784, and the following year he was ordained a priest by Bishop Seabury.

Subsequently, he went to Rowan County, North Carolina, where he officiated as a clergyman in a section which was then being opened for settlement. On February 27, 1794, he entered his claim with the Land Grant Office for six acres on the waters of Crooked Run. On March 24, 1795, he purchased from Lewis McCartney, of Rowan County, land lying on the north side of the Yadkin River, and on April 29, same year, he bought additional land on Second Creek from Alexander Long.[3]

He returned to Maryland and became the principal of Charlotte Hall Academy. On April 27, 1797, the vestry of All Faith's Parish called him as their priest, an office which he filled until his death.

The will of the Rev. Hatch Dent was dated September 7, 1799, and admitted to probate in Charles County on April 29, 1800. He devised his entire realty to his wife Judith during life, then to be sold and the money divided equally. He referred to land in North Carolina sold to Thomas Carson of that place by Thomas H. Dent in his behalf. His named heirs were children—Lucinda Dyson, Mary Dent, Priscilla Anne Dent, William Hatch Dent, Catherine Amelia Judith Dent, and Julianna Chapman Dent.[4]

The final settlement of the estate was made in February 1806, and distributed between the widow and the following children: Mary Dent, Priscilla Anne Dent, William H. Dent, Catherine A. J. Dent, and Julianna Chapman Dent—the latter three being under age.[5]

His widow died on March 3, 1814. Her will, dated September 13, 1811, was proved in Charles County on March 23, 1814. She bequeathed personalty to her daughters Priscilla Anne Dent, Catherine Amelia Judith Dent, and Julianna Chapman Dent. The residue of the estate was to be divided equally among her four daughters, William Hatch Dent, and the children of her daughter Lucinda Dyson.[6]

On July 28, 1817, William Hatch Dent, Catherine Amelia Judith Dent, Lucinda Dyson (the foregoing residents of Charles County) and William Good and Priscilla Anne his wife, of District of Columbia, conveyed to George Dent Parnham, William H. Smoot, William Matthews, Edward Turner, John I. Estep, William Good, and Clement Dorsey the tract "Goodwill Enlarged" and "Trifle". The former tract had been patented by Priscilla Poston and the latter on May 6, 1808, by Judith Dent. Katherine Dent, the wife of William H. Dent, acknowledged the transfer.[7]

On July 26, 1819, Lucinda Dyson, Catherine A. J. Dent, Julianna C. Dent and Nathan Dent her husband, and Priscilla A. Dent and William Good her husband conveyed "Property" to William Good.[8]

---

[1] Wills, Liber A K no. 11, folio 418.
[2] Archives, vol. 12.
[3] Deeds, Liber 13, folios 905, 907, Salisbury, N. C.
[4] Wills, Liber A K no. 11, folio 569.
[5] Liber 1806, folio 288, La Plata.
[6] Wills, Liber H B no. 13, folio 289.
[7] Deeds, Liber J B no. 12, folio 96, La Plata.
[8] *Ibid.*, Liber J B no. 13, folio 213, La Plata.

ENSIGN JOSEPH MANNING DENT[4]

(1750 - 179-)

Joseph Manning Dent, son of Michael, was born about 1750 at "Dent's Inheritance", Trinity Parish, Charles County. In 1775 as constable of Newport West Hundred he conducted the census for that hundred. At the beginning of the Revolutionary War, he enlisted in the militia and served as sergeant.[1] On May 28, 1779, he was commissioned an ensign and assigned to the 12th Battalion of Charles County Militia.[2] His services consisted chiefly of guarding the coast of southern Maryland from plunder of the British vessels which were constantly in the Potomac or Chesapeake Bay.

Before the close of the war he married Mary Manning ————, but whose last name is unknown to her many descendants.

Children of Joseph and Mary Dent

1. Elizabeth Dent.
2. John Turner Dent. *q.v.*
3. Michael Lawson Dent married Sarah Heard. *q.v.*
4. Joseph Manning Dent. *q.v.*
5. Sarah Dent married Thomas Dent. *q.v.*
6. Priscilla Dent.

At the tax list of 1783, Joseph Manning Dent was the head of a family in Newport Hundred, with four in family, but without land. Undoubtedly he was living upon a portion of the parental estate, the dwelling-plantation of which he was to inherit at the death of his father, according to the latter's will dated 1786. The first census of 1790 showed that Joseph was still a resident of Charles County. Before the probation of his father's will in 1795, however, Joseph Manning Dent had died intestate, and inasmuch as his father failed to alter his will, several complications presented themselves at the settlement of the estate.

On January 4, 1806, John Dent, of Franklin County, North Carolina, by deed recorded in Charles County, relinquished all claims in the plantation of his late father, Michael Dent, in order that the heirs of his brother Joseph Manning Dent might enjoy the same. On January 16, same year, Benjamin Edward and Mary his wife deeded to Mary M. Dent a portion of "Dent's Inheritance", their share of the estate of Michael Dent.[3]

From the above deeds it is evident that the widow of Joseph Manning Dent was a resident of Charles County as late as 1806, but sometime after that year she and her children migrated to Wilkes County, Georgia, and settled near the town of Washington where many other Maryland families had previously migrated.

Her will was dated July 1822, and proved at Washington Courthouse, Wilkes County, on November 4, 1822, with her son John Turner Dent as the executor. She named the following children: Michael Lawson Dent, John Turner Dent, Joseph Manning Dent, Sarah Dent, and Pricy Dent.

On March 14, 1824, Joseph Manning Dent II, conveyed to his brother Michael Lawson Dent his entire interest in the estate of "Joseph M. Dent, late of Maryland, deceased, and Mary M. Dent, late of Georgia, deceased".

---

[1] Unpub. Md. Rec., vol. 2, p. 265, DAR.
[2] Archives, vol. 21.
[3] Liber J B no. 6, folio 540, La Plata.

John Dent[4]

John Dent, son of Michael, was born at "Dent's Inheritance", Charles County, Maryland. Prior to the Revolutionary War or during its early stages he migrated with his brother Michael to the Halifax District of Franklin County, North Carolina. He was active during the conflict, and it is shown that he received for services rendered £18/5/– from William Hunt, Treasurer of Granville County.[1]

On January 4, 1806, as a resident of Franklin County he relinquished all claims in "Dent's Inheritance" and "Dent's Addition" willed to his deceased brother, Joseph Manning Dent, by his father Michael Dent, in order that the heirs of Joseph Manning might enjoy the devise.[2] Consequently, as John Dent, Sr., he conveyed all his rights in his father's

estate to Mary Manning Dent, and appointed Henry Dent, of Charles
County, his attorney.[3]

---

[1] Revolutionary Accounts, vol. 7, p. 58, f. 1, N. C., Hist. Comm., Raleigh.
[2] Deeds, Liber J B no. 4, folio 534, La Plata.
[3] *Ibid.*, Liber J B no. 9, folio 428.

ENSIGN MICHAEL DENT[4]

Michael Dent, son to Michael, was born at "Dent's Inheritance",
Charles County, Maryland. Prior to the Revolution or at its very beginning, he with his brother John settled in the Halifax District of
Franklin County, North Carolina. On August 28, 1778, he applied for
a land grant and was subsequently granted on October 13, 1784, 640
acres bordering Richland Creek. Likewise, on August 28, 1780, he filed
another claim and was granted 320 acres on the waters of Little River,
the certificate being dated October 13, 1784.

During the war Michael Dent served as an ensign of the State
militia and was attached to the Company of Captain Robert Goodloe.
In 1777 he received £10 from Jacob Blount, Paymaster of the North
Carolina Militia, and in April 1780, he received £12/10/- for expenditures under "Sundries furnished and cash paid the militia of North
Carolina, South Carolina, and Virginia". And on August 31, 1781, he
was the receiptant of £12 from the Comptroller Office of North Carolina.[1]

According to the 1800 census, Michael Dent was the head of a family
in Franklin County, North Carolina, both him and his wife being more
than 45 years of age. At home were a boy and girl between the ages of
10 and 16, and one girl less than 10.

A Captain Michael Dent served from Georgia in one of the early
Indian Wars, and under the Lottery Act of 1819 received land acquired
from the Creek and Cherokee Indians.

---

[1] Revolutionary Accounts, vol. 8, f. 2; vol. A, p. 53; vol. B, p. 223; vol. 1,
p. 84, f. 2; and book 1-6, f. 341; North Carolina Historical Commission, Raleigh.

GIDEON DENT[4]

(17— - 1814)

Gideon Dent, son of Benjamin, was born at "Dent's Inheritance",
Charles County. At the death of his mother he received a portion of the
home plantation, where his seat was maintained, located in what was

known as Newport West Hundred, of Charles County. In 1783 he was taxed for 143 acres of "Dent's Inheritance" and 10 acres of "Cooksey's Barren". In that year he had three in family. His wife was Mary ———.

Children of Gideon and Mary Dent

1. Theophilus Dent, born 1781, married Drusilla ———. He and his wife were communicants of Trinity Parish 1832; in 1850 living alone with realty appraised at $10,000. Served as 1st Lieut. 1st Md. Regt., War of 1812.
2. Anne Dent.
3. Martha Dent married Rezin Smoot.*
4. Mary Dent.
5. Cecilia Dent married ——— Harrison. Their son Gideon Dent Harrison married Emily Dent, May 30, 1843, Trinity Parish.

During the Revolutionary War, Gideon Dent served as a private in the Company of Captain Clarkson of Charles County Militia.[1]

On December 31, 1794, Gideon Dent purchased "Higdon's Chance" from Henry Gardner and Catherine his wife, John Edelen and Monica his wife, and Ignatius Gardner and Anne his wife.[2]

On June 9, 1800, there was filed with the high court of chancery a bill of complaint by which Gideon Dent instituted action against Anne and Kezia Burch. The bill set forth that Oliver Burch, deceased, by his will of December 29, 1793, devised to Anne Burch and Kezia Burch, of Charles County, "Bowling's Plain Resurveyed", lying in Charles County during their natural lives, then to his son Henry Burch. On April 17, 1799, Henry Burch sold the land to Gideon Dent and since then settled in Kentucky. Anne Burch and Kezia Burch continued to live upon the land, but were tearing down the out-houses and destroying trees.[3]

The will of Gideon Dent was dated August 5, 1808, and admitted to probate in Charles County on February 15, 1814. Theophilus received the dwelling-plantation, but in the event that he died without issue then to daughter Anne Dent. Martha Smoot was willed the land leading from Bryan Town and intersecting with the road leading to Port Tobacco. Mary Dent was devised "Higdon's Chance" and "Dent's Slip". Cecilia Dent received the residue of the realty. His wife Mary, however, was to have full power over the estate during life. By a codicil dated October 9, 1811, the daughter Cecilia Harrison was devised certain land.[4]

---

[1] Unpub. Md. Records, vol. 2, p. 262, DAR.
[2] Deeds, Liber N no. 4, folio 338, La Plata.
[3] Chancery Papers no. 1576.
[4] Wills, Liber H B no. 13, folio 282.

---

*For descendants *see* Newman's "The Smoots of Maryland and Virginia."

JOHN BREWER DENT*

(1759 - 1838)

John Brewer Dent, son of Benjamin, was born May 9, 1759, in Charles County. In 1783, as a bachelor, he was seized of no land but was taxed for personal property. According to family tradition, he married his kinswoman Priscilla Elizabeth, the daughter of John and Violetta (Winnett) Dent.

Children of John Brewer and Priscilla Dent

1. John Benjamin Dent. *q.v.*
2. Violetta Dent married Alexander Dent. *q.v.*
3. Susannah Attawa Dent married Zachariah Dent. *q.v.*
4. Levi Dent married Pamelia ————. *q.v.*
5. Priscilla Elizabeth Dent married William Keech, Jan. 6, 1847, Trinity Parish.

During the Revolutionary War he served as a private in the militia company of Captain Thomas H. Marshall of Charles County.[1]

At one time John Brewer Dent conveyed "Brawner's Risque" to his son John Benjamin for natural love and affections. Priscilla Dent his wife waived dower rights.*

The National Intelligence of May 1, 1838, carried the following notice: "On the 24th ultimo at his residence in Charles County, Mr. John Brewer Dent, (died) in his eighty-seventh year".** He was interred at "Good Will", and his headstone, still standing, reads "In Memory of John B. Dent of Maryland who departed this life April 24, 1838, aged 79 years, 5 months, and 9 days".

The will of John Brewer Dent was dated April 26, 1834, and proved in Charles County on September 3, 1839. John Benjamin was devised "Johnson's Purchase" of 28½ acres and "Johnson's Trifle". Priscilla Elizabeth Dent received "Bird's Head", "Woods Wilderson", "Davis Wilderson", "Great Worth", "Water Race", "Water Range", "Poverty", "Waters' Addition", "Dispute", "Loving Brothers", "Wilful Destruction", "Arabiah", "Bartholomew's Lot", "Whord's Mountain", the latter being the plantation whereon the testator lived, also a portion of "Dent's Inheritance", "Dent's Addition", "Oneal's Desert", "Dyson's Addition", and "Partnership", land formerly owned by the late Alexander Dent.

---

* Deeds, Liber J B no. 14, folio 108, La Plata.

** NOTE: Discrepancy of age in newspaper and on tombstone.

Violetta Dent and Susannah Attawa Dent were bequeathed $5.00 each, while Levi received certain slaves. Priscilla Dent was named as executrix.[2]

The headstone of his widow reads "Priscilla Dent of Maryland, died 1845, aged 84". Her will was dated May 17, 1845, and proved in Charles County on June 25, same year. Her daughter Priscilla Elizabeth Dent was the only named heir.[3]

---

[1] Unpub. Md. Rec., vol. 2, folio 375, DAR.
[2] Wills, Liber D J no. 16, folio 168.
[3] *Ibid.*, folio 372.

BENJAMIN DENT[4]

(17— - 1835)

Benjamin Dent, son of Benjamin, was born at "Dent's Inheritance", Charles County. He married perhaps before 1775, for in that year he was the head of a family in Newport West Hundred. His wife was Anne ————.

Children of Benjamin and Anne Dent

1. Wilson Dent married Elizabeth ————.
2. William Benjamin Dent.
3. Eleanor Dent.
4. Susan Cecilia Dent.
5. Jane Dent married ———— Penn.

During the Revolutionary War, Benjamin Dent served as a private in the militia of Charles County.[1] In 1783 he was assessed for taxes on 100 acres of "Stephen" and "Coleman", with two in his immediate household.

The will of Benjamin Dent was dated January 20, 1835, and proved in Charles County on March 26, 1835. To his wife, Anne, he devised all property real and personal during life. After her death certain articles of personal property were willed to his grandchildren—Benjamin Dent Penn, Rezin Manual Penn, and Elizabeth Jane Penn—all children of his daughter Jane Penn. His dwelling-plantation "St. Stephen" and "Coleman" after the decease of his wife was to revert to his sons, Wilson Dent and William Benjamin Dent. The residue of his estate was then to be divided among his four children—William Benjamin Dent, Wilson Dent, Eleanor Dent, and Susan Cecilia Dent.[2]

---

[1] Unpub. Md. Rec., vol. 2, p. 265, DAR.
[2] Wills, Liber D J no. 16, folio 33.

ZACHARIAH DENT⁴

(17— - 1828)

Zachariah Dent, son of Benjamin, was born at "Dent's Inheritance", in Trinity Parish. During the Revolutionary War, he served as a sergeant in the militia of Charles County.¹ In 1778 he took the oath of allegiance and fidelity to the State of Maryland in Charles County before John Parnham.²

His wife was Elizabeth ————. In 1783 he was the head of a family with four, including himself, and the owner of 100 acres of land lying in Bryan Town Hundred. His realty consisted of 96 acres of "Turner's Forest", and 4 acres of "Church Over".

Children of Zachariah and Elizabeth Dent

1. William Dent.
2. George R. Dent.
3. Zachariah Dent. *q.v.*
4. Catherine Dent married Benjamin Swann.
5. Elizabeth Sophia Dent married Benedict L. Higdon.

The will of Zachariah Dent was dated June 21, 1828, and proved in Charles County on December 27, 1828. He devised his daughter, Elizabeth Sophia Dent, the dwelling-plantation being portions of "Turner's Forest" and "Church Over".

Zachariah received the plantation whereon he was then living, being portions of "Burches' Reserve", "Chesham", and "Boarman's Manor". Catherine Swann received slaves, while William and George each received $1. The property which was bequeathed by the testator's wife, Elizabeth, during her life was to be delivered to Zachariah who was named executor. The residue of the estate was to be divided among Zachariah, Catherine, and Elizabeth.³

After the death of Zachariah Dent and his widow Elizabeth Dent, their son Zachariah Dent, Jr., in August 1834, instituted action in the high court of chancery against his sister Elizabeth Sophia and her husband Benedict Higdon. Elizabeth Sophia Higdon previously had obtained judgement against her brother Zachariah Dent for $278.27 as executor of the will of their deceased father.

In the bill it was stated that Zachariah Dent, Sr., had died testate on December 18, 1828, and had bequeathed to his daughter Elizabeth certain property subject to the life interest of his widow who had died in the spring of 1830. It was also stated that during and after the death of the widow, Elizabeth and her husband had dissipated the estate. The daughter Elizabeth lived with her mother until her death, and after her decease she and her husband claimed the tobacco and other crops upon the land.

Many witnesses and depositions were made which brought out some interesting connections. John F. S. Higdon and John Thomas Higdon were both brothers of Benedict Higdon, the husband to Elizabeth. Theophilus Dent stated that he heard Mrs. Elizabeth Dent, widow, say before her death that Benedict Higdon had "stripped her of everything and had carried off wheat, meat, corn, and tobacco".

Wilson Dent stated that the daughter Elizabeth had the keys to the chest where money was kept belonging to the widow. Zachariah Dent, Jr., the complainant, stated that he was not residing with his father nor his mother at time of their death, but that he had been present in his mother's home when his sister had taken money from the chest. Dr. Stouton W. Dent was another witness. The case also showed that Zachariah Dent's dwelling-plantation lay at Centreville, and that Elizabeth Sophia Dent had married Benedict L. Higdon on February 26, 1829. Furthermore, Catherine Swan with her brother Zachariah and sister Elizabeth were residuary heirs in the estate of their father after the death of the widow. And that Benjamin Swan had also been an executor of the will of Zachariah Dent, Sr.[4]

---

[1] Unpub. Md. Records, vol. 2, p. 265, DAR.
[2] *Ibid.*, vol. 5.
[3] Wills, Liber W B M no. 15, folio 300.
[4] Chancery Papers nos. 7531, 7589.

TITUS DENT[4]

(17— - 1811)

Titus Dent, son of Benjamin, was born at "Dent's Inheritance", in Charles County. During the Revolutionary War he served as a private in the militia of Charles County.[1] He married Mary ————.

Children of Titus and Mary Dent

1. Leonard G. Dent married Isabella C. ————. *q.v.*

According to the tax list of 1783, Titus Dent was the head of a family in Trinity Parish and was seized of 50 acres of "St. Stephen" and "Colemar". He died intestate in Charles County, the inventory of his personal estate being made on October 1, 1811, and being appraised at $986.30. The final account and distribution were made by his widow

Mary Dent in 1816 and divided between her and the only child Leonard
G. Dent.[2]

On September 23, 1825, Leonard G. Dent, of Charles County, conveyed to Theophilus Dent "St. Stephen" and "Colemar", at which time
his wife Isabella C. Dent waived dower.[3]

---

[1] Unpub. Md. Records, vol. 2, p. 265, DAR.
[2] Adm. Accts., Liber 1816, folio 135, La Plata.
[3] Deeds, Liber J B no. 16, folio 470, La Plata.

JOHN DENT[4]
(1753 - 1828)

John Dent, son of John and Mary Dent, was born in St. Mary's
County, Maryland. He disposed of his parental estate there, and prior
to the Revolutionary War he settled in Montgomery County where he
married Verlinda Beall. She was born about 1758, the daughter of
Robert and Hannah Beall. She was made an heir in her father's will
of 1796, while her husband was granted permission to dwell upon the
land on which they lived and made executor with the testator's widow
Hannah.

Children of John and Verlinda.(Beall) Dent*

1. Robert Dent married Mary Hays. *q.v.*
2. Hannah Dent married Andrew Foreman. License Montg. Co.,
   Aug. 17, 1802.
3. Rebecca Dent.
4. Lucy Dent, died spinster.
5. Mary Dent married Daniel Gill.
6. Asa Dent married Martha, dau. of Notley Hays. License Montg.
   Co., Mar. 20, 1804.
7. Nancy Dent married William Foreman.
8. Elizabeth Dent, born 1795, died 1878, married Thomas Foreman.
9. John Dent, born 1797, died 1876, married Margaret Snyder and
   Sarah Hopkins.

During the Revolutionary War he served as a private in the 6th
Company of Montgomery County militia, 29th Battalion.[1] During 1778
he subscribed to the oath of fidelity and allegiance to the State of Maryland in Montgomery County.

The tax list of 1783 showed that he was seized of realty appraised
at £160 lying in Middle Potomac, Lower Potomac, and Georgetown
Districts. His entire property was appraised at £460, and he had eleven
in his immediate family.

---

*NOTE: Names of children and marriages given by members of the family.

As the executor of Robert Beall, he conveyed to Kinsey Beall a portion of "Hannah's Inheritance", and at the same time Kinsey Beall deeded a portion of the same tract to John Dent. Charlotte Beall, wife of Kinsey, waived dower rights.[2] In 1795 John Dent and Verlinda his wife, with other heirs of James Beall, shared in the proceeds from the sale of "Beckwith's Range". In 1805 he deeded a portion of "Hannah's Inheritance" to Samuel Magruder. Verlinda Dent, his wife, waived her third.[3]

Shortly after he disposed of his estate in Montgomery County, he and his family settled at St. Clairsville, Belmont County, Ohio. There he conducted a school on his farm until his death in 1828. His wife had died five years earlier.

---

[1] Unpub. Md. Rec., vol. 5, p. 109, DAR.
[2] Deeds, Liber E, folios 208, 210, Rockville.
[3] Deeds, Liber M, folio 409, Rockville.

CAPTAIN GEORGE DENT[4]

(1756 - 1842)

George Dent, son of Thomas and Elizabeth Dent, was born December 21, 1756, in All Faith's Parish, St. Mary's County. At the beginning of the Revolutionary War, he was a student at Charlotte Hall Academy, when he and other boys formed a militia company at the academy under Captain Henry Sothoron. Later, on May 25, 1778, he enlisted in the Maryland Line under Captain Carberry. With about 70 volunteers and draftees he was marched by Captain Carberry and Sergeant King to Annapolis. After a few days at that port, they embarked in small boats under Sergeant King for the head of the Elk. Upon arrival Lieutenant James, of Baltimore, took command and marched them to headquarters in New Jersey.

They heard the firing in the distance during the battle of Monmouth, but failed to reach the battlefield in time for actual combat. While in New Jersey, he, Jonathan Woodburn, and Norman Burroughs were transferred to Captain John Davidson's Company in order that they may be with their friends, Richard Hall and Henry Spalding, of St. Mary's County. His company marched to White Plains, had frequent skirmishes with the British, and then marched with a detachment to strengthen the fort at West Point. He was discharged on April 3, 1779.

Upon his return to St. Mary's County, he volunteered under Captain Mills, Lieut. William Cartwright, and Ensign Henry Swann to guard the coast in the lower part of the county. He also had service under

Lieut. Benjamin Edwards, at which time he marched to Llewellyn's warehouse on the Potomac and guarded the shore for about two weeks. Within two months he was taken ill and was prevented from being present with his company at Yorktown.

In 1818 upon his application for a revolutionary pension, it was stated that he had received a discharge at Middlebrook, New Jersey, in April or May 1779, from Captain Davidson. About one mile from camp he and his comrades met General Baron de Kalb. "He accosted us in the following manner: Where are you going soldiers? I being ahead told him we were going home. He asked me if we had been discharged. I told him we had and I gave him my discharge to look at. While looking at it his horse threw his head down which caused the discharge to be torn in two pieces. He remarked that it would answer, and I brought it home with me, but it has long since been lost or mislaid".[1] He furthermore stated that he was known to three-fourths of the respectable men of his county and referred to the Rev. John Claxton, the rector of his parish, for character.

About 1790 he married Elizabeth Temperance Mills, born about 1767. The following children survived:

Children of George and Elizabeth (Mills) Dent

1. William Dent. *q.v.*
2. Hezekiah Dent married Martha Matilda Hammett. *q.v.*
3. Mary Anne Dent married John Duke, Jr. License St. M. Co., Feb. 10, 1824. Issue: Susanna M.; Mary P.; George Dent; James; John.
4. Elizabeth Dent married Feb. 3, 1816, Joseph B. Burroughs.
5. Elizabeth Temperance Dent married Feb. 3, 1816, John Amary Burroughs.
6. Harriet Dent married George Burroughs. License St. M. Co., Feb. 14, 1814; removed to Kentucky.

On August 22, 1807, George Dent purchased "Scegby" from Clement Dorsey, of Charles County, who had received it as judgement against the heirs of the late John Johnson Sothoron.[2] On December 18, 1809, George Dent conveyed "Trent Fork" adjacent to the land of John Chappelear to John Horrell, Benjamin M. Horrell, Rebecca C. Weems, Thomas Horrell, and Maximilliam Horrell, of Calvert County.[3]

In 1810 when he petitioned the courts to perpetuate the boundaries of "Scegby", he was referred to as Captain George Dent. The court appointed a commission consisting of John Chappelear, William Kilgour, John Kilgour, and Neale H. Shaw. The land lay at "the door of the parish church" in All Faith's Parish. Thomas Greenfield, aged 37 years in 1811, said that about 25 years ago he was present on a commission when a stone was fixed near Beaver Dam Branch of Indian Creek a little west of the road from All Faith's Church towards Benedict. Other testimonies were those of Henry Burroughs, aged about 41 years, son of Hezekiah; Hanson Burroughs, aged about 39 years, son of Hezekiah; Henry Burroughs, aged about 41 years, referred to an old well shown him by Richard Sothoron, deceased, grandfather to the present Dr. William Sothoron, and that it was the boundary between his land and that of James Burroughs and John Johnson Sothoron.[4]

The will of George Dent was dated November 14, 1839, and admitted to probate in St. Mary's County on December 14, 1842, by Thomas C. Dent, Enoch Hammett, and John R. Lusby. The dwelling-plantation "Urquhart's Gift" was devised to the eldest son, William, while other tracts were left to Hezekiah and Mary, the wife of John Dukes, Jr. Bequests were made to Elizabeth T. Burroughs, wife of John A. Burroughs, and the following grandchildren, all children of Joseph B. Burroughs: G. S. M. Burroughs, Mary A. E. Burroughs, Charles C. Burroughs, John M. Burroughs, Elizabeth Burroughs, Rebecca Burroughs, William T. Burroughs, Catherine C. Burroughs, and Jane M. Burroughs. His granddaughter, Elizabeth Burroughs, daughter of George and Harriet Burroughs, was bequeathed the negro that her parents carried with them to Kentucky.[5]

The estate was distributed in St. Mary's County on April 19, 1844, to all heirs named in the will.

---

[1] Revolutionary Pension Claim; Archives, vol. 18, p. 329.
[2] Deed Digest, Liber 2, folio 98.
[3] *Ibid.*, Liber 2, folio 286.
[4] Petitions, Liber J H no. 1, folio 491, Leonardtown.
[5] Wills, Liber G C no. 2, folio 66, Leonardtown.

WILLIAM DENT[4]

(1756 - 1816)

William Dent, son of Thomas and Elizabeth (Edwards) Dent, was born 1756 in Charles County. His wife was Margaret Rettea Smoot whom he married about 1777.*

Children of William and Margaret (Smoot) Dent

1. Alexander Dent married Violetta Dent. *q.v.*
2. Thomas Dent married Sarah Dent. *q.v.*

---

*DAR papers incorrectly state that his wife was the daughter of William Barton Smoot. For her authentic lineage, *see*, Newman's "The Smoots of Maryland and Virginia."

3. Jane Dent.
4. Catherine Dent.
5. Nathan Smoot Dent married Juliana Dent. *q.v.*

During the Revolutionary War, William Dent served as a private in Captain Clarkson's company of Charles County Militia. And during 1778 he took the oath of fidelity and allegiance to the State of Maryland in Charles County under Joshua Sanders.[1]

In 1783 he was domiciled in Newport Hundred, with seven in family. His landed estate consisted of "Smith's Reserve" of 100 acres and "Simkin Crow Back" of 50 acres.

On April 2, 1803, as William Dent of Thomas, he conveyed to his son Alexander Dent for natural love and affections a portion of "Dent's Inheritance", lying on the north side of Main Swamp which emptied into Pile's Freshlet at the head of Dent's Mill dam, and also a portion of "Dent's Addition", lying on the edge of Gilbert Swamp. No wife relinquished her dower.[2]

The will of William Dent was dated July 28, 1816, and proved in Charles County on August 21, 1816. He devised his wife Margaret Rettea Dent his entire realty during life, then the dwelling-plantation "Dent's Inheritance" and "Dent's Addition" to his son Alexander. Thomas received one dollar, but all children of his son Thomas, born to Sarah his wife, were to inherit "Simkin's Comeback," of 100 acres, but in the event that Thomas desired to remove to another State, then the land could be sold and a home in the new State be bought. His daughters, Jane and Catherine, were devised all land whereon Jane was then living, that is, "Church Over" and "Bowling's Plains". His son Nathan S. Dent was willed "Smith's Reserve", of 100 acres.[3]

The inventory of the personal estate was taken on April 14, 1819, with Alexander Dent as the executor. The first and final account was filed at court on May 23, 1829, by Alexander Dent and Nathan Smoot Dent.

---

[1] Unpub. Md. Records, vol. 2, p. 263, DAR.
[2] Deeds, Liber J B no. 5, folio 481, La Plata.
[3] Liber H B no. 13, folio 480.

HENRY DENT[4]

(17— - 1815)

Henry Dent, son of Thomas and Elizabeth (Edwards) Dent, was born in Charles County. During the Revolutionary War, he served as a private in the company of Captain Clarkson of the militia.[1] In March

1778 he subscribed to the patriot's oath in Charles County before Magistrate Joshua Sanders.[2] Circumstances indicate that he married late in life Charity, the daughter of Sarah Cox, of Charles County.[3]

Children of Henry and Charity Dent

1. Thomas Samuel Dent; 1850 census shows his living Hill Top, Chas. Co., with his wife Matilda. Headstones at Durham Churchyard state that he was born Sept. 19, 1809, died Dec. 21, 1878; Matilda, his wife, born Aug. 5, 1822, died Nov. 6, 1884.
2. Henry Story Dent, died May 29, 1887, aged 72, buried Durham Churchyard.

He died intestate. The inventory of his personal estate was filed at court on August 8, 1815, showing a value of $4,544.33. His widow, Charity Dent, was the administrator.[4] Distribution was made on June 17, 1823, to the widow and two named children.[5] The widow died shortly afterwards, for on November 18, 1823, the inventory of her estate was taken in Charles County, with Robert Guest and Anne C. Guest as the administrators.

---

[1] Unpub. Md. Records, vol. 2, p. 262, DAR.
[2] *Ibid.*, vol. 5.
[3] Inventories & Accounts, 1812-15, folio 250.
[4] Inventories 1815, folio 468.
[5] Accounts, Liber 1834, folio 320.

THOMAS DENT[4]

Thomas Dent, son of Thomas and Elizabeth (Edwards) Dent, was born sometime before 1765. On October 14, 1799, he secured license in St. Mary's County to marry Rebecca, the daughter of James and Elizabeth (Dent) Chappelear. Her bachelor brother Nathan Chappelear died in St. Mary's County during 1807, and by his will he bequeathed $30 to his sister Rebecca Dent "which her husband has in his hands", who also shared in the residuary estate.[1] The will of her father, James Chappelear, was proved in St. Mary's County on October 11, 1808, when it was stated that his heirs all lived in the State of Virginia. His daughter Rebecca Dent was bequeathed $100.[2]

A complete list of the children of Thomas and his wife has not been found, however, Thomas E. Dent who married Susan Hammett is proved as a son. (*q.v.*)

Thomas Dent settled in Frederick County, Virginia, where he was domiciled in 1810—the first census available for Virginia. In that year he was the head of a family with a wife, born sometime between 1765 and 1784, three females and one male, all born between 1800 and 1810.

In 1810 Thomas Dent and Rebecca his wife, of Frederick County, Virginia, acknowledged the receipt of $50 from James Harrison as administrator of the estate of James Chappelear. In 1820 he received negroes from the estate of John Chappelear, late of St. Mary's County, Maryland, and at the same time he appeared as attorney for James Riley, of Winchester, Virginia, whose infant children—Elizabeth Anne, James Previs, Addison Briscoe, and Casandra Mary Riley—were entitled to a portion of their uncle, John Chappelear's estate.

At the 1820 census, he was the head of a family in Frederick County, Virginia, with seven children at home.

[1] Wills, Liber J J no. 2, folio 157, Leonardtown.
[2] *Ibid.*, folio 184.

JOHN CHILTON DENT[5]
(1792 - 1816)

John Chilton (Shelton) Dent, son of John and Anne Dent, was born October 12, 1792, in Charles County. After the death of his father, he was placed under the guardianship of Hatch Dent.[1] He died intestate, the inventory of his personal estate being made on June 11, 1816, with an appraisement of $1,747.63. His administrator, Wilfred Dent, distributed the balance on February 1, 1819, to the widow, Anne Dent, and only child, Martha Anne Dent.[2]

[1] Guardians (1790-1806), folio 196, La Plata.
[2] Adm. Accounts, Liber 1819, folio 101.

JOHN BLACKMAN EDWARDS DENT[5]

John Blackman Edwards Dent, son of Hatch and Susannah (Edwards) Dent, was born at "Dent's Inheritance", Charles County. During the War of 1812 he served as sergeant of the 1st Maryland Regiment.[1] He married Maria, the daughter of William and Kitty Turner, who shared in the distribution of her father's estate on February 10, 1818.[2] On August 7, 1816, he purchased from Mary Manning Dent and Hatch Dent portions of "Dent's Inheritance" and "Dent's Addition".[3] On July 3, 1817, he and Hatch Dent conveyed to John Brewer Dent these tracts at which time Maria Dent, wife of John B. E. Dent, waived dower.[4]

[1] U. S. War Department.
[2] Liber 1798-1806, folio 486, La Plata.
[3] Deeds, Liber J B no. 11, folio 413.
[4] Deeds, Liber J B. no. 12, folio 82.

STOUGHTON WARREN DENT[5]

(1806 - 1883)

Stoughton Warren Dent, son of Hatch and Susannah (Edwards) Dent, was born January 15, 1806, at "Dent's Inheritance", Charles County, Maryland. He married first Lydia B. Watts,[1] and after her death he married Mary Catherine Smoot.*

Children of Stoughton Warren Dent

1. Catherine Dent.
2. Stouten Hubert Dent married Anna Beall Young.
3. Hugh B. Dent.
4. Lydia S. Dent married Frederick L. Dent.
5. Mary Smoot Dent, born Aug. 1, 1840, died June 23, 1890, married J. Marion Freeman.
6. George H. Dent, said to have migrated to Alabama.
7. Columbia Dent.
8. Ella Dent, died spinster Apr. 1940, aged 81.
9. Emma Smoot Dent.
10. Julia C. Dent married William J. Naylor.

Dr. Stoughton Warren Dent was a well known physician of medicine in southern Maryland of the last century. He lived in Allen's Fresh District of Charles County, where he was domiciled at the 1850 census, with his wife Mary Catherine and the following children at home: Catherine, aged 22 years; Stouten, aged 17; Hugh aged 18; Lydia S., aged 14; Mary, aged 10; George H., aged 7, and Columbia, aged 1. In his household was also Andrew Smoot, a student, aged 22. Dr. Dent died on October 7, 1883, and was buried in a now abandoned burying grounds near Newtown.

His will was dated August 17, 1882, and admitted to probate in Charles County on October 30, 1883, by the oaths of George B. Lancaster, J. E. Ware, and R. S. Corry. He bequeathed his personal estate to his wife Mary Catherine Dent and stated that his unmarried daughters, Emma Smoot Dent and Ella Dent should have a home with their mother in the family homestead. At the death of the widow, all realty was to revert to Emma and Ella. As his sons expressed no desire for their portions of the estate, he failed to provide for them. He mentioned three married daughters of their husbands—Lydia S., wife of Frederick L. Dent; Mary, wife of James M. Freeman; and Julia C., wife of William J. Naylor. He appointed his son-in-law, James M. Freeman, and his daughter, Emma, as executors.[2]

---

*See, "The Smoots of Maryland and Virginia," by Newman.

His widow died on October 6, 1894, and was interred beside the remains of her deceased husband.

---

[1] The Morgue, Peabody Libr., Balto.
[2] Wills, Liber M T no. 18, folio 238.

THOMAS HATCH DENT[5]
(1760 - 1817)

Thomas Hatch Dent, son of John and Margaret (Dyson) Dent, was born about 1760 in Trinity Parish, Charles County. In 1778 he took the oath of fidelity and allegiance to the State of Maryland in Charles County before Magistrate Joshua Sanders.[1] He also served as a private in the militia of Charles County.[2]

In 1790 as the eldest son of his deceased father, he was the head of the family in Charles County. Shortly after this date, he migrated to Rowan County, North Carolina, where on November 21, 1796, he secured license to marry Anne Trott. His bondsmen were John Rogers and Samuel Trott.

Children of Thomas Hatch and Anne (Trott) Dent

1. Josiah Dent, removed West.
2. John Henry Dent, removed West.
3. Thomas Dent.
4. Rebecca Dent married Joseph Owens. Issue: Joseph Franklin; Henry Caswell; James; Jane; Rufus; Thomas.
5. Dorcas Dent married William Heathman.
6. Sarah Dent married John Todd.
7. Elizabeth Dent married Scott Trott.
8. Anne Dent married Rand Watson.
9. Margaret Dent married ——— McAtee.
10. Catherine Dent married ——— Brown.
11. Wilfred Dent married Rachel Smith. *q.v.*

On February 10, 1794, Thomas Hatch Dent purchased from Charles Burroughs and Anne his wife, all parties being of Rowan County, North Carolina, 102 acres of land lying on the south side of Second Creek.[3] The witnesses were Joseph Renshaw and Joseph Owens. On February 1, 1802, he bought of Sarah Wood for £100 a tract of 80 acres on the south side of Second Creek "beginning at Thomas Dent's corner".[4] Likewise, on February 6, 1804, he purchased from Thomas Biles other land on the south side of Second Creek, beginning at "Dent's Corner". The witnesses were John Turner and Stephen Biles.[4] On September 20, 1815, he purchased 43 acres of land in Rowan County from Benjamin Trott. In 1816 Thomas H. Dent and John Trott and Nancy his wife conveyed to John B. Todd and Thomas Todd, all parties of Rowan County, land on Grant's Creek" being a portion of the realty of James Todd, deceased, which was left the said James Todd by the last will of his grandfather John Todd". The witnesses were Josiah Dent and Thomas Todd.[5]

Thomas Hatch Dent died in Rowan County during 1817, and was interred near South River in that county. His will, dated March 12, 1817, was proved during the September session of the court. He devised his wife Nancy the plantation during widowhood, and granted his sister Nancy the privilege of residing with his widow during life. To his son John Henry he bequeathed $50. At the death or remarriage of his widow, the estate was to be divided equally among all children except Josias. He appointed his wife and brother-in-law Samuel Trott the executors.

The will of his widow Anne Dent was dated April 21, 1838, and proved in Rowan County during November 1838, by A. C. Winders and Tabert T. Trott. She named her daughters Margaret Anne Dent, Elizabeth Dent, and Nancy Dent; son Thomas H. Dent; and granddaughter Clementine "now living with me". She named James Owens as the executor.

---

[1] Unpub. Md. Rec., vol. 5.
[2] *Ibid.*, vol. 2, p. 266.
[3] Rowan Co. Deeds, Liber 13, folio 970.
[4] *Ibid.*, Liber 18, folios 263, 928.
[5] *Ibid.*, Liber 24, folio 583.

JOHN BAPTIST DENT[5]
(1771 - 1816)

John Baptist Dent, son of John and Margaret (Dyson) Dent, was born on June 1, 1771, in Charles County, Maryland. He joined his older brother in North Carolina and there he died intestate. Letters of administration upon his estate were granted on May 25, 1816, by the court of Rowan County to David Fraly "the widow having relinquished her right". The bondsmen were Isaac Linster and James Kincaid.

TOWNSEND DENT[5]
(1776 - 18—)

Townsend Dent, son of John and Margaret (Dyson) Dent, was born January 25, 1776, at "Dent's Inheritance", Charles County, Maryland. He migrated to Rowan County, North Carolina, and there on

May 12, 1797, he negotiated a bond to marry Mary Hightower. John Rogers and Turner Pinkston were the sureties. In 1816 he was one of the constables of the county.

HEZEKIAH DENT[5]
(1770 - 1809)

Hezekiah Dent, son of Hezekiah and Martha his wife, was born in Charles County about 1770. He studied medicine and practiced his profession in St. Mary's County. In that county he secured license to marry Larena Milburn on June 16, 1803.

Children of Hezekiah and Larena (Milburn) Dent
1. Lucinda Evelina Dent married Thomas Loker.* License St. M. Co., Sept. 2, 1826.

On June 7, 1804, Hezekiah Dent purchased from William Richardson, of St. Mary's County, "Green Hills", of 362 acres, lying in Elizabeth and Hally's Manor.[1]

His will was dated St. Mary's County, December 5, 1809, and was witnessed by James White, Benjamin Tabbs, and John White. He devised his daughter, Lucinda Evelina, the land inherited from his father and the dwelling-plantation "Green Hills" purchased from William Richardson. His wife, Larena, was bequeathed one-third of the personal estate, while other heirs were his mother, Martha Dent, and brothers Wilfred and Hatch. He also referred to the property bequeathed his daughter by her grandmother, Anne Milburn, late of St. Mary's County.[2]

The inventory of his personal estate was filed on May 24, 1810, showing an appraisement of $6,287.51. Robert Milburn and John Mackall, Jr., were the executors. The former as the "surviving executor" rendered the sixth account of the estate on June 13, 1817.

His widow married Peter M. Thompson, according to license issued in St. Mary's County on January 24, 1815.

---

[1] Digests, Liber 1, folio 415, Annapolis.
[2] Wills, Liber J J no. 3, folio 227, Leonardtown.

JOHN TURNER DENT[5]

John Turner Dent, son of Joseph Manning and Mary Dent, was born in Charles County, Maryland. He joined his brother, Michael

---

*A descendant of this union possesses a silver pitcher with the Dent coat-of-arms once owned by Captain Hezekiah Dent.

Lawson, in Wilkes County, Georgia, where he is found as the head of a family at the census of 1820. In that year he was between the ages of 26 and 45, likewise, his wife. Other members of his household were a male and female under 10 years, and a female between 16 and 26. He owned three slaves. In 1831 he was named as the executor of Jane Stathan, late of Wilkes County.

MICHAEL LAWSON DENT[5]
(1780 - 1847)

Michael Lawson Dent, son of Joseph Manning and Mary Dent, was born about 1780 at "Dent's Inheritance", Charles County, Maryland. In 1803 he was named in the will of his aunt, Victory Dent, of Charles County. He migrated to Wilkes County, Georgia, and there on October 15, 1807, he secured license to marry Sarah Heard. According to her descendants, she was born about 1784 and was the daughter of Jesse and Judith (Wilkerson) Heard. Her father had been a captain in the Virginia Continental Line and had migrated to Georgia prior to 1784. He was reputed to be the son of Steven Heard, an Irishman, and Mary Faulkner his wife.

Children of Michael and Sarah (Heard) Dent

1. Mary S. Dent married ———— Binns.
2. Anne Dent married Lorenza Biggers. *q.v.*
3. Joseph Manning Dent, born *c* 1815 Wilkes Co., Ga., married Frances ————, born 1820.
4. Alexander Lawson Dent married Martha ————. *q.v.*
5. Richard Dent. *q.v.*
6. Margaret Anne Dent married ———— Mullen.
7. Robert Lawson Dent.
8. John Michael Lawson Dent, born 1831, Wilkes Co., Ga.
9. William Hatch Dent.
10. Caroline Dent married James Biggers.

Michael Lawson Dent served under his kinsman, Captain Michael Dent, in one of the early Indian Wars and for his services shared in the Lottery Act of 1819, by which he received land taken from the Creek and Cherokee Indians.

On March 3, 1824, he was one of the bondsmen for John Rich when he administered on the estate of Margaret Dyson, late of Wilkes County. And in 1828 he was the administrator of the estate of Rebecca Montgomery, late of Wilkes County.

At the census of 1820, he was listed as Lossen Dent, and in 1830 as Michael Lawson Dent—being a resident of Wilkes County at both census. By 1840 he had removed to the newly opened lands of Muscogee County, Georgia, where he died during 1847.

By his will, dated June 11, 1847, he devised the dwelling-plantation as well as certain personalty to his wife during life, then to his minor son, William Hatch Dent, placing him under the guardianship of his elder brother Joseph Manning Dent. Richard, another minor, was placed with John Michael Dent, with the understanding that Richard receive sufficient schooling. Negroes were bequeathed to the following children: Mary S. Binns, Elizabeth Biggers, Margaret Anne Mullen, Richard Dent, Robert Lawson Dent, and Alexander Lawson Dent. A codicil bequeathed $50 to the widow of John H. Dent.

JOSEPH MANNING DENT[5]
(17— - 1822)

Joseph Manning Dent, son of Joseph Manning and Mary Manning Dent, was born in Maryland. He served under Captain Michael Dent in one of the early Indian Wars, and for his services he participated in the Georgia Land Lottery of 1819, when the land taken from the Creek and Cherokee Indians in western Georgia was partitioned. He also shared in the land lottery of 1821. He died in Wilkes County, and on November 5, 1822, Michael L. Dent was granted letters of administration on his estate.

JOHN BENJAMIN DENT[5]
(17— - 1841)

John Benjamin Dent, son of John Brewer and Priscilla Dent, was born in Trinity Parish, Charles County. He married Catherine Petrie. In 1832 both he and his wife were registered communicants of Trinity Parish.

Children of John and Catherine (Petrie) Dent

1. Catherine Dent.
2. Sarah E. Dent.
3. Rosanna S. Dent.
4. Elizabeth M. Dent married Joseph H. Jones. License Dec. 2, 1850, St. M. Co.
5. Valeria I. Dent.
6. Walter L. Dent married Elizabeth A. Posey. License Apr. 15, 1850, St. M. Co.
7. Alexander C. Dent.
8. John F. Dent married Lillia D. Blackistone.

According to the press, "Mrs. Catherine Dent, died 20 September 1838, in the 48th year of her age, consort of John Benjamin Dent, of Charles County, Maryland".[1]

The will of John Benjamin Dent was proved in Charles County on November 23, 1841. He devised his daughters — Catherine, Sarah, Rosanna, Elizabeth, and Valeria—the dwelling-plantation "Brawner's Rest" during their single lives as well as the mill, providing that they give their two youngest brothers, Walter and Alexander, each two years' education. The residue was to be divided equally among the five daughters and the following sons: John, Walter, and Alexander.[2]

At Walnut Hill are the following tombstone inscriptions: "In Memory of Catherine Petrie Dent born July 16, 1791, died Sept. 20, 1838"; "In Memory of John B. Dent born July 10, 1786, died Sept. 20, 1841"; "In Memory of Eliza[h] Mary 5th daughter of J. B. Dent and wife of Jos. H. Jones who departed this life June 3, 1853, aged 26 years and 1 mo."

---

[1] The Morgue, Peabody Libr., Balto.
[2] Wills, Liber D J no. 16, folio 241.

LEVI DENT[5]

(18— - 1842)

Levi Dent, son of John Brewer and Priscilla Dent, was born in Trinity Parish, Charles County. He married Pamelia ————.

Children of Levi and Pamelia Dent

1. Anna E. Dent married ———— Carrico.
2. Robert M. Dent.
3. Verlinda Dent married ———— Hatton.
4. Frederick L. Dent married Lydia Dent.
5. Walter B. Dent.

Levi Dent practiced medicine in southern Maryland, where he died on June 14, 1842. The 1850 census shows his widow, Pamela Dent, the head of a family with realty appraised at $5,000. The son Walter Brewer Dent was baptized at Trinity Church on September 17, 1830. Children at home in 1850 were Frederick, aged 19; Robert, aged 18; Anne E., aged 15; and Priscilla Verlinda, aged 14.

The will of his widow, Pamelia A. Dent, was dated April 18, 1872, and proved in Charles County on May 19, 1874, by Thomas Carico, Francis L. Higdon, and Joseph R. Harrison. She devised her daughter

Anna E. Carico the farm lying in Gilbert Swamp then occupied by the testatrix's son Robert M. Dent containing 200 acres. To her daughter Velinda P. Hatton she devised the land purchased from Walter B. Dent, being one-fifth of the farm then occupied by Peter Hatton. Silverware was bequeathed to son Frederick L. Dent, and $25 to the children of son Walter B. Dent. Son Robert M. received the farm on which he lived, and she mentioned a grandson George T. Carico. Dr. Thomas H. Carico was appointed executor.

ZACHARIAH DENT[5]

Zachariah Dent, son of Zachariah and Elizabeth Dent, was born in or near Centreville, Charles County. It has already been shown that he sued his sister and brother-in-law over the estate of their mother in 1834. Records of Charles County fail to show whom he married, but in 1845 a case in chancery developed which proved that he had a daughter Priscilla M. who married in March 1840 George T. Richards.[1]

On August 23, 1845, John Hughes for his wards Benjamin Swann, Samuel Swann, and Theophilus Swann filed a bill of complaint against Zachariah Dent, George T. Richards and the latter's wife Priscilla. Zachariah Dent had filed bankruptcy in 1845 and had formerly been the guardian of his nephews—Benjamin, Samuel, and Theophilus Swann— the sons of his sister Catherine Swann and her husband Benjamin Swann. On July 15, 1844, Zachariah Dent had deeded land that had been willed him by his father and other lands consisting of 176 acres to his daughter Priscilla Richards as well as about $5,000 worth of personal property.

It was stated that George T. Richards had come to Charles County in 1840, opened a tavern in Bryan Town, then became a merchant, and had no visible property upon settlement in Charles County. He was born in Charles County, but was raised in Prince Georges County, had also lived on the Eastern Shore and in the District of Columbia. He was a brother to Samuel T. Richard and had filed bankruptcy in 1836.

Arthur D. Smoot, a witness, stated that he lived within two miles of Zachariah Dent. Richard T. Robertson, aged 15, stated that he lived with his uncle George Richards.

The following data from Trinity Parish register may or may not be connected with Zachariah Dent of Centreville:

> Maria, daughter of Zachariah and Attaway Dent, was buried Sept. 2, 1830.
>
> Sarah Maria, daughter of Zachariah and Attaway Dent, was born May 8, 1833.

Zachariah Walter Brewer Dent, born 1834, was baptised January 16,
  1836, at Zachariah Dent's home.
Zachariah Dent was confirmed 1831 by Bishop William Murray
  Stone.
Attaway Dent was buried November 10, 1846.

¹ Chancery Papers no. 11,314.

LEONARD DENT[5]

Leonard G. Dent, son of Titus and Mary Dent, was born in Trinity
Parish, Charles County. He married Isabella C. ————.

Children of Leonard and Isabella Dent

1. Charles H. Dent.
2. Samuel C. Dent.
3. Isabella C. Dent married Robert R. Rye.
4. Mary Dent married George K. Posey.
5. Margaret Jane Dent.

The will of Isabella C. Dent was dated January 27, 1850, and admitted to probate in Charles County on February 21, 1850, by William
Smith, Richard Price, and Thomas X Posey as the witnesses. She devised her son, Charles H. Dent, all land, and various slaves to the
following children: Samuel C. Dent; Isabella C., wife of Robert R. Rye;
Mary, wife of George K. Posey; and Margaret Jane Dent. She appointed her son, Charles, the executor.¹

The 1850 census shows Charles H. Dent as the head of family in
Hill Top District of Charles County, aged 22, and with realty appraised
at $400. In his home were Margaret Dent, aged 18, and Samuel Dent,
aged 14.

¹ Wills, Liber D J no. 16, folio 497, La Plata.

ROBERT BEALL DENT[5]

(1777 - 1853)

Robert Dent, son of John and Verlinda (Beall) Dent, was born
December 12, 1777, in Montgomery County, Maryland. In that county
he secured license on April 4, 1801, to marry Mary Hays. She was born
February 16, 1785, the daughter of Notley Hays.

Children of Robert and Mary (Hays) Dent

1. John Peter Dent married Rachel Helms.
2. William Dent, died young.

3. George Hays Dent married Marie Snyder.
4. Elizabeth Dent, born 1810, married Sylvester, son of David and Margaret (Scoles) Creamer, born Feb. 22, 1811, Washington Co., Md., died Apr. 4, 1894, in Belmont Co., Ohio. Issue: Cynthia and George Dent.
5. Sarah Dent married William Meek, of Monroe Co., Ohio.
6. Robert Beall Dent, born 1815, died 1888, married 1840 Sarah Jane Chapman McMurray, born 1818, died 1892.
7. Mary Anne Dent, spinster.

On April 10, 1802, Robert Dent was deeded by Vachel Hall and his wife a portion of "Jeremiah's Park", lying on the north side of the road in Montgomery County, which had once been the property of William Hays, the grandfather of Mary (Hays) Dent.[1] On December 5, 1805, Robert Dent conveyed this tract to John Plummer. Mary Dent his wife waived dower.[2] Shortly afterwards, he and his father settled at St. Clairville, Belmont County, Ohio. Robert taught school for a time, was at one time magistrate, and the proprietor of the first merchantile establishment in St. Clairville. His wife died on February 16, 1840; he died on November 12, 1853, and was interred in Belmont County.

---

[1] Deeds, Liber K, folio 283, Rockville.
[2] Deeds, Liber M, folio 216, Rockville.

WILLIAM DENT[5]

(18— - 1869)

William Dent, son of George and Elizabeth (Mills)) Dent, was born in St. Mary's County.

Children of William Dent

1. Jane Maria Dent married James E. Heard. License St. M. Co., Aug. 1845.
2. Susan Elizabeth Dent.

In 1833 William Dent appeared as the legal guardian of Jane Maria and Susan Elizabeth Dent, with Hezekiah Dent and James Hebb as his bondsmen.

The will of William Dent was dated December 14, 1857, when he named Tial Heard and Charles E. Dent as trustees for the estate of his daughter Susan Dent. The dwelling-plantation was devised to his daughter Jane Maria Heard. By a codicil he appointed Charles E. Dent sole trustee. The instrument was proved in St. Mary's County on August 10, 1869.[1]

---

[1] Wills, Liber J T M R no. 1, folio 245, Leonardtown.

Hezekiah Dent[5]

(1791 - 1863)

Hezekiah Dent, son of George and Elizabeth (Mills) Dent, was born in or about 1791 in St. Mary's County. On October 16, 1821, he secured license in that county to marry Martha Matilda Hammett.

Children of Hezekiah and Martha (Hammett) Dent

1. James Thomas Dent, born Oct. 24, 1822.
2. Charles Dent married Sarah Hammett. *q.v.*
3. Susan Matilda Sophia Dent, born Dec. 27, 1828, married George Edward Hammett. License Nov. 9, 1847, St. M. Co.
4. Mary Elizabeth Dent, born 1831, married Clarke J. Durant. License May 15, 1851, St. M. Co.
5. George B. Dent, born 1833.
6. Hezekiah Dent, born 1835.
7. Martha Anne Dent, born 1840, married James T., son of John and Mary (Dent) Duke. License May 22, 1860, St. M. Co.

In 1842 Hezekiah Dent by the court was appointed the guardian of Martha Anne Dent, Susan S. Dent, and Mary Elizabeth Dent. His bondsmen were William Dent and Mary Ann Dukes. He died in St. Mary's County during 1863; his widow died in 1872.

Alexander Dent[5]

(17— - 1830)

Alexander Dent, son of William and Margaret Rettea (Smoot) Dent, was born at "Dent's Inheritance", Charles County. He married Violetta, daughter to John Brewer and Priscilla Dent.

Children of Alexander and Violetta (Dent) Dent

1. John Dent married Sophia Herbert.
2. Henry Dent married Sarah Porter.
3. Deborah Dent married James Mankin. License Dec. 31, 1838, D. C.
4. Margaretta Dent married James Mankin. License Feb. 13, 1833, D. C.
5. Grace Ann Dent, *d.s.p.*

On December 2, 1813, Alexander Dent and Hatch Dent of John purchased from Henry Watson of Monongalia County, Virginia, "Oneal's Desert" and "Dyson's Addition". The said Henry Watson, according to the deed, was one of the co-heirs of Anne Watson whose maiden name was Anne Dyson and who first married Henry Swann of

Charles County, deceased, and then James G. Watson, formerly of Charles County, but then of Monongalia County, Virginia.[1]

On March 29, 1817, Alexander Dent of Charles County conveyed to John Blackman Edwards Dent of the same county "Oneal's Desert" and "Dyson's Addition" of 11 acres, and "Partnership" of 3 acres, the "latter patented to the said Alexander Dent and a certain Hatch Dent father to John B. E. Dent on October 16, 1807". Violetta Dent wife of Alexander waived her dower rights.[2]

On December 4, 1817, Alexander Dent and Nathan S. Dent of Charles County, executors of the will of William Dent . . . "whereas William Dent late of Charles County did on 28 July 1816 by will . . . to the children now born of my son Thomas and Sarah his wife . . . 100 acres of Simpkin Coatback, but if my son Thomas wishes to remove to any of the new States then my executors are to sell land for the benefit of the children", sold the said land inasmuch as Thomas was about to migrate to another State. Sarah Dent the wife of Thomas acknowledged the transfer.

The will of Alexander Dent was dated September 1829, and proved in Charles County on March 18, 1830. He devised his wife Violetta during life one-third of his two plantations which was then occupied by him, one lying on the east side of Gilbert Swamp and the other on the west side of the same swamp, and one-third of the personal estate. The land which he had purchased from Thomas M. Swann, of St. Mary's County, and from Lucy and Bennett Dyson, of Charles County, was to be sold to cover all indebtedness. The remaining realty was not to be sold or divided so long as his daughters (unnamed) remained single, thereby giving them a livelihood. He appointed his wife Violetta and son John as the executors.[3]

At the probation of the will, Nathan Smoot Dent testified that he prepared the will in writing and that it was approved by the testator.

In 1832 Violetta Dent, the relict of Alexander, was listed as a communicant of Trinity Parish. The parish register also shows that Mrs. Mankin, the daughter of Mrs. V. Dent was buried April 27, 1837, on the plantation of Brewer Dent.

The will of the spinster daughter, Grace Ann, was dated April 2, 1845, and proved in Charles County on June 10, 1845, by William K. Dent, Priscilla E. Dent, and Sophia A. Dent. She named her mother, Violetta Dent, as the executrix and bequeathed her negroes and all interest in the estate of her deceased father Alexander Dent.

[1] Deeds, Liber J B no. 10, folio 380, La Plata.
[2] Deeds, Liber J B. no. 12, folio 12.
[3] Liber W D M no. 15, folio 342.

THOMAS DENT[5]

(1778 - 1862)

Thomas Dent, son of William and Margaret Rettea (Smoot) Dent, was born about 1778 in Charles County, Maryland. By the terms of his father's will of 1816, the children born to him and his wife Sarah were to inherit "Simkin's Comeback". This proviso was made owing to his well known dissipation. In or about 1800 he married his cousin Sarah Dent, the daughter of Joseph Manning and Mary Dent.

Ten children were the result of this union, but the most prominent was William Barton Wade Dent. Thomas Dent disposed of his Maryland land and settled first in Pittsylvania County, Virginia. Later he removed to the village of Franklin in Heard County, Georgia. His wife died in 1859; he died in 1862.

Their son, William Barton Wade Dent, was born at Bryantown, Charles County, Maryland, on September 6, 1806. In 1823 he was graduated from Charlotte Hall Military Academy and soon afterwards settled at Mallorysville, Wilkes County, Georgia. On February 22, 1827, he married Eliza Hinton at the residence of her father on Newford Creek, Wilkes County, where she was born. During the Creek Indian War, he was commissioned a colonel and was actively engaged in the campaign. In 1843 he was elected to the State Legislature, and five years later he served as judge of the inferior court of Coweta County. On November 4, 1853, he was elected to the 33rd Congress, but was not a candidate for renomination in 1854. He died at Newnan, Georgia, on September 7, 1855, and was interred in Oak Hill Cemetery. His widow died on June 18, 1881.

Twelve children were born to him and his wife. Their fourth child, Mary Sophia Dent, was born November 13, 1831, in Heard County, Georgia, and married John T. Pace. *q.v.*

NATHAN SMOOT DENT[5]

(1791 - 18—)

Nathan Smoot Dent, son of William and Margaret Rettea (Smoot) Dent, was born 1791 in Charles County. He married a kinswoman, Julia Chapman, daughter to Hatch and Judith (Poston) Dent.

Children of Nathan Smoot and Julia (Dent) Dent

1. Juliana Chapman Dent, bur. Oct. 29, 1830.
2. William Hatch Dent, bap. Oct. 28, 1825.
3. Addison Dent.

4. Alexander Dent.
5. Lucy Dent.
6. Walter Chapman Dent.

Nathan Smoot Dent served as a sergeant in Colonel Hawkins' First Maryland Regiment during the War of 1812 and later as ensign in the same regiment.[1] On June 28, 1824, he filed a bill of complaint in the chancery court against Townley Robey over accounts between Smoot who was Deputy Sheriff and Robey the Sheriff. Nicholas Stonestreet and Henry Brawner were appointed by the court to arbitrate.[2] In 1832 he was a communicant of Trinity Parish.

---

[1] U. S. War Dept.
[2] Chancery Papers no. 7437.

THOMAS E. DENT[5]
(1806 - 18—)

Thomas E. Dent, son of Thomas C. and Rebecca (Chappelear) Dent, was born about 1806 in Frederick County, Virginia. He, however, settled in St. Mary's County where his ancestors had lived for several generations and where on December 14, 1827, he obtained license to marry Susan Hammett. His dwelling-plantation lay in St. Andrew's Parish, where the births of several children are recorded.

Children of Thomas and Susan (Hammett) Dent

1. Sarah M. Dent, born 1829 in Va., married Joseph N. Harrison. License Oct. 19, 1854, St. M. Co.
2. James Hammett Dent, born May 6, 1833.
3. Joseph Chappelear Dent, born Mar. 13, 1835, married Emeline R. Hammett. License Sept 26, 1859, St. M. Co.
4. Martha Anne Dent, born Sept. 20, 1837.
5. Thomas Dent, born Oct. 21, 1839.
6. Benjamin Dent, born June 12, 1842.

WILFRED DENT[6]

Wilfred Dent, son of Thomas Hatch and Anne (Trott) Dent, was born in Rowan County, North Carolina. There on May 11, 1837, he negotiated a bond to marry Rachel Smith, with H. Belton and Pharley Ellis as his sureties. On September 18, 1839, Wilfred Dent and Rachel his wife conveyed to James Smith, of Rowan County, land lying on Third Creek adjoining Richmond Pearson. Wilfred Dent made his X mark, while Rachel signed her name.

ANNE ELIZABETH DENT[6]
(1815 - 1900)

Anne Elizabeth Dent, daughter of Michael Lawson and Sarah (Heard) Dent, was born May 13, 1815, in Georgia. On March 17, 1835, she married Lorenza Madison Biggers in Muscogee County, Georgia. She died September 2, 1900.

Children of Lorenza and Anne Elizabeth (Dent) Biggers

1. Joseph Lawson Biggers.
2. Lorenza John Biggers.
3. Frances Anne Louisa Biggers married ———— Kimbrough.
4. Sarah Elizabeth Biggers.
5. Margaret Jackson Biggers married ———— Crane.
6. Mary Anna Biggers married ———— Anthony.
7. Josephine Augusta Biggers married ———— David.
8. Madeline Virginia Biggers married Miles Green Wade. *q.v.*
9. Lavonia Walton Biggers married ———— Jones.

Their daughter, Madeline Virginia Biggers, was born December 20, 1852, and at present is one of the oldest living descendants of Michael Lawson Dent. On November 28, 1875, in Muscogee County, Georgia, she was married to Miles Green Wade. He was born January 6, 1851, the son of Thomas Henry Wade who was born March 1, 1815, and married June 2, 1844, to Mary Comfort Robinson, born September 12, 1823. Thomas Henry Wade died April 24, 1883, and was buried at Smith Station, Alabama, near his wife who had died on July 17, 1872. Miles Green Wade, the husband of Madeline Virginia, died October 5, 1903.

Children of Miles Green and Madeline (Biggers) Wade

1. Howard Madison Wade, born Aug. 21, 1876, Muscogee Co., Ga., married Nov. 22, 1900, Rosalie Tarver, of Columbus, Ga. Issue: Isabelle, born Feb. 16, 1911, Charlotte, N. C., married June 5, 1937, at Charlotte to Morgan Ayres Reynolds, the parents of Rosalie Wade Reynolds, born Nov. 1, 1939.
2. Thomas Henry Wade.
3. Miles Lovett Wade.
4. Julia Wade married ———— Fletcher.
5. Albert Brown Wade.
6. Madeline Wade married ———— Cox.
7. Annie Ruth Wade.

ALEXANDER LAWSON DENT[6]
(1818 - 18—)

Alexander Lawson Dent, son of Michael Lawson and Sarah (Heard) Dent, was born about 1818 in Wilkes County, Georgia. His wife was

Martha ————, born about 1822, in Putnam County, same State. They lived for a time in Harris County, where their children, Richard and Mary, were born. In 1850 he was the head of a family in Muscogee County, Georgia, and in his household were Richard, born 1844; Mary, born 1846; and Michael, born 1848.

RICHARD DENT[6]
(1821 - 18—)

Richard Dent, son of Michael Lawson and Sarah (Heard) Dent, was born about 1821 in Wilkes County, Georgia. He accompanied his parents to Muscogee County, where he was domiciled at the 1850 census. His wife was Mary A. ————, born 1828 in Harris County, Georgia. In his household were also his widowed mother, and John H. Dent, born 1831 in Wilkes County.

CHARLES DENT[6]

Charles Dent, son of Hezekiah and Martha (Hammett) Dent, was born in St. Mary's County in or about 1827. In that county on May 18, 1852, he secured license to marry his kinswoman Sarah Margaret Hammett.

Children of Charles and Sarah (Hammett) Dent
1. Catherine Ruth Dent, born Apr. 9, 1853, died 1894, married 1882 J. Edward Evans.
2. Molly Dent, born Aug. 5, 1855, died 1938, married 1887 J. Parran Crane.
3. Charles Francis Dent, born 1858, died 1868.
4. Martha Jane Dent married Walter Hanson Briscoe Wise. *q.v.*
5. Hezekiah Enoch Dent, born Apr. 25, 1862, married Ella Harp.
6. Sophia Amanda Dent, born 1865, died 1868.
7. George Frank Dent, born Apr. 7, 1868, married Susan E. Keyworth and Frances Hatfield.

ROBERT BEALL DENT[6]
(1815 - 1888)

Robert Beall Dent, son of Robert and Mary (Hays) Dent, was born 1815, and in 1840 married Jane Chapman McMurray who was born 1818. He died in 1888 and his widow in 1892.

Children of Robert and Jane (McMurray) Dent
1. William Dent, born 1841, died 1875, married Monica Porterfield.
2. Robert Middleton Dent, born 1844, died 1893, married Elizabeth Simpson.

3. Narcissa Dent, born 1846, died 1928, married Robert McF. Fulton.
4. Sarah Emmaline Dent, born 1848, died 1920, married 1869, William King. Issue: James Robert; Myrtle Alice; William; Ida Ethel; Gertrude; Delbert Dent; Roy C.; George.

Myrtle Alice King, the second child of William King and his wife Sarah Dent, was born in 1872, and married Dr. Harry Myers, of Columbus, Ohio. Their daughter Elizabeth Monica Myers married Herbert G. Mote.

MARTHA JANE (DENT) WISE[7]

Martha Jane Dent, daughter of Charles and Sarah (Hammett) Dent, was born January 31, 1860. On December 2, 1883, she married Walter Hanson Briscoe Wise, a banker of Leonardtown, Maryland. Their son, Walter Dent Wise, was born May 18, 1885, at Patuxent Beach, Maryland. On October 20, 1914, he married Agnes Gordon Whiting, of Baltimore, who was born December 7, 1888.

Children of Walter and Agnes (Whiting) Wise

1. Marian Gordon Armistead Wise, born Nov. 24, 1916, at Baltimore.
2. Agnes Whiting Wise, born Dec. 20, 1918, at Baltimore.

His wife died on January 27, 1919. He married secondly on July 27, 1921, Josephine McMillan, widow, the daughter of Thomas W. Warfield, of Maryland.

Walter Dent Wise attended the College of Medicine of the University of Maryland, receiving his medical degree in 1906. Since that year he has practiced medicine and surgery in Baltimore, and is at present (1940) chief surgeon of Mercy Hospital. In 1937 he was appointed professor of clinical surgery at the University of Maryland, a position which he has since held, and in the same year he was appointed visiting surgeon at the Union Memorial Women's Hospital and the South Baltimore General Hospital. He holds fellowships in the American College of Surgeons as well as the American Surgical Association and the Southern Surgical Association. He frequently contributes articles on surgery to various medical journals throughout the country.

His mother now a widow resides (1940) at Leonardtown.

DENT-BURRELL DESCENDANTS

Peter Dent — Mary Brooke

d. 1757.

Eleanor Dent — Alexander Burrell

d. 1784.

Alexander Burrell was born in England in or about 1740 and came to Maryland as a young man, settling at Piscataway, Prince Georges County.* He was in Maryland by March 25, 1756, inasmuch as on that date he was a witness at the sale of personal effects of Nicholas Dawson to Francis King and John Glassford & Co., to satisfy debts against Dawson.[1]

Very little is known about his antecedents in England, but he was probably a younger son of a country gentleman who without a landed estate from his parent sought adventure in America. He was not without capital upon his settlement in Maryland and soon contracted marriage with Eleanor Dent, a maiden of proud lineage.

The marriage is recorded in St. John's Piscataway Parish, but no date is given. From the dates before and after the entry, it is concluded that the event occurred about 1758. Circumstances, however, place it somewhat later, inasmuch as the marriages of his daughters did not occur until after 1790. Furthermore, if he gave his age correctly in 1781 as 38 years, he was slightly immature for marriage in 1758.

Children of Alexander and Eleanor (Dent) Burrell

1. Alexander Hawkins Burrell married Susannah Wood. License Mar. 18, 1789, Pr. Geo. Co.
2. John Burrell.
3. William Burrell.
4. Mary Burrell married James Wells. License Pr. Geo. Co., Feb. 6, 1795.
5. Anne Burrell married Absalom Anderson. License Pr. Geo. Co., June 6, 1794.
6. Catron Burrell.
7. Sarah Burrell married John Baughman Denune. q.v.

---

*Archives, vol. 18, p. 381. His name has been incorrectly printed in several secondary sources as *Allen*. A study of his signatures shows that he frequently signed as *Aller* Burrell, the *r* now faded and indistinct is easily taken for an *n*. Other times he signed as Allex[r].

On May 7, 1765, Alexander Burrell purchased from John Noble, son of Joseph Noble, late of Piscataway, Prince Georges County, a portion of "Littleworth" for £125. The deed read "whereas by the last will of Joseph Noble he gave his wife Mary during life two acres of land bought of Edward Edelen being a portion of Littleworth in Piscataway Town the land on which my dwelling house stands and at her decease to my son John Noble". No wife waived dower; the witnesses were Alexander Symmes and David Crawford.[2] On June 1, 1771, he leased from Thomas Lancaster, of Prince Georges County, Gent., for 21 years the land adjoining Queen Anne Town on the Patuxent River below the house built by Jeremiah Crabb for a granary. Both Thomas Lancaster and Alexander Burrell signed the lease which was witnessed by Richard Duckett, Jr., and David Crawford.[8]

On November 4, 1771, he conveyed to Thomas Dent for £400 a portion of "Littleworth" adjoining "Leith" then in the possession of George Hardy and adjacent to the land of Edward Pye. Eleanor Burrell his wife waived dower, the witnesses being John Bayne and George Hardy, Jr.[4]

On January 21, 1778, Alexander Burrell took the oath of allegiance and fidelity to the State of Maryland in Prince Georges County.[5] His resentment against the mother country was amply exemplified by his enlistment at the age of 38 on May 25, 1781, in Prince Georges County for active service against the British.[6]

The will of Alexander Burrell was dated December 5, 1783, and proved in Prince Georges County on June 26, 1784, by Joseph Richardson, Richard Toggett, and Richard Elliott. He devised to his wife Eleanor and son Alexander Hawkins Burrell the lot of land and houses in Queen Anne Town whereon he then lived with all improvements which was leased from Thomas Lancaster. In the event that his son, Alexander Hawkins Burrell, did not return to Maryland, then the above property was to revert to son John after the death of the widow. John was willed the land in Queen Anne Town whereon the granary stood, leased from Thomas Lancaster. Son William was devised a portion of "Knaves Disappointment" lying in Georgetown, Montgomery County. The personal estate was to be sold at public auction and the proceeds divided equally among his wife Eleanor and the four daughters—Mary, Ann, Catron, and Sarah. He named his wife Eleanor Burrell, son Alexander Hawkins Burrell, and friend Richard Dent, the executors.[7]

---

[1] Deeds, Liber N N, folio 431, Marlboro.
[2] *Ibid.*, Liber T T, folio 406.

* *Ibid.*, Liber A A no. 2, folio 411.
* *Ibid.*, Liber A A no. 2, folio 411.
* Brumbaugh's Md. Rec., vol. 2, p. 296.
* Archives, vol. 18, p. 381.
* Wills, Liber T no. 1, folio 196, Marlboro.

SARAH (BURRELL) DENUNE

Sarah Burrell, daughter of Alexander and Eleanor (Dent) Burrell, married John Denune. He was born about 1766, the son of John and Elizabeth (Forrest) Denune, of the same county, and as a lad of not more than fourteen years of age served as both drummer and fifer to the Maryland Line.

On March 1, 1780, John Denune enlisted as a drummer in the Sixth Maryland Regiment for one year. The muster of that regiment in October 1780, after the regiment had been practically decimated in the southern campaign showed that the surviving members had been formed into a company of the Second Battalion and attached to Colonel Williams' regiment of infantry. He was discharged on November 1, 1780, at the termination of his enlistment. On January 1, 1782, he enlisted as a fifer in the 1st Company, 2d Battalion, commanded by Captain Alexander Trueman, Lieutenant Jacob Crawford, and Ensign Charles Skirvins. He was later assigned to the company of Captain Edward Spurrier, with Lieutenants Joshua Rutledge and Robert Halkerson.[1]

After the war he returned to his home in Prince Georges County and there on January 17, 1798, he secured license to marry Sarah Burrell.

Children of John and Sarah (Burrell) Denune

1. William Forrest Denune.
2. John Duval Denune.
3. Alexander Denune married Mary Ann Agler. *q.v.*
4. Mary Anne Denune.
5. Lucy Washington Denune.
6. Sarah Anne Denune.
7. James Perry Denune.
8. Nancy Brown Denune married Hiram Loy.
9. Barbara Denune.
10. Willia Harrison Denune.
11. Elizabeth Denune.
12. Susannah Denune.
13. Caroline Denune.

The first three children were born in Maryland, but about 1806 he and his young family migrated westward and ultimately settled in Franklin County, Ohio, now a part of the city of Columbus.

Under the Pension Act of 1818, he applied in May 1818 for a pension by rights of his service in the Maryland Line. At that time he stated that he was 52 years of age, and had enlisted about March 1, 1780, at Bladensburg in a foot company as a musician of the 6th Maryland Regiment under Captain Henry Dodson. At the battle of Eutaw Springs his captain was killed and John Lynn, his lieutenant, was wounded. After the battle his company retired to the hills of Santic, where he received an indefinite furlough. He returned to his home in Prince Georges County and there in about two or three months he enlisted in Captain Edward Spurrier's company and was stationed at Baltimore. With several companies, his outfit marched under Major Lansdale to Newburg where General Washington was in command. He was discharged at Baltimore during June 1783. Other battles in which he was actively engaged during the southern campaign were Camden and Guilford Court House.

At the time he applied for a pension, his wife's first cousin, William Dent Beall, late a captain in the Maryland Line, certified that John Denune enlisted with him and served at one time under his command.[2]

John Denune died on November 28, 1838, in Mifflin Township, Franklin County, Ohio. His grave marked with an impressive monument states that he was a Revolutionary soldier.

At the adjustment of the proceeds of his pension claim in 1850, it was shown that the following were his surviving heirs: William Denune; A. B. Denune; Elizabeth Ballinger; Nancy Loy; Lucy Agler; Susannah Stott; Mary Anne Denune; and Caroline Denune.

Alexander Bond Burrell Denune, third son of John and Sarah (Burrell) Denune, was born May 18, 1807, in Prince Georges County, Maryland. As an infant he accompanied his parents to Ohio and there he matured into manhood. On December 1, 1831, he married Mary Ann Agler, born May 10, 1814, near Columbus, Ohio. His wife died on September 7, 1882, while his death occurred several years later on May 18, 1886. Both were interred in Riverside Cemetery in Franklin County, Ohio.

Sarah Melissa Denune, daughter to the above, was born March 4, 1836, in Franklin County. On July 6, 1855, she married Swan Innis Rankin who was born on March 26, 1832, near Gahanna, Ohio. One of the issue of this union was Lewis Lincoln Rankin, born August 4, 1860, in Mifflin Township, Franklin County, Ohio. He married Hattie

[1] Archives, vol. 18, pp. 201, 347, 439, 531.
[2] Pension Claim, Revolutionary, S 44133.

Rathnell, born September 16, 1861, at Lockborne, Ohio, and in 1940 was living in Columbus, Ohio. Lewis Rankin died December 27, 1918, at Columbus.

Bertha Rankin, their daughter was born August 16, 1887, at Lockborne, Ohio, and was graduated from Wellesley College. On October 5, 1910, she married James Edgar Kinney, born January 15, 1887, at Belmont, Ohio.

Children of James and Bertha (Rankin) Kinney

1. James Lewis Kinney, born Oct. 7, 1911, Columbus, Ohio; graduated Ohio Wesleyan 1932, B.A.; Harvard Business School 1935, M.B.A.
2. Richard Rankin Kinney, born June 3, 1913, Columbus, Ohio; graduated Ohio Wesleyan 1934, B.A.; Harvard Law Sch., 1937, LL.B.
3. Harriet Martha Kinney, born Jan. 27, 1915, Columbus, Ohio; graduated Ohio State Univ. 1936, B.A., 1940, B.Sc.
4. Dorothy Kinney, born Nov. 30, 1916, died Apr. 7, 1919.

DENT-PACE DESCENDANTS

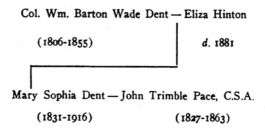

Col. Wm. Barton Wade Dent — Eliza Hinton

(1806-1855)   d. 1881

Mary Sophia Dent — John Trimble Pace, C.S.A.

(1831-1916)   (1827-1863)

Mary Sophia Dent was born November 13, 1831, at Franklin, Heard County, Georgia, where her parents were then residing before their removal to Coweta County. At Newnan on July 5, 1855, she was married to John Trimble Pace, born 1827, also a native Georgian. About 1857 they settled at London, Texas, where the young husband for a time was engaged in business. Later he and his family removed to Omen, Smith County, where he became the proprietor of a merchandise establishment. On January 8, 1863, he enlisted as a private in Co. C, 7th Regt. Texas Infantry. His services with the Confederate forces were brief, for the muster roll of the regiment for June 30, 1863, shows that he died near Canton, Miss., on June 3, 1863.* His widow survived him many years and died on October 25, 1916, at Troup, Texas.

Children of John and Mary Sophia (Dent) Pace

1. William Dent Pace married Ida Orr. *q.v.*
2. Henry Barnabas Pace, born 1858, died 1859.
3. Loulie Ellen Dent Pace married William Woldert. *q.v.*
4. Helen Lucy Pace, born Dec. 14, 1861, Omen, Tex.; died Oct. 27, 1890, married Feb. 21, 1883, J. R. Eskridge. Issue: Forest Wade, born 1884, died 1885; Wadrick Waddell, born 1886, died young; Lillian Eskridge, born Feb. 5, 1888, married Ralph Gibbs; Helen Lucy, born and died 1890.

WILLIAM DENT PACE[8]

(1857 - 1918)

William Dent Pace, son of John Trimble and Mary Sophia (Dent) Pace, was born January 15, 1857. He married Ida Orr on November 8, 1880. He maintained his residence at Troup, Texas, where all of his children were born and where he was engaged in business. He died at

---

*U. S. War Dept., Washington.

Troup on October 3, 1918, leaving a widow (living 1940) and seven children.

Children of William Dent and Ida (Orr) Pace

1. Pearl Pace, died in infancy.
2. Pansy Pace, born Nov. 23, 1883, married R. B. Walthall and Jabez Curry Nelson.
3. John Walton Pace, born Apr. 27, 1885, married Aug. 1914, Bess Whittaker. Issue: Mary Katherine; John Walton; Betty Barton; Richard Dent.
4. Pattie Mary Pace married Aug. 4, 1909, Rufus Roy Ruff. Issue: Elizabeth, born Oct. 28, 1911.
5. Bonnie Pace, born Dec. 26, 1889, unmarried.
6. William Dent Pace married Azile Fox. *q.v.*
7. Charles Pace, born Mar. 11, 1894, married Apr. 18, 1925, Harriet Okie.
8. Edgar Pace, born Nov. 26, 1899, married July 10, 1929, Rose Rutledge. Issue: Martha.

LOULIE ELLEN PACE[8]

(1860 - 1898)

Loulie Ellen Dent Pace, daughter to John Trimble and Mary Sophia (Dent) Pace, was born March 12, 1860, at Omen, Texas. There on January 7, 1883, she was married to William Albert Woldert who was born May 1, 1855. She died on January 19, 1898. Her husband survived her many years, dying on February 26, 1937.

Children of William and Loulie Ellen (Pace) Woldert

1. Alma Mary Woldert married twice. *q.v.*
2. William Albert Woldert, born Apr. 6, 1886, married May 19, 1923, Edel Weiss Bedford. Issue: Marion Wilma; Dorothy May; Carolyn Jean.
3. Bonnie Loulie Woldert, died in infancy.
4. Christine Ellen Woldert, Feb. 7, 1890, married William Walter Campbell and Morton P. Briggs. Issue: (first) Christine; William Walter; Albert William.
5. Nina Dent Woldert, died in infancy.

WILLIAM DENT PACE[9]

William Dent Pace, son of William Dent and Ida (Orr) Pace, was born January 26, 1892, at Troup, Texas. In 1917 he married Azile Fox, by whom one son, William Dent Pace III, was born, aged 14 years in 1940. He maintains his residence in Tyler, Texas, and from 1933-1940 he has been a member of the Texas Senate. He is also known for his civic leadership, not only in his county but throughout the Southwest.

ALMA MARY WOLDERT[9]

Alma Mary Woldert, daughter to William Albert and Loulie Ellen (Pace) Woldert, was born May 21, 1884. At Tyler, Texas, on June 1, 1905, she was married to Richard Ransom Mc LeRoy, who was born April 29, 1880, at Vienna, Louisiana.

Children of Richard and Alma Mary (Woldert) Mc LeRoy

1. Richard Ransom Mc LeRoy married Polly Minton. *q.v.*

Her husband died on May 6, 1910, at El Paso, Texas. On January 4, 1912, at Tyler, Texas, she married secondly Robert Spence, a native of San Diego, Texas.

Children of Robert and Alma Mary (Woldert) Spence

1. Elizabeth Margaret Spence married Carol Emil Recknagel. *q.v.*
2. Robert William Spence, born Feb. 7, 1918, at Tyler; B.B.A., Univ. of Texas; at present (1940) studying law at Univ. of Texas.

She is well known as a writer of prose and poetry as well as a civic leader in her community. She appears frequently on the radio and on the lecture platform, and resides at Tyler, Texas.

Her eldest son, Richard Ranson McLeRoy, was born June 23, 1909, at El Paso, and was later graduated from the Agricultural and Mechanical College of Texas as a mechanical engineer. On August 22, 1936, at Hemphill, his home State, he married Polly Minton. A son— Richard Ransom McLeRoy, III—was born at Dallas on September 12, 1940.

Her only daughter, Elizabeth Margaret Spence, was born February 11, 1913, at Tyler, and was graduated from the State University at Austin. On June 29, 1932, at Tyler, she was married to Carol Emil Recknagel, formerly a lieutenant of the 90th Squadron, United States Air Corps, but now a captain in the reserve. He was graduated from the University of Ohio, and at present (1940) is a pilot for the United Air Lines of Chicago. One child—Margaret Ann Recknagel—was born December 28, 1933, at Chicago.

MISCELLANEOUS

John Dent enlisted on May 1, 1777, as a private in Captain Waters' Company, 3rd Maryland Regiment, for three years under Colonel Peter Adams. He served at one time as body guard to General Washington, and data pertaining to him in this capacity are filed with the Manuscript Division in the Library of Congress. At the expiration of his enlistment, he returned to his home in Maryland wounded.

On January 19, 1777, he married Eleanor Cecil, of Anne Arundel County, at St. James Parish, by the Rev. Mr. MacGowan.

Children of John and Eleanor (Cecil) Dent

1. Arasmus Dent.
2. John Dent, migrated to Ohio.
3. Richard Dent, married Maria ————. *q.v.*
4. James Dent.
5. Elizabeth Maria Dent married Richard Owens.
6. Walter Dent, *d.s.p.*

John Dent died intestate in Anne Arundel County during March 1808. His widow and administratrix, Eleanor Dent, filed an account on October 20, 1806, in Anne Arundel County, by which she accounted for an inventory of $1,752, taken on July 19, 1808, and a balance of £496/11/11, due to the heirs. (Liber J G no. A, folio 674.)

The General Assembly of Maryland on March 4, 1835, passed a resolution to pay Eleanor Dent, widow of John, a private in the 3rd Maryland Regiment, the half pay of a private during life.

In 1842 his widow, aged 82, applied for a Federal pension by right of her deceased husband's service in the Revolution. She stated that she was at that time a resident of Anne Arundel County, but formerly lived in Prince Georges County. Rezin Lowman, aged 77, in 1842, stated that he knew that John Dent served in the war and lost an eye in battle. Furthermore, that he and John Dent were boys together and that John Dent and his wife lived at a place near Buck Tavern. In correspondence with the Commissioner of Pensions, Richard Owens, of Baltimore, stated that he was a son-in-law to Mrs. Eleanor Dent.

Richard Dent, son to John and Eleanor, died intestate in Baltimore County, when on July 23, 1821, letters of administration were issued to his widow, Maria Kirby, then the wife of Joseph Kirby. The final account was rendered in 1828, when the widow received $65.80, and the daughter Anne Dent $131.61.

Walter Dent, another son, died a bachelor testate. His will dated May 14, 1836, proved June 7, 1836, in Anne Arundel County, by James Newburn and Owen Disney, bequeathed his estate to his mother, Eleanor Dent, then to Charles Walter Owens, son of "my" brother-in-law Richard Owens. Owen Cecil was named executor.

Chancery case (no. 7265) showed that the personal estate was insufficient to satisfy the creditors and that the land "Support" of 80 acres had to be sold to satisfy the creditors. Among the heirs noted were mother Eleanor Dent, Maria wife of Richard Owens, and Anne Dent daughter of his brother Richard Dent.

A lawsuit filed with the High Court of Chancery on July 27, 1821, showed that John Dent, of Anne Arundel County, was indebted to his brother Walter Dent for $600, and his sister Elizabeth Maria Dent for $400, and it was agreed between him and his brother Richard Dent that he (John Dent) should dispose of the land in Anne Arundel County. John Dent accordingly conveyed "Trusty Friend", lying in Anne Arundel County, to Richard Dent. No wife waived dower; Archibald Dorsey and Thomas Worthington witnessed the transfer. John Dent soon afterwards migrated to Ohio. Richard Dent was taken suddenly ill with yellow fever and within a few days, July 16, 1821, died leaving a widow Maria and an infant daughter Nancy, aged 1 year. (Ref. Chancery papers no. 7393.)

Another lawsuit filed on July 3, 1828, stated that Thomas Bicknell, late of Anne Arundel County, died seized of "Fowler's Range" of 108 acres, which he had contracted to sell John Dent through Benjamin Gaither. The tract lay in the forks of the Patuxent adjoining the lands of Benjamin Gaither and Francis Bealmear and was possessed formerly by Matthew Robinson. Walter Dent stated that William Cecil, uncle to Walter and John Dent, had purchased in 1825 "Trusty Friend" from John Dent who was very young at that time, had his mother to support, and who had been "talked into the sale". (Chancery papers no. 7988.)

Charles Dent, by his will dated February 1, 1847, and proved on April 1, same year, in Baltimore County, devised the brick house on Holland Street in Baltimore City to his wife Sophia during widowhood, then to the children (unnamed) begotten of her body. The first and only account, showing no distribution, on October 10, 1850, displayed a balance of $2,381.98. (Ref.: Wills, Liber 21, folio 401.)

Anne Dent, by her will dated March 20, 1802, and proved August 1, 1803, in Charles County, Maryland, bequeathed her entire estate to her daughter, Frances Anne Dent, and named her executrix.

George Dent, by his will dated October 28, 1843, and proved in Fauquier County, Virginia, on November 25, 1844, named his nephew William Massey Simmes as the sole legatee, and appointed his friend Granville I. Kelly as the executor. The witnesses were Jackson Garrison, Jacob Jacobs, and Aquilla W. Jacobs. (Ref.: Liber 19, folio 97, Warrenton.)

John Dent, died intestate in Baltimore County, when letters of administration were issued to William Morrow, with Hugh Crea and Joseph Carey as the sureties, on April 13, 1813. The first account on April 20, 1816, showed a balance due the heirs of $300.55.

George Dent was married to Susannah Davis on January 28, 1779, at St. Paul's Church, Baltimore Town. He died intestate in Baltimore County. Letters of administration were issued to his widow, Susannah Dent, and Walter Simpson on November 26, 1798. The inventory of his personal estate was appraised at £659/8/10. The first account was rendered by Walter Simpson in 1800 when he was the guardian to Eleanor and Susannah Dent, daughters of the deceased. Nathan Levering, however, completed the administration on February 23, 1826, when $533.68 each were distributed to the three representatives—Martha Harrison, Eleanor Dent, and Nathan Levering in right of his wife Susannah.

Edellin

EDELEN FAMILY

The Edelen family is of Continental origin and had its seat during the fourteenth century at Nantes—then in the Province or Dukedom of Bretagne. There about fourteen hundred or so Rolland Edellin rose to prominence and wealth as a *marchand* and in recognition of his ability and position in the State he was granted armorial bearings for the use of him and "his descendants for ever".[1] The armorial emblazonment was the characteristic *poisson* and it would not be unwise to assume that he were a *poisson marchand* and had large interest in the fishing industries of the Briton peasantry operating from the River Loire, on which Nantes is located, out along the waters of the Brittany coast.

At that time Brittany was claimed by the King of England as a vassale state—though France at various times refused to recognize the English claims. The Bretons racially were of the same Celtic stock as the Scotch, Welsh, and Irish, and during that period Bretons settling in England were not in the true sense of the word emigrants. They spoke the Celtic tongue, but from their close proximity to the French they had absorbed many French customs. They, however, were regarded by the pro-Anglican party of England as foreigners and were generally unpopular with the masses.

Further up the Loire in the ancient Province of Beauce settled a descendant of Rolland Edellin who married the sole heiress of an armorial house of Beauce and by his acquisition of her ancestral estates he quartered his arms with the rose, the emblazonment of her house. This branch is known as the Edeline of Beauce and the characteristic *poissons* of early Edellin arms are retained according to the laws governing the use and practice of heraldry. Beauce was at one time a separate province of France with the town of Chartres as its principal historic and commercial center, but later became absorbed into the Province of Orleanais.

A century or so later the descendants of Rolland Edellin around Nantes became identified with the Protestant movement in France and were powerful factors politically as well as religiously in France of that day. Persecutions were common and even before the Masacre of St. Bartholomew which began on August 24, 1572, several of the Edelens had fled to England. One of the first references to the family in England was that of Henry Edlin in the third year of the reign of Elizabeth (1561). It was said that ". . . for three months following the said day and even till now, Henry Edlin late of Hendon, County Middlesex, husbandman, has had neither bow nor arrow for shooting against the form of the statue in this case provided".[2]

As persecutions continued, more Edelens sought safety and refuge in England as is testified by the records of the Huguenot churches around Kent, Middlesex, and London. The register of Thread Needle Street shows Abraham, Jean, Orsel, Sarah, Assle, and Marie Edlin as well as other members with varied spellings.[3]

In 39th Elizabeth (1597) Reginald Gurney late yeoman of London stole two white sheep worth 13 shillings from John Edline.[4] And in 42nd Elizabeth (1600) Henry Edlyn of St. Stephen's Alley in Westminster, County Middlesex, yeoman, refused to "keep Watches" at the alley.[5]

Some of the Edelens of a later period became members of the English Church. The register of St. James' Clerkenwell, of London, records the baptisms and marriages of several. And on August 5, 1669, Henry Edlin was married to Mary Edlin.[6]

In 1613 William Finch, the Elder, of Watford, Diocese of London, by will named his son-in-law John Edlin. Thomas Burnell, of London, by will of 1661 named his cousin Sarah Edlin, while Hester Burnell, of Spittle, Middlesex, named in her will of 1693, her cousin Sarah Edlin, widow. Dr. John Hammond whose wife was Joan, of Chelmsford Parish, by his will of 1612 proved at the Court of Essex and Herts bequeathed £40 to his grandson Richard Edlinge, son of his daughter Joan. Henry Edlin, of St. Margaret, Westminster, Gent., bachelor, aged 27, was married on October 26, 1672.

The *Edelinge de Beauce* maintained a prominent position in French society of the sixteenth century and several rose in favor at the royal court in Paris. They were loyal to their birthrights in every respect and being affluent and conservative they naturally remained staunch in their allegiance to the Church of Rome and in sympathy with the politics of the court party. The Huguenot Edlins for the most part through vicissitudes degenerated to the yeomanry and therefore did not occupy the position in England or France as their distant kinsman in the Province of Beauce.

Early in the seventeenth century Richard Edlin and Philip Edlin, members of the gentry, were domiciled in England, and their position and contacts would indicate that they had little in common with the protestant Edelens. Both intermarried with ancient armorial houses of Old England and while it is not known, insofar as this research was carried out, why they became British subjects or whether they definitely were scions of the *Edelinge de Beauce* their social position would indicate such. Circumstances are quite strong that they were brothers, and with the characteristic given name of Richard, it may not be unwise to surmise that they were the sons of a Richard Edlin.

Richard Edlyn (*sic*) before 1634 had married Jane, the youngest daughter of Thomas Reding, of Cannons in the Parish of Pinner, County Middlesex, whose ancestry is recorded in the Visitation of Middlesex.[7] It is interesting to note that the Redings were seated at Pinner in Middlesex—the name of one of the Edelen's estates in Maryland. Pinner, however, was not an original Edelen grant, but came into the family through a marriage with the Jones family. And it may be pointed out that the naming of the Jones' plantation Pinner leans a possible clue to the English home of Moses Jones, the progenitor of that family in Maryland.

About 1623 Philip Edlin, of Middlesex, Gent., married Catherine Offley, a member of an old English armorial house. Adam Thorowgood, a prominent character of Virginia, also married an Offley maiden, so consequently the Thorowgoods of Virginia and the Edelens of Maryland were of near kinship. The tomb of the widow of Adam Thorowgood at Princess Anne, Virginia, shows distinctly the Offley coat-of-arms—carved almost 300 years ago. The following Offley lineage is taken from the 1633 Visitation of London:[8]

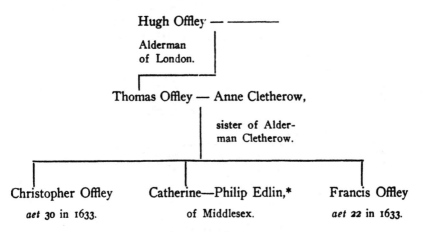

Hugh Offley ———

Alderman of London.

Thomas Offley — Anne Cletherow,

sister of Alderman Cletherow.

Christopher Offley   Catherine—Philip Edlin,*   Francis Offley

aet 30 in 1633.   of Middlesex.   *aet* 22 in 1633.

Of the several children born to Philip and Catherine (Offley) Edlin, of Middlesex, one Richard was born about 1635, and it was he who emigrated to Maryland and founded the only known Edelen family in America.

The Maryland Edelens were conscious of their birthrights and used their coat-of-arms and crest like the many gentry families of Provincial Maryland. Mrs. John A. Hamilton, daughter of Colonel James Noble

---

*Parents of Richard Edelen of Maryland.

Edelin, U.S.M.C., who lived until 1923, recalled as a child the emblazonments on the doors of pre-Revolutionary carriages in the coach house at her ancestral home near Piscataway. The crest was a swan which was also used on the silver of a later generation.

The emigrant to Maryland like the *Edelinge de Beauce* was a member of the Catholic Church, as Edward Watson, of Calvert County, stated in Council "Rychard Edelen was a knowe Papist". In Maryland the Edelens for the most part intermarried into the ancient Catholic families, but occasionally they wedded with an Anglican house which accounted for a small branch becoming members of the Established Church. In general they were staunch Catholics, many of whom accepted Holy Orders.

Like all names, and as it has already been shown, several variations of spelling occurred, but a document examined by the compiler and which bore the signature of the emigrant showed that he wrote thusly "Rich: Edelen". And inasmuch as many colonists were unable to write their names, it is a source of pride to the many descendants that their ancestor was not only able to sign his name but to write freely in his mother tongue. Consequently, Edelen was the original spelling in this country, but some members of the family had adapted Edelin. The emigrant was styled "Gent." on official documents—an exception was not recalled by the compiler.

---

[1] Bibliothique Nationale (Manuscript Division), Paris.
[2] Middlesex Records, vol. 1, p. 41, pub. by Middlesex County Records Soc., 1886.
[3] Huguenot Society of London Publications, vols. 1, 2.
[4] Middlesex Records, vol. 1, p. 236.
[5] *Ibid.*, vol. 1, p. 264.
[6] St. James Clerkenwell, vol. 1, p. 194, pub. by Harleian Soc.
[7] Middlesex Pedigrees, Harleian Soc., vol. 65, p. 87.
[8] Visitation of London 1633, Harleian Soc., vol. 2, p. 130.

RICHARD EDELEN, GENT.[1]

(1635 - 1694)

Richard Edelen, younger son of Philip and Catherine (Offley) Edelen, was born about 1635 in Middlesex, England. About 1664 he married Elizabeth ————, and left for Maryland perhaps in the same year. They were in the Province, however, by February 1664/5, as proved by the following document:

> "I Richard Edelen do from me and my heirs assign and make over unto Daniel Jenifer and his heirs all my full rights title and interest of mine and Elizabeth's my wife's right to land for either of

our transportation unto this Province as Witness my hand this ninth day of February one thousand six hundred and sixty-four".[1]

Witness by   (signed) Richard Edelen
Edward Savage.

In 1665 he declared his intentions of returning to England before a session of the Provincial Court. All indications point to the fact that his wife Elizabeth accompanied him and there their first son, Philip, was born. He returned to the Province before the spring of 1669, at which time he established headrights for his wife and son.[2]

"6 May 1669. Richard Edelen proved rights to 100 acres of land for Elizabeth his wife and Philip his son proved in Common form".

(signed) John Blomfield.

Children of Richard and Elizabeth Edelen*

1. Philip Edelen, probably *d.s.p.*
2. Catherine Edelen.
3. Richard Edelen married Sarah Hagoe. *q.v.*
4. Thomas Edelen married Comfort Barnes. *q.v.*
5. Edward Edelen married Elizabeth Jenkins. *q.v.*
6. Christopher Edelen married Jane Jones. *q.v.*

In 1670 Richard Edelen was appointed Deputy Surveyor of the Province by Baker Brooke, then the Surveyor General. It is believed that he held the position continuous until after the establishment of the Church of England as the State Church with the consequence that all Roman Catholics were disenfranchised and prohibited from holding office. In 1693 by order of the Council he was requested to continue as Deputy Surveyor of St. Mary's County until further orders.[3] During the session of the Assembly from November 14 to December 8, 1688, he officiated as doorkeeper and for his services he received 1,200 pounds of tobacco.

In 1674 Richard Edelen and Justinian Funnis were appointed by the Prerogative Court to appraise the estate of Captain William Boreman (Boarman), late of St. Mary's County.[4] About this time "Richard Edelen of St. Mary's County, Gent.," was requested by the court to make returns of the verbal will of Thomas Matthews, Jr., late of St. Mary's County.[5]

In 1675 he with James Bowling was ordered to appraise the estate of Daniel Russell, late of St. Mary's County,[6] and on February 4,

---

*Note the family names. Philip was named after his paternal grandfather; Catherine after her grandmother; Christopher after his uncle Christopher Offley.

1675/6, he appeared in court as the executor of the estate of Samuel Cressey.[7] Subsequently, the Deputy Commissary issued citation against him as the executor of Samuel Cressey.[8] On October 8, 1677, Richard Edelen, Gent., appeared in court as the "executor of the will of Samuel Cressey, late of Charles County who was the executor of Daniel Russell late of St Mary's County".[9]

On August 10, 1682, Richard Edelen served judgement upon Samuel Raspin, late of Charles County.[10] On August 26, 1683, before the Prerogative Court he stated that Henry Aspinwall of Charles County died intestate and that Elizabeth his widow desired letters of administration, but not being able to travel to court appointed him her attorney.[11] In December 1686, he was ordered to appraise the estate of John Clarke, late of St. Mary's County.[12] On October 28, 1687, Richard Edelen and George Butler, Gent., were summoned to appear at the November Court. And in February 1687/8, he and Maramaduke Semmes were ordered to appraise the estate of Dennis Husculos.[13]

Richard Edelen survived his wife by several years. On March 5, 1694/5, he made his will, dying shortly afterwards. On July 31, of the same year, the will was admitted to probate in St. Mary's County, by John Bowling, James Hogan, and Bowling Speake.[14]

He requested that the dwelling-plantation in St. Mary's County be divided equally among his five surviving children. In addition Richard was devised 100 acres of land purchased from Major Boarman and 86 acres of "St. Christopher". Edward and Christopher received equally 200 acres of "Dublin" then lying in Charles County. Thomas was devised 250 acres of unnamed land, while Catherine, his only daughter, was bequeathed personalty.

The court appointed the two sons, Richard and Edward, as the executors, but only Richard appeared at court in August 1695 to receive the official letters of administration. The inventory of the personal estate was exhibited at court on May 16, 1696, by Richard Edelen "under the hands and seal of William Boarman, Jr., and Anthony Sims".

Of the four sons of Richard Edelen, Sr., who matured, Thomas was the only one to die without issue. He was born in or about the year 1672 in St. Mary's County, according to a deposition of 1720. He settled in Piscataway Parish of Prince Georges County, and there after 1720 he married Comfort Barnes, the widow of Patrick Dyer. The following children were born to Patrick Dyer and Comfort his wife: Sarah; Penelope; William; Elizabeth, born Jan. 22, 1711/12; Rebecca, born March 12, 1714/15; Thomas, born Dec. 12, 1715; James, born Oct. 14, 1717; and Edward, born Dec. 29, 1719.

On November 10, 1715, Thomas Edelen purchased from Thomas Edgerton, Randolph Edgerton, and James Edgerton, of St. Mary's County, a portion of "Calvert or Piscattaway Manor", containing 2,400 acres. The deed read as follows: ". . . granted to William Calvert, Esq., 11 February 1662 containing 3000 acres and which William Calvert settled 600 acres on the marriage of his daughter Elizabeth with James Neal of Charles County the remainder 2400 acres being by Charles Calvert son and heir of William Calvert Esq. made over by conveyance 14 January 1689 to Charles Edgerton, Merchant, of St. Mary's, and by will 11 November 1689, gave to his four sons, John, Thomas, Randolph, and James". It adjoined land belonging to Randall Hanson. No wives waived dower, and the witnesses were Richard Edelen and George X Hardy.

In 1724 when he administered on the estate of William Nugent, late of Prince Georges County, his nephew Thomas Edelen, Jr., and Edward Stephens were his bondsmen.

He died without issue in Prince Georges County during 1749. By his will his widow Comfort received the dwelling-plantation "Edelenton" and "Edelenton's Addition" during life, then to his goddaughter Catherine Spalding. His brothers Richard, Edward, and Christopher were devised 800 acres of "Edgerton's Manor", while 400 acres of the same were devised to his step-son Thomas Dyer. The latter also received "Stone Hill" of 300 acres, "Edelen's Thickett", "Edelen's Hogpen", and slaves. Certain pieces of silver plate were given to his step-daughters Elizabeth Green and Sarah Sanders after the decease of their mother. Wearing apparel was left to "cousin" Francis Sims.[16]

The inventory of the personal estate was exhibited on November 22, 1749, and showed an appraisement of £1,305. Edward Edelen and Christopher Edelen signed as the next of kin, while Thomas Dyer signed as executor. Thomas Thompson and John Thompson, Jr., were the bondsmen.

Comfort Edelen, his widow, died testate in 1760. She made a number of bequests to the following heirs: Children—Edward Dyer, Penelope Howard, Thomas Dyer, Elizabeth Green, and Rebecca Sanders; grandchildren — Thomas and Anne Dyer of Edward, Elizabeth Dyer of Thomas, and Thomas Edelen Green of James, and the children of her deceased son William Dyer; and great-grandchild Anne the daughter of Basil and Catherine Spalding.[17]

The signatories at the inventory were Elizabeth Green and Thomas Dyer as the kinsmen, and Edward Dyer as the executor.

The following was filed at court on December 3, 1760: "Comfort Edelen's Will & Penelopy Howard's tenure to Executorship & testamentary bond by Edward Dyar Executor with Joshia Winn and Francis Green of Prince Georges County sureties for £1000. 22 September 1760."

His widow or her executor paid quit rents on "Edelenton" of 250 acres and "Edelen's Addition" of 90 acres, both tracts lying in Prince Georges County, through 1762, according to the Debt Books.

---

[1] Liber 7, folio 508, Land Office.
[2] Liber 7, folio 210, Land Office.
[3] Archives, vol. 51, pp. 294, 306; vol. 20, p. 34.
[4,5] Test. Pro., Liber 6, folios 333, 501.
[6,7] Test. Pro., Liber 7, folios 274, 198, 219.
[8,9] Test. Pro., Liber 4c, folios 1, 34.
[10] Test. Pro., Liber 12, folio 59.
[11,12] Test. Pro., Liber 13, folios 71, 436.
[13] Test. Pro., Liber 14, folio 43.
[14] Wills, Liber 7, folio 84.
[15] Wills, Liber 27, folio 35.
[16] Wills, Liber 31, folio 53

Edeline

RICHARD EDELEN, GENT.[2]

(1671 - 1760)

AND

HIS DESCENDANTS

Richard Edelen, son of Richard and Elizabeth Edelen, was born in or about 1671, according to his deposition in 1752 when he declared himself 82 years of age. He failed to pursue the occupations of his brothers, that is, gentlemen planters, but became an architect, contractor, and builder which in that day was designated as "carpenter". Many of the early eighteenth century homes of Charles County, some of which are still standing, are no doubt examples of his craftsmanship.

He is sometimes credited with three wives.* His first wife, however, was Sarah, daughter of Thomas and Mary Hagoe, of Charles County, whom he married prior to 1713. Thomas Hagoe died testate in 1716, and named his daughter Sarah Edelen.[1] She was perhaps the mother of most of his children, inasmuch as her death occurred after 1727. His widow, however, was Anne, daughter of Ignatius and Sophia (Beedle) Craycroft, who had previously been the wife of Luke Gardiner. At court in 1747, an Ann Edelen gave her age as 58 and declared herself to be the wife of Richard Edelen.

It has been difficult to compile a complete list of his children. Several predeceased him and the numerous granddaughters whom he mentioned in both deeds and will were matrons and thus carried the name of their spouse. The following are only those whom the compilers have been able to prove by documents:

Children of Richard Edelen

1. Richard Edelen married Margaret Neale. *q.v.*
2. Mary Edelen married Benjamin, son of James and Elizabeth (Lord) Neale. Issue: Bennett; James; Elizabeth; Mary; Anne.
3. Philip Edelen married Jane Gardiner. *q.v.*
4. Edward Edelen married Susannah Wathen. *q.v.*
5. Thomas Edelen married Mary Blandford. *q.v.*
6. Winifred Edelen married William, son of William and Monica Boarman. Issue: William; Mary Anne; Edward.
7. ———— Edelen married Bennett Neale.
8. Jane Edelen married Thomas James, son of William and Mary (Pile) Boarman. Issue: Jane; Thomas; Raphael.

---

*The Semmes papers at the Maryland Historical Society claim that his second wife was Ann, daughter to Raphael Neale.

Shortly after Richard obtained his majority, that is, in 1687, he patented 258 acres of land in Charles County which was given the name of "Friendship". By his father's will, he received the tract "St. Christopher", and in 1749 he inherited 400 acres of "Egerton's Manor" from the estate of his childless brother Thomas. From time to time he added to his landed estate by numerous purchases as the following deeds will show:

On November 1, 1708, Richard Edelen, of Charles County, Carpenter, for 2,400 pounds of tobacco purchased from Robert Hagoe, Sr., of Charles County, Planter, and Elizabeth his wife, and Robert Hagoe, the eldest son, the tract known as "St. George the First" lying in St. Mary's County on the west side of Piles Fresh. Robert Hagoe, Sr., and Robert Hagoe, Jr., signed the deed, while Elizabeth made her mark.[2]

On July 10, 1713, Richard Edelen, of Charles County, Carpenter, and Sarah his wife, conveyed to Edward Edelen of Prince Georges County, "Thomas Chance" which had been purchased from John Hawkins. Richard Edelen signed his name, while his wife made her X mark. The witnesses were J. Lemon and John Rozer.[3]

On November 9, 1714, he purchased from Ebsworth Bayne, of Charles County, Gent., "Irving". Catherine Bayne, wife, waived her dower rights, while Gerard Fowke, Thomas Stone, and Daniel Dulaney witnessed the deed. On August 24, of the same year, he purchased from Luke Gardiner, Gent., of Prince Georges County, and Anne his wife, for 6,000 pounds of tobacco the tract "Frankland", adjoining "Dublin", John Abington witnessed the conveyance.[4]

On December 2, 1717, he purchased from Thomas Dent and Anne his wife for £25 and 4,000 pounds of tobacco "Laurel Branch", lying on Mattawoman Fresh. The deed was witnessed by Gerard Fowke, Thomas Stone, and James X Russel.[5]

On February 8, 1717/8, Richard Edelen, of Charles County, and Sarah his wife, sold "Irving" lying in Prince Georges County next to "Locust Thickett" to John Abington for 7,000 pounds of tobacco. The witnesses were J. Leman, Edward Edelen, and John X Jones.[6]

On November 12, 1718, he purchased from John Baptist Boarman of Charles County, Gent., for £30 and 5,000 pounds of tobacco "Lanterman" except the 60 acres which were devised by Major William Boarman by codicil to Thomas Hagan, lying on the north side of the runn into Zachariah Swamp. Philip Hoskins and John Fendall witnessed the conveyance, while Elizabeth Boarman, wife, waived her rights. Within a few days he purchased from Giles Hill, of St. Mary's County, for 3,000 pounds of tobacco "Simpsons' Supply". Margaret, the wife of Giles Hill, relinquished her third.[7]

Richard Edelen, Gent., on December 20, 1720, bought of John Hill, of St. Mary's County, Carpenter, "Addition to Smith's Addition", adjoining "St. George". Anne, wife, waived her dower, while the witnesses were John Fendall and John Chum, Jr.[8]

On April 6, 1722, Richard Edelen, Gent., purchased from Benedict Leonard Boarman, Gent., for 5,000 pounds of tobacco "Hardshift" lying in Zachaiah Swamp. Anne Boarman, wife, waived dower, while the conveyance was witnessed by Thomas Stone, Jr., and Josias Fendall. A few days later he bought of George Brett and Susannah his wife, of Charles County, for 6,000 pounds of tobacco 50 acres which had been conveyed by Thomas Gerard to Robert Drown and taken out of Westwood Manor. John Fendall and Robert Hanson witnessed the transfer. On November 13, 1722, Richard Edelen, Gent., and Sarah his wife deeded this tract back to George Brett for the same amount of tobacco. Robert Hanson and John Briscoe witnessed.[9]

On April 16, 1725, Richard Edelen, Sr., of Charles County, Gent., for natural love which he had unto "my sister-in-law Mrs. Elizabeth Neale wife to James Neale, Sr.", 4 negroes during life then to be divided equally between the two youngest sons and two youngest daughters of the said James Neale husband to Elizabeth. Walter Story and Thomas Taney were the witnesses.[10]

On October 4, 1726, he purchased from Richard Sheppard, of Prince Georges County, Carpenter, "Quarities", lying partly in Charles and St. Mary's Counties, which had been granted to John Sheppard, deceased, and inherited by his son the grantor. John Williams and Thomas Edelen, Sr., witnessed the conveyance.[11]

On August 7, 1727, Richard Edelen purchased for a consideration of £50 and 6,000 pounds of tobacco from Thomas Sympson, Sr., and Thomas Sympson, Jr., a tract taken up by Thomas Sympson, Sr., known as "St. Thomas". The witnesses to the transfer were George Dent and John Wathen. On the same day is recorded another indenture for the same tract for a consideration of £18 and 3,500 pounds of tobacco. At this time George Dent and John Philpott were the witnesses. At both times Sarah, the wife of Thomas Sympson, Jr., waived dower.[12] On the same day he conveyed to Benedict Leonard Boarman, Gent., for 5,000 pounds of tobacco and other good causes "Asenton", lying on the east side of Zachiah Swamp. Sarah his wife waived all dower rights, and the witnesses were John Boarman and Richard Edelen, Jr.[12]

On August 28, 1732, he purchased from Benjamin Douglas, Gent., for £40 and 6,000 pounds of tobacco "New York", lying on the north side of Cuckhold's Creek, formerly called Back Creek, being a portion of a tract taken up by John Mansell and conveyed by him to James Turner who died without issue and which became escheat. Elizabeth Douglas, wife, waived all rights.[13]

Richard Edelen, Gent., on November 27, 1735, conveyed a portion of "St. Thomas" to Peter Wood. Anne Edelen, wife, waived dower. The witnesses were John Howard and Samuel Chunn.[14] On February 12, 1747, for the love which he had for his grandchildren—Mary Boon, Sarah Boarman, and Thomas Boarman—he deeded them a portion of "Boarman's Manor". No wife waived dower, but the witnesses were George Dent and Edward Edelen.[15]

On February 20, 1749/50, he sold to William Digges, of Prince Georges County, Gent., a portion of "Frankland". No wife waived dower, while the witnesses were George Dent and Charles Edelen.[16]

On October 23, 1752, Richard Edelen bought for £20 "Simkin" from Richard Bennett Boarman and Maryann his wife, of Charles County. John Winter and James Nivison were the witnesses. On the same day he and his wife Anne conveyed to Hudson Wathen for £70 land taken up by Thomas Sympson, Sr., deceased, called "St. Thomas". Both Richard and his wife signed the deed.[17]

On July 19, 1757, Richard Edelen, Sr., Gent., conveyed to John Corry, Surgeon, for 10,500 lbs. of tobacco a 115-acre portion of "St. Thomas". Anne Edelen, wife, relinquished her third, while John Winter and James Nivison witnessed the transfer.[18] On October 24, 1757, he purchased from Richard Bennett Boarman for £100 the tract "Sympson's Supply", containing 138 acres. Mary Boarman, wife, waived her dower rights.[19] On January 14, 1759, he conveyed to William Simpson, Planter, a 112-acre portion of "St. Thomas". No wife relinquished her interest, but the witnesses were Walter Hanson and George Dent.[20]

The last deed before his death was on March 11, 1760, when he conveyed to his son Philip for natural love and affections the plantation whereon Philip was then residing called "Lanterman" which lay on the north side of Zachiah Swamp and consisted of 635 acres. The deed was witnessed by John Winter and Robert Horner.[21]

According to the Debt Books of Charles County, Richard Edelen in 1753 paid quit rents on the following tracts: "Edelen's Amendment", of 104 acres; "St. Thomas and Simkin", of 168 acres; "Westwood Lodge", of 100 acres; "Aslington", of 630 acres; "Formby", of 200 acres; and "Sympson's Supply", of 164 acres. In St. Mary's County, he paid rents on "Truman's Hunting Quarter", of 200 acres; and "Hope", of 64 acres.

The will of Richard Edelen was dated July 16, 1760, and proved by Bennett Semmes, James Campbell, John Urquhart, and Randolph

Brandt.[22] He devised his wife Anne during life the dwelling-plantation near Zachaiah Swamp and the lower plantation "Edelen's Admentment" of 104 acres and various personalty. To his son Edward he willed the remainder of the plantation which was purchased from Kenelm Chiseldyne lying on the south side of Gerard's Runn, "Truman's Hunting Quarter" in St. Mary's County which was purchased from Adley Davies, "Assington" of 630 acres in Charles County, and "Westwood Lodge" of 100 acres. His grandson Richard Edelen of Philip was devised the upper portion of "Lanturnham" of 150 acres bought from John Baptist Boarman and personalty. To his son Philip he willed the 200 acres of "Lanturnham" which he purchased from John Ball and also the residue of the tract which he bought of John Baptist Boarman. His grandson James Edelen of Thomas received 120 acres of "Sympson's Supply" where Richard Higdon lived, with the residue of the tract going to his grandson Edward Edelen of Edward.

To Richard Edelen of Thomas he devised the land acquired from Luke Gardiner in Prince Georges County near the north branch of the Piscataway, containing 100 acres. The Rev. George Hunter and his successors were willed one acre of land at "St. Thomas" near Newport where his family burying ground and chapel stood.

His granddaughter Mary Anne, the daughter William Boarman and the testator's daughter Winifred, was devised the land purchased from John and James Hills. His grandson Philip Edelen of Thomas was willed 200 acres of "Calverton Manor" where Thomas Hally and Joseph Crown lived. His grandson Thomas Edelen of Thomas received the plantation whereon lived Alexander Steel. His granddaughters Henrietta Thompson and Susannah Edelen, daughters of his son Thomas Edelen, were devised "Thornsley" of 200 acres. And his grandson Edward Edelen of Edward after the decease of the testator's widow inherited the dwelling-plantation "Askington" near Zachaiah Swamp, while the grandson Francis Edelen of Edward was to inherit "Edelen's Admentment" after the decease of the widow.

Negroes were bequeathed to Eleanor, the daughter of Bennett Boarman, but no relationship was stated. His granddaughters Elizabeth Corry and Mary Lancaster* were devised 200 acres of "Laurel's Branch", and portions of "Venture" and "Friendship" on the Mattawoman. Another granddaughter Anne Neale, daughter of Benjamin Neale, and his granddaughter Charity Edelen of Thomas were willed the

---

*It has been said that Richard Edelen had daughters who married a Corry and a Lancaster, but they were the married daughters of Mary Edelen by her marriage to Benjamin Neale.

residue of the land at Mattawoman. And grandson Philip Edelen of Thomas received three tracts on the Mattawoman.

Personalty were bequeathed to his grandsons: Raphael Boarman, Thomas Edelen of Thomas, Richard Edelen of Philip, Edward Edelen of Edward, James Neale of Bennett, and James Edelen of Thomas; granddaughters Susannah Edelen of Thomas, Anne Edelen of Philip, Mary Edelen of Philip, Charity Edelen of Thomas, and an unnamed granddaughter the youngest daughter of Philip Edelen; son Edward.

An unnamed granddaughter who was the wife of Charles Boone and the daughter of Thomas James Boarman was devised 180 acres of "Boarman's Manor".

The will of his widow Anne Edelen was dated May 12, 1765, and proved in Charles County on October 17, 1765. She named her four Gardiner children—Ignatius; Richard; Mary (Gardiner) Chum; Jane (Gardiner) Edelen; and grandchildren — Henrietta Smith; Clement Smith; Mary Smith; Joseph Mudd; and Richard Edelen.[23]

The inventory of the personal estate was returned on January 7, 1767, by Richard Gardiner, executor, at which time Ignatius Gardiner and Jane Edelen signed as the next of kin. Distribution of the balance on March 24, 1768, by Richard Gardiner, the executor, showed disbursements to Henrietta Smith, Clement Smith, Mary Smith, George Hunter, and Jane Edelen. Charles Love and Joshua Sanders were the bondsmen.

The estate of Richard Edelen was unsettled as late as 1775. In that year the court requested an account from Edward Edelen "the surviving executor". The sureties were James Campbell and Charles Love.

---

[1] Wills, Liber 14, folio 213.
[2] Deeds, Liber C no. 2, folio 119.
[3] Deeds, Liber E, folio 350, La Plata.
[4] Deeds, Liber E, folios 418, 434, Marlb.
[5] Deeds, Liber H no. 2, folio 117, La Plata.
[6] Deeds, Liber F, folio 46, Marlb.
[7] Deeds, Liber H no. 2, folios 210, 216, La Plata.
[8] Deeds, Liber H no. 2, folio 413.
[9] Deeds, Liber L no, 2, folios 31, 33, 54.
[10] Deeds, Liber L no. 2, folio 212.
[11] Deeds, Liber L no. 2, folio 214.
[12] Deeds, Liber L no. 2, folios 331, 385, 387, 391.
[13] Deeds, Liber M no. 2, folio 306.
[14] Deeds, Liber O no. 2, folio 114.
[15] Deeds, Liber Z no. 2, folio 212.
[16] Deeds, Liber P P, folio 32, Marlb.
[17] Deeds, Liber A no. 1, folios 35, 94, La Plata.
[18][19][20][21] Liber G no. 3, folios 93, 150, 336, 403.
[22] Wills, Liber 31, folio 279.
[23] Wills, Liber 33, folio 419.

RICHARD EDELEN[3]

(17— - 1738)

Richard Edelen, son of Richard and Sarah (Hagoe) Edelen, was born in Charles County during the early part of the eighteenth century. About 1734 he married Margaret, daughter of James and Elizabeth (Lord) Neale, of Wooleston Manor. She was mentioned as Margaret Neale in her father's will of 1733, and as Margaret Edelen in her mother's will of 1734.[1]

Children of Richard and Margaret (Neale) Edelen

1. Joseph Edelen married Catherine Queen. *q.v.*
2. Richard Edelen, born 1735, living 1768.
3. Mary Anne Edelen.

Richard Edelen established his seat in St. Mary's County. On June 2, 1736, he and James Swann were bondsmen for Ann Hayes, the widow and executrix of John Hayes, late of St. Mary's County.

His will was admitted to probate in St. Mary's County on August 15, 1738, by James Taylor, Thomas Barber, and William Stewart. He named his wife Margaret, brother Philip, and father Richard—all of whom were appointed trustees to have power to rectify any mismanagement of his estate that was detrimental to his children (unnamed).[2]

William Neale and Henry Neale, of Charles County, were sureties to the amount of £700 for the executors Margaret Edelen and Philip Edelen.[3]

His widow married Zachary Bond who with his wife and Philip Edelen closed the estate, when the balance was distributed to the widow Margaritt Bond, and Joseph, Richard, and Mary Anne Edelen "the orphans of the deceased".

---

[1] Wills, Liber 20, folio 160.
[2] Wills, Liber 21, folio 909.
[3] Test. Proc., Liber 30, folio 452.

PHILIP EDELEN, GENT.[3]

(17— - 1761)

Philip Edelen, son of Richard, was a native of Charles County. In 1760 his father deeded him 635 acres of "Lanterman", where he had already established his dwelling-plantation. This gift was confirmed by his father's will, and in addition Philip's son, Richard, received 150 acres of the same tract. He married his step-sister Jane, the daughter of Luke and Anne (Craycroft) Gardiner, of Prince Georges and Charles Counties.

Children of Philip and Jane (Gardiner) Edelen

1. Richard Edelen married Sarah Harrison. *q.v.*
2. Sarah Edelen, resided in France.
3. Anne Edelen married Edward, son of Alexius Semmes.
4. Mary Edelen married Charles, son of Leonard Boarman.
5. Elizabeth Edelen married Thomas Courtney Reeves.*

On June 13, 1744, Philip Edelen, Gent., purchased from William Boarman, Gent., 29 acres of "Boarman's Manor". No wife waived dower, while John Winter and Robert Yates witnessed the conveyance.[1] On August 23, 1748, Philip Edelen, Gent., bought of him another portion of "Boarman's Manor". Again no wife waived dower, but the witnesses were George Dent and Margaret Gosdin.[2] On February 19, 1754, he purchased another portion of "Boarman's Manor", but this time from Bowling Speake. No wife waived dower.[3]

On June 17, 1758, he purchased from Edward Speake for 2,000 pounds of tobacco "Speake's Meadow", adjoining the upper portion of "Boarman's Manor". Arthur Lee and Daniel of St. Thomas Jenifer witnessed the deed, but no wife waived dower.[4]

In 1753 Philip Edelen paid quit rents on 635 acres of "Lanterman", while his heirs after his death continued to remit through the year 1769.

Philip Edelen died intestate. Letters of administration upon the estate were issued to his widow, Jean Edelen, when her bond in the value of £1000, dated January 14, 1761, was signed by James Middleton and John Gardiner. The signatories at the inventory of the personal estate, recorded June 22, 1761, were Edward Edelen and Richard Boarman as the kinsmen, and Jane Edelen as the administratrix. The final account was rendered on July 6, 1768, and distributed to the widow and five children—Richard, Sarah, and Anne who were of age, and to Mary and Elizabeth, minors.[5]

The will of the widow Jane Edelen was dated December 9, 1790, and proved in Charles County on December 2, 1793. She bequeathed slaves and other personalty to her four children—Richard Edelen, Anne Semmes, Mary Boarman, and Elizabeth Reeves on the condition that

---

*St. Peter's R. C. Church, Charles Co., "Sacred to the Memory of Thomas C. Reeves whose Ashes rest here, a true Christian, zealous for the promotion of Religion. In peace with God and his neighbor he died in the 70th year of his age on the 28 November 1823". . . . "Sacred to the Memory of Elizabeth Reeves, widow of Thomas Reeves, whose mortal remains rest here beneath, A pattern of charity and adorned with all the mild virtues of religion. She died as full of merits as of years in the 85 year of her age on 18 April 1840".

they each pay their sister, Sarah, a resident of France, £5 annually. Slaves were also willed to her three granddaughters—Elizabeth Boarman, Jane Boarman, and Rachel Gardiner. She left a dwelling to the Roman Catholic Church and 1,000 pounds of tobacco to the Catholic clergy of Charles County, appointing her son Richard Edelen and son-in-law Charles Boarman the executors.[6]

The inventory of her personal effects was recorded on December 9, 1793, and was appraised at £591/2/2½. Edward Semmes and Thomas C. Reeves signed as the next of kin. [7] The final account was not rendered by Richard Edelen and Charles Boarman, executors, until the year 1803; disbursements were made to Thomas C. Reeves in "right of his wife" and to Edward Semmes in "right of his wife".

---

[1] Deeds, Liber X no. 2, folio 155.
[2] Deeds, Liber Z no. 2, folio 284.
[3] Deeds, Liber A no. L, folio 153.
[4] Deeds, Liber G no. 3, folio 201.
[5] Balance Book, Hall of Records.
[6] Wills, Liber A K no. 11, folio 194.
[7] Liber 1793, folio 226.

EDWARD EDELEN, GENT.[3]

(17— - 1780)

Edward Edelen, son of Richard, was born in Charles County. From his father's estate, he received "Truman's Hunting Quarter" in St. Mary's County, 630 acres of "Assington" and 100 acres of "Westwood Lodge", both lying in Charles County. His wife was Susannah, the sister of Clement Wathen.

Children of Edward and Susannah (Wathen) Edelen

1. Edward Edelen married Eleanor Boarman. *q.v.*
2. Richard Edelen, *d.s.p.*
3. John Edelen married Monica Boarman. *q.v.*
4. Oswald Edelen married Mary Thompson. *q.v.*
5. Francis Edelen married Sarah Thompson. *q.v.*
6. Philip Edelen, *d.s.p.*
7. Joseph Edelen. *q.v.*
8. Leonard Edelen, *d.s.p.*
9. Clara Edelen married Nathan Thomas. License May 10, 1782, Fred. Co.
10. Sarah Edelen.
11. Minta Edelen married Philip Knott. License Fred. Co., Jan. 12, 1801.
12. Anne Edelen married ———— Carrick.
13. Elizabeth Edelen married Thomas Knott.

Edward Edelen maintained his seat as "Assington" lying in Newport Hundred of Charles County. During the Revolutionary War he subscribed to the patriot's oath, his name appearing upon the returns of His Worshipful John Parnham.[1]

According to the Debt Books of Charles County, he first paid quit rents in 1764 as the proprietor of "Edelen's Amendment" of 104 acres, "Westwood Lodge" of 100 acres, "Assington" of 630 acres, and "Simpson's Supply" of 164 acres. He continued to remit rents on these tracts through 1774, with the addition of "Toom Bitt" of 50 acres.

On February 6, 1767, Edward Edelen, Gent., purchased from Gerard Boarman, Gent., "Green's Rest" and a portion of "Boarman's Manor", both tracts lying in Charles County, for a consideration of £100 and 100 pounds of tobacco. Susannah Boarman, wife, waived all dower rights, while the witnesses were John Winter and Robert Horner.[2]

On August 26, 1767, he bought of Joseph Jameson, of Charles County, for £21 "Hall's Lot", adjoining the lands of the said Joseph Jameson and Benjamin Jameson in Zachia Swamp. Anne Jameson, wife, gave her consent.[3] On May 13, 1768, Joseph Jameson granted him by purchase another portion of "Hall's 'Lott".[4]

On July 11, 1772, Edward Edelen, Planter, conveyed "Hall's Lot" to Benjamin Jameson, of Charles County, for a consideration of £107. His wife, Susannah Edelen, waived dower, while the witnesses were John Winter and John Briscoe. On February 14, 1775, he sold to Benjamin Lusby Corry, Planter, for £40 "Tombit" of 50 acres. Susannah his wife, again waived dower. John Winter and Philip Briscoe witnessed the transfer.[5]

He negotiated his will on October 21, 1779, which was admitted to probate on March 25, 1780. His wife Susannah was granted during life the dwelling-plantation, being 200 acres of "Asslington", a number of slaves, and the water mill. At her death the aforesaid bequests were to revert to his three minor sons—Philip, Joseph, and Leonard—who were to attain their majority at the age of 18 years. To sons of this brother (unnamed) and his son Philip, he devised 200 acres of "Asslington" and "Westward Lodge". John received "Green's Rest", and Richard was devised an unnamed tract of land. Edward was willed personalty. Slaves and other personalty were bequeathed to his five daughters, while the four unmarried ones were to have two rooms, one with a fireplace, in the dwelling during their single lives. They were to share equally in the residuary estate.[6]

The inventory of the personal estate was rendered on May 17, 1780, by the executors John Edelen and Raphael Boarman. The appraisement amounted to £624/12/3, and signed by Francis Edelen and Edward Edelen as the next of kin.[7]

The tax list of 1783 in Charles County showed that his widow Susannah Edelen owned 178 acres of land in Newport Hundred and had six in family. John Edelen, her son, held 289 acres in the same hundred for the "heirs of Edward Edelen".

The will of Richard Edelen, the bachelor son, was dated January 13, 1805, and proved in Charles County on April 23, 1805. He named his brothers: Francis, Oswald, Leonard, and Philip; sisters Anninta Knott, Elizabeth Knott, Anne Carrick, and Clare Thomas; nephews Oswald and Leonard sons of Oswald; niece Elizabeth Simpson daughter of Oswald Edelen; and the family of his uncle Clement Wathen.[8]

The final account was rendered to the court on December 10, 1811, by his brother and executor, Philip Edelen, when the balance of $1369 was distributed according to the will.

The will of the bachelor son Philip Edelen was dated July 27, 1823, and proved August 26, the same year, in both Montgomery County, Maryland, and the District of Columbia, with Nacy Griffith as the executor. He devised his dwelling to Mary, Priscilla, and Betsy Mathews, and $50 to James Mathews. Other heirs were his brother Leonard Edelen, the four unnamed children of Philip Knott, and the eight unnamed children of Thomas Knott.

On April 26, 1797, Leonard Edelen, another unmarried son of Edward Edelen, purchased from Thomas M. Simpson, of Charles County, a portion of "St. Thomas" for £11. Judith Simpson, wife, waived dower, while the witnesses were William D. Briscoe and Walter Dyson.[9] On May 13, 1799, he conveyed to John B. Wathen of Bennett for a consideration of £2000 portions of "Westwood Manor" and "Assington". The witness was Daniel Jenifer.[10]

His will was dated May 28, 1827, and proved June 18, 1827. He devised his nephew Leonard Edelen the house and lot in Montgomery County then in the possession of John P. Knott. The legacy left him by his brother Philip Edelen was bequeathed to John P. Knott, with the residue of the estate going to Elizabeth Edelen.[11]

[1] Unpub. Md. Rec., vol. 5, DAR.
[234] Deeds, Liber O no. 3, folios 168, 251, 421.
[5] Deeds, Liber V no. 3, folio 17.
[6] Wills, Lliber A F no. 7, folio 457.
[7] Liber A F no. 7, folio 528.
[8] Wills, Liber A L no. 12, folio 297.
[9] Deeds, Liber I B no. 2, folio 154.
[10] Deeds, Liber I B no. 3, folio 2.
[11] Wills, Liber W D M no. 15, folio 234.

THOMAS EDELEN[3]

(17— - 1752)

Thomas Edelen, son of Richard, was born in Charles County. He settled in Piscataway Parish, Prince Georges County, and there according to the parish register he married on February 9, 1719, Mary Blandford. She was named as an heir in the will of her father Thomas Blandford in 1749.[1]

Children of Thomas and Mary (Blandford) Edelen

1. Thomas Edelen married Priscilla Clements. *q.v.*
2. Richard Edelen married Mary ————. *q.v.*
3. Charles Edelen married Catherine ————. *q.v.*
4. Philip Edelen married Mary Howard. *q.v.*
5. Susan Edelen married Thomas P. Edelen. *q.v.*
6. Christopher Edelen married Elizabeth ————. *q.v.*
7. James Edelen married Susannah Hagan. *q.v.*
8. Charity Edelen.
9. Henrietta Edelen married ———— Thompson.
10. Edward Edelen. *q.v.*

On April 23, 1739, Thomas Edelen, Jr., was deeded by his father Richard Edelen, Sr., of Charles County, referring to him as "beloved son" 320 acres of "Apple Doore". Anne Edelen, the wife of Richard, joined in the deed, and the conveyance was witnessed by John Addison and Christopher Edelen.[2]

The will of Thomas Edelen was dated August 13, 1751, and probated in Prince Georges County in 1752. He devised his wife one-third of the tracts "Apple Door" and "Rome", while Thomas, the eldest son, received the dwelling-plantation of 120 acres and portions of "Apple Door" and "Rome". Christopher was to receive portions of "Apple Door" and "Rome" at the death of his brothers. Other children were not mentioned. Two barrels of corn and wearing apparel were bequeathed to James Atchinson, Jr. On July 2, 1753, the bond of Mary Edelen, his relict and executrix, in the amount of £2000 was signed by Benjamin Musgrove and Charles Edelen.[3]

The inventory of the personal estate was rendered January 25, 1754/5, with Charles Edelen and James Edelen signing as the kinsmen, and his widow as the executrix.

The widow died intestate. An inventory of her estate was recorded on December 11, 1754, when Christopher Edelen and Richard Edelen signed as the next of kin. Ten unnamed children shared in the final distribution.

At the time of the widow's death, the estate of Thomas Edelen was unsettled, thereupon the administration fell to Thomas, the eldest son. On August 12, 1754, he filed his bond, with Benjamin Musgrove and Charles Edelen as sureties. The final account was rendered on September 19, 1762, when distribution was made to ten unnamed children.[4]

[1] Wills, Liber 27, folio 13.
[2] Deeds, Liber Y, folio 27, Marlborough.
[3] Wills, Liber 28, folio 419.
[4] Balance Books, Hall of Records.

JOSEPH EDELEN[4]

(17— - 1775)

Joseph Edelen, son of Richard and Margaret (Neale) Edelen, was born in Charles County, Maryland. On May 9, 1759, he received from his grandfather "Richard Edelen of Charles County, Gent." for the natural love and affections which he had for his grandson and also for 5 shillings "New York", lying on the north side of Cuckhold's Creek, being a portion of the tract taken up by John Mansell and conveyed to James Turner who died possessed of it without heirs. It became escheat and was then conveyed to Benjamin Douglas by deed on May 28, 1732. Anne Edelen, the wife of Richard, waived her dower rights, while John Winter and James Nivison witnessed the gift.[1]

Joseph Edelen married Catherine, the daughter of Samuel and Sarah (Edelen) Queen, who was born in or about the year 1731. At the death of her brother Henry Queen in 1768, Catherine inherited "Pinner" lying in Prince Georges County, according to the terms of her grandfather's will.[2] Her mother, Sarah Queen-Pye, by her will proved July 29, 1773, named her daughter Catherine Edelen, grandchildren Elizabeth and Henry Edelen, and son-in-law Joseph Edelen whom she appointed executor.[3] The administration bond was signed on July 29, 1773, in the amount of £1500, with Benjamin Jameson and Jesse Matthews as the sureties.

Children of Joseph and Catherine (Queen) Edelen

1. Henry Edelen, d.s.p. q.v.
2. Samuel Edelen, d.s.p. q.v.
3. Margaret Edelen, died young.
4. Elizabeth Edelen, died young.
5. Joseph Edelen, born Feb. 3, 1764.
6. Teresa Edelen, born Jan. 10, 1767, married Walter Jameson.
7. Sarah Edelen, born Feb. 3, 1769.
8. Catherine Alice Edelen married Joseph Edelen. q.v.

The debt books of Charles County show that Joseph Edelen paid quit rents from 1753 to 1770 on 185 acres of "New York" and 38 acres of "Maiden's Point". In 1771 he remitted rents, in addition to the above named tracts, on "Tompkins Purchase" and "Good Luck", bought of John Smoot, Jr., and "Dawkins' Delight", bought of George Scroggin. He continued to pay rents on these tracts through 1774, the last year for which the debt books are available. During this period he also paid rents on "New Design", lying in St. Mary's County.

On May 18, 1769, he purchased from George Scroggin, of Charles County, planter, for 6200 pounds of tobacco the land laid out for Thomas Walker called "Docket's (Dawkins) Delight" in William and Mary Parish. Charity Scroggin, wife, waived dower, while the deed was witnessed by John Winter and Edward Smoot.[4]

His will was dated June 26, 1772, and admitted to probate in Charles County on October 13, 1775, by the oaths of Jezreel Penn, Joseph Shaw, and Thomas Evans. He devised the dwelling-plantation "New York" to his wife Catherine during life also the adjacent tract "Maiden's Point" during life then to his son Joseph. The latter received immediately two small tracts—"Tomkins Purchase" which had been bought from John and Edward Smoot and "Good Luck". If Joseph died without issue, then these tracts to son Henry. Samuel was devised land at Coole Springs called "Wood's Inclosure" and "Duckeet's Delight" purchased from George Scroggin. Henry was willed "New Design" in St. Mary's County. His daughter Sarah was devised "Pinner" lying in Prince Georges County, while Margaret and Elizabeth were to receive a negro upon the death of their mother.[5]

The will was exhibited in court by his widow and executrix on October 13, 1775, with Benjamin Jameson and William Leigh as her bondsmen. She died within a short time, consequently the administration of the estate was granted to the sureties. They executed a bond on January 2, 1777, when Thomas Semmes and Thomas Jameson became sureties.[6]

The will of Catherine Edelen, the widow, was proved in Prince Georges County on June 12, 1776. She devised her son Henry "New Design", but in the event that he died without issue then to her daughters Teresa and then to Alcey. Sarah received "Pinner". John Digges, Widow Martindale, and Widow Buchanan were remembered with minor bequests. The residue of the estate was bequeathed to her daughters— Teresa, Alcey, and Sarah—with "brother" Benjamin Jameson as their guardian. The executors so named were Benjamin Jameson and Walter Pye.[7]

Letters of administration were issued on May 8, 1779, to Benjamin Jameson, with his bond fixed at £3000 by William Queen and Henry Joshua Jameson. Walter Pye, the other executor, refused to act. The inventory was returned on March 14, 1780, with William Queen and Margaret Matthews signing as the next of kin.[8]

The inventory of the personal estate of Joseph Edelen was returned on June 3, 1777, by Benjamin Jameson and William Queen as administrators *d.b.n.* The appraisement was £1580/1/6, and was agreed to by Bennett Neale and Edward Edelen who signed as the next of kin, and by Thomas Smoot, the Youngest, and Henry Barnes as the greatest creditors.[9]

On December 8, 1778, Joseph Edelen of Joseph appeared in court, being aged 14 years February 3, last, and chose Benjamin Jameson as his guardian. At the same time Teresa Edelen, daughter of Joseph, aged 12 January 10, next; Sarah aged 9, February 3, last; and Alice aged 6, the 10th of December were placed under the guardianship of Benjamin Jameson.[10]

A valuation of the lands of Joseph Edelen in possession of Benjamin Jameson his guardian was recorded in court and showed that he was seized of all tracts where his father, Joseph Edelen, formerly lived containing one dwelling house of brick 45 feet long and 30 feet wide, with a kitchen 18 feet long and 14 feet wide, a milk house 10 feet square, meat house 12 feet square, hen house 16 feet long and 10 feet wide—all in very good condition. Also a chair house 16 feet long and 10 feet wide, corn house 20 feet long and 12 feet wide, a meat house 8 feet square in need of repair, a tobacco house 30 feet long and 24 feet wide, another tobacco house 30 feet long and 20 feet wide, a servant quarter 20 feet square in need of repair. There was also other improved property.

The final accounts on the estate of Joseph Edelen were rendered on November 24, 1778, and June 4, 1779, by Benjamin Jameson and William Queen as the executors and showed a balance of £2338/5/4 to be distributed according to the will.[10]

The estate of Katherine Edelen was distributed in Charles County on April 11, 1788, to son Henry; daughters Teresa, Sarah, and Alcy; John Diggs; and Widows Martindale and Buchanan.[11]

Henry Edelen died a bachelor in 1777 and by his will bequeathed his estate to sisters Teresa, Sarah, and Alcey whose property was to be held in trust by Edward Edelen, Sr., until they arrived at the age of 16 years. Edward Edelen was named as executor and bequeathed negroes as well as the latter's son John.[12]

The inventory was taken on July 10, 1778, and appraised at £214/1/3. Samuel Edelen and John Edelen signed as the kinsmen.

The final account was rendered on April 20, 1782, with John Edelen as executor. On August 23, 1783, however, "John Edelen executor of Edward Edelen who was executor of Henry Edelen late of Charles County, deceased" showed a disbursement of £146/12/8 to Walter Jameson and Teresa his wife and the like amount to Alice Edelen.[13]

Samuel Edelen, also a bachelor, died testate in 1778. He devised to his sisters Teresa, Sally, and Alicy the use and profits from the lands bought by their father from Thomas Smoot and Thomas Wheeler. The residue of the estate was to be divided among his brother Joseph and three sisters.[14]

The inventory was recorded on November 23, 1779, and appraised at £169/16/–. Walter Jameson was the executor, and William Queen and Benjamin Jameson signed as the kinsmen.[15]

---

[1] Deeds, Liber G no. 3, folio 334.
[2] Wills, Liber 36, folio 336.
[3] Wills, Liber 39, folio 284.
[4] Deeds, Liber O no. 3, folio 567.
[5] Wills, Liber 40, folio 483.
[6] Test. Pro., Liber 47, folios 1, 143.
[7] Wills, Liber 40, folio 659.
[8] Liber A F no. 7, folios 358, 453, 481.
[9] Liber A F no. 7, folios 17, 263, 525.
[10] Liber A F no. 7, folios 252, 363.
[11] Liber 1788, folio 484.
[12] Wills, Liber 41, folio 280.
[13] Liber B no. 1 (1782-1785).
[14] Wills, Liber A F no. 7, folio 224.
[15] Liber A F no. 7, folios 192, 420, 426.

RICHARD EDELEN, GENT.[4]

(17— - 1803)

Richard Edelen, son of Philip and Jane (Gardiner) Edelen, was born in Charles County. He married Sarah, the daughter of Rachel Harrison, of Anne Arundel County. His mother-in-law died intestate and at the inventory of the personal effects in 1793, it was shown that her daughter Sarah, one-time wife of Richard Edelen, was deceased.

On April 2, 1803, David Weems and Richard Edelen, sons-in-law of Rachel Harrison, and Susan Hoxton, daughter, instituted action in the chancellery court against Richard Harrison and Samuel Harrison of Samuel who had been granted letters of administration on the estate. The case showed that the inventory of the personal estate was appraised at £1,605, with Samuel Harrison, Jr., and Benjamin Harrison signing as the kinsmen. The complainants accused the defendants of mismanaging the estate and improper accounts. The lawsuit was called off by mutual consent on January 21, 1817.[1]

Children of Richard and Sarah (Harrison) Edelen

1. Richard Edelen married Anne Gough. *q.v.*
2. Philip Edelen, *d.s.p.*
3. Samuel Edelen, *d.s.p.*
4. Elizabeth Edelen married Thomas Semmes.
5. Aminta Edelen, entered convent.
6. Rachel Edelen married Charles Gardiner.
7. Jane Edelen married Alexius Mudd.
8. Dorothy Edelen married Apr. 14, 1793, Joseph Benedict, son of Richard and Catherine (Boarman) Gardiner.

Richard Edelen received from his father's estate the dwelling-plantation "Lanterman" of 635 acres on which he paid quit rents beginning in 1770. He also remitted rent on 17 acres of "Speake's Meadows". His land transactions were many and varied.

On November 2, 1774, he purchased from John Hagan, of Fairfax County, Virginia, bricklayer, a portion of "Lanterman"—"the dwelling-plantation of my father Ignatius Hagan containing 65 acres". Mary Hagan, wife of John, relinquished her third, while the witnesses were Philip Briscoe and Samuel Briscoe.[2]

On August 7, 1777, Richard Edelen, Gent., conveyed to Benedict Leonard Boarman, Gent., for a consideration of 5,000 pounds of tobacco a portion of "Assington", lying on the east side of Zachia Swamp on the south side of Great Beaver Dam. Sarah Edelen, wife, waived dower, while the witnesses were John Boarman and Richard Edelen, Jr.[3]

On August 12, 1779, he purchased from Samuel Hanson 159 acres of "Boarman's Reserve", adjoining the land of William Hardy which had been conveyed by a certain Mary Gardiner to Bowling Speake on August 6, 1718. The consideration was £2,385. Richard Barnes and Joshua Sanders witnessed the conveyance.[4]

On September 22, 1789, he bought of Henry Hardy, of Prince Georges County, for £70 a portion of "Boarman's Manor". John Smith Brookes and Thomas Boyd witnessed the deed.[5]

On August 20, 1794, Richard Edelen of Philip conveyed to Thomas Mundell, of Prince Georges County, on behalf of Alexander Henderson, Robert Ferguson, and John Gibson, creditors of the said Richard, "Lanterman" of 1,111 acres which had been resurveyed for him on January 3, 1772, also 219 acres of "Boarman's Manor" which had been conveyed to Philip Edelen by Bowling Speake on February 19, 1754, and to Richard Edelen from Samuel Hanson on August 12, 1779, and 39 acres of "Boarman's Manor" conveyed to Philip Edelen by William Boarman on June 13, 1744. No wife waived dower, but the witnesses were John Dent and William D. Briscoe.[6]

On November 2, 1795, he conveyed to Alexander McPherson land sold by William Boarman to William Hardy on May 20, 1686, called "Boarman's Manor". William D. Briscoe and Walter Dyson witnessed the deed.[7]

On April 25, 1796, he being a creditor of Vernon Smith received personal property to the value of £40/5/2½.[8] His last conveyance was on March 23, 1798, when he deeded to Alexander McPherson for £144 a portion of "Boarman's Manor" adjoining the land of the said McPherson near Bryan Town, originally deeded Bowling Speake by Mary Gardiner. No wife waived dower, while William H. McPherson and Robert Brent were witnesses.[9]

During the Revolutionary War Richard Edelen took the oath of allegiance and fidelity to the State of Maryland, his name appearing upon the returns of His Worshipful Joshua Sanders, a magistrate of Charles County.[10] The tax list of 1783 showed him the head of a family in Bryan Town Hundred with seven in his family and seized of 970 acres of land.

The will of Richard Edelen was dated December 16, 1801, and proved on November 29, 1803, in Charles County. To his three sons— Richard, Philip, and Samuel—he devised "Lanterman" of 1,111 acres which he had patented in 1772, 29 acres of "Boarman's Manor" whereon a water mill was located, and "Boarman's Reserve" of 60 acres. Richard was to have that portion of "Lanterman" whereon the testator was then living, Philip was to have the portion which was the dwelling-plantation of the testator's mother. Six slaves were bequeathed to his daughter Elizabeth Edelen, and a legacy to Aminta, a Catholic nun. The residue of the estate was to be divided among Richard, Philip, Samuel, Rachel Gardiner, Jane Mudd, Dorothy Gardiner, Elizabeth Edelen, and Aminta.

"Whereas my son Samuel doth give me great grief and fear that he may or will spend or waste what I have given him by my will, in order to prevent I appoint my brother-in-law Thomas Courtney Reeves trustee of his estate. If he acts obstinate, then everything is null and void".

He added a codicil on behalf of his single daughter Elizabeth who was to have the use of a room in the dwelling "the one called the girl's room or Betsy's room".[11]

Samuel Edelen, the bachelor son, dated his will April 2, 1807, it being probated in Charles County on May 19, same year. He named his sisters; Ninty Edelen and Dorothy Gardiner; brother Philip; nephews Thomas Alexander and Henry Mudd, sons of Alexius Mudd, James Edelen of Richard, and Philip Gardiner of Charles; and nieces Teresa daughter of Thomas Semmes, and Sarah daughter of Charles Gardiner. One thousand pounds of tobacco were bequeathed to Father Auger and the like amount to the poor of the parish. The children of Joseph Gardiner were devised the mill lot. Henry Thomas Mudd was devised a portion of "Landterman", while another portion was willed to his nephew Thomas Alexander Mudd.[12]

The will of Philip Edelen was dated August 19, 1818, and probated in Charles County five days later. He devised to his brother-in-law Joseph Gardiner the mill lot which he had received from his father. Other heirs were sisters Dorothy Gardiner, Arrayminta Edelen "now in the monastery", and Elizabeth Semmes; nephews Philip Gardiner and Richard Gardiner; niece Teresa Gardiner; and brother Richard Edelen.

[1] Chancery papers no. 5544.
[2] Deeds, Liber S no. 3, folio 645.
[3] *Ibid.*, Liber L no. 2, folio 391.
[4] *Ibid.*, Liber V no. 3, folio 387.
[5] *Ibid.*, Liber D no. 4, folio 585.
[6,7] *Ibid.*, Liber N no. 4, folios 285, 489.
[8,9] *Ibid.*, Liber I B no. 2, folios 3, 335.
[10] Unpub. Md. Rec., vol. 5, DAR.
[11] Wills, Liber A L no. 12, folio 142.
[12] Wills, Liber A L no. 12, folio 425.

EDWARD EDELEN[4]

(17— - 1834)

Edward Edelen, son of Edward and Susannah (Wathen) Edelen, was born in Newport Hundred, Charles County. On January 24, 1777, he enlisted in the First Maryland Regiment, and was subsequently discharged on December 27, 1779.[1] During March 1778, he subscribed to the oath of fidelity and allegiance to the State of Maryland in Charles County before Magistrate John Parnham.[*]

On February 12, 1782, by the Rev. John Bolton, of Charles County, he was married to Eleanor Boarman. The 1783 tax list shows that they were living in Newport Hundred, seized of 364 acres of land, and that he and his wife were the only members of the household.

Children of Edward and Eleanor (Boarman) Edelen

1. Benedict Edelen married Elizabeth ———. *q.v.*
2. Rosalie Edelen married ——— Stonestreet. Issue: James; Edward Noble; Eleanor; Catherine.
3. Sarah Edelen.
4. George Edelen.

By the will of his grandfather, he received a portion of "Assington", but he was devised no realty by the will of his father in 1780. His name,

[*] Unpub. Md. Rec., vol. 5, DAR.

however, figured in numerous land transactions. His first purchase was made on January 25, 1773, when he bought "Westwood Manor" from John Brooke, of Charles County, Gent., for a consideration of £111. George Dent and John Winter witnessed the conveyance.[2]

He made no further additions to his landed estate until November 9, 1790, when he purchased from Joseph Boarman son of Thomas James Boarman, of Charles County, a portion of "Boarman's Manor", lying on the edge of Zachia Swamp. The consideration was £400 and was paid by John Hoskins Stone. Walter Hanson and Henry Barnes witnessed the transaction.[8]

On January 28, 1792, Edward Edelen deeded to Francis Edelen for 10,000 pounds of tobacco and one pistol "Simpson's Supply" adjoining "Simpson's Coatback". No wife waived dower, but the witnesses were Benjamin Dyson and William D. Briscoe.[4]

On November 13, 1793, he purchased from Philip Edelen, of Washington County, Maryland, for £275 portions of "Assington" and "Westwood Lodge", lying on the east side of Zachia Swamp. B. Fendall and William D. Briscoe witnessed the conveyance.[5]

On October 29, 1799, Edward Edelen purchased from Jesse Jameson, Michael Boarman, Henry Boarman, and John C. Boarman, all of Charles County, for £450 a portion of "Boarman's Manor", where Michael Boarman was then living. No wives waived dower; the witnesses were Walter Dyson and Henry A. Smith.[6]

On March 15, 1802, he purchased from John H. Boarman "Boarman's Enlargement". No wife waived dower, while the witnesses were Benjamin Lancaster and Ignatius Middleton.[7]

Edward Edelen on April 24, 1804, sold to Samuel Cox for £54 "Fortune's Retreat". Eleanor, wife of Edward Edelen, waived her third, while the witnesses were Benjamin Douglas and John Digges.[8] On January 12, 1807, he bought of John Haw, of Charles County, "Charles Borough's Hills".[9]

On February 17, 1808, he sold to Benedict Edelen, of Charles County, for £1,000 a portion of "Boarman's Rest", portion of "Hard Shift", and portion of "Westwood Lodge" which said tracts "were devised unto the before mentioned Edward Edelen in Tail by his grandfather Richard Edelen and which since been resurveyed and reduced to one tract called "Assington Resurvey". No wife waived dower, and the witnesses were Benjamin Douglas and John Digges.[10]

On February 18, 1808, he purchased from Benedict Edelen for £1000 a portion of "Asslington". No wife waived dower.

On March 11, 1809, he purchased from Joseph Wathen, of Charles County, "St. Thomas" of 18½ acres which had been conveyed to Wathen by Smith Hawkins. Mary Ann Teresa Wathen, wife, gave her consent. Benjamin Douglas and John Digges were the witnesses.[11]

He purchased on December 13, 1813, from Thomas Lancaster, of Charles County, for £447/5/4 land that had been purchased by Thomas Lancaster of Ignatius, Baker Brooke, Leonard Brooke, and William Corry called "St. Thomas", "Wood Addition", and "Hawkins' Addition". No wife waived dower, while the witnesses were Walter Dyson and Lawrence Posey.[12]

On November 29, 1817, Edward Edelen, Sr., sold "Simpson's Supply", beginning at "Simpson's Coatback" to Vinstant Cooksey, of Charles County. No wife waived dower.[13] On September 29, 1818, he sold to Nathan S. Dent another portion of "Simpson's Supply". The witnesses were John B. Wills and Joseph Wathen.[14]

On November 10, 1820, he sold to Rebecca Wathen a portion of "Assington". Joseph N. Stonestreet and John B. Wills witnessed the conveyance, but no wife waived dower.[15] On November 27, 1822, he conveyed to Calistus Lancaster a portion of "St. Thomas". No wife gave consent; the witness was Philip King.[16]

On June 12, 1827, Edward Edelen, Sr., deeded to George Edelen for natural love and affections a portion of "Boarman's Manor". No wife waived dower, while the witnesses were Henry C. Brice and Charles McCann. Four days later he sold to Thomas Shorter, of Charles County, for $50 a portion of "St. Thomas".[17]

On September 8, 1827, he conveyed to his grandson, Benedict Joseph Edelen, and his daughter-in-law, Elizabeth Edelen, and mother of the said Benedict Joseph for the love he had for his grandson and his mother 300 acres of unnamed land adjacent to the estate of Dr. Stonestreet, John T. Hawkins, and John F. Gardiner. No wife waived dower.[18]

On May 12, 1829, Edward Edelen, Sr., conveyed to Edward Miles a portion of "St. Thomas". No wife waived dower.

The will of Edward Edelen, Sr., was dated January 16, 1834, and proved in Charles County on December 23, 1834. He devised his wife Eleanor one-third of the real and personal property during life, with the residue to his "infant" daughter Sarah. In the event that Sarah died without issue, then the dwelling-plantation was to revert to his grandsons James Stonestreet and Edward Noble Stonestreet. The lot and tavern in Newport was devised to two named grandsons, and "St. Thomas", "Woods Addition" and "Hawkins' Addition", containing 115 acres were

devised to his granddaughters Eleanor Stonestreet and Catherine Stonestreet. He appointed his wife and Edward Edelen the executors.[19]

---

[1] Archives, vol. 18, p. 106.
[2] Deeds, Liber S no. 3, folio 354.
[3][4] Deeds, Liber K no. 4, folios 172, 382.
[5] Deeds, Liber N no. 4, folio 178.
[6] Deeds, Liber I B no. 3, folio 81.
[7] Deeds, Liber I B no. 5, folio 118.
[8] Deeds, Liber I B no. 6, folio 113.
[9] Deeds, Liber I B no. 7, folio 273.
[10][11] Deeds, Liber I B no. 8, folios 9, 256.
[12] Deeds, Liber I B no. 10, folio 497.
[13][14] Deeds, Liber I B no. 12, folios 214, 492.
[15] Deeds, Liber I B no. 14, folio 3.
[16] Deeds, Liber I B no. 15, folio 110.
[17][18] Deeds, Liber I B no. 17, folios 301, 369, 377.
[19] Wills, Liber D J no. 16, folio 24.

JOHN EDELEN[4]

(17— - 1803)

John Edelen, son of Edward and Susannah (Wathen) Edelen, was
born presumably at "Assington", Charles County. He married Monica,
daughter of Leonard and Elizabeth Boarman.

Children of John and Monica (Boarman) Edelen

1. James Edelen.
2. Leonard Edelen, born 1783, died 1823, entered priesthood.
3. Walter Edelen.
4. Robert Edelen married Mary Catherine ————. q.v.
5. John M. Edelen.
6. Elizabeth Hester Edelen married Basil Smith.
7. Elizabeth Cecilia Edelen married John C. Gardiner.
8. Wilfred Edelen.

In 1778 John Edelen took the oath of allegiance and fidelity to the
State of Maryland in Charles County before His Worshipful John
Parnham.[1]

According to the tax list of 1783, he was the head of a family of
four in Newport Hundred of Charles County and was seized of 241
acres of land. In 1787 he patented "Edelen's Neglect".

On May 11, 1789, John Edelen purchased from Zephaniah Turner
and Joseph Millburn Semmes, the authorized trustees for the sale of
"Hall's Lot" the latter of 41 acres. The witnesses were Richard Barnes
and George Lee.[2]

On February 6, 1792, John Edelen, Planter, of Charles County, conveyed to Oswell Edelen, Philip Edelen, Joseph Edelen, and Leonard

Edelen for £20 "Assington", "Westward Lodge", "Westward Manor", and "Hardship" "as directed by my father Edward Edelen's will". The witnesses were Benjamin Dyson and William D. Briscoe.[3]

On January 31, 1794, John Edelen and Monica his wife, Henry Gardiner and Catherine his wife, and Ignatius Gardiner and Anne his wife, all of Charles County, conveyed to Joseph Boarman of Leonard for a sum of £82/10, inasmuch as some doubt existed over the tracts, "Boarman's Rest", "Calvert Hope", and "Hardship" one-half of the land which was conveyed by Leonard Boarman "father of Catherine Gardiner, Monica Edelen, and Ann Gardiner to his son Leonard Boarman, Jr., by deed of 13 May 1785" and which were devised by the will of Leonard Boarman, the father, October 14, 1791. Alexander McPherson and William D. Briscoe witnessed the transaction.[4]

On the same day John Edelen and Monica his wife, Henry Gardiner and Catherine his wife, Ignatius Gardiner and Anne his wife, Sylvester Baker Boarman of Harford County, Charles Boarman, and Joseph Boarman all figured in a land transaction over "Westward Manor", "Boarman's Folly", and a portion of "Boarman's Rest", at the head of Holly Bush Branch, containing 25 acres. Mary Boarman, wife of Charles, and Sarah Boarman, wife of Joseph, waived dower.[4]

On December 31, 1794, John Edelen and Monica his wife, Henry Gardiner and Catherine his wife, and Ignatius Gardiner and Anne his wife, all parties being of Charles County, conveyed "Higdon's Chance" to Gideon Dent, of the same county.[4]

The will of John Edelen was dated July 19, 1803, and proved in Charles County on October 18, 1803. He was seized of "Green's Rest" which he had received from his father in 1780, and portions of "Hall's Lot", "Toombit", and "Edelen's Neglect". He bequeathed to his wife, Monica, numerous slaves. To each of the following children, Elizabeth Hester, Elizabeth Cilly, Walter, Robert, John Michael, and Wilfred (minor), he bequeathed £35. The residue of the estate was to be divided among his eight children.[5]

The first account to the court showed personalty valued at £1,322-/1/3. Edward Edelen and Joseph Boarman of Leonard were sureties for the widow. She died before 1809, inasmuch as by that year her son, Walter, appeared as administrator *d.b.n.* On November 11, 1809, an account showed a balance of $2,657.53.[6]

Distribution of the personal estate was not made until January 1811, when the balance of $1,739 was divided by Walter Edelen, administrator *d.b.n.* among the eight heirs—James Edelen, Elizabeth H. Smith, Leonard Edelen, John Gardiner in right of his wife Elizabeth, Walter Edelen, John M. Edelen, Robert Edelen, and Wilfred Edelen.[6]

On March 20, 1811, Wilfred Edelen, minor, by Robert Edelen his guardian filed action in the High Court of Chancery for an equitable division of the realty, i. e., "Green's Rest", and portions of "Hall's Lot", "Toombit", and "Edelen's Neglect", 340 acres in all. The heirs were James Edelen, Leonard Edelen, Walter Edelen, Robert Edelen, John Michael Edelen, Wilfred Edelen, Elizabeth Hester, wife of Basil Smith, and Elizabeth Creacy wife of John C. Gardiner.[7]

Robert Edelen, son, though he married, died without issue. On August 8, 1815, he purchased from Wilson Smoot, of Charles County, portions of "George's Rest", "Noe's Desert", and "Betty's Delight Enlarged". Ann Smoot, wife, waived dower, while the witnesses were Daniel Smallwood and Horatio Moore. On the same day Somerset Posey and Robert Edelen figured with John B. Knott and Susan Knott over a mortgage which covered "Hitching", "Meadows Growing", and portions of "Lumley", "Burches' Help", "Penury" and "Ash Swamp". Samuel Ogden and Thomas H. Reeder witnessed.[8]

On December 1, 1816, Robert Edelen, of Charles County, deeded to William B. Smoot for $1,840 "George's Rest", "Strife", "Noe's Desert", and "Betty's Delight Enlarged", all containing 230 acres except ½ acre retained as a burying ground of the Smoot family. Mary Catherine Edelen, wife, waived dower, and the witnesses were Horatio Clagett and Stephen Latimer.[8]

The will of Robert Edelen was dated August 7, 1817, and proved in Charles County on September 22, same year. He named his sister Cecilia Gardiner, nephews Walter Smith and John Leonard Smith, and niece Monica Carolina Smith. To his brother Walter Edelen he bequeathed $500 "trusting in his virtue to be appropriated to pious purposes with the direction of my Rev. Brother Leonard Edelen who knows my mind on this affair". He devised his sister Elizabeth Smith "New Design", lying in the neighborhood of Newport, and to his wife, Mary Catherine, "all property real and personal which she owned when I married her".[9]

The will of Leonard Edelen who took Holy Orders was dated January 6, 1823, and proved in St. Mary's County on February 3, 1824, by Lewis Ford, George W. Neale, and Thomas Boothe. He named the Rev. Francis Neale of St. Thomas' Manor, the Rev. Enoch Fenwick of Georgetown College, and his sister Elizabeth Smith.

James Edelen, son of John and Monica, on July 28, 1784, purchased from Edward Boarman for £30 a portion of "Boarman's Manor". No wife waived dower; the witnesses were Joshua Sanders and John Morton.[10] On November 17, 1806, he sold to Basil Smith, of Charles County, for £160 his one-eighth interest in the dwelling-plantation of his late father. No wife waived dower, and the witnesses were Gerard Briscoe and Thomas Rogerson.

John M. Edelen, another son, on October 29, 1808, conveyed to Basil Smith his one-eighth portion of the dwelling-plantation of his late father. No wife waived dower, and the witnesses were Benjamin Douglas and Walter Dyson.[11]

Wilfred Edelen, another son, on December 20, 1814, conveyed to James Jameson for $500 portions of "Edelen's Neglect", "Hall's Lot", and "Boarman's Manor". No wife waived dower.[12]

Walter Edelen, also a son, settled in Prince Georges County, and as a resident of that place he conveyed to Basil Smith, of Charles County, for $490 "one-eighth of the dwelling-plantation of the late John Edelen, of Charles County, and which was devised by the said John Edelen to his son Walter". No wife waived dower, and the witnesses were Ignatius Middleton and Ignatius Semmes.[13]

[1] Unpub. Md. Rec., vol. 5, DAR.
[2] Deeds, Liber D no. 4, folio 470.
[3] Deeds, Liber K no. 4, folio 207.
[4] Deeds, Liber N no. 4, folios 212, 338.
[5] Wills, Liber A L no. 12, folio 135.
[6] Inv. and Accts. (1808-12), folios 190, 477, 392.
[7] Chancery papers 1637.
[8] Deeds, Liber I B no. 11, folios 133, 136, 503.
[9] Wills, Liber H B no. 13, folio 531.
[10] Deeds, Liber Z no. 3, folio 110.
[11] Deeds, Liber I B no. 8, folio 261.
[12] Deeds, Liber I B no. 11, folio 57.
[13] Deeds, Liber I B no. 7, folio 471.

OSWALD EDELEN[4]

Oswald Edelen, son of Edward and Susannah (Wathen) Edelen, was born in Newport Hundred, Charles County. His name does not appear upon the magistrate's lists as taking the oath of allegiance and fidelity in 1778, which apparently indicates that he was less than 18 years of age at that time. According to the tax list of 1783, he was seized of 66 acres of land in Newport Hundred.

On October 25, 1787, he was married to Mary Thompson by the Rev. Father Henry Pile, of Charles County. A complete list of his children has not been proved.

Children of Oswald and Mary (Thompson) Edelen

1. Oswald Edelen.
2. Leonard Edelen.
3. Elizabeth Edelen married ———— Simpson.

On November 27, 1793, Oswald Edelen and Philip Edelen had recorded in Charles County that they agreed to the division of the land left them by the will of their father. John S. Haw and Richard Edelen witnessed the indenture.[1] On January 7, 1807, he conveyed to John Haw of Charles County a portion of "Assington". No wife waived dower, but the witnesses were John Digges and Benjamin Douglas.[2] On March 17, 1823, Oswald Edelen, of Charles County, conveyed to Leonard Edelen, of the same county, personal property. Nathan Smoot Dent and Francis Edelen witnessed the sale.[3]

---

[1] Deeds, Liber N no. 4, folio 177.
[2] *Ibid.*, Liber I B no. 7, folio 271.
[3] *Ibid.*, Liber I B no. 15, folio 189.

FRANCIS EDELEN[4]

(17— - 1830)

Francis Edelen, son of Edward and Susannah (Wathen) Edelen, was born in Newport Hundred, Charles County. By the terms of his paternal grandfather's will in 1760, he was to receive "Edelen's Admentment" upon the decease of his grandfather's widow.

At the beginning of the Revolutionary War he volunteered for service with the Flying Camp and was enlisted by Captain Belain Posey, of Charles County, and passed on July 8, 1776, by John Marshall.[1] In 1778 he took the oath of allegiance and fidelity to the State of Maryland, under Magistrate John Parnham.[2]

On November 8, 1779, in Charles County, he was married to Sarah Thompson, by the Rev. John Bolton.[3]

Children of Francis and Sarah (Thompson) Edelen

1. William Edelen.
2. Francis Hoskins Edelen.
3. Catherine Edelen.
4. Mary Edelen married ——— Boarman.
5. Edward Edelen.

The tax list of 1783 shows him a resident of Newport Hundred of Charles County, seized of 180 acres of land, and with four in family including himself.

On February 28, 1828, Francis Edelen, of Charles County, conveyed to William Edelen for $2,000 "Simpson's Supply" and "Edelen's Amendment" "not already conveyed by the said Francis Edelen to Francis Hoskins Edelen". No wife waived dower, but the witnesses were Nathan Smoot Dent and James A. Middleton. During the same year he conveyed personal property to Francis Hoskins Edelen.[5]

Francis Edelen dated his will October 7, 1826, it being proved in Charles County on March 16, 1830. He devised his son William a portion of "Simpson's Supply", and his wife Sarah "Edelen's Amendment", the dwelling-plantation, during life then to his son Francis Hoskins Edelen, but reserved one-half of the dwelling for the use of his single daughter Kitty and his widowed daughter Mary Boarman and her children. Edward received various bequests. He appointed his sons William and Edward the executors.[6]

---

[1] Archives, vol. 18, p. 32.
[2] Unpub. Md. Records, vol 5, DAR.
[3] Brumbaugh's Md. Rec., vol. 2, p. 488.
[4] Deeds, Liber V no. 3, folio 503.
[5] Deeds, Liber I B no. 17, folios 477, 527.
[6] Wills, Liber H B no. 14, folio 234.

JOSEPH EDELEN[4]

Joseph Edelen, son of Edward and Susannah (Wathen) Edelen, was born in Charles County. On January 5, 1796, he conveyed to Edward Edelen for £75 portions of "Hardship", "Westward Manor", and "Assington", beginning at "Boarman's Rest". William D. Briscoe and Walter Dyson witnessed the deed, but no wife waived dower.[1]

---

[1] Deeds, Liber N no. 4, folio 523.

THOMAS EDELEN[4]

(1720 - 17—)

Thomas Edelen, son of Thomas and Mary (Blandford) Edelen, was born November 12, 1720, according to the records of Piscataway Parish. He completed the administration on the estate of his father in 1762, from which he received portions of "Apple Door" and "Rome".

On August 2, 1768, Thomas Edelen of Prince Georges County "grandson and heir of Richard Edelen late of Charles County deceased" conveyed to Philip Edelen "brother of the said Thomas Edelen whereas Richard Edelen by will devised to the said Philip Edelen grandson land whereon Thomas Hally and Joseph Crown lived being a portion of 3,000 acres granted to William Calvert known by the name of Piscataway Manor . . . but Thomas Edelen being sensitive gave fee to Philip Edelen". No wife of Thomas waived dower, while the witnesses were John Baynes and George Hardy.[1] The exact significance of this assignment is not clear, but it looks as if Thomas Edelen was relinquishing all claims in this tract, thus giving his brother Philip a clear, uncontested title.

The Debt Books of Prince Georges County show that as Thomas Edelen, Jr., he paid quit rents beginning in 1753 on 279 acres of "Apple Door" and 28¾ acres of "Rome". In 1761, however, he remitted only for 100 acres of "Apple Door" and continued to do so throughout 1772. On January 9, 1775, he purchased from Thomas Clagett, merchant, "Something and Merry Thought Enlarged" for £29/9/-. Mary Meek Clagett, wife, waived dower, while the witnesses were John Baynes and Luke Marbury.[2]

Raphael Semmes of the past generation from his tireless research stated that Thomas Edelen married first Mary Ann ———— by whom he had Edward, Elizabeth, Eleanor, and Richard, and secondly Priscilla Clement by whom he had Jeremiah and Jacob. The census for Piscataway Parish of 1776 shows a Thomas Edelen aged 56 and in his household was Mary Ann Edelen aged 51, but no children.

However, Priscilla, the daughter of Francis and Elizabeth Clements, was a Mrs. Edelen as early as 1760. Francis Clements who referred to his deceased father Francis in his will of 1760 bequeathed property to his sister Priscilla Edelen, and a ring to Eleanor Clement Edelen (no stated relationship).[3] Elizabeth Clements, widow, by her will dated November 4, 1771, named her daughter Priscilla Edelen and granddaughter Mary Edelen as heirs.[4] And both received their share at the distribution in 1773.[5] On May 16, 1778, Priscilla Edelen as a sister of George Clements late of Charles County deceased shared in the distribution of his estate.[6] Furthermore, Mrs. Mary (Clements) Jenkins, who died without issue, by her will dated June 26, 1787, and proved in Charles County in 1795, bequeathed her sister Priscilla Edelen certain negroes during life then to her daughter Elizabeth Edelen. Among other heirs were brother John Clements and sister Henrietta Dyer.[*] It is therefore quite obvious that the Thomas and Mary Anne Edelen in 1776 could not be the Thomas Edelen, spouse to Priscilla.

Children of Thomas and Priscilla (Clements) Edelen

1. Eleanor Clements Edelen married Thomas Mitchell. License Pr. Geo. Co., Nov. 9, 1778.
2. Mary Edelen.
3. Elizabeth Edelen married Dennis Osborn. License Pr. Geo. Co., Feb. 7, 1800.
4. Jeremiah Edelen married Anne Sarah Jenkins. *q.v.*

---

* Liber A K no. 11, folio 303.

5. Jacob Edelen married Mary Osborn. License Pr. Geo., Dec. 23, 1806.
6. Joseph Edelen. *q.v.*
7. Francis Edelen. *q.v.*
8. Richard Edelen married Mary Anne ————. *q.v.*

In 1778 Thomas Edelen took the oath of allegiance and fidelity to the State of Maryland in Prince Georges County.[7] He died intestate in Prince Georges County. The administration bond was dated February 11, 1783.

The will of his widow, Priscilla Edelen, was dated November 26, 1804, and proved in Prince Georges County on February 19, 1805.[8] She bequeathed slaves to the following children: Elizabeth Osborn, Jeremiah Edelen, Eleanor Mitchell, and Jacob Edelen. The residue of the estate was willed to Jacob whom she named as executor and to her daughter Elizabeth Osborn.

[1] Deeds, Liber B B no. 2, folio 452.
[2] *Ibid.*, Liber C C no. 2, folio 95.
[3] Wills 1760-1763, folio 28, La Plata.
[4] Wills, Liber 38, pt. 2, folio 452.
[5] Balance Book no. 6, folio 280.
[6] Liber 1777-1782, folio 151, La Plata.
[7] Brumbaugh's Md. Records, vol. 2, p. 264.
[8] Wills, Liber T no. 1, folio 598.

RICHARD EDELEN[4]

(1723 - 1810)

Richard Edelen, son of Thomas and Mary (Blandford) Edelen, was born in or about 1723 in Prince Georges County. He married Mary ————, born about 1723, according to the 1776 census of St. John's Parish. In that year there were in his household five females and two males, all under the ages of seventeen, and eight slaves.

His dwelling-plantation was 100 acres of "Long Land als Frankland", on which he remitted quit rents regularly beginning with 1753. He was recorded in the Debt Books as Richard Edelen, Jr.

Children of Richard Edelen

1. Susannah Edelen, spinster.
2. Thomas Edelen, died prior to 1810.
3. Bartholomew Edelen. *q.v.*
4. Basil Edelen. *q.v.*
5. Mary Edelen married Jachin Jenkins.
6. Walter Edelen, *d.s.p.*

7. Rebecca Edelen married Bennett Gwinn. License Pr. Geo. Co.,
   Aug. 29, 1807.
8. John Edelen.
9. Clara Edelen married Jesse Edelen. *q.v.*

Richard Edelen in 1778 took the oath of allegiance and fidelity to
the State of Maryland in Prince Georges County.[1] On September 13,
1791, as Richard Edelen of Thomas, he purchased from Edward Lloyd
Wailes, Sheriff of Prince Georges County, "Aix (Ayr)", formerly belonging to George Hardy. William Baker and Joseph Noble Bayne
witnessed the conveyance.[2] On August 20, 1796, he purchased another
portion from Clothia Keech, of Montgomery County, which had been
devised by the will of Thomas Thompson to his son, Thomas, and sold
by the latter to Clothia Keech. Joseph N. Bayne and Nicholas Young
witnessed.[3]

The will of Richard Edelen was dated January 11, 1810, and proved
in Prince Georges County on May 2, 1810, by Giles Dyer, Ignatius
Lovelace, and Jeremiah Edelen. To his daughter Susan he devised the
dwelling-plantation "Frankland", containing 100 acres during her single
life, then to his son Walter. To the heirs of his deceased son, Thomas,
he bequeathed £30. Walter received 130 acres of unnamed land, while
the residuary estate was to be divided among the following children:
Basil Edelen, Mary Jenkins, Walter Edelen, Bartholomew Edelen, Rebecca Gwinn, Susan Edelen, and John Edelen.[4]

The testamentary bond on the estate of Richard Edelen, Sr., was
dated May 2, 1810, with Jeremiah Edelen and Ignatius Lovelace as the
sureties. Walter Edelen was the executor.

The bachelor son Walter Edelen dated his will January 16, 1816, it
being probated in Charles County on December 5, same year. He bequeathed his nephews John Aloysius, Richard James, and Walter Alexander Edelen each $100 at 21 years, while the residue of the estate real
and personal were devised to his brother Barton Edelen, sister Susannah Edelen, and nephew Richard Lloyd Jenkins whom he appointed
executor.

Susannah Edelen, daughter, died a spinster and by her will she bequeathed each child of her deceased brother Thomas Edelen $50. To
her nephew Lewis Edelen, son of her late brother Basil Edelen, she
willed $100, and to Richard L. Jenkins $50 toward repairing the chapel
at Piscataway or Mattawoman. Her brother Barton Edelen was to receive $50 annually during life, while small legacies were given to Richard
L. Jenkins, Charles Jenkins, John A. Edelen, Richard J. Edelen, and

Walter A. Edelen. Richard L. Jenkins and Charles Jenkins were to support "my sister their mother Mary Jenkins" during her widowhood.

¹ Brumbaugh's Md. Rec., vol. 2, p. 267.
² Deeds, Liber I R M no. 4, folio 598.
³ Deeds, Liber I R M no. 6, folio 96.
⁴ Wills, Liber T T no. 1, folio 28.

CHARLES EDELEN⁴
(1727 - 1790)

Charles Edelen, son of Thomas and Mary (Blandford) Edelen, was born about 1727 in Piscataway Parish. According to the Debt Books, he became a tax payer in 1758, when he remitted quit rents on 162 acres of "Apple Door". Beginning in 1772, he remitted in addition to this tract rent for "Edelen's Rest", and continued to pay rents on these tracts throughout 1775.

His wife was Catherine ————, born about 1729. According to the 1776 census, he was the owner of 10 slaves and had the following children at home: four males, born 1760, 1763, 1769, and 1771; and two females born 1764 and 1767. His son, Samuel who married Mary Suit (*q.v.*), is the only child who has been identified.

Charles Edelen died intestate in Prince Georges County, when letters of administration upon his estate were issued to his son, Samuel, on October 12, 1790.

PHILIP EDELEN⁴
(1731 - ——)

Philip Edelen, son of Thomas and Mary (Blandford) Edelen, was born about 1731 near Piscataway. In 1762 or thereabouts he married Mary, daughter of Penelope (Dyer) Howard, who according to the 1776 census, was born about 1743. Penelope Howard by her will, dated January 15, 1763, and proved October 17, 1763, made her daughter Mary Edelen the residuary heir and named her son-in-law Philip Edelen the executor.¹

The 1776 census for St. John's or Piscataway Parish shows the following children in the home of Philip Edelen: three males born 1763, 1765, and 1771; and four females born 1767, 1769, 1773, and 1775. Of the males, two have been identified—John Baptist (*q.v.*) and Joseph.

During March 1778, Philip Edelen took the oath of fidelity and allegiance to the State of Maryland in Prince Georges County.²

Philip Edelen received from his brother, Thomas, a portion of Piscataway Manor, according to deed recorded August 2, 1768, i. e.,

"Thomas Edelen of Prince Georges County, grandson and heir of Richard Edelen, late of Charles County, deceased, conveyed to Philip Edelen, brother of the said Thomas, whereas Richard Edelen by will devised to the said Philip Edelen his grandson land whereon Thomas Halley and Joseph Crown lived it being a portion of 3,000 acres granted to William Calvert known as Piscattaway Manor providing that his said brother Thomas Edelen died without issue". The deed furthermore stated that Thomas Edelen was "sensitive" and thus conveyed the land in fee to his brother Philip. No wife of Thomas Edelen waived dower, but the witnesses were John Bayne and George Hardy.[3]

[1] Wills, Liber 31, folio 1000.
[2] Brumbaugh's Md. Rec., vol. 2, p. 289.
[3] Deeds, Liber B B no. 2, folio 452.

CHRISTOPHER EDELEN[4]

Christopher Edelen, son of Thomas and Mary (Blandford) Edelen, was born about 1723 near Piscataway. By his father's will he received a portion of "Apple Door" on which he paid quit rents of 136 acres from 1760 through 1769. In or about 1758 he married Elizabeth ————, born about 1734. The 1776 census shows the following children in his household: two males, born 1759 and 1774; and five females, born 1760, 1762, 1764, 1767, and 1770. Son, Joseph, born 1759, is the only one who has been placed (*q.v.*).

JAMES EDELEN[4]

James Edelen, son of Thomas and Mary (Blandford) Edelen, was born in Prince Georges County. By the will of his paternal grandfather Richard Edelen in 1760, he received "Sympson's Supply" in Charles County. By 1771 he had married Susan, the widow of Basil Hagan, and daughter of Ignatius Gardiner. The latter by his will, dated January 17, 1777, named his daughter Susannah Edelen. On January 29, 1773, James Edelen and Susan his wife rendered an account upon the estate of Basil Hagan, late of Charles County, deceased.[1] The final account was passed on March 8, 1773, when the balance of £212/0/3 was distributed to the widow Susannah Edelen and the three children—Raphael, Teresa, and John Barton Hagan.[2] One of their children, James, settled in Montgomery County. (*q.v.*)

[1] Test. Proc., Liber 45, folios 1, 29.
[2] Adm. Accts., Liber 10, folio 173.

EDWARD EDELEN[4]

(17— - 1825)

Edward Edelen, son of Thomas and Mary (Blandford) Edelen, was born in Prince Georges County. By the will of his father in 1752, he failed to share in any portion of the landed estate. On October 31, 1787, he who described himself in the deed as Edward Edelen of Thomas purchased from Zephaniah Wade, of Prince Georges County, "Stoney Harbour", lying near Tinker's Branch as it intersected the line of Robert Wade's portion of the same tract, adjoining the house of Elisha Harrison and the land of William Jenkins. No wife waived dower, while the witnesses were David Crawford and Rindall Johnson. On November 12, 1798, again as Edward Edelen of Thomas he purchased for £815 another portion of "Stoney Harbour" from Benoni Hamilton Wade. No wife waived dower, and the witnesses were Francis C. Dyer and Nicholas Young. This conveyance was the occasion for a lawsuit in 1802 instituted by Edward Edelen against Bryan Hampson.[1]

He died intestate in Prince Georges County. On August 9, 1825, Jeremiah and Jacob Edelen as the "administrators *d.b.n.* of Edward Edelen of Thomas" rendered an account, showing an inventory of the personal estate valued at $6,651.21, and after certain disbursements recorded a balance of $6,230.63. Among the expenditures were shoes for Joseph T. Edelen.[2]

---

[1] Deeds, Liber H H, folio 588; Liber I R M no. 7, folio 51; Chancery papers no. 1620.
[2] Adm. Acts., Liber T T no. 3, folios 424, 540.

RICHARD EDELEN[5]

(1774 - 1835)

Richard Edelen, son of Richard and Sarah (Harrison) Edelen, was born about 1774 at "Lanterman", in Bryan Town Hundred, Charles County.* He settled in St. Mary's County and in 1800 was the only Edelen residing in that county. He and his wife were both between the ages of 26 and 45 in that year. His first wife was Clara whose headstone in Newton graveyard reads "Clara Edelen wife of Dr. Richard

---

* The Athenaeum, of Apr. 25, 1835, carried his death as "14 April 1835 at his residence in St. Mary's County, Dr. Richard Edelin, in his 61 year". The National Intelligence, of Apr. 21, 1835, carried "Dr. Richard Edelen died 14 April 1835, aged 71, of Prince Georges County". It does not seem probable that two Dr. Richard Edelens died the same day.

Edelen died 28 April 1802, aged 30 years". On August 3, 1803, in St. Mary's County, he secured license to marry Anne Gough.

Children of Richard Edelen

1. William Joseph Edelen married Ellen Leigh. License St. M. Co., Jan. 23, 1827.*
2. James Stephen Edelen, *d.s.p.*
3. Anne E. Edelen married Bennett Gough. License St. M. Co., Feb. 28, 1832.
4. Clara Edelen.
5. Sarah Edelen married James C. Gough.**
6. Jane M. Edelen married Nicholas Goldsborough. License St. M. Co., May 17, 1831.
7. Philip R. Edelen.

The will of Richard Edelen was dated January 3, 1835, and proved June 10, 1835, by S. Gough, C. Thompson, and John S. Gough in St. Mary's County. He bequeathed his son William Joseph $1,200, and the residue of his estate to his wife Anne during widowhood, but in the event that she remarried, than only her third. He mentioned other children (unnamed) and appointed his wife and son James Stephen Edelen executors.[1]

The will of his widow was dated September 23, 1850, and proved in St. Mary's County during September 1853, by James Y. Blackistone, R. Ford, and John S. Gough. She bequeathed personalty to her son James S. and her daughters Clara Edelen and Anne E. Gough, wife of Bennett Gough. The residue was divided among the following children: James S. Edelen, Sarah C. Gough, Anne E. Gough, Jane M. Goldsborough, Clara Edelen, and Philip R. Edelen. She placed money in the hands of Judge Bryce I. Goldsborough for the use of her daughter Jane Goldsborough, and appointed her son, James, the executor.[2]

The will of the bachelor son, James S. Edelen, was dated January 6, 1860, and proved in St. Mary's County on March 1, 1860. He named his brothers Dr. William J. Edelen and Philip R. Edelen; niece Anne P. Gough; and sisters Clara Edelen, Sarah C. Gough, Jane M. Goldsborough, and Anne E. Gough.[3]

---

[1] Wills, Liber E I M, folio 310, Leonardtown.
[2] Wills, Liber G C no. 2, folio 456.
[3] Wills, Liber J T M R no. 1, folio 57.

---

* "Married at the Cathedral 5 February 1850, William J. Edelen, M.D., to Ellen, daughter of the late Peter Gough, of St. Mary's County". Balto. Amer., 8 Feb. 1850. Died 31 December 1891, at his residence 807 North Fulton St., Balto.
** "Sally Catherine Edelen, daughter of Dr. Richard Edelen, married 31 July 1832, James C. Gough". (Nat. Intel., 7 Aug. 1832.)

BENEDICT EDELEN[5]

(18— - 1832)

Benedict Edelen, son of Edward, was born at Newport, Charles County. On September 8, 1827, he received from his father for natural love and affections portions of "Assington" and "Westwood Lodge", adjoining the land of William Penn, also 10 acres of the tract "St. Thomas", near the village of Newport adjacent to the lands of Dr. Calistus Lancaster, Capt. James Saxton, and Thomas Shorter. No wife waived dower, while the witnesses were James H. A. Middleton and John B. Wills (Wells).[1]

On June 28, 1830, he sold to Thomas and Susanna E. Turner for $1,000 a portion of "St. Thomas", adjoining the village of Newport, and adjacent to the land of Dr. Edward Miles, John J. Cordell, and Thomas Shorter.[2]

The will of Benedict Edelen was dated January 21, 1832, and proved on March 2, 1832, in Charles County. He devised his unnamed wife all real and personal property during life, but in the event that his wife gave birth to an heir within 9 months after his death, then the estate was to revert to his heir. In case there were no heir then the property was to be invested in the children of his sister Rosey Stonestreet, that is, Eleanor, Catherine, and James Noble Stonestreet. He named his wife and Alexius Lancaster the executors.

[1] Deeds, Liber I B no 17, folios 413, 415.
[2] Deeds, Liber I B no. 19, folio 147.

JOSEPH EDELEN[5]

(17— - 1804)

Joseph Edelen, son of Thomas, was born in Prince Georges County His marriage has not been placed, but he referred to children in his will which was dated September 7, 1804, and proved in Prince Georges County on December 11, 1804. He bequeathed slaves to his brother Jeremiah Edelen and personalty to Charles Osborn. The residue of the estate was to be divided between his brother Jacob and "my" children (unnamed). In the event that his children died without issue, then their estate to brother Jacob.

JEREMIAH EDELEN[5]

Jeremiah Edelen, son of Thomas and Priscilla (Clements) Edelen, was born in Prince Georges County. On February 11, 1792, he secured license in Prince Georges County to marry Sally Jenkins. In 1822 his brother, Francis Edelen, of Charles County, bequeathed property to "my nephew Harwood Edelen son of Jeremiah".

FRANCIS EDELEN[5]

(17— - 1823)

Francis Edelen, son of Thomas Edelen, was born in Prince Georges County. He settled in Charles County, however, and it was ,in that county in 1778 that he subscribed to the oath of allegiance and fidelity to the State of Maryland.[1] His wife was Martha ————.

On January 15, 1781, he purchased from Arnold Elder and Clotilder his wife, of Frederick County, a portion of "Green's Inheritance", lying on Portobacco Creek for 11,000 pounds of tobacco. According to the deed, the tract had been willed by Robert Doyne, late of Charles County, in 1760 to Clotilder, the daughter of Francis Green, but in the event that she died without issue then to Robert Doyne, son of the testator, and to Benedict Green, son of Frances and brother to Clotilder. Both Arnold Elder and his wife signed the deed, while the witnesses were Daniel Jenifer and W. H. Jenifer.

The will of Francis Edelen was dated May 8, 1822, and proved in Charles County on January 17, 1823. He devised his wife Martha "Green's Inheritance" as well as negroes and other property. He men-' tioned his nephew, Harwood Edelen, the son of Jeremiah Edelen.

The will of his widow, Martha Edelen, was dated May 8, 1835, and proved in Charles County, on May 24, 1836. She bequeathed negroes to her sister Priscilla, the wife of Luke Pentoney, of Martinsburg, Virginia; to her niece Martha Pentoney; to her nephew Thomas Pentoney, of Wheeling, Virginia; and to her nephew John E. Taylor, living near Baltimore.

RICHARD EDELEN[5]

(17— - 1815)

Richard Edelen, son of Thomas, was born in Prince Georges County. His wife was Mary Anne ————.

Children of Richard and Mary Ann Edelen

1. Edward C. Edelen married Sarah Maone (Malone). License Dec. 8, 1801, Pr. Geo. Co.
2. Francis Edelen.
3. ———— Edelen married ———— Jenkins.

The will of "Richard Edelen of Thomas" was dated March 7, 1815, and proved in Prince Georges County on April 5, 1815, by Notley Young, Walter Edelen, William Marshall, and Jeremiah Edelen. He bequeathed his entire estate to his wife Mary Ann Edelen during life, except a negro girl whom he bequeathed to his granddaughter Elizabeth Ann Edelen. Other grandchildren mentioned were Priscilla Jenkins and Sally Jenkins. After the decease of his widow, the estate was to be divided between his two sons—Edward C. and Francis Edelen—whom he named as executors.[1]

A lawsuit was instituted in the court of chancery on June 29, 1819, by which it was shown that Cave W. Edelen, of Baltimore, had sold a slave to Benjamin McCeney. It was claimed that the slave was the property of Mary Ann Edelen, widow of Richard Edelen, who died testate in 1815. Cave Edelen was the widow and administratrix of Thomas H. Edelen, late of Anne Arundel County. The inventory of his estate, filed by his widow on March 25, 1816, displayed a value of $1,140.15.[2]

[1] Wills, Liber T T no 1, folio 112.
[2] Chancery papers no. 9599.

BARTHOLOMEW EDELEN[5]

(1748 - 18—)

Bartholomew Edelen, son of Richard and Mary Edelen, was born about 1748 in Prince Georges County. About 1775 he married Monica ————. In 1776 he was living in Frederick County, aged 28, his wife Monica aged 24, and daughter Ann, aged 1. In his household was also his brother Thomas Edelen aged 26. On July 13, 1776, Bartholomew Edelen was enrolled by Captain Leonard Deakins for service in the militia of Frederick County.[1] In the will of his father he was referred to as Bartholomew, but as Barton in the will of his spinster sister Susannah and that of his brother Walter in 1816.

[1] Archives, vol. 18, p. 43.

BASIL EDELEN[5]

Basil Edelen, son of Richard and Mary Edelen, was born in Prince Georges County. He enlisted as corporal on May 27, 1778, in the Third Maryland Regiment and was "discharged at the termination of service".[1] On April 13, 1779, he "a 9 months discharged soldier" was placed on recruiting duty.[2] A Basil Edelen was the head of a family in Charles County in 1790 with 2 males over 16 (including himself), one male under 16, two females, and 21 slaves.

[1] Archives, vol. 18, p. 107.
[2] Archives, vol. 21, p. 344.

JOSEPH EDELEN[5]

(1759 - 18—)

Joseph Edelen, son of Christopher and Elizabeth Edelen, was born about 1759 near Piscataway. During March 1778, as Joseph Edelen of Christopher he subscribed to the patriot's oath in Prince Georges County. He was probably the Joseph Edelen who on April 3, 1786, secured license in Prince Georges County to marry Catherine Watkins. At the census of 1790 he was domiciled near Piscataway with a male under 16, one female, and two slaves.

SAMUEL EDELEN[5]

(1763 - 1835)

Samuel Edelen, son of Charles and Catherine Edelen, was born about 1763 in or near Piscataway. On December 14, 1787, he secured license in Prince Georges County to marry Mary Suit.

Children of Samuel and Mary (Suit) Edelen

1. Alexander Edelen.
2. Charles Edelen married Anne Morland. *q.v.*
3. Cynthia Edelen married Richard Smith, Jr. License Feb. 19, 1814, Wn Co., Ky.
4. Teresa Edelen.
5. Cecilia Edelen.
6. Nancy Edelen married ———— Philipps.
7. Edward H. Edelen.
8. Christopher Edelen.
9. Martina Edelen married ———— Ball.

On April 12, 1796, as "Samuel Edelen of Charles" he conveyed to George Robert Peiper for £400 "Appledore", lying on the main branch of the Piscataway. And on the same day he deeded to Edward Edelen land lying on Piscataway Branch being a portion of "Edelen's Rest" which adjoined "Hawkins' Rest". Mary Eleanor Edelen, his wife, waived dower on both occasions, while Francis C. Dyer and Nicholas Young were the witnesses.[1]

Shortly after these indentures, Samuel Edelen migrated to Washington County, Kentucky. The 1810 census, first available for Kentucky, shows him to be over 45 years of age as well as his wife. There were 7 slaves.'

The will of Samuel Edelen was dated February 18, 1835, and proved in Washington County, Kentucky, on March 23, 1835. He requested that he be buried at St. Rose. All property was devised to his wife Mary during life, then to his sons Christopher and Edward H. Edelen, both of whom he named as executors. He mentioned the following: sons Alexander and Charles F.; daughters Cynthia Smith, Teresa Edelen, Cecilia Edelen, Nancy Philips, and Mary Ball; and granddaughter Mary Philipps.[2]

His widow was the head of her household in 1850, aged 83 years and born in Maryland. Other members of her household were Horace Edelen, aged 38, born in Kentucky; Teresa Edelen, aged 42, born in Kentucky; and Nancy Philip, aged 17, born in Kentucky.

---

[1] Deeds, Liber I R M, folio 387, 390.
[2] Wills, Liber F, folio 162, Wash. Co., Ky.

JOHN BAPTIST EDELEN[5]

(1763 - 1822)

John Baptist Edelen, son of Philip and Penelope (Howard) Edelen, was born in or about 1763 in Prince Georges County. He married twice. His first wife was Susannah ————, whom he married prior to 1790. His second wife and ultimate widow was Ann Helen (Helena), the only daughter and heir of Jacob and Elizabeth (Neale) Clements. Jacob Clements died 1769 in Charles County and his widow Elizabeth, daughter to William Neale, married secondly Henry McAtee. He died in 1782 and left his widow and among other children William McAtee who was therefore half-brother to Helena (Clements) Edelen. Mme. Clements-McAtee died in 1814.

Children of John Baptist Edelen

1. John Henry Edelen married Susan ————.
2. Elizabeth Harriet Edelen married William, son of William and Mary (Semmes) Clark. License Oct. 9, 1810, Montg. Co., Md.
3. Stanislaus Edelen.
4. Mary Henrietta Edelen married Andrew M. Kirk. License D. C. Dec. 17, 1818.
5. Dennis Edelen.
6. Sarah Anne Edelen.

On May 14, 1790, as John Baptist Edelen "son and heir" of Philip Edelen, of Charles County, deceased, he deeded to Hezekiah Johnson for £23 "Friendship", beginning at the line of the heirs of Elizabeth Tarwin and the heirs of Richard Edelen. His wife Susannah waived dower.[1]

His will was dated March 22, 1819, but it was not proved in Charles County until October 3, 1822. He bequeathed his wife Helena one-third of the estate, and to his son John Henry $60 for his education. One-third of the estate was bequeathed to his four children—Harriett Clarke, Stanislaus Edelen, Mary Henrietta Kirk, and Dennis Edelen—and the other third to his children—Sarah Ann Edelen and John Henry Edelen. He named his brother Joseph Edelen and "the half brother to my wife William McAtee" as executors.[2]

Joseph Edelen, the brother and executor, died in December 1823 or January 1824. William McAtee, the half brother-in-law, continued as sole executor until his death in September or October 1824. The administration was then taken up by the testator's son Joseph (John) Henry Edelen who also died shortly afterwards leaving a widow Susan. On June 13, 1827, she rendered an account on the estate of her deceased husband as well as that of her husband's father John Baptist Edelen.

---

[1] Deeds, Liber J J no. 2, folio 259.
[2] Wills, Liber H B no 14, folio 214.

JAMES EDELEN[5]

(1777 - 1852)

James Edelen, son of James and Susan (Gardiner) Edelen, was born March 27, 1777, probably in Charles County. On February 23, 1804, he married Eleanor Davis.

A complete list of their children has not been established, but it is known that Amos, born Apr. 13, 1813, who married on September 1, 1836, Caroline Streaker, was a son. Nathan who was living with him in 1850, and who married Mary Shipley by license in Montgomery County on April 9, 1849, may possibly be a younger son.

He was domiciled in Montgomery County, Maryland, by the winter of 1839, inasmuch as on December 17, that year, he purchased from John H. T. Hays, of that county for a consideration of $1,397.74, portions of four contiguous tracts—"Resurvey on Hanover, Friendship, Hobson's Choice" and "Second Resurvey on Wolf's Cow". Ellen May Hays, wife, waived dower rights, while the witnesses were Leonard Hays and William E. Murphey. On May 13, 1843, he increased his holdings by the purchase of "Drane's Purchase" for $63.75 from Daniel Heffer, Sr. His wife Mary Ann Heffner joined in the deed, with Thomas C. Lannan and Elias Spalding as the witnesses.

According to the 1850 census, James Edelen, aged 73, was a farmer in the Third Election District of Montgomery County, with his wife Eleanor aged 69, Nathan Edelen aged 27, and Mary Edelen aged 23, comprising his household.

Obituaries state that he was born March 27, 1777, and died on March 21, 1852, in Montgomery County, and that his widow Eleanor was born November 18, 1780, and died September 28, 1852.

On April 8, 1852, his widow renounced the administration of the estate and requested that letters be granted to John W. Darby. The returns of the personal estate on April 20, showed an appraised value of $1,427.47½. The sale brought $1,658.18, with Nathan R. Edelen the only purchaser bearing the name of Edelen.

On May 4, 1852, Nathan Edelen acknowledged in court that he had an unsettled claim against the estate of James Edelen, by which the court appointed Nathan S. White and William J. Johnson to investigate. The court ultimately declared and ordered John W. Darby, the administrator, to pay Nathan Edelen $1,000 in full payment of his claim. It was furthermore declared at court that $80 was a fair annual rental for the realty of James Edelen, deceased.

On June 6, 1852, Nathan R. Edelen conveyed to John W. Darby, livestock, agricultural implements, blacksmith's tools, household furniture, etc., "for and in consideration that John White of B hath become security for me . . ." The price received for the personalty was $563.03 and $1.00.

CHARLES EDELEN[6]

(1794 - 18—)

Charles Edelen, son of Samuel and Mary (Suit) Edelen, was born about 1794 in Maryland. He migrated with his parents to Kentucky as a youngster, and there in Washington County he secured license on April 11, 1818, to marry Anne, the daughter of Henry Morland (Worland).

At the census of 1850, he was the head of a family, aged 56, and his wife Charity A., aged 55 and born in Maryland. Other members of his household, all born in Kentucky, were Henry D. Boone, aged 34; Mary C. Boone, aged 30; Charles H. Boone, 12; Thomas J. Edelen, 10; Christopher Edelen, 7; Maritina Edelen, 6; and Elizabeth Edelen, aged 3.

EDWARD EDELEN, GENT.[2]
(1676 - 1756)
AND
HIS DESCENDANTS

Edward Edelen, son of Richard and Elizabeth Edelen, was born about 1676 in St. Mary's County, inasmuch as in 1730 he declared himself to be about 54 years of age. By his father's will he inherited a portion of "Dublin", where he established his dwelling-plantation and which in 1695 became incorporated in the new county of Prince Georges.

About 1707 he married Elizabeth, the widow of Moses Jones, of Prince Georges County, and the daughter of Thomas and Anne Jenkins, of Charles County. Moses Jones died in 1706, and left besides his widow six minor children—John, Thomas, Notley, Jane, Anne, and Elizabeth.[1] The tracts "Thomas Chance" and "Pinner" held by Edward Edelen at his death were formerly a part of the estate of Moses Jones.

In 1708 Edward Edelen "who marryed Elizabeth the executrix of Moses Jones" petitioned the court to pass his account upon the estate.[2] It seems as if the estate was not settled until many years thereafter. In April 1715 he submitted an account, and others in May 1725, and December 1726.[3]

At an account filed on May 7, 1727, it distinctively states "Edward Edelen who married the relict of Moses Jones". He accounted for a disbursement to "Christopher Edelen who married the said Jones' daughter" as well as one to "Robert Innis who married another daughter". The balance due the heirs on that date was 13 shillings and 5 pence.[4]

Children of Edward and Elizabeth (Jenkins) Edelen

1. Sarah Edelen, born Feb. 18, 1705/6, married Feb. 17, 1723/4, Samuel Queen. Issue: Samuel, born Jan. 13, 1724/5; Edward, born Jan. 15, 1726/7; Catherine, born Oct. 2, 1731; Sarah, born Oct. 1734. He died testate 1734, and widow married Feb. 25, 1735/6, Edward Pye. Issue: Elizabeth, born Dec. 15, 17—; Walter; Margaret. (Births from Rock Creek Parish.)
2. James Edelen married Salome Noble. *q.v.*

Thomas Jenkins, the father of Elizabeth Jones-Edelen, died in 1727, and bequeathed his daughter Elizabeth Edelen a portion of the personal estate.[5] At the final account on April 28, 1731, it was shown that the estate had been overpaid by the executors, Edward Jenkins and William Jenkins, "who were the executors of Ann Jenkins who was the executrix of Thomas Jenkins".[6]

At this time it was also shown that the wife of Edward Edelen was deceased and that her share of her father's estate was paid to "James Edelen one of the said Elizabeth Edelen's children" and to "Samuel Queen husband to Sarah Queen daughter of Elizabeth Edelen".[6]

In 1726 Edward Edelen was the administrator of the estate of Christopher Scaines, at which time Peter Dent and John Stoddert were his bondsmen.[7] On August 17, 1727, he and Edward Jenkins signed the bond of Susannah Jenkins, the administratrix of George Jenkins. On September 13, 1742, he and Walter Pye signed the bond of Edward Pye, the administrator of Walter Pye. And on January 28, 1745/6, he and William Neale, Jr., signed the bond of Mary Neale, the executrix of Benjamin Neale.

On July 10, 1713, Edward Edelen, of Prince Georges County, purchased from Richard Edelen and Sarah his wife 'Thomas Chance" which had been purchased at one time from John Hawkins. John Rozer and J. Lemon were the witnesses.[8]

On February 15, 1719, Thomas Jenkins, of Charles County, yeoman, and Anne his wife conveyed to Edward Edelen, of Prince Georges County, carpenter, for the love which they held for their daughter, Elizabeth Edelen, wife of said Edward, "Pinnar" in Prince Georges County, which had been patented by George Shenst and assigned to Thomas Jenkins on November 20, 1674. It adjoined "Locust Thickett". The witnesses were William Machenchie, Robert Hanson, and Thomas Stone.[9]

On June 15, 1728, Edward Edelen assigned to James Reed, of Prince Georges County, a portion of "Calvert Manor", lying on Ackakick Branch.[10] On March 21, 1736/7, Edward Edelen, planter, assigned "Pinner" of 200 acres at Piscataway to Edward Pye to be held in trust for Henry Queen until he arrived at majority. John Addison and Charles Willett witnessed the trust.[11]

Edward Edelen, of Prince Georges County, Gent., on October 9, 1741, leased a portion of "Calvert Manor" to Robert Thompson, of Charles County, for the consideration of rent. The witnesses were Thomas Marshall, Thomas Owen, and Thomas Bates.[12]

On February 24, 1742/3, Edward Edelen, Gent., deeded to Joseph Noble, Gent., a portion of "Littleworth", lying in Piscataway Town. The witnesses were Peter Dent and John Hawkins, Jr.[13] On the same day, he deeded to Edward Pye for one shilling a lot in Piscataway Town.[14] On July 15, 1749, he conveyed to John Baynes for a consideration of £8 a lot in Piscataway, being a portion of "Littleworth". Henry Queen and Charles Blandford were the witnesses.[15] On March 6,

1753/4, he assigned a portion of "Calvert alias Elizabeth Manor" to Ignatius Wheeler. Peter Dent and George Fraser were the witnesses.[16]

According to the Debt Books, Edward Edelen in 1755, the last year before his death, paid quit rent on the following tracts: "St. Thomas' Chance" of 100 acres, "Little Ease" of 140 acres, "Littleworth" of 28 acres, "No Name" of 300 acres, and "Never Fear" of 15 acres. In addition he paid rent on "Pinner" of 200 acres which was being held for his grandson Henry Queen.

Edward Edelen made his will on February 22, 1745, but the latter was not admitted to probate until March 30, 1756.[17] His son James was devised "Thomas Chance" of 200 acres, "Little Ease" of 140 acres, and "Littleworth" of 29 acres. He left his brother Christopher that portion of "Dublin" upon which Christopher was then living. He bequeathed his daughter Sarah Pye £15, and devised his grandson Henry Queen "Pinner", but in the event that Henry died without issue then to Henry's sisters Catherine and Sarah.* Numerous slaves and other personalty, including silver plate, were bequeathed to the following grandchildren: Catherine Edelen, Edward Edelen, Elizabeth Edelen, Mary Edelen, Salome Edelen, Walter Pye, and Margaret Pye.

[1] Wills, Liber 3, folio 637.
[2] Test. Pro., Liber 21, folio 3.
[3] *Ibid.*, Liber 22, folio 458.
[4] Adm. Accts., Liber 8, folio 167.
[5] Wills, Liber 19, folio 251.
[6] Adm. Accts., Liber 10, folio 695.
[7] Test. Pro., Liber 27, folio 371.
[8] Deeds, Liber E, folio 350, Marlboro.
[9] Deeds, Liber F, folio 287.
[10] Deeds, Liber M, folio 295.
[11] Deeds, Liber T, folio 454.
[12][13][14] Deeds, Liber Y, folios 413, 608, 644.
[15] Deeds, Liber B B, folio 666.
[16] Deeds, Liber N N, folio 108.
[17] Wills, Liber 30, folio 58.

JAMES EDELEN, GENT.[3]

(1710 - 1768)

James Edelen, son of Edward and Elizabeth (Jenkins) Edelen, was born April 14, 1710, in Piscataway Parish, Prince Georges County. About 1740 he married Salome Noble. She was born April 23, 1724, in Piscataway Parish, the daughter of Joseph Noble, Gent. The latter was born April 17, 1689, at Cockemouth, County Cumberland, England, the

* Henry Queen died in St. Mary's County in 1768 and devised "Pinner" to his sisters—Catherine Edelen and Sarah Jameson.

son of Joseph Noble and Catherine his wife. In Maryland on February 2, 1708/9, he was married to Mary Wheeler, born November 14, 1693, the daughter of Francis and Winifred (Green) Wheeler.

Joseph Noble, by his will dated December 6, 1747, and proved in Prince Georges County on January 15, 1749/50, devised his dwelling-plantation "Littleworth", which he had purchased from Edward Edelen to his wife Mary during life, then to his son John Noble. The personal estate was bequeathed to his widow during life, then to be divided equally among his named children among whom was Salome Edelen.[1] At the administration of the estate on March 9, 1750/1, cash was delivered to James Edelen and John Bayne, merchants, and it was shown that Salome Edelen was one of the heirs.[2] The will of his widow, Mary Noble, was proved in Prince Georges County on April 14, 1766, at which time her daughter Salome was an heir.[3]

Children of James and Salome (Noble) Edelen

1. Elizabeth Edelen married Thomas Dent. *q.v.*
2. Mary Noble Edelen married Henry Stonestreet, Adjutant of Md. Militia Rev. War, son of Butler and Jane (Edelen), Stonestreet. Issue: Jane; Mary Noble; Lewis; Henry; Nicholas; Joseph Noble.
3. Edward Edelen, born 1747, *d.s.p. q.v.*
4. Samuel Edelen, born 1762, *d.s.p. q.v.*
5. James Edelen, born 1764, *d.s.p. q.v.*
6. Catherine Salome Edelen, born 1754, died spinster 1786, naming mother; sister Margaret and her dau. Jane Stonestreet; brothers Samuel and James.
7. Margaret Edelen, born 1756, married Richard, son of Butler and Jane (Edelen) Stonestreet.
8. Joseph Edelen married Catherine Alice Edelen. *q.v.*
9. Sarah Edelen, born 1760, married Charles Pye. Issue: Charles; Caroline; James B.
10. Martha Edelen.

On February 27, 1739/40, James Edelen and Edward Pye signed the bond of Elizabeth Innis, the administratrix of Dr. Robert Innis. And on July 16, 1750, he and Henry Queen, the latter of Charles County, became bondsmen for Sarah Pye, the executor of Edward Pye.

On April 23, 1743, James Edelen purchased from an attorney for Charles Pye, of Prince Georges County, "Marian's Disturbance". George Fraser and John Hawkins signed the deed as witnesses.[4] On November 2, 1748, James Edelen, Gent., purchased from Catherine Plasay, of Prince Georges County, Innholder, for 10 shillings "Craft", near Piscataway Town. Luke Marbury and John Hawkins, Jr., witnessed. On the same day he bought a portion of "Partnership" from John Jones "son of John Jones who was son and heir to Moses Jones who in company with a certain William Hutcherson" had patented that tract. Elizabeth Jones, wife of John, waived dower, while John Wheeler and John Sutton witnessed the conveyance. On the same day he also purchased another portion of "Friendship" from Nehemiah Wade and Eleanor his wife. Henry Truman and John Hawkins, Jr., witnessed.[5] On June 9, 1750, he leased a portion of "Friendship", lying near Broad Creek to Joseph Simpson for 20 years and another portion to James Thorn, carpenter, for the same period. James Mullikin and John Wheeler witnessed.[6]

In 1759 James Edelen conveyed to Thomas Marshall, of Charles County, for £15 a portion of "Calvert's Manor" which had been granted originally to William Calvert. J. Hepburn and William Elson signed the deed as witnesses.[7] On June 24, 1761, he deeded to George Harding a portion of "Littleworth" in Piscataway which began "at the post of Mrs. Mary Noble's garden". Nathaniel Magruder and Thomas Williams were the witnesses.[8]

On August 26, 1761, he sold to Robert Todd, of Prince Georges County, Merchant, another portion of "Littleworth".[9] And on November 25, same year, he conveyed to Joseph Boarman, planter, "land lately possessed by Edward Edelen, Sr., being granted to William Calvert, Esq., called Piscattaway Manor otherwise Calvert alias Elizabeth Manor" adjoining the land of Thomas and George Noble. Thomas Williams and David Crawford signed as witnesses.[10]

On October 22, 1766, he purchased from Jesse Lanham and Eleanor his wife of Prince Georges County the tract known as "Two Johns". John Contee and James Kirk were the witnesses.[11] On February 10, 1768, he bought of Notley Jones, of Prince Georges County, "Lyon's Hole", of 50 acres. Eleanor Jones, wife, waived her rights, while Thomas Hanson Marshall and George Hardy, Jr., witnessed.[12] On the same day, he sold to Thomas Dyer "Edelen's Rest", lying on Tinker's Creek. Salome Edelen, his wife, waived her dower rights.[13]

On December 13, 1755, James Edelen, planter, purchased from William Smallwood, of Charles County, for £32 "Friendship". Mary Smallwood, wife, granted consent, while Thomas Stone and Daniel of St. Thomas Jenifer were the witnesses.[14]

In 1753 according to the Debt Book, James Edelen remitted rents on the following tracts in Prince Georges County: "James" of 166 acres; "Partnership" of 25 acres; "Hazard" of 5 acres; and "Friendship" of 200 acres. In 1758 his estate had increased considerably—"James" of 166 acres; "New Ship" of 25 acres; "Hazard" of 5 acres; "Friendship" of 200 acres; "Little Ease" of 140 acres; "Littleworth" of 27 acres; "No Name" of 300 acres; "Never Fear" of 15 acres; and "St. Thomas' Chance" of 200 acres. In 1771 his heirs paid rents on "James" of 166 acres; "Littleworth" of 27 acres; "Littleease" of 140 acres; "Never Fear" of 15 acres; "Friendship" of 200 acres; and "Edelen's Enlargment" of 215 acres. The latter tract James Edelen had patented in 1762.

The will of James Edelen was dated March 7, 1768, and proved in Prince Georges County on June 28, 1768.[15] His eldest son Edward received "Edelen's Enlargement" of 215 acres, "Little Ease" of 140 acres, "Littleworth" of 27 acres, "Never Fear" of 15 acres, and "Hazard" of 5 acres.

Joseph was devised "Friendship" lying near Broad Creek containing 200 acres, "Two Johns" of 18 acres, "Lyon's Hole" of 50 acres, and numerous slaves. Samuel received tracts on the Mattawoman in Charles County, a portion of "Friendship", a portion of "Smallwood's Meadows" of 106 acres, and also one-half of his father's interest in the mill, including the land, and also a lot in Piscataway Town where Mr. Burrell formerly lived, but if he died without issue then his share to his brother James. The latter was devised "Apple Door" consisting of 110 acres, "Rome" of 27 acres, but in the event he died without issue then to Samuel. The sons were to be of age at 19 years.

The following daughters — Elizabeth, Mary, Catherine, Salome, Margaret, and Sarah—all were to receive £30 each at 16 or day of marriage. After the widow had deducted her third from the personal estate, the residue was to be divided among the children.

The inventory of the personal estate was returned by Edward Edelen, the executor, on November 21, 1768, and showed an appraisement of £991/15/2. Sarah Pye and Christopher Edelen signed the papers as the next of kin.

The final account was rendered to the court on January 4, 1770, by Edward Edelen, Jr., the executor, and showed distribution to the following—the widow, and children—Elizabeth, Mary, Salome, Martha, Sarah, Joseph, Samuel, and James.

At the census of 1776 in St. John's Parish, Salome Edelen was the head of the house. In addition to her daughters, Catherine S. Edelen, Margaret Edelen, and Sarah Edelen, and her sons Edward, Joseph, Samuel, and James, there were in her immediate family Betty Gill aged 44 and Catherine Curtain aged 60. She also owned 24 slaves.

Their bachelor son, James Edelen, became a well known and affluent physician of southern Maryland. On September 28, 1790, he sold to Thomas Clagett, merchant, "Apple Door" adjoining "Hawkins' Lott" and "Rome", being the line between the lands of Thomas and Christopher Edelen and containing 110 acres. Thomas Marshall and William Baker witnessed the sale.* On April 13, 1792, he purchased from Hoskins Hanson and Ignatius Matthews, trustees for Walter Pye, land on Cornwallis Neck known as "Hall's Lease". The witnesses were Henry Barnes and James Freeman.[16] On September 3, 1796, Henry Stonestreet, of Charles County, conveyed to Dr. James Edelen, of Charles County, "Cornwallis' Neck". Mary Stonestreet, wife, waived dower, while John Dent and William H. McPherson witnessed the deed.[17] Five days later Dr. James Edelen purchased from Charles Pye, of Charles County, a portion of "Cornwallis' Neck". Sarah Pye, wife, relinquished her third.[18]

James Edelen died a bachelor at the age of 60 years. His will, dated August 13, 1813, was proved in Prince Georges County on January 8, 1814. He requested that his realty be sold for the benefit of the estate and bequeathed more than $22,000 to various kinsmen. From his will, one can obtain several marriages of his sisters. His heirs were brothers: Joseph and Samuel; sisters: Elizabeth Dent, Margaret Stonestreet, Sarah Pye, and Mary Stonestreet; nieces and nephews: Jane Digges, Mary N. Stonestreet, Lewis Stonestreet, Nicholas Stonestreet, Joseph N. Stonestreet, James B. Pye, Charles Pye, Caroline Pye, and William Lewis Dent. George W. Dent, no relationship stated, was bequeathed $250 and named executor. Legacies were also left to Walter S. Parker, Nehemiah Crawford, and the Rev. John Fenwick.[19]

On October 4, 1819, Joseph Edelen, Sr., and Nicholas Stonestreet, the executors of Dr. James Edelen, deeded to Richard L. Jenkins for a consideration of $3,124 "Cornwallis Neck".[20]

---

[1] Wills, Liber 27, folio 141.
[2] Adm. Accts., Liber 29, folio 222.
[3] Wills, Liber 34, folio 193.
[4] Deeds, Liber Y, folio 687, Marlborough.
[5] Deeds, Liber BB, folios 557-560.
[6,7] Deeds, Liber PP, folios 55, 57, 287.
[8,9,10] Deeds, Liber R R, folios 140, 153, 218.
[11] Deeds, Liber T T, folio 652.
[12,13] Deeds, Liber B B no. 2, folios 202, 203.
[14] Deeds, Liber A no. 3, pt. 2, folio 421, La Plata.
[15] Wills, Liber 36, folio 593.
[16,17] Deeds, Liber K no. 4, folio 437, La Plata.
[18] Deeds, Liber I B no. 2, folios 55, 56, La Plata.
[19] Wills, Liber T T no. 1, folio 80.
[20] Deeds, Liber I B no. 13, folio 264, La Plata.

---

* Deeds, Liber I I no. 2, folio 454.

EDWARD EDELEN[4]

(1747 - 1811)

Edward Edelen, son of James and Salome (Noble) Edelen, was born in or about the year 1747, near Piscataway. By the will of his father in 1768, he received "Edelen's Enlargement", "Little Ease", portions of "Littleworth", "Never Fear", and "Hazard". He was a staunch patriot during the Revolutionary War. He and Thomas Dent were among those present who attended a meeting of the Committee of Observation for Prince Georges at the home of Richard Carnes in Piscataway on Friday, August 4, 1775.

On October 25, 1772, Edward Edelen purchased from Barton Philphott and Martha his wife, of Prince Georges County, "Locust Thickett" for £700, adjoining the lands of Benjamin Musgrove and Elizabeth Simpson. John Baynes and George Fraser Hawkins witnessed the sale.[2]

On January 6, 1775, he purchased from Thomas Clagett, of Prince Georges County, merchant, for £18/8/9 "Something and Merry Thought Enlarged". Mary Meek Clagett, wife, waived dower, while the witnesses were John Baynes and Luke Marbury.[3]

On June 18, 1779, as Edward Edelen, Jr., he purchased from John Wynn, of Prince Georges County, "Addition to Edelen's Courtesy", then called Wynn's Middle Lot for a consideration of £2,000. No wife waived dower, while the witnesses were Thomas Clagett and William Lyles, Jr.[3]

On December 8, 1785, he sold to Henrietta Dyer for £75 a lot in Piscataway Town. Thomas Clagett and H. Rozer witnessed the sale, but no wife waived dower.[4] On June 26, 1786, he sold to Henry Hardey, Jr., a lot in Piscataway Town, being a portion of "Littleworth". No wife waived dower, while the witnesses were Fielder Bowie and Samuel Hepburn.[4]

It was recorded on November 27, 1792, that Richard Carnes, of St. Mary's County, was bound unto Edward Edelen, of Prince Georges County, for 7200 pounds of tobacco upon the condition that "Richard Carnes shall make over by a sufficient deed portion of two tracts 'Littleworth' and 'Leith', containing 1¼ acres, now in the possession of Richard Edelen as lenient". The land had been assigned by Edward Edelen on June 22, 1781, to Bennett Edelen. The indenture was attested to by Thomas Dent and Bennett Edelen.[5]

On March 25, 1802, he purchased from Charles Pye, of Charles County, for £20,000 land which had been patented by Thomas Cornwallis on September 11, 1665, called "Cornwallis Neck" or "Mattawoman Neck". R. Sprigg and James Edelen witnessed the deed.[6] The next day he transferred this tract to Charles Pye.[6] And September 20, 1804, there is another deed of Edward Edelen, of Prince Georges County, transferring "Cornwallis Neck" to Charles Pye, of Charles County.[7]

There is also a deed in Prince Georges County of Edward Edelen and Elivira Hardy, widow of George Dent Hardy, of Prince Georges County, selling negroes to Richard Ponsonby for £115.

The will of Edward Edelen was dated March 27, 1809, and proved in Prince Georges County on April 3, 1811, by Walter Edelen, Gavin Hamilton, and William Marshall, Jr. He bequeathed his entire estate to his brother James.[8]

---

[1] Archives, vol. II.
[2] Deeds, Liber B B no. 3, folio 94.
[3] *Ibid.*, Liber C C no. 2, folios 102, 641.
[4] *Ibid.*, Liber H H, folios 43, 142.
[5] *Ibid.*, Liber I R M no. 1, folio 372.
[6] *Ibid.*, Liber I B no. 5, folios 134, 135, La Plata.
[7] *Ibid.*, Liber I B no. 6, folio 228.
[8] Wills, T T no. 1, folio 39.

SAMUEL EDELEN[4]

(1752 - 18—)

Samuel Edelen, son of James and Salome (Noble) Edelen, was born in or about the year 1752 near Piscataway. By the will of his father in 1768, he received land on the Mattawoman in Charles County, namely "Friendship" and "Smallwood's Meadow".

On October 2, 1792, "Samuel Edelen of James" purchased from Elixis Hagan, of Prince Georges County, the land known as 'Strife" which adjoined the land of Joseph Clark and which had been willed to Thomas Edelen Green by his father. David Crawford and Samuel Hepburn witnessed the sale, but no wife waived dower.[1]

On November 1, 1793, he sold "Friendship" and "Hopewell" to Walter Bayne Smallwood, of Charles County. No wife waived dower, while the witnesses were Joseph Noble Baynes and Nicholas Young.[2] On the same day, he sold for a consideration of £500 several tracts to Henry Smallwood, of Charles County. The land was originally granted on November 20, 1766, to Nathaniel Hally, another portion had been granted on May 6, 1748, to John Hally known as "Costly's Addition", and a portion of "Hopewell" granted on July 3, 1699, to William Dent, and "Meadows Enlarged" granted to him (Samuel Edelen) on February 21, 1789.[3]

On February 6, 1798, "Samuel Edelen of James", of Prince Georges County, conveyed to John H. Beanes, of the same county, for a consideration of £586 "Strife" which had formerly been assigned to Thomas Edelen Green by his father.[4] No wife waived dower.

On February 11, 1802, he purchased from William L. Bowling, of Prince Georges County, for the consideration of 5 shillings land on the Mattawoman. No wife waived dower; the witnesses were William Marshall and Robert A. Beall. On June 10, of the same year, he purchased from James F. Green, of Prince Georges County, for £104 land adjoining the estates of Thomas Bowling and Thomas Green.[5]

On January 21, 1804, Samuel Edelen, of Prince Georges County, conveyed to Walter B. Smallwood for £550 "Meadow's Enlarged". No wife waived dower, while the witnesses were Richard S. Briscoe and Benjamin Cawood.[6]

---

[1] Deeds, Liber J R M, folio 325, Marlboro.
[2] *Ibid.*, Liber N no. 4, folios 215, 216, La Plata.
[4] *Ibid.*, Liber I R M no. 6, folio 6, Marlboro.
[5] *Ibid.*, Liber I R M no. 9, folios 198, 249.
[6] *Ibid.*, Liber I B no. 6, folio 15, La Plata.

JOSEPH EDELEN[4]

(1757 - 1833)

Joseph Edelen, son of James and Salome (Noble) Edelen, was born in or about 1757 in Prince Georges County. During 1778 he took the oath of allegiance and fidelity to the State of Maryland in that county.[1] On February 26, 1788, he secured license in Prince Georges County to marry his kinswoman Catherine Alice, born December 10, 1772, daughter of Joseph and Catherine (Queen) Edelen.

Children of Joseph and Alice (Edelen) Edelen

1. William Marshall Edelen married Barbara Gantt, Ann Blake, and Jane Blake.
2. Joseph Edelen, *d.s.p.*
3. James Noble Edelen married Margaret Tolson. *q.v.*
4. Henry Alfred Edelen, *d.s.p.*
5. Aloysius Noble Edelen married Eleanor Kirby. License Pr. Geo. July 14, 1831.
6. Edward Charles Edelen, *d.s.p.*
7. Horace Edelen married Eleanor Tolson. *q.v.*
8. Mary Olivia Edelen, born June 8, 1808, married Thomas Felix, born about 1793 near Port Tobacco, son of Benedict Joseph and

Henrietta (Thompson) Semmes.* Issue: Thomas Felix; Alfred; Celestia; Mary Josephine; James Hall; Emily Edelen;
Thomas Felix, II.

9. Teresa Celestia Edelen married Samuel Chapman McPherson.
License July 15, 1828, Pr. Geo. Co.

10. Emily Elizabeth Edelen, born Mar. 22, 1800, died Feb. 5, 1853,
married Nov. 11, 1823, Benedict Joseph, son of Benedict Joseph
and Henrietta (Thompson) Semmes. Issue: Henrietta; Charlotte; Benedict Joseph, I; Matilda; Eugenia; Benedict Joseph,
II; Alice; Celestia.

11. Salome Caroline Edelen married William Mason, of Va. License
June 30, 1817, Pr. Geo. Co.

12. Margaret Matilda Edelen married Theodore William Maurice.
License July 16, 1819, Pr. Geo. Co.

13. Catherine Queen Edelen married John H. Bean. License Jan. 29,
1817, Pr. Geo.

14. Samuel Edelen.

15. George Washington Edelen, *d.s.p.*

The seat of Joseph Edelen was at Mt. Airy near Piscataway. On
November 30, 1779, he purchased from Elisha Lanham, of Prince
Georges County, for £275 "Fox's Hole" and "Dickinson Lott". No
wife waived dower; the witnesses were Thomas Clagett and William
Lyles, Jr.[2] On June 19, 1781, he conveyed to Edward Magruder "Friend-
ship", at which time William Lyles, Jr., and H. Rozer witnessed.[3]

On September 9, 1790, Joseph Edelen purchased from John Magruder Burgess, Gent., of Prince Georges County, and Eleanor his wife,
land which had been willed to the said Eleanor by her father Enoch
Magruder. David Crawford and John Hepburn were the witnesses.[4]

On August 2, 1792, he conveyed to Giles Dyer several tracts near
Piscataway adjoining the land of Richard Stonestreet. Catherine Edelen,
his wife, waived dower, while the witnesses were John Smith Brookes
and Samuel Hepburn. On November 27, same year, Dyer assigned the
same tracts to him, at which time his wife, Susannah Dyer, waived her
dower rights.[5]

On March 30, 1796, Joseph Edelen and Alice his wife, conveyed to
John Tompkins, of Charles County, "Tompkins' Purchase", formerly
sold to Edward Turner, to Ralph Smith, and also to Newman Tompkins
and George Dent. Francis C. Dyer and Nicholas Young witnessed the
transfer.[6]

On November 20, 1824, Joseph Edelen and Alice his wife, of Prince
Georges County, sold "Docker's Delight" to William Bateman, of

---

* Mary Olivia Edelen married 2 June 1835, at Mount Air, Prince Georges
County, Thomas F. Semmes of Washington. (Natl. Intelligence, 5 June 1835.)

Charles County, inasmuch as Alice Edelen was "one of the sisters and co-heiresses of Joseph Edelen, late of Charles County, deceased". B. I. Semmes and Raphael C. Edelen signed the deed as witnesses.[7]

He died at his seat Mount Air near Piscataway on January 4, 1833. The notice was carried in the National Intelligence as of January 12, 1833.

His will was dated May 11, 1827, and admitted to probate on February 20, 1833, in Prince Georges County. He provided that certain portions of his estate were to be maintained by his executors for the support of his widow and three single children—two daughters and a son. Funds were arranged for the education of his son William until twenty-one years of age. Seven years after his death certain personalty were to be divided among his five daughters. Joseph was devised the land on the west side of the road leading from Colonel Samuel Coe to Piscataway beginning at "Locust Thickett". James was devised the land lying near to that of Dr. William Marshall and Philip J. Ford. Henry Alfred was willed a portion of "Locust Thickett" which had been purchased by Edward Edelen from Samuel Edelen and also the tract "Edelen's Courtesy". Aloysius was devised the forest land or Gater's Place being portions of "Marlow's Resurvey" and "Wynn's Middle Lot." His son Dr. Horace Edelen was also willed realty as well as William M. Edelen. Slaves were bequeathed to the following children: Joseph, James, Henry Alfred, Aloysius, Horace, Mary Olivia, and Teresa Celestia. Sons Joseph and Alfred were named as executors.[8]

The following notice was carried in the National Intelligence on January 20, 1847, upon the death of the widow. "Mrs. Catherine A. Edelen died on 12 instant at the residence of her son Dr. Horatio Edelen near Piscataway, Prince Georges County, in the 77th year, widow of the late Joseph Edelen".

[1] Brumbaugh, vol. 2.
[2] Deeds, Liber C C, folio 694.
[3] *Ibid.*, Liber F F no. 1, folio 157.
[4] *Ibid.*, Liber II no. 32, folio 409.
[5] *Ibid.*, Liber J R M no. 1, folios 376, 436.
[6] *Ibid.*, I B no. 2, folio 63.
[7] *Ibid.*, I B no. 16, folio 208.
[8] Wills, Liber T T no. 1, folio 509.

COLONEL JAMES NOBLE EDELIN, U.S.M.C.[5]

(1790 - 1869)

James Noble Edelen, son of Joseph and Alice (Edelen) Edelen, was born in 1790 at Mount Airy, near Piscataway, Maryland. Shortly after the ratification of the Treaty of Ghent which concluded the War of 1812, he was commissioned a second lieutenant in the United States Marine Corps by President Madison. His commission was dated March 1, 1815, with his name inadvertently spelled Edelin—rather than change it, he continued to use this spelling which was later adapted by his brothers and sisters.

Within a short time he was ordered to sea duty and while in France a British naval officer by the name of Edelen visited his ship during his absence and expressed the desire to be presented to the young American officer who bore his name. It was only a short time after the cessation of hostilities between the two countries and feeling against the British was then quite intense. When his commanding officer related the incident to him, he replied, "Damned glad I was not here. I do not wish to meet him even if he is a distant kinsman". The officers present on the ship remarked about the physical resemblance between the two Edelens.

On April 18, 1817, he was promoted to first lieutenant, and on April 18, 1827, he was brevetted captain, owing to legislation enacted in July 1812, whereby the President was empowered "to confer brevet rank on such officers of the Army or the Marine Corps, as shall have served ten years in any one grade". On July 1, 1834, he received full recognition and compensation as captain.

On March 1, 1836, while stationed at the Marine Barracks in Washington, he was ordered to the field with the Army. And it was during this time that he participated in the Seminole Indian War of 1835 to 1842, the fiercest of all wars waged by the United States against the Indians. On April 28, 1837, he was ordered to sea duty on the U.S.S. Macedonian. During the Mexican War of 1846-48, he was the commanding officer of the Marine guard on board the U.S.S. Independence of the Pacific Squadron. On September 14, 1847, he was advanced to the rank of major.

At four different periods he was commandant of the Marine Barracks in Washington—from November 1835 to June 1839, October 1841 to August 1846, August 1848 to October 1853, and August 1857 to February 1859. Among the various vessels on which he served at sea were the U.S.S. Brandywine in 1828, U.S.S. Macedonian in 1837, U.S.S. Independence in 1846, and the U.S.S. Erie in 1847.

At the beginning of the Civil War he was stationed at the Marine Barracks at Norfolk, Virginia. On April 26, 1861, he was ordered to the barracks at Philadelphia and remained there until June 1, 1861, when he was detached and ordered to Boston. On November 15, 1861, at the age of 70 he was placed on the retired list with the rank of lieutenant colonel. His retirement owing to age at that time avoided embarrassments during the War Between the States—as his native section of Maryland was strongly Confederate in sympathy and action.

On December 29, 1829, he had secured license in Prince Georges County to marry Margaret McPherson Tolson, a maiden of distinguished lineage. The ceremony was performed a few days later in Charles County. The Tolsons of Maryland descend from Henry Tolson, of Woodhall, Brightchurch Parish, County Cumberland, England, while the McPhersons were scions of one of those two well known clans of Scotland—the Macphersons of Invereshie and Macphersons of Ballindalloch. The present residence of the Cluny (chief) is Cluny Castle, Kingussie, Inverness-shire, Scotland.

Children of James and Margaret (Tolson) Edelin

1. Emily Edelin, born 1831, died 1856, at Norfolk, Va., married Dr. Charles Williamson, U. S. N.
2. Thomas Boyd Edelin, born Sept. 1833, died Feb. 1902, married Isabella Lee Whiting.
3. Margaret Tolson Edelin married James Hamilton. *q.v.*

His wife died in 1843 in Prince Georges County while he was Commandant of the Marine Barracks at Washington. He afterwards married Nancy, the daughter of Overton and Cloe (Lea) Carr. She died on September 5, 1852, leaving no issue. Colonel Edelin died on July 13, 1869, at Piscataway at the age of 79.

DR. HORACE EDELEN[5]

(1804 - 1882)

Horace Edelen, son of Joseph and Catherine Alice (Edelen) Edelen, was born June 12, 1804, at Mount Airy, Prince Georges County. On February 13, 1827, he secured license in Prince Georges County to marry Eleanor Catherine Tolson.

Children of Horace and Eleanor (Tolson) Edelin

1. Alfred Edelin, born 1828, Col., U.S.A., *d.s.p.*, married Sidney Bradley, of Washington.
2. Edmonia Edelin, married John Beatty Semmes. *q.v.*
3. Horace Edelin, born 1832, *d.s.p.* 1870.
4. Francis Edelin, born 1835, *d.s.p.* 1859.
5. Margaret Alice Edelin, born 1836, *d.s.p.* 1851.
6. James Alexander Edelin, born 1837, *d.s.p.* 1857.
7. George Augustus Edelin, born 1838, *d.s.p.* 1852.
8. Thomas Edelin, born 1839, *d.s.p.* 1860.
9. Eleanor Catherine Edelin, born Oct. 31, 1842, died Jan. 31, 1899, married Dr. Walter Clarke Briscoe, son of Richard Gerard and Anna (Clarke) Briscoe. Only surviving issue, Rosalie Edelin.

10. Rosalie Edelin, born Dec. 23, 1844, died spinster June 29, 1927.
11. Robley Dungleson Edelin, born 1845, *d.s.p.* Jan. 12, 1899.

Horace Edelin was a well known physician of southern Maryland and resided at the old Edelin estate "Mount Airy" near Piscataway. To demonstrate the losses which the Southern Maryland gentry sustained during the War Between the States, Dr. Edelin in 1860, according to the census, had realty appraised at $20,000 and personalty, including slaves, at $15,000. The 1870 census recorded realty at $18,000, and through the emancipation of slaves his personal estate had declined to $2,000.

The *Baltimore Sun* of January 16, 1875, carried the following notice: "Died at Mount Airy, Prince Georges County, 11 January 1875, Mrs. Eleanor C., wife of Dr. Horace Edelin in her 68th year".

Dr. Edelin died on June 26, 1882.

Margaret Tolson Edelin[6]
(1843 - 1923)

Margaret Tolson Edelin, daughter to Colonel James Edelin and Margaret his wife, was born July 14, 1843, in Prince Georges County. On November 12, 1867, at Washington she was married to James Alexander Hamilton, the son of George Ernest and Sarah Anne (Boone) Hamilton. He was born in 1836 near Port Tobacco, Maryland, where his Scotch Hamilton ancestors had lived for more than a hundred years.

Children of James and Margaret (Edelin) Hamilton
1. Alexander Edelin Hamilton, *d.s.p.*
2. James Noble Edelin Hamilton, of Montana and Washington, D.C.
3. Mary Louise Hamilton married twice. *q.v.*

James Alexander Hamilton was a prominent financier of Washington, D. C., and died there on March 12, 1915. His widow continued to maintain her residence in the National Capital and died there on February 5, 1923.

Their daughter, Mary Louise, married first Littell Wilson, of Richmond, Virginia, by whom were born: Alexander Hamilton Wilson and Margaret Edelin Wilson. The son is an outstanding architect of the National Capital and married Isabelle Murphy, by whom were born Alexander Hamilton, II; Mary Louise; Littell Edward; James Montgomery; Marguerite Isabelle; and Donna Edelin. Littell Wilson died on February 18, 1903. His widow married secondly Henry Spencer Powell, of Cincinnati, Ohio, son of Henry Spencer Powell, I. He died on September 14, 1917, leaving one son—Henry Spencer Powell, III, who married Eulalie Mehlhop.

EDMONIA EDELEN[6]
(1829 - 1903)

Edmonia Edelen, daughter of Horace and Eleanor (Tolson) Edelen, was born at Mount Airy, near Piscataway, December 26, 1830. On February 1, 1860, at Mount Airy, she was married to John Beatty Semmes, who had secured license in Prince Georges County on January 27, 1860. He was born December 14, 1826, in Georgetown, D. C., the son of Alexander and Eleanor Harrison (Beatty) Semmes. He died on November 19, 1865, leaving a young widow who survived until April 13, 1903.

Children of John and Edmonia (Edelen) Semmes
1. Son, died young.
2. Alexander Harrison Semmes. *q.v.*
3. Eleanor May Semmes, born 1864, died 1865.

Alexander Harrison Semmes, the only surviving issue, was born December 7, 1861, at Washington, D. C., and was thus only a youngster at the death of his father in 1865. On April 15, 1891, at Washington, he married Mary Hodges who was born June 6, 1861, at La Grange, Georgia, the daughter of Henry and Anna Elizabeth Hodges.

Two children were born—Henry Hodges, born January 18, 1892, and Helen Edelin, born and died 1901.

Harry Hodges Semmes, the son, spent his childhood in Washington, and was graduated from Darmouth in 1913 and from the Law College of George Washington University in 1916. He married Juanita Hopkins of Texas.

Children of Harry and Juanita (Hopkins) Semmes
1. Harry Hodges Semmes, II.
2. Raphael Semmes.
3. John Gibson Semmes.
4. David Hopkins Semmes.

During the World War he served as Captain in the United States Army Tank Corps, was wounded, and for bravery under fire he received the Distinguished Service Cross and the Oak Leaf Cluster for a second citation, also the Purple Heart, and Croce Al Merito Di Guerra from the King of Italy. He resides (1940) at Chevy Chase, Maryland, and is a senior member of the patent law firm of Semmes, Keegin & Semmes, of Washington.

CHRISTOPHER EDELEN[2]'
(1682 - 1771)
AND
HIS DESCENDANTS

Christopher Edelen, son of Richard and Elizabeth Edelen, declared himself to be 50 years of age in 1732, therefore, making his birth about 1682. His share of the parental estate in 1694 included a portion of "Dublin" which became his dwelling-plantation. It is not known whether he forsooth the Roman faith of his parents, but his marriage and the births of his children are recorded in St. John's Piscataway Parish which somehow indicate that he became a member of the Established Church.

In 1707 he married Jane, daughter of Moses and Elizabeth (Jenkins) Jones, and a step-daughter of his brother Edward. Moses Jones by his will, dated July 1704 and proved March 1704/5, devised his daughter Jane Jones 100 acres of land on Port Tobacco Creek.

On July 27, 1727, Christopher Edelen and Jane his wife and Dr. Robert Innis and Elizabeth his wife, both of Prince Georges County, conveyed to Edward Edelen the tract "Thomas' Chance". The deed stated that "whereas Moses Jones late of Prince Georges by his last will and testament bequeathed a moiety of Thomas Chance to his son Thomas Jones who died without issue and intestate and it then became the right of his son Notley Jones who likewise died without issue and intestate and therefore the land became the right of Jane and Elizabeth Jones co-heiress and sisters of the said Thomas and Notley Jones, and the said Jane intermarried with Christopher Edelen and the said Elizabeth intermarried with Dr. Robert Innis". Christopher Edelen and Robert Innis both signed the deed, while their wives made their marks. The witnesses were George Noble and John Magruder.[2]

On April 28, 1731, his wife Jane Edelen shared in the distribution of the estate of her maternal grandfather Thomas Jenkins.[3]

Children of Christopher and Jane (Jones) Edelen

1. Elizabeth Edelen, born Oct. 10, 1708, married Clement, son of Francis and Winifred (Green) Wheeler, Feb. 5, 1732/33. Issue: Katherine, born July 25, 1734; Susan, born Jan. 2, 1735/6; Clement, born Mar. 13, 1737/8 . . .
2. Anne Edelen, born Sept. 2, 1710, married ——— Garner (Gardiner).
3. John Edelen married Sarah ———. *q.v.*
4. Richard Edelen married Sarah Stonestreet. *q.v.*

5. Benjamin Edelen, born Dec. 5, 1720.
6. Jane Edelen, born Dec. 12, 1718, married Butler, son of Thomas and Christian Stonestreet, and secondly Clement Wheeler. Issue: (first) Verlinda, born Apr. 12, 1744; Catherine born Apr. 8, 1747; Eleanor, born Apr. 4, 1749; Henry born Sept. 11, 1752; Richard; Butler Edelen, born Feb. 8, 1756.
7. Christopher Edelen married Rebecca Johnson. *q.v.*
8. Eleanor Edelen married Edward, son of Thomas and Christian Stonestreet. Issue: Thomas; Joseph; Christian; John; Edward; and Basil William.
9. Catherine Edelen.

On May 3, 1737, Christopher Edelen purchased from William Wheeler of Prince Georges County, carpenter, "Major's Choice" for 4,200 pounds of tobacco. The witnesses were John Addison and Robert Wade, Jr., but no wife waived dower.[4] On August 8, 1748, for natural love and affections which he maintained for his son Richard, he deeded him "Edelen's Addition" and "Edelen's Folly", containing improvements. His wife Jane consented while the witnesses were John Hawkins, Jr., and Luke Marbury.[5]

On September 7, 1765, Christopher Edelen, Sr., deeded to John Edelen, of Prince Georges County, for 1,012 pounds of tobacco a portion of "Piscattaway Manor" otherwise "Calvert alias Elizabeth's Manor" beginning at the land of Philip Edelen and running to the line of Joseph Boarman and John Bowling which portions were formerly in the possession of Thomas and George Noble, deceased. No wife waived dower; the witnesses were Thomas Hanson Marshall and Thomas Addison, Jr.[6]

On September 14, 1765, he purchased from Joseph Noble, of Prince Georges County, planter, land in that county which was lately in the possession of Francis Wheeler and Winifred his wife, being a portion of "Major's Choice". Martha Noble, wife, waived all dower rights, while the witnesses were Thomas Hanson Marshall and Thomas Addison, Jr.[7]

The various Debt Books of Prince Georges County from year to year show his landed estate. In 1753 he paid quit rents on 200 acres of "Dublin" and 19 acres of "Major's Choice". By 1759 his share of "Major's Choice" had been increased to 99 acres. No further changes were noted on the debt books.

He frequently became bondsman for his neighbors and friends. On August 7, 1718, he and Richard Connor were sureties for Mary Sewell, the administratrix of Charles Sewell. In 1721 he and Thomas Stonestreet were bondsmen for Elizabeth Tyler, the executrix of William Tyler, and on May 10, 1725, he and Thomas Athey were bondsmen for Jane Mac Queen, the administratrix of Timothy MacQueen. On May

2, 1727, he and Luen Jones signed the bond of Elizabeth Barnes, the administratrix of Henry Barnes.

He administered upon the estate of William Lee, at which time Edward Edelen and John Jones were his sureties. On March 5, 1727/8, he and Francis Tolson signed the bond of Henry Massey, the executor of Robert Rearson. In 1731 he, Nehemiah Wade, Zephanial Wade, and William Thomas were sureties for Henry Tolson, the executor of Francis Tolson, late of Prince Georges County, deceased. In 1734 he and Edward Edelen were sureties for Sarah Queen, the executrix of Samuel Queen, late of Prince Georges County. In 1734 he and John Dickinson were sureties for Anne Jenkins, the administratrix of Enoch Jenkins. In 1736 he and John Edelen were sureties for Elizabeth and Thomas Clarkson, the executors of William Clarkson.

On February 10, 1749/50, Christopher Edelen and John Hawkins signed the bond of Mary Noble, the executrix of Joseph Noble, late of Prince Georges County. And on August 14, 1750, he and John Edelen signed the bond of Elizabeth Wheeler, the administratrix of Clement Wheeler. On April 8, 1756, he and John Edelen likewise signed the bond of Jane Stonestreet, the executrix of Butler Stonestreet. The bond was fixed at £1500. On July 4, 1757, he was granted letters of administration upon the estate of Christopher Parker, when John Dunn and Thomas Dent, of Prince Georges County, were his sureties.

The will of Christopher Edelen was probated in Prince Georges County during 1771. He devised his widow the homestead "Dublin" during life, then to his son Christopher. His grandson James Edelen was willed "Major's Choice", of 96 acres, which had been purchased from William Wheeler. Personalty was left to his granddaugter Catherine Stonestreet. After the decease of his widow, the personal estate was to be divided among his grandson James Edelen and the following children: Anne, John, Richard, Elizabeth, Christopher, and Catherine.[8]

The bond of his widow and son John Edelen as executors of his estate in the amount of £1000 was signed by Thomas Edelen and Edward Jenkins on December 20, 1771. The inventory of his personal effects was exhibited at court on March 7, 1772, by John Edelen, while Richard Edelen, Sr., and Elizabeth Wheeler signed as the next of kin.

His widow died shortly afterwards, and by March 8, 1773, James Edelen with John Edelen administered on the estate.

[1] Wills, Liber 3, folio 637.
[2] Deeds, Liber M, folio 226, Marlborough.
[3] Adm. Accts., Liber 10, folio 695.
[4] Deeds, Liber T, folio 582.

° *Ibid.*, Liber B B, folio 491.
°' *Ibid.*, Liber T T, folios 469, 471.
° Wills, Liber 38, folio 623.

JOHN EDELEN[3]

(1712 - 1786)

John Edelen, son of Christopher and Jane (Jones) Edelen, was born on December 16, 1712, at "Dublin", Piscataway Parish, Prince Georges County. His wife was Sarah ————, and inasmuch as she gave the family name of Pannewell to her first son, it lends a possible relationship.

Children of John and Sarah Edelen

1. Thomas Pannewell Edelen married Susannah Edelen. q.v.
2. Jane Edelen, born 1744.
3. Christopher Edelen married Mary ————. q.v.
4. Mary Edelen, bap. May 3, 1752, married John Spalding.
5. Sarah Edelen married ———— Lindsay.
6. William Edelen, d.s.p. 1791, naming brother Thomas as sole legatee.
7. John Edelen.
8. Richard Edelen.
9. Benjamin Edelen married Sarah ————. q.v.
10. Elizabeth Edelen, born 1758, married May 12, 1779, Ezekiah Mudd.

His wife died sometime before 1776. At the census of that year his daughter, Jane Edelen, born in 1744, was the chatelaine of his household. During March 1778, he took the oath of fidelity and allegiance to the State of Maryland in Prince Georges County.[1]

John Edelen died testate in Prince Georges County during 1786. He devised the dwelling-plantation "Piscataway Manor", containing 150 acres to his daughter Jane, but at her decease it was to be divided among his five sons—Thomas, William, John, Christopher, and Benjamin. In addition Jane received numerous negroes and other personalty, but in the event that she married Joseph Blandford, then the personalty would revert to her brother Christopher.

Negroes were bequeathed to the following grandchildren: Anne Mudd, John and Mary Spalding, and Sarah and Susannah Lindsay. Negroes were also bequeathed to his son John, but if he married either of the daughters of John Halley, then the slaves were to revert to the testator's grandson Robert P. Edelen. Other slaves were left to his children—Christopher, Richard, Benjamin, and Elizabeth Mudd. The residuary estate was to be divided among the four daughters.[2]

[1] Brumbaugh's Md. Records, vol. 2, p. 289.
[2] Wills, Liber T no. 1, folio 242.

RICHARD EDELEN[3]

(1715 - 1791)

Richard Edelen, son of Christopher and Jane (Jones) Edelen, was born August 4, 1715, at "Dublin", Piscataway Parish. He married Sarah, the daughter of Butler Stonestreet by his first wife.[1] According to the census of Prince Georges County in 1776, Sarah was born about 1731. She was an heir in the will of her father, proved in Prince Georges County in 1755.[2]

Children of Richard and Sarah (Stonestreet) Edelen

1. Anna Edelen, spinster.
2. Frances Edelen, spinster.
3. Mary V. Edelen, spinster.
4. Jane Cordelia Edelen married Joseph, son of John Baptist and Elizabeth (Edelen) Boarman.
5. Elizabeth Anamentia Edelen, spinster.
6. Christopher Butler Edelen, born 1759, *d.s.p.*
7. Benedict Joseph Edelen, born 1754. *q.v.*
8. Jesse Edelen married Clara Edelen. *q.v.*
9. George Stonestreet Edelen married Sarah Edelen. *q.v.*
10. Electius Edelen, *d.s.p.* 1808.

Richard Edelen manifested his political views during the Revolution by taking the oath of allegiance and fidelity in 1778 to the State of Maryland.[3]

The Debt Books for Prince Georges County in 1758 show that he was seized of "Major's Choice" of 23 acres, "Edelen's Addition" of 15 acres, and "Edelen's Folly" of 100 acres. The returns for 1771 show no changes from the earlier year.

On August 5, 1767, Richard Edelen, planter, for the consideration of 5 shillings leased from Benedict Calvert, Esq., of Prince Georges County, a portion of "His Lordship's Kindness" during his life and that of his wife Sarah and the natural life of their son Benedict. The witnesses were Alexander Symmes and David Crawford.[4]

On August 14, 1790, he conveyed to Butler Edelen for the sum of £20 "Maiden's Mistake", lying in Prince Georges County next to "Maiden Bradley". No wife waived dower; the witnesses were William Baker and T. Marshall.[5]

His will was proved in Prince Georges County during February 1791. He devised his wife all realty during widowhood, then to his four spinster daughters—Anna, Frances, Mary, and Elizabeth. In the event that his daughters married, then their share would become void. The five named sons shared in certain items of his personal estate, with the residue going to his wife.[6]

Christopher Edelen, a bachelor son, died testate in Prince Georges County in 1794. He devised "Strife" of 250 acres to his four unmarried sisters during life then to his brothers George, Jesse, and Elexius. His brother Benedict was willed "Maiden's Mistake" of 28½ acres, and his sister Cordelia Boarman slaves. He named his brother-in-law Joseph Boarman as the executor.[7]

The will of Electius Edelen, another bachelor son, was dated March 7, 1808, and proved on March 21, 1808. He devised his sister Dolly Boarman 150 acres of land in Charles County, with the residue of the realty to his four sisters—Fanny, Nancy, Mary, and Any. Suits of mourning were bequeathed to Joseph Boarman and his wife, George Edelen and his wife, and Jesse Edelen and his wife. He appointed Walter Edelen the executor.[8]

The three spinster sisters—Anna, Elizabeth Anamenta, and Mary V.—negotiated their wills on July 15, 1808, all being probated in Prince Georges County on April 28, 1815.[9]

Anna devised to her sister Jeanne Delia Boarman during life 250 acres of land in Charles County which had been willed by her late brother Electius Edelen. At her decease the land was to revert to her three children—Anna Maria Boarman, Raphael Harris Boarman, and Carolina Matilda Boarman. The residue of the realty was devised to her sisters—Frances, Mary Velinda, and Elizabeth Anamentia. Various legacies and silver plate were left to the three children of her sister Mrs. Boarman, while $20 was bequeathed to her nephew Caleb Edelen and $30 to her brother Jesse Edelen; and $8 was bequeathed annually to the Bishop of the Roman Church.

The wills of Elizabeth and Mary were practically identical. The 250 acres of land in Charles County devised them by their brother Electius Edelen were left to the Boarman nieces and nephews, and similar legacies were bequeathed to the Church.

The will of Frances Edelen was dated November 2, 1825, and proved in Prince Georges County on December 8, of the same year. She devised her nephew John B. Edelen the store house and lot, where Dr. B. I. Semmes maintained his office opposite the post office, which was received from the estate of "my late sister Elizabeth Anamentia Edelen", silver plate, and numerous slaves for "the support of my sister Delia Boarman and at her death to her daughter Catherine Anamentia". To Benedict Joseph Edelen, the son of her nephew John B. Edelen, she willed the tract of 250 acres in Charles County which formerly belonged to her brother Electius. The house and lot bought of Samuel and James Edelen and the brick house in Washington formerly the property of Electius Edelen, slaves, and other realty were devised to her three nephews—John Aloysius Edelen, Richard James Edelen, and Walter Alexander Edelen. Slaves were left to her brother George S. Edelen and to her niece Elizabeth Queen; also personalty to her niece Caroline Matilda Edelen the wife of John B. Edelen. Legacies were bequeathed to the Roman Catholic Church.[10]

---

[1] Adm. Accts., Liber 41, folio 270.
[2] Wills, Liber 30, folio 35.
[3] Brumbaugh's Md. Records, vol. 2, p. 267.
[4] Deeds, Liber B B no. 2, folio 190, Marlborough.
[5] Deeds, Liber J J no. 2, folio 290, Marlborough.
[6] Wills, Marlborough.
[7] Wills, Liber T no. 1, folio 351.
[8] Wills, La Plata.
[9] Wills, Liber T T no. 1, folio 119.
[10] Wills, Liber T T no. 1, folio 388.

CHRISTOPHER EDELEN, GENT.[8]

(1723 - 1786)

Of the descendants of Richard Edelen, Christopher Edelen of Frederick County became by far the most distinguished during the colonial and revolutionary periods—perhaps because he failed to adhere to the ancient faith of his house and thus gained civil advantages in the Province. He was born 1723, the son of Christopher and Jane (Jones) Edelen, of Prince Georges County, and occasionally signed his name as Christopher Edelen, III. In manhood he followed the tide of migration from the southern counties into western Prince Georges later to become Frederick County.

He settled there sometime prior to December 4, 1754, when he, described as of Frederick County, Merchant, and Christopher Lowndes, of Prince Georges County, Merchant, were the mortgagees of 104 acres of land called "Abin's Choice" from John Radford, of Frederick County, Joyner. The witness was Reverdy Ghiselin. On June 18, 1755, the same parties mortgaged from John Radford 104 acres of "Henry". At this time the witnesses were J. Darnall and James Dickson.[1]

He was well established in Frederick Towne by the year 1756, as is evident by the following advertisement:

> "On December 30, 1756, Christopher Lowndes advertised to let by the year or for a term, and to be entered upon on the beginning of the following March, a very good public house with all necessary outbuildings, situated in the middle of the town, and then in the

occupation of William Beall, and that any person inclined to rent said house might know the conditions by applying to Christopher Edelin on the premises or to him".

This public house was formerly a tavern in which the county court had met until the completion of the first court house.

Christopher Edelen married Rebecca, the daughter of George Johnson, in All Saint's Parish, Frederick County, on July 24, 1757. The birth of three children is recorded in the parish register.

Children of Christopher and Rebecca (Johnson) Edelen

1. Elizabeth Edelen, born June 7, 1760.
2. Eleanor Edelen, born Oct. 19, 1762, married John Lynn. License Fred. Co. Feb. 26, 1784.
3. Rebecca Edelen, born Oct. 10, 1765, married John Hodge Bayard. License Fred. Co., April 15, 1784.

The interest of Christopher Edelen in the welfare of Frederick County and the Province consisted not only in the judiciary, but it reigned from minor civic enterprises to military services to his King. During the French and Indians Wars, he fought in the company commanded by Captain Peter Butler, of Frederick County.[2]

In December 1768, he was one of the managers for the lottery to raise funds for completing the market house and town hall in Frederick Town. He was also on the committee for the lottery in 1760 to raise money for building the first engine house in Frederick. And in 1769 he was one of the managers in the lottery which raised revenue for the erection of the school house.

He became one of the early patriots of Western Maryland for the cause of liberty and was outspoken for the independence of the Colonies. He was one of the judges at the election on July 12, 1776, in the Middle District which resulted in his election to the First State Convention. He took his seat, representing Frederick County, on August 14, 1776, at Annapolis.[3] He also represented Frederick County at the Provincial Convention of 1777.

During the early days of the Revolution he was placed upon the Council of Safety for Frederick County, and it is believed that he remained a member of that body until its dissolution. On July 19, 1776, he was entrusted with money for the purchase of munitions and blankets for the Maryland Militia.[4] On August 28, 1776, he was paid £250 for the use of the Committee of Observation for Frederick County in order that it may be used for the support of the prisoners from North Carolina. He at one time served as chairman for the Committee of Observation.[5]

His age perhaps prevented his pursuing a military career during the conflict, but he held many important county offices. He was Justice of the Peace of Frederick County in 1777 as well as in 1778, Judge of the Orphan's Court in 1778 and 1779, and High Sheriff of the county in 1779 and 1785.[6] On November 13, 1781, he was in correspondence with Governor Lee regarding money matters for Frederick County.

On July 2, 1777, Christopher Edelen was paid by the Treasurer of Maryland £308/11/2 for the removal of British prisoners from Frederick Town to Burlington.

The following letter to Christopher Edelen from the Privy Council in 1781 shows that he was entrusted by the State:

> "If you have any linen or cloth or any other Article in your Possession belonging to the State, we wish you to embrace the first opportunity of sending them to this Place, as the Soldiers here are much distressed for Cloathing".

The name of Christopher Edelen figures in a number of land transactions in Frederick County. On December 6, 1763, "Christopher Edelen the Third" conveyed to Gilbert Kemp, farmer, the "Resurvey on Fountain Low", containing 380 acres for a consideration of £190. His wife, Rebecca Edelen, waived all dower, and the deed was witnessed by J. Dickson and Thomas Price.[7]

On March 1, 1765, he purchased from Fielder Gaunt, of Frederick County, Gent., for 1 shilling "Fielderia", lying in Frederick County, adjoining "Salisbury Plains". No wife waived dower, but James Dickson and Thomas Price signed as witnesses.[8]

On April 27, 1765, he bought of Christopher Lowndes, of Prince Georges County, merchant, for £30 the tract "Salsbury Plains". Elizabeth Lowndes, the wife of Christopher, relinquished her third, and Elizabeth Scott and J. Hepburn signed as witnesses.[9]

On August 8, 1765, it was shown that William Kimball, of Frederick Town, saddler, was indebted to Christopher Edelen, merchant, to the amount of £30/13/7, therefore, Kimball conveyed to him a negro woman. The transaction was witnessed by Thomas Price and Benjamin Ogle.[10]

On July 12, 1768, Charles Beatty, of Frederick Town, merchant, sold to Christopher Edelen, Conrad Grosh, John Cary, Casper Shaff, Thomas Schley, and Arthur Charlton land in Frederick Town whereby a merchant house was to be erected. Martha Beatty, wife of Charles, waived her dower rights.[11]

On April 18, 1769, Christopher Edelen, merchant, purchased land in Frederick Town from Valentine Shroiner, saddler, and Casper Shaaff. The witnesses were Thomas Price and Eli Williams.[12]

On July 21, 1770, he bought of Charles Beatty and George Fraser Hawkins, the latter being of Prince Georges County, for £6 a lot in Georgetown, being a portion of "Knaves Disappointment". Susanna Truman Hawkins, wife to George Fraser Hawkins, relinquished her third. The witnesses were Joseph Wood and Thomas Price.[13]

On March 21, 1771, Christopher Edelen, Michael Ramer, John Sellman, and Casper Shaaff, all parties being of Frederick County, conveyed to Dr. Philip Thomas land in Frederick County. Charlotte Ramer, Margaret Sellman, Rebecca Edelen, and Alice Shaaff, wives, all gave their consent. The transaction was witnessed by Evan Shelby and Eneas Campbell.[14]

On March 22, 1771, Christopher Edelen, merchant, purchased from Dr. Philip Thomas, Gent., lot no. 30 with dwelling house in Frederick Town for a consideration of £542/7/10.[15]

It is recalled that Christopher Edelen under the provisions of his father's will was to inherit the parental homestead upon the decease of his mother. Accordingly, "Christopher Edelen of Frederick Towne Gent." conveyed to Enoch Magruder of Prince Georges County, Gent., for £7500 land lying on Tinker's Branch in Prince Georges County originally granted to Matthew O'Bryan of Charles County, deceased, known by the name of "Dublin" consisting of 200 acres with all buildings, outhouses, etc. . . . except the burying place of one-quarter acre "for the dead of the family and ancestors of Christopher Edelen". Rebecca Edelen, wife to Christopher, waived dower, and the witnesses were Jacob Young and P. Thomas.*

On May 22, 1779, he conveyed to Sebastian Dorr, farmer, a lot in Frederick Town. His wife, Rebecca, waived her rights, while the deed was witnessed by Jacob Young and Philip Thomas.[16] Likewise, on July 22, same year, he deeded to Alexander Brandenbergh for £270 the tract known as "Chance", lying in Frederick County which had been resurveyed for Solomon Turner. Rebecca Edelen, his wife, gave her consent.[17]

During 1781 Christopher Edelen as sheriff for the county sold a number of tracts of land resulting from various foreclosures.

On December 10, 1785, he conveyed to Mountjoy Bayley, of Frederick Town for a consideration of £863/2/6 the lot in said town "whereon Christopher Edelen now lives on the street which leads through

---

*Deeds, Liber C C no. 2, folio 196, Marlboro.

Frederick Towne aforesaid to Conococheague". The transaction was
witnessed by George Murdock and George Scott. No wife waived dower.
On December 21, of the same year he sold two negroes to Montjoy
Bayley and other negroes to John Lynn, of Washington County.[18]

From these various conveyances it indicates that Christopher Edelen
in later life sustained financial reverses. He died intestate in Frederick
County during 1786, when on May 12, of that year, the court issued
letters of administration to Mountjoy Bayley, his greatest creditor.
Presumably, he acquired all the assets of the estate, inasmuch as no
accounts were rendered the court.

[1] Deeds, Liber E, folios 616, 759, Frederick.
[2] Md. Hist. Mag., vol. 9.
[3] Scharf's History of Western Maryland, vol. 1, p. 479.
[4] Archives, vol. 12.
[5] Md. Hist. Mag., vol. 11, pp. 59, 313.
[6] Archives, vols. 12, 21.
[7] Deeds, Liber J, folio 19, Frederick.
[8] *Ibid.*, Liber J, folio 1059.
[9] *Ibid.*, Liber J, folio 1141.
[10] *Ibid.*, Liber J, folio 1288.
[11] *Ibid.*, Liber L, folio 383.
[12] *Ibid.*, Liber M, folio 187.
[13] *Ibid.*, Liber N, folio 376.
[14] *Ibid.*, Liber P, folio 76.
[15] *Ibid.*, Liber P, folio 78.
[16] *Ibid.*, Liber W R no. 2, folio 49, Frederick.
[17] *Ibid.*, Liber W R. no. 2, folio 101.
[18] *Ibid.*, Liber W R no. 6, folios 230, 250, 251.

THOMAS PANNEWELL EDELEN[4]

(1739 - 1810)

Thomas Pannewell Edelen, son of John and Sarah Edelen, was born
about 1739, in Prince Georges County. Before 1765 he married his
cousin Susannah, born 1741, daughter to Thomas and Mary (Blandford) Edelen. A daughter of this union was married to Smith Mudd
by 1792, but if any heirs survived Thomas Edelen and his wife, they
were not mentioned in their wills. On June 9, 1777, Thomas P. Edelen
and Charles Fenley signed the bond of John Harris Gibbs, the administrator of Ann Gibbs, late of Prince Georges County. During March
1778, he took the oath of fidelity and allegiance to the State of Maryland in Prince Georges County.[1]

The will of Thomas P. Edelen was probated on September 7, 1810,
in Prince Georges County. He devised the dwelling-plantation to his
wife Susannah during widowhood, then to his nephew Robert Pannewell
Edelen of Christopher. After the decease of his widow a tract of land

in Charles County, purchased from Raphael Mudd, was to revert to Thomas Pannewell Lindsay (undoubtedly the son of his sister Sarah) and also certain negroes to Thomas Pannewell Spalding of James. Other heirs were his nieces Sarah and Anne 'Edelen.[2]

His widow survived him nearly eleven years, dying in 1821. Her will probated in Prince Georges County on April 2, of that year, bequeathed her estate for the most part to the nieces and nephews of her late husband. They were: Mary Spalding, Raphael C. Edelen, Mary Boarman, Thomas P. Edelen of Robert, Robert P. Edelen, and Catherine Edelen of Philip.

[1] Brumbaugh's Maryland Records, vol. 2, p. 279.
[2] Wills, Liber T T no. 1, folio 31.

CHRISTOPHER EDELEN[4]

(1748 - 18—)

Christopher Edelen, son of John and Sarah Edelen, was born about 1748 in Prince Georges County. His wife was Mary ————, also born about 1748. The census of St. John's Parish shows him the head of the house, with his wife, a male aged 21, and two females aged 3. One son Robert Pannewell (*q.v.*) has been proved. During March 1778, he took the oath of allegiance and fidelity to the State of Maryland in Prince Georges County.[1]

He migrated to Fayette County, Kentucky, where on August 22, 1798, as "Christopher Edelen of John of Fayette County, State of Kentucky", he deeded to Thomas Pannel Edelen of Prince Georges County 138¼ acres of land "all that land entitled to me by the will of my father John Edelen", near Piscataway Creek. Both he and his wife Mary signed the conveyance which was witnessed by Andrew McCalla and C. Beatty.[2]

The 1810 census, the first preserved schedule for Fayette County, fails to show him the head of a family in that year.

[1] Brumbaugh's Maryland Records, vol. 2, p. 267.
[2] Deeds, Liber J R M no. 6, folio 594, Marlboro.

BENJAMIN EDELEN[4]

(17— - 1791)

Benjamin Edelen, son of John and Sarah Edelen, was born in Prince Georges County, but later settled in Port Tobacco Hundred of Charles County. During March 1778, he subscribed to the patriot's oath of allegiance and fidelity in Charles County before Magistrate William Harrison.[1] His wife was Sarah ————.

Children of Benjamin and Sarah Edelen

1. Robert Edelen married Elizabeth Lewis. *q.v.*
2. John Edelen.
3. Elizabeth Edelen married Edmund Turley.

Shortly before his death in 1791 Benjamin Edelen settled in Brunswick Parish of King George County, Virginia, which was directly across the Potomac from his ancestral home in Maryland. He negotiated his will on November 17, 1790, and bequeathed £200 Maryland currency to his wife Sally Edelen to purchase land in Virginia which was to be retained by her and his three children during her life. Upon her decease the land was to be sold and the proceeds divided equally between his two sons, Robert and John. Slaves and other personal property were bequeathed to his three children—Robert, John, and Elizabeth. All three children were under age. He named his wife and John. Perry as executors. It was witnessed by John Beverly, James Tyler, and Daniel McCarty Fitzhugh.

Inasmuch as Benjamin Edelen maintained personal property in both Charles County and King George County, his will was admitted to probate in Maryland and Virginia. It was proved in King George County on April 7, 1791, before Lawrence Berry, clerk.

The inventory of his personalty in Charles County was recorded on December 16, 1791, by John Perry as the acting executor and manifested an appraised value of £575. Thomas Perry, Sr., and William Perry were bondsmen for the executor.[2] He owned ten slaves, the most valuable one being Ben appraised at £70. An infirm girl, Sarah, was worth only £2/10.

His estate was not settled until May 11, 1801, by a commission in Loudoun County, Virginia, composed of Joseph Lewis, Charles Lewis, and Vincent Davis. At that time it was shown that the widow was deceased and that his daughter Elizabeth was the wife of Edmund Turley.

---

[1] Unpub. Md. Rec., vol. 5, DAR.
[2] Inv. & Acts. (1791-98), folios 58, 99.

BENEDICT JOSEPH EDELEN[4]

(1754 - 1800)

Benedict Joseph Edelen, son of Richard and Sarah (Stonestreet) Edelen, was born about 1754 in Prince Georges County. In 1778 he took the oath of allegiance and fidelity to the State of Maryland in his native county.[1]

On April 4, 1783, he received from the Treasurer £35/14/10 in connection with services during the Revolutionary War.[2] He married after the war, but the name of his wife is unknown. In 1790 he was the head of a family with three females, and seven slaves.

Proved Children of Benedict Joseph Edelen

1. John Baptist Edelen married twice. *q.v.*
2. Raphael Caleb Edelen. *q.v.*

In 1794 Benedict Joseph Edelen received by the will of his brother, Christopher, 28½ acres of "Maiden's Mistake".

He died intestate in Prince Georges County. Letters of administration upon his estate were issued to his brother, Jesse Edelen, on April 8, 1800. An account was rendered to the court on August 11, 1801, by which the administrators, Jesse and Electius Edelen, accounted for a balance of £353/11/11, and with various receipts due the estate brought the assets to £794/13/3.[3]

[1] Brumbaugh's Md. Records, vol. 2, p. 265.
[2] Archives, vol. 48, p. 394.
[3] Adm. Accts., Liber S T no. 3, folio 263.

JESSE EDELEN[4]

(17— - 1815)

Jesse Edelen, son of Richard and Sarah (Stonestreet) Edelen, was born at the ancestral estate "Dublin". On February 7, 1800, he married his kinswoman Clara, the daughter of Richard Edelen.

Children of Jesse and Clara (Edelen) Edelen

1. John Aloysius Edelen married Maria ————. *q.v.*
2. Richard James Edelen married Harriet Dyer. *q.v.*
3. Walter Alexander Edelen married twice. *q.v.*

He negotiated his will on December 20, 1814, and died in the early months of 1815. The instrument which was probated in Prince Georges County on April 5, 1815, named his brother-in-law Walter Edelen as the executor and made his three sons—John Aloysius, Richard, and Walter Alexander—the sole legatees.[1]

[1] Wills, Liber T T no. 1, folio 112.

GEORGE STONESTREET EDELEN[4]

(1760 - 18—)

George Stonestreet Edelen, son of Richard and Sarah (Stonestreet) Edelen, was born 1760 in Prince Georges County. On July 27, 1776, he was enlisted by Captain Bowie for services in the Flying Camp, at which time it was stated that he was aged 17, born in Prince Georges County, and 5 feet 7½ high.[1] He saw active service around New York during that summer and fall, after which he recruited for the American army.[2]

On May 14, 1785, by the Rev. Father Pile he was married to his cousin Sarah Edelen.

On July 27, 1791, he purchased from William Robinson, Sr., of Charles County for £40 "Robinson's Tryal". Linder Robinson waived dower, and the witnesses were John Dent and George Lee.[3] On August 6, 1803, he bought of Samuel A. Berry of Charles County "Berry's Hazard", lying on the main fresh of Piney Branch. No wife waived dower, but the witnesses were Ignatius Middleton and Benjamin Cawood.[4]

---

[1] Archives, vol. 18, p. 36.
[2] *Ibid.*, vol. 21, p. 308.
[3] Deeds, Liber K no. 4, folio 338.
[4] *Ibid.*, Liber I B no. 5, folio 535.

ROBERT PANNEWELL EDELEN[5]

(1783 - 1830)

Robert Pannewell Edelen, son of Christopher and Mary Edelen, was born in or about 1783 in Maryland. He failed to accompany his father to Kentucky, but remained in Maryland where he married Charity ————.

Children of Robert and Charity Edelen

1. Susannah Edelen.
2. Elizabeth Edelen married ———— Hunter.
3. Louis Edelen.
4. Benedict Edelen married Johana Posey. *q.v.*

He died intestate prior to 1830, when his widow administered upon his estate. An account on August 9, 1830, showed a value of $4,385.34, and after various disbursements a balance of $2,586.77 remained. A final account was rendered on September 14, 1841, leaving $2,585.77 to be distributed among unnamed heirs.[1]

The 1850 census shows that Charity Edelen, aged 67, born in Maryland, was the head of a family in the Piscataway District, with Lewis Edelen aged 33; Elizabeth Edelen aged 29; Benedict Edelen aged 27; and Susannah Edelen aged 25.

The will of Charity Edelen was dated April 17, 1858, and proved on March 10, 1863, in Prince Georges County by Francis O. Medley, Edgar D. Hurtt, and William Handey. She devised her daughter Susanna the dwelling-plantation and numerous negroes and named her the executrix. Negroes were also bequeathed to her daughter Elizabeth Hunter and sons Louis and Benedict Edelen. To her granddaughter Lena Edelen he willed $100.[2]

On March 6, 1863, Susanna Edelen appeared at court and renounced the executorship of the estate of her mother and requested that letters be issued to her brother Benedict.[3]

The first and final account upon the estate was rendered by Benedict Edelen on May 16, 1864, showing a balance of $2,431.70 to be distributed.

---

[1] Adm. Accts., Liber P C no. 2, folios 204, 511.
[2] Wills, Liber W A J no. 1, folio 238.
[3] *Ibid.*, Liber W A J no. 1, folio 240.

ROBERT EDELEN[5]

(1782 - 1849)

Robert Edelen, son of Benjamin and Sarah Edelen, was born in Charles County, Maryland, on March 10, 1782, according to his family Bible (printed 1837). His early youth was spent in King George County, Virginia, at the home of his parents, but later he settled in Loudon County, Virginia.

In the latter county he met and wooed Elizabeth, the fifth child of George and Violet (Gist) Lewis, whom he married March 10, 1803. Her mother was of distinguished Maryland lineage and was born on March 13, 1755/6, in St. Thomas Parish, Baltimore County, the daughter of William and Violetta (Howard) Gist. She was baptized Violetta after her mother who was a descendant of Edith Cromwell who married Christopher Gist.

Children of Robert and Elizabeth (Lewis) Edelen

1. Sarah Edelen, born Loudon Co., died Nov. 16, 1840, Parkersburg, Va., married John Stephenson Mar. 4, 1821; he died Portland, Oreg., Oct. 16, 1871, aged 74 yrs., 7 mos., 6 days.
2. Catherine Edelen, born Loudon Co., died Feb. 6, 1845, Wood Co., Va., married Aug. 13, 1829, John A. Bailey, born Wood Co., June 24, 1804, died Mar. 9, 1885.
3. Lucy Edelen, born Nov. 20, 1806, Wood Co., died Belleville, Va., May 17, 1840, married Feb. 9, 1826, John Kincheloe, born Wood Co. Oct. 24, 1799, died Martinsville, Tex., Oct. 1879.

4. Benjamin Edelen married Susan Clark. *q.v.*
5. Elizabeth Edelen, born Dec. 23, 1809, Wood Co., died Jan. 29, 1896, married Dec. 24, 1829, William Logan, born Fairfax Co., Va., June 5, 1809, died Dec. 27, 1895.
6. Violet Edelen, born Nov. 19, 1811, died spinster Mar. 11, 1836.
7. Ann Matilda Edelen, born July 24, 1813, died Oct. 6, 1831. Married Albert G. Leonard, born Oct. 14, 1807, Loudon Co., Va.
8. Jane Edelen, born Nov. 26, 1814, died Belleville, Sept. 9, 1847, married Dec. 7, 1832, Allen Davis, born Wood Co., Sept. 30, 1811, died Oct. 3, 1869.
9. Frances Edelen, born Nov. 16, 1816, died Oct. 20, 1863, married Apr. 13, 1837, Stephen Chester Shaw, born Lewis Co., N. Y., Oct. 7, 1808, died at Leafly Glen near Parkersburg, June 30, 1890.
10. John Edelen, born July 10, 1818, married May 23, 1843, Mary E. Timms, born Wood Co., Sept. 30, 1818, died June 26, 1883, at Washington Bottom.
11. Mary Edelen, born Apr. 9, 1820, died June 24, 1883, married Feb. 22, 1838, Francis M. Keene, born Fairfax Co., Va., Feb. 14, 1808, died June 20, 1880, at Washington Bottom.

Under the leadership of his father-in-law, George Lewis, in October 1806, he was a member of a group from Loudon County, Virginia, who settled on the banks of the Ohio River in Wood County, Virginia, known as Washington Bottom. George Lewis purchased from Charles Carter and Betty Lewis, his wife, the latter having inherited the tract upon the death of her uncle George Washington, 1186 acres of land which had been granted to Washington for his services in the colonial wars. The tract was originally 2314 acres and had been granted to George Washington on December 15, 1771, by John Murray, Earl of Dumore, the last Royal Governor of Virginia.

George Lewis assigned 100 acres to his son-in-law, Robert Edelen, where he established his dwelling-plantation. George Lewis died on November 11, 1811, and his widow died on July 28, 1817, at the home of her son-in-law Robert Edelen. She was interred in the Edelen burying grounds.

The will of George Lewis was proved in Wood County, Virginia, in January 1812, by Barnes Beckwith, John Keys, and Susanna House. Among his heirs were his sons-in-law John Harwood and Robert Edelen who received equaled portions of the home place and his daughters Sarah Neale, Elizabeth Edelen, and Nancy Harwood.

Robert Edelen became a civil leader in Wood County, holding several offices of trust. His wife died at Washington Bottom on April 1, 1835, and was buried in the private burying grounds, now reputed to be the oldest at Washington Bottom. He died on May 7, 1849, and was buried beside his wife.

The family Bible stated that Robert Edelen migrated to Washington Bottom, Wood County, West Virginia, with his wife and two children in October 1806, and died of inflammation of the lungs 7 day of May 1849, aged 67 years, 1 month, and 27 days.

A notation stated that his wife belonged to the Baptist Church, but he had no religious affiliations—was 6 feet, 4 inches, and weighed about 180 pounds. Another entry stated that he died of bilious fever at his residence on Washington Bottom.

His will was dated May 2, 1849, and proved on May 21, by Lewis Neale, William Harwood, and Isaac Neale. He named his son John, heirs of his daughter Sarah Stephenson, granddaughter Catherine Bailey, heirs of his daughter Lucydean Kincheloe, heirs of his daughter Jane Davis, daughter Elizabeth Logan, daughter Frances Shaw, daughter Mary Keene, and son Benjamin. His son John and Chester Shaw were named as executors.

JOHN BAPTIST EDELEN[3]

(1793 - 1836)

John Baptist Edelen, son of Benedict Joseph and his wife, was born about 1793 in Prince Georges County. According to license issued in Prince Georges County on July 29, 1819, he married Cornelia M. Boarman,* the daughter of Joseph and Cordelia (Edelen) Boarman.

Children of John Baptist and Caroline (Boarman) Edelen

1. Joseph Benedict Edelen married Clara Edelen. *q.v.*
2. Lewis Edelen.
3. Amanda Edelen.
4. Susannah Edelen, born 1825.
5. Elizabeth Edelen, born 1821, married ———— Hunter.
6. Son.**

In 1825 John Baptist Edelen received from the will of his aunt, Frances Edelen, the store and lot in Piscataway, silver plate, and numerous slaves, and his son, Joseph Benedict Edelen, was willed 250 acres of land in Charles County which the testatrix had received by the will of her brother Electius Edelen.

After the death of his wife, Caroline, he married Cecilia Jane Anderson. The license was issued in Prince Georges County to Jane Anderson on October 15, 1834.

John Baptist Edelen died at Piscataway on March 16, 1836, aged 43, according to National Intelligence of March 18, 1836. His will was

---

*The script in the will of his aunt reads more like Caroline Matilda.
**Possibly an issue of the second marriage.

dated March 9, 1836, and admitted to probate in Prince Georges County on March 29, 1836, by the oaths of John W. Ward, James H. Griffin, and B. J. Semmes.[1]

He bequeathed numerous slaves to his daughter Amanda Edelen and his son Joseph Benedict Edelen, with the residue of his estate to his wife and three children (all unnamed). He appointed his "brother" Raphael C. Edelen and "friend" Walter A. Edelen the executors.

On May 3, 1836, his widow Cecilia J. Edelen appeared at court and denounced the provisions in the will and likewise demanded her third. At the same time Raphael C. Edelen renounced the executorship in favor of Walter A. Edelen.[2]

His widow married William Nailor. The license was issued in Washington, D. C., on June 4, 1839.

The will of his spinster daughter, Susannah Edelen, was dated January 8, 1870, and proved on April 2, 1872, in Prince Georges County by William G. Hardy, Matilda M. Hardy, and John O. Hill.[3] She appointed her sister, Elizabeth Hunter, the executrix and willed her real and personal property for the benefit of her brother, Lewis Edelen, during his life, and at his death the bequests were to be divided equally between the sister, Elizabeth Hunter, and the heirs of the deceased brother, Benedict Edelen. All interest in the estate of her deceased brother (unnamed) in Louisiana was devised to St. Dominic Church, Washington, D. C. Her niece, Pauline Edelen, was bequeathed $200.

[1] Wills, Liber P C no. 1, folio 52.
[2] *Ibid.,* folio 53.
[3] Wills, Liber W A J no. 1, folio 477.

RAPHAEL CALEB EDELEN[5]

(1793 - 1851)

Raphael Caleb Edelen, son of Benedict Joseph and his wife, was born in or about 1793 in Prince Georges County. He wife was Sarah Ann ———.

Children of Raphael and Sarah Edelen

1. Mary A. Edelen married Walter Edelen. q.v.
2. Eleanor Edelen married Bennett F. Gwynn, son of John and Ann Eliza (Dyer) Gwynn.*

*NOTE: The *American* of Feb. 22, 1843, carried the following: "Eleanor G. Edelen, 4th daughter of Raphael C. Edelen, was married 31 January 1843 to Bennett F. Gwynn, eldest son of Captain John H. Gwynn, all of Prince Georges County." The 1860 census shows Bennett F. Gwynn a resident of Surrattsville, Maryland, aged 35, with realty appraised at $15,000, and personalty at $11,000. His wife Eleanor was aged 30, and the following were at home: Clarence aged 16; Edward 12; Raphael 10; John 4; Laura 2.

3. William Henry Harrison Edelen, aged 10 in 1850.
4. Sarah Virginia Edelen, aged 13 in 1850.
5. Olivia Edelen married Joseph Parker.
6. Raphael Caleb Edelen.

During the War of 1812 Raphael Edelen served as Ensign in Captain Clagett's Company, 17th Regiment.[1]

The will of Raphael Caleb Edelen was dated September 5, 1844, and proved in Prince Georges County on July 7, 1851, by Will H. Tuck, Joseph B. Edelen, and Thomas A. Wheaton.[2] He devised his son Raphael Caleb the dwelling-plantation known as "Stoney Harbour", and the land on the public road from Piscataway to Upper Marlborough except for that portion which he had sold to Walter A. Edelen. To his son William Henry Harrison he devised his lands lying on the public road near Mrs. Lanham. He provided for the education of his three younger children (unnamed) and bequeathed the residue of the estate to his wife Sarah Ann Edelen whom he appointed executrix.

The will of his widow, Sarah Ann Edelen, was dated June 24, 1851, and proved on August 13, 1851, by Martin A. Wells, G. H. Hunter, and Walter Wilkinson.[3] She bequeathed negroes to her daughters Sarah Virginia Edelen, Olivia Parker, and Eleanor Gwynn, and to her sons Raphael C. Edelen and William Henry Harrison. She referred to two colts given to her two sons by their grandfather, and also negroes given to her daughter Eleanor Gwynn by her father "my late husband". She appointed her son Raphael C. Edelen the executor.

The will of the spinster daughter, Sarah Virginia Edelen, was dated November 24, 1852, and proved in Prince Georges County on February 15, 1853, by Richard L. Jenkins and George H. Thompson.[4] She bequeathed the entire estate to her sister Eleanor Gwynn and at her death it was to be divided equally among her children. Bennett F. Gwynn was named as executor.

---

[1] Marine's British Invasion of Maryland, p. 276.
[2] Wills, Liber P C no. 1, folio 464.
[3] *Ibid.,* folio 466.
[4] *Ibid.,* folio 493.

JOHN ALOYSIUS EDELEN[5]

John Aloysius Edelen, son of Jesse and Clara (Edelen) Edelen, established his seat in Prince Georges. In 1815 he and Walter Edelen sold to Edward Edelen, Sr., of Charles County, for $800 "Semmes' Fragments" containing 103 acres. No wives relinquished thirds, but George D. Parnham and Lawrence Posey were the witnesses.[1]

On October 21, 1818, he purchased from Francis L. Mudd, Clement A. Mudd, and Balthozzar Mudd, all of Charles County, for $970 the tract on which Anne Mudd, mother of the grantors lived, and which had been assigned her as dower rights from the estate of her deceased husband Joshua Mudd. The witnesses were Thomas Rogerson, Daniel Smallwood, John Edelen, and John Meredith. The area was 270 acres; no wives waived dower.[2]

On March 11, 1820, Aloysius Edelen, of Prince Georges County, bought for $250 "Strife", "Sharp", portion of "Friendship", "Costley's Addition", "Smallwood's Palace", all containing 272 acres which "were allotted to Ann Mudd widow of Joshua Mudd, Sr." Anne Robey, wife of Townley Robey the grantor, waived dower, while the witnesses were Daniel Smallwood and Hezekiah M. Robinson.[3]

On January 29, 1829, Aloysius Edelen, of Charles County, was assigned by Peter D. Hatton, of Charles County, attorney for Benjamin S. Mudd, son of Joshua, the "widow's dower in the land of Joshua Mudd". On the same day Aloysius Edelen sold the above to Sylvester F. Gardiner, of Charles County, for $2000 described as the "land laid out as the dower for the widow of Joshua Mudd". Maria Edelen, wife, relinquished her third.

---

[1] Deeds, Liber I B no. 12, folio 2, La Plata.
[2] *Ibid.*, Liber I B no. 13, folio 31.
[3] *Ibid.*, Liber I B no. 13, folio 461.

JAMES RICHARD EDELEN[5]
(1806 - 18—)

James Richard Edelen, son of Jesse and Clara (Edelen) Edelen, was born in the Piscataway District of Prince Georges County in or about 1806.* On June 16, 1829, he obtained license in the National Capital to wed Harriet E. Dyer. She was born in or about 1811 in Virginia, the daughter of Thomas Baker and Mary Pamelia (Davis) Dyer.

Children of Richard and Harriet (Dyer) Edelen

1. Clara Edelen married Benedict Edelen. *q.v.*
2. Thomas Baker Edelen, born 1835.
3. Mary Ellen Edelen.
4. Mary Pamelia Edelen.
5. James Richard Edelen.
6. John M. Edelen.
7. Harriet Edelen.

---

*Present members of the family state that his name was James Richard, but he usually appeared in public records as Richard J.

On July 16, 1833, Richard J. Edelen received letters of administration upon the estate of Francis Edelen, late of Prince Georges County. On July 1, 1839, he and Thomas H. Edelen filed suit against Thomas N. Burch for the sum of $72. The 1850 census shows that Richard J. Edelen was domiciled in the Piscataway District of Prince Georges County, aged 44, and his wife Harriet E., aged 39. In the household were Thomas B. Edelen, aged 15; Mary E. Edelen, aged 13; Mary P., aged 10; James, aged 7; and John M., aged 3—also Daniel R. Dyer, aged 32.

The 1860 census shows his widow, Harriet Edelen, born in Virginia, the head of the family at her estate near Piscataway. At home were the following: Mary Ellen, aged 24; Mary P., aged 18; James R., aged 16; Harriet, aged 9; and also Albert Jenkins, aged 13.

WALTER ALEXANDER EDELEN[5]

(1807 - 18—)

Walter Alexander Edelen, son of Jesse and Clara (Edelen) Edelen, was born in or about 1807 in the Piscataway District of Prince Georges County. He married his kinswoman, the license being issued to Mary A. R. Edelen on May 20, 1833. The National Intelligence of June 15, carried the following: "Mary A. Edelin, daughter of Raphael C. Edelin, was married 21 May 1833 to Walter A. Edelin, both of Prince Georges County".

Children of Walter and Mary (Edelen) Edelen

1. Walter Edelen.
2. Susan Edelen.
3. Jesse Edelen.

After the death of his first wife he married Emily Gwynn. The license was obtained in Prince Georges County on October 15, 1849.

Children of Walter and Emily (Gwynn) Edelen

4. Alexander Edelen, born 1851.

The 1850 census shows him domiciled in Piscataway District aged 43, with the following comprising his immediate household: Emily aged 25; Susan aged 12; Walter aged 10; and Jesse aged 5.

He died before 1860, for in that year his widow Emily Edelen, aged 36, was the head of a household at Surrattsville, with her son Alexander

Edelen, aged 9. She owned realty appraised at $6,000 and personalty at $5,000. In that year Walter Edelen, the son by the first union, was living with Henry D. Edelen, aged 53, and had realty valued at $4,000 and personalty of $2,000.

BENEDICT EDELEN[6]

(1823 - 1867)

Benedict Edelen, son of Robert and Charity Edelen, was born in Prince Georges County in or about 1823. On November 21, 1854, he secured license in Prince Georges County to marry Johanna Posey, widow.

Children of Benedict and Johanna Edelen

1. Paulina E. Edelen married Francis M. Finotti. License Pr. Geo. Co., Nov. 4, 1879.
2. Elizabeth Edelen.
3. Mary Naomi Edelen.
4. Sally Edelen married Ballard J. Galloway.
5. Benjamin Edelen.

The 1860 census shows Benedict Edelen the head of a family in Piscataway District, aged 37, planter, with realty appraised at $10,000 and personalty at $30,000. Other members of his household were Joanna Edelen, aged 30; Paulina Edelen, aged 4; Elizabeth Edelen, aged 2; Francis A. Posey, aged 10; and Lemuel Penn, aged 8. Adjoining lived his mother Charity Edelen, aged 77, with realty valued at $4,000 and personalty at $2,000.

The will of Benedict Edelen was proved in Prince Georges County on March 28, 1867, by John H. Bayne, G. H. Hunter, and A. D. Brooke. He left a legacy of $400 to his brother Lewis Edelen, and the remainder of his property to his wife Joana and unnamed children. He named his wife and Samuel B. Hance as the executors.[1]

The will of his widow Joana Edelen was dated July 31, 1889, and proved in Prince Georges County on December 9, 1897. She styled herself as widow of Fort Foot. She bequeathed $300 to her daughter Elizabeth Z. Edelen, and the residue to her daughters Mary Naomi Edelen and Sarah M. Galloway wife of Ballard J. Galloway of Baltimore County. She stated that she had already provided for her son Francis A. Posey and daughter Paulina Finotti, the wife of Frank Finotti.[2]

---

[1] Wills, Liber W A J no. 1, folio 356.
[2] Wills, Liber J B P no. 1, folio 396.

BENJAMIN EDELEN[6]

(1808 - 18—)

Benjamin Edelen, son of Robert and Elizabeth (Lewis) Edelen, was born July 19, 1808, at Washington Bottom, Wood County, Virginia. On May 25, 1834, he married Susan Clark who was born in Loudon County, Virginia, on May 24, 1811.

Children of Benjamin and Susan (Clark) Edelen

1. Delos Marcellus Edelen married Sarah Elizabeth Smith. *q.v.*
2. Sarah Edelen married Elias Booher.
3. Annie Edelen married Frank Miller.
4. Stephen Wallace Edelen, born Wood Co., Oct. 28, 1847, married Nov. 5, 1879, at Parkersburg, Emma, born Feb. 25, 1857, dau. of William and Elizabeth (Chancellor) Harwood. Issue: Lillian, born July 1, 1881.
5. Richard H. Edelen, served in Civil War, married first Martha, dau. of Frank and Marietta (Simpson) Lewis. Issue: Francis, born Aug. 12, 1869; George, born Oct. 18, 1871.

Benjamin Edelen, being the eldest son and heir, inherited the parental farm at Washington Bottom. He was a member of the Southern Methodist Episcopal Church.

JOSEPH BENEDICT EDELEN[6]

(1822 - ——)

Joseph Benedict Edelen, son of John Baptist and Caroline (Boarman) Edelen, was born in or about 1822 in Prince Georges County. He married his kinswoman Clara E., born about 1831, the daughter of James Richard and Harriet (Dyer) Edelen.

The 1870 census shows that Joseph Edelen, aged 48, was the head of a family in Piscataway District, with realty appraised at $10,000 and personalty at $15,000. In his household were Clara Edelen aged 36; William aged 14; Blanch aged 11; and Charles aged 8.

Children of Joseph Benedict and Clara (Edelen) Edelen

1. William Edelen.
2. Blanch Edelen.
3. Charles Jenkins Edelen married Olivia Attawa Middleton. *q.v.*

DELOS MARCELLUS EDELEN[7]
(1836 - 1887)

Delos Marcellus Edelen, son of Benjamin and Susan (Clark) Edelen, was born November 22, 1836, at the old place on Washington Bottom. On August 23, 1864, at Marietta, Ohio, he was married to Sarah Elizabeth Smith. She was born March 29, 1839, at Parkersburg, the daughter of Robert Saurin and Lucy Lord (Brooks) Smith.

Children of Delos and Sarah Elizabeth (Smith) Edelen

1. Charles William Edelen married twice. *q.v.*
2. Mary L. Edelen, born 1866, died 1876.
3. Richard H. Edelen, born 1868, died 1873.
4. Sarah Elizabeth Edelen, born Jan. 13, 1880, spinster.

Delos Marcellus Edelen was not only a slave owner as his forefathers had been before him, but he was an intense sympathizer of the Confederate Cause. It is even reported that he trained soldiers for the Army. He died on June 14, 1887; his widow died December 26, 1913.

CHARLES JENKINS EDELEN[7]
(1863 - ——)

Charles Jenkins Edelen, son of Benedict and Clara (Edelen) Edelen, was born in or about 1863 at Piscataway, Maryland. He married a kinswoman Olivia Attawa Middleton, the daughter of Dr. Elexius Llewellyn Middleton. The latter was born December 4, 1833, the son of Elexius and Elizabeth Attawa (Jameson) Middleton. The mother of Olivia, wife to Charles Jenkins Edelen, was Ada Pauline Parker, born 1845 in Maryland, the daughter of Judge Joseph Messenger Parker, of Prince Georges County, and Olivia Edelen his wife.*

Children of Charles and Olivia (Middleton) Edelen

1. Blanche Middleton Edelen, died Mar. 1, 1930, married Clinton A. Baden. Issue: Mary.
2. Pauline Edelen married Pembroke Jones.
3. Alexius Middleton Edelen married Bertie Baden.
4. Joseph Benedict Edelen, U. S. Army, World War, died in service, Oct. 16, 1918.

---

*The 1860 census of Prince Georges County showed that Joseph M. Parker, aged 45, was born in Maryland and had realty valued at $10,000 and personalty at $15,000. His wife was Olivia aged 38, with the following children: Ada aged 15; Florence aged 14; Edelen aged 13; Mary aged 11; Laura aged 9; Joseph aged 6; and Olivia aged 1.

5. David Middleton Edelen married Eloise Berry. Issue: David; Clifford.
6. Charles Jenkins Edelen married Felicie Atlee. Issue: Mabel; Charles Jenkins, III.
7. Clara Edelen married John M. Spadala. Issue: Joan.
8. Attawa Edelen married Thomas Hamilton Webb.
9. William Alexander Dent Edelen.
10. Edgar Hurtt Edelen.
11. Mary Elizabeth Edelen married Francis L. McFarren.

CHARLES EDELEN[8]

Charles William Edelen, son of Delos Marcellus and Sarah (Smith) Edelen, was born June 13, 1865, at Washington Bottom, West Virginia. After his father's death he removed to Parkersburg and ultimately became identified with hardware, banking, and the Parkersburg Transfer & Storage Co. On April 11, 1889, he married Lena L. Leachman. She died on December 24, 1910, and on October 13, 1919, he married Ruth Kilton Caldwell.

Children of Charles and Lena (Leachman) Edelen

1. Barbara Edelen married Frederick Perkins. *q.v.*
2. Charles Brooks Edelen, resident of Cleveland, U. S. Air Corps, World War.
3. John Richard Edelen, U. S. Navy, World War, attached to the fleet which laid Allies' mines in North Sea.
4. Eugene Elliott Edelen, U. S. Navy, World War.
5. Rama May Edelen.
6. Elizabeth Edelen.
7. Isabell Edelen.

BARBARA EDELEN[9]

Barbara Edelen, daughter to Charles and Lena (Leachman) Edelen, was born at Parkersburg, West Virginia. She married Frederick Wallace Perkins, the son of Archer and Henrietta (Layne) Perkins, of West Virginia. He is at present (1940) a journalist of the National Capital and resides in Chevy Chase, Maryland. Three children were born— Frederick Wallace Perkins, II, graduate of University of Maryland; Charles Henry Perkins; and Penelope Perkins.

MISCELLANEOUS

Susannah Edelen made her will on October 1, 1813, being proved in the District of Columbia on November 15, same year. She named her sons Elextius, John, and Ignatius, and daughters Mary Ann Craycroft, and Catherine Bowman. To her granddaughter Lucinda Ann Craycroft she bequeathed $80 which was owed her by James Welch, of Washington. She also referred to money owed her by Robert Long of Washington, and by James Wood and John Gardner, both of Charles County. Her son-in-law, Thomas Craycroft, was named as executor.

Susannah Edelen made her will on November 19, 1818, being admitted to probate in Charles County on December 8, same year. She bequeathed slaves and other personalty to four children—Elizabeth, Lewis, Edward, and John Horatio.

John Edelen dated his will February 14, 1832, it being proved in Charles County on May 24, 1837. He named his wife Eleanor and daughter Elizabeth Jane, but in the event that his wife were with child at the time of his death, then all were to share equally. He appointed his wife and friends John Ferguson and Henry Brawner as executors.

Robert Edelen was born about 1785 in Maryland. On February 20, 1808, in Washington County, Kentucky, he secured license to marry Hetty Riney—born about 1789 in Maryland. The census of 1850 shows that he had realty appraised at $16,400.

His will was dated August 10, 1855, and proved in Washington County, Kentucky, on September 3, same year, by M. R. Hardin, and John Semmes. He requested that he be buried in the churchyard at St. Rose. To his wife Elizabeth Hester he devised 170 acres of the dwelling-plantation situated on Springfield and Perryville Road and the Knod Lick Road, also land of about 36 acres on the Molly Miles' tract, lying on the south side of the last mentioned road, one-half of which had been conveyed to him by R. F. Parrott, and also one-third of all slaves and household effects. He requested his executor to place an iron railing around the burial spot and to erect suitable tombstones for himself and wife. At the death of his widow the land and slaves were to be divided among his children (unnamed). To his son James he devised realty, and mentioned his son George, and sons-in-law Thomas Y. Fenwick and Benedict J. Simms. He appointed his friend Levy J. Smith as executor.

Edward Edelen, son of Robert, predeceased his father, having made his will on May 26, 1846. He bequeathed his wife Priscilla $6,000, and left negroes to his brothers James, Leonard, and George; sisters

Sarah Fenwick, Matilda Semmes, Elizabeth Fenwick, and Harriet Edelen. Also $100 to the Rev. C. D. Bowling for the use of St. Rose Church. Smith Edelen was another heir, but no relationship was stated. At the probation his father Robert Edelen gave his approval.

Clement Edelen was born in or about 1753 in Maryland. On January 24, 1777, he enlisted at Port Tobacco, Charles County, in the company of Captain Nathaniel Ewing of the First Maryland Regiment commanded by Colonel John H. Stone.* Most of his services were in the States of New York and New Jersey part of the time under the command of Major Mordecai Gist. In the same regiment were Edward Edelen and John Edelen. He participated in the battles of White Plains, Germantown, and Brandywine, and was discharged at the termination of his enlistment on December 27, 1779, with the rank of sergeant, near the town of Kumbley, New Jersey. His discharge was signed by Captain Alexander Roxburgh.

He returned to Maryland and on November 6, 1780, he obtained license in Prince Georges County to marry Anne Simpson.[2]

After the war he removed to Breckinridge County, Kentucky, where he pursued the occupation of farmer. Under the Act of 1818 he applied for a Revolutionary pension as a resident of Kentucky. His immediate household at that time consisted of his wife aged 70, and a maiden daughter Anne aged 36. He subsequently settled at the home of a son-in-law in White County, Illinois. At the age of 74 he was married to Lucy Aud at Carmi, Illinois, by John Craw, a Justice of the Peace. He died in White County on May 25, 1839. His widow being much his junior married on May 10, 1840, Adolphus Ammons. Her second husband died in White County on December 18, 1841. On February 18, 1862, Lucy Ammons, aged 56, as the widow of Clement Edelen, Revolutionary soldier, applied for bounty land under the Act of 1855.

---

*Although he stated under oath that he enlisted Dec. 10, 1776, the official records state Jan. 24, 1777. (Archives, vol. 18, p. 6.)

Hanson

HANSON FAMILY

Few families of Maryland have been the subject of more tradition and myth than the Hansons. And while tradition plays its part in history and genealogy, it means very little to the searcher of the truth unless that tradition can be substantiated by State or private documents.

According to tradition, the Hansons of both the Eastern and Western Shores of Maryland all descend from an English gentleman who settled in Sweden and married a lady of noble birth. The name or house of this distinguished lady, however, has never been cited. Both died young, leaving an orphan boy who in manhood became an officer in the Swedish Army and was killed at the battle of Luttzen in 1632. He left four minor sons who in 1642 were sent by Queen Christiana as her special wards to the Governor of New Sweden in America, afterwards the Colony of Delaware. In 1653 the four Hansons—Andrew, William, Randolph, and John—removed to Kent Island in the Province of Maryland. Andrew became the progenitor of the Hansons of the Eastern Shore, William and Randolph died without male issue, while John became the father of the Hansons of Charles County.

Regarding the truths of the above traditions, the compiler of these chronicles does not wish to enter into any controversy, but the records which have been preserved in Maryland somehow seem to contradict the narrative. In the seventeenth century the family name of Hanson in England was as common as its Swedish equivalent Hansen. Many of the baptismal records of the early seventeenth century parishes of England have been searched and the name of Hanson appears most frequently.

Disregarding the traditions of the Maryland family, a review of the early entries of settlers bearing the surname of Hanson is essential. In September 1658, Andrew Elina demanded land for the transportation of Andrew Hanson, Anibeck Hanson, Margaret Hanson, Hance (Hans) Hanson, Frederick Hanson, and Catherine Hanson into Maryland. His Lordship's clerk therefore ordered the Deputy Surveyor of Kent County to lay out for Andrew Elina 350 acres of land on the east side of Chester River and the north side of Corsica Creek adjoining the land of Henry Coursey.[1]

From the above record, it is ascertained that the six Hansons were all in Maryland by the year 1658 and had expressed their intentions to become subjects of Lord Baltimore. Inasmuch as all six were transported by a single person, it can be assumed that they were closely related and probably all arrived in the same vessel. It is also noted that two had given names not common to most English families. By 1666 it was shown that Margaret Hanson had become the wife of Alexander Waters.

Hans Hanson left quite a distinguished record for his descendants. In 1671 he applied for naturalization and stated that he was "borne in Delaware Bay of Swedish parents". He represented Kent County at the General Assembly in 1692, 1693, 1694, and beginning in 1695 he was referred to as Colonel Hans Hanson. He continued to serve throughout the 1697 session.

In 1659 Randle (Randolph) Hanson appeared at His Lordship's Land Office at St. Mary's City and requested 50 acres of land which was due him as a former redemptioner of Dr. Luke Barber. At this event it was not only shown that Randle Hanson had performed a certain period of service to Dr. Barber but that he had in 1657 on his own volition transported a certain John Davis into the Province to inhabit. It is therefore proved that Randle was a freeholder in 1657 and apparently was in Maryland prior to 1650.

Randle Hanson was sometimes enscribed on the records as Henson and Hinson, and was most likely the first bearing the name of Hanson to settle in Maryland. He was domiciled in Charles County, but after a thorough search there is no suggestion nor fact to indicate that he was of any blood relationship to John Hanson who is the ancestor of the Hanson family with whom these chronicles are directly concerned.

The family of John Hanson gained fame and fortune in Colonial Maryland and ranked among the first families of the Province in culture as well as in society of that period. It was entitled to bear arms, inasmuch as Robert Hanson, presumably the eldest son of the supposed emigrant, in his will bequeathed to a son "my sword, pistols, and silver seal".

Perchance, it would not be wholly impossible to prove some day that John Hanson were of near relationship or even son to Sir Robert Hanson, one-time Lord Mayor of London. It is frankly admitted, however, that in the preparation of this discourse no research was conducted to prove or disprove this point. But it is significant that John Hanson gave the name Robert to his believed-eldest son.

The following is taken from the records of the Prerogative Court of Maryland for 1674 and clearly shows that Sir Robert had official relations with some of the Maryland subjects:[2]

> "To all persons to whom these presents shall come Sir Robert
> Hanson, Knight, Lord Mayor of the Citty of London and the alder-
> man of the same citty send Greeting at the instance and humble re-

quest of John Keynes of Marleborough in the County of Wilts, Gent., wee the said Lord Mayor and Aldermen doe certify for undoubted truth that the said John Keynes is sole executor of the last will and testament of Joseph Burgess, late of Marleborough, and of Anne Arundel County in the province of Maryland, Merchant, deceased, and . . . have, proved his will under the seal of the Prerogative Court of the Archbishop of Canterbury bearing date of 27 November . . . and Thomas Taylor have administered on the estate in the Province to the behalf of the said John Keyns . . . "

---

[1] Liber Q, folio 365; Liber 10, folio 312, Land Office.
[2] Test. Pro., Liber 6, folio 233.

JOHN HANSON[1]

(16— - 1714)

The first reference to John Hanson in Charles County was of June 1672, when he witnessed the will of Stephen Montague—though a John Hanson, with no county given, was named as the overseer of the estate of John Pain in 1671. From the former fact, it is concluded that in 1672 John Hanson had attained at least his eighteenth birthday, the required age for witness, consequently his birth occurred prior to the year 1654.

In 1676 John Hanson became the heir to the residuary estate of Richard Midgely, of Charles County, who, besides Hanson, named his wife Elizabeth Midgely and brother-in-law John Lewager. The will was formally proved in the Prerogative Court before John Stone, Gent., when John Wright and Edward Price were ordered to appraise the estate. Although the will failed to name an executor, the instrument was administered by John Hanson and Elizabeth Midgely as "executors" at its initial probation and at a return of the inventory early in 1677. At subsequent accounts, namely, in 1678 and 1679, John Hanson appeared as the sole executor.

In 1675 he purchased land from Thomas Cosker, and in 1677 he bought additional land from William Lowday and Joan his wife, the latter conveyance being witnessed by Thomas Jenkins and Joseph Wolff.[1] These are practically the only knowledge of land ownership. He failed to exercise his rights to 50 acres of land upon his intentions to become a subject. And from the fact that he patented no land may offer the suggestion that he were of the second generation in the Province. Furthermore, if he had been of foreign birth, he would have come under the Act of Naturalization which affected all residing in :he

Province after a certain year. While record exists of the naturalization of Hans Hanson, none is found for John.

In January 1678/9, John Hanson was sued in court by Rando Hinson, executor of Zachary Wade, late of Charles County, deceased, for 623 pounds of tobacco. He was represented at court by Nehemiah Blackston, and subsequently lost the suit.[2]

On August 24, 1680, Elizabeth Maris, the daughter of Thomas Maris, deceased, was placed by the court under John Hanson "until she arrives at 16 or marriage, if not then married, then to 18, she being about 4 years of age".[3]

His participation in the punitive expedition against the Nanticoke Indians of the Eastern Shore was the occasion for the receipt of 830 pounds of tobacco by His Lordship's Assembly in 1678, and this seems to be the only record of his activity in military affairs—though his two sons both distinguished themselves in that field. In 1682 an additional 60 pounds of tobacco were awarded for public service by vote of the Assembly.[4]

In 1684 John Hanson witnessed the will of Henry Hickson, of Nanjemoy Hundred, and in 1704 he, with his son Robert, likewise witnessed the will of George Britt, of Charles County. In 1697 he and John Addison were appointed by the court to appraise the estate of George Tubman, and in 1704 he and John Theobald were likewise appointed to appraise the estate of John Stone.

These are practically all recorded references to his public or private career which, when compared to those of his immediate descendants, were rather unimportant. It is also significant that in no instance was his name followed by the courtesy title of "Gent.", which after the first generation in Maryland implied affluence rather than birth. He, however, was superior to many of his Maryland compatriots by the fact that he could inscribe his name, but from the absence of civil positions of trust and prominence and the designation of Gentleman somehow lead one to draw the conclusion that it took the stamina of the second generation and their marriages with gentry houses to place the family among the elite of Southern Maryland.

The only reference to his wife is in the County Court record which registers the birth of "Anne, the daughter of John Hanson and Mary his wife, of Portobacco, was born on 18 January 1692".

Children of John and Mary Hanson

1. Robert Hanson married four times. *q.v.*
2. Benjamin Hanson. Died intestate Chas. Co; inventory Aug. 1719; appraised £188; Josh Douglas, executor; George Dent and Douglas Gifford, presumably greatest creditors.

3. Mary Hanson married William Maconchie and Theophilus Swift.
4. Anne Hanson, born 1692.
5. Sarah Hanson.
6. John Hanson married twice. *q.v.*
7. Samuel Hanson married Elizabeth Story. *q.v.*

The will of John Hanson was dated December 12, 1713, and proved in Charles County on July 5, 1714, by Jane Rose, Alexander Contee, and John Cockain. Robert was devised the dwelling-plantation and named as the executor. Other heirs were his children—Benjamin, Mary the wife of the the Rev. William Maconchie, Anne Hanson, Sarah Hanson, John Hanson, and Samuel Hanson—and his grandson Samuel Hanson.[5]

The bond of Robert Hanson in the amount of £300 was filed at the Prerogative Court on July 5, 1714, with John Rogers and Alexander Contee as his sureties. The inventory of the personal estate was appraised at £142/9/4, by Thomas Lewis and Matthew Barnes.

[1] Deeds, Liber F no. 1, folio 165, La Plata.
[2] Liber H no. 1, folio 120, La Plata.
[3] *Ibid.*, folio 325.
[4] Archives, vol. 7.
[5] Wills, Liber 13, folio 719.

COLONEL ROBERT HANSON, GENT.[2]

(16— - 1748)

Robert Hanson, son to John, was born at a date prior to the year 1686 in Port Tobacco Hundred, Charles County, and was probably the eldest son as he was entrusted with the administration of his father's estate. In 1704 he witnessed a will and in 1705 he negotiated his first land patent—"Hanson's Discovery" of 51 acres. No other patents were made until 1719 when "Hanson's Hills" of 136 acres was surveyed. Then several appeared in rapid succession—"Hanson's Plains" of 75 acres in 1725; "Hansonston" of 600 acres in 1726; "Robertus" of 345 acres in 1727; and "Addition to Robertus" of 28 acres in 1728, but the certificate to the latter was issued to George Dent.

Robert Hanson married four times—from his numerous wives and the loss of the parish register, it has been extremely difficult to establish the maternal parent of each child. No issue occurred, however, from the fourth and last union.

His first wife was Mary, daughter of Colonel Philip Hoskins, a neighbor and an important figure of his day in Southern Maryland.[1] Colonel Hoskins negotiated his will on June 20, 1714, and provided for his daughter Mary who was perhaps a maiden at that time. At the probation of the will, however, she had become Mrs. Hanson.

On June 16, 1718, Robert Hanson with Philip Hoskins, II, as next of kin, signed the inventory papers of the personal estate of his father-in-law. Likewise, on August 12, 1720, Robert Hanson and Thomas Stone, both being brothers-in-law to the deceased, signed the inventory of Philip Hoskins, II.

Children of Robert and Mary (Hoskins) Hanson

1. Robert Hanson, *d.s.p.* 1734, willing brother Samuel house—lot in Charles Towne; brother William "Hanson Green"; and personalty to mother Violetta* and Mistress Elizabeth Story.
2. William Hanson married Mary Stone. *q.v.*
3. Samuel Hanson married Mary Fendall. *q.v.*

By 1721 the first wife of Robert Hanson was deceased and he had married Dorothy, the widow of John Parry (Perry) with a son Thomas. John Parry died intestate in Charles County during 1719, when on November 11, his widow and administratrix filed the administration bond in common form to the value of £3,000, with Robert Hanson, Daniel Jenifer, Bernard White, and Luke Barber as her sureties. On March 2, 1720/21, at the proceedings of the Prerogative Court George Dent and Daniel Jenifer were ordered to pass the account of "Robert Hanson and Dorothy his wife, administrators of John Parry late of Charles County, deceased".[2]

The following three children are believed to be of this union: Dorothy was named from her mother, and inasmuch as Benjamin was a minor at the death of his father, he could not possibly be an issue of the first marriage.

Children of Robert and Dorothy Hanson

4. Dorothy Hanson married Richard Harrison.**
5. Benjamin Hanson, *d.s.p.*
6. Mary Hanson married Daniel, son Daniel Jenifer and Elizabeth his wife. Issue: Walter Hanson; Warren Dent; Daniel.†

---

*Although he named Violetta as his mother, it is believed that it was through affections rather than blood, for if he were the son of Violetta, he would have been too young to have negotiated a will in 1734.

**"Died on 5 of last month (Mar. 5, 1752) Dorothy wife of Col. Richard Harrison, of Charles County, and daughter of Col. Robert Hanson, aged 31 years" (Md. Gazette). "In memory of Dorothy Harrison a sincere christian who was the daughter of Col. Robert Hanson and Dorothy his wife of Port Tobacco and wife of Col. Richard Harrison of Nangemoy who was born September 19, 1721, and died March 5, 1752, aged 30 years, 3 months, and 25 days, had issue Robert Hanson, William, Walter Hanson, . . ." (remainder illegible). Reference: Durham Churchyard.

†Former genealogists, somewhat reliable, have stated that she married John Briscoe. Furthermore, Myers Cary Wilson, well known and careful genealogist of the past generation, stated that Daniel Jenifer married Elizabeth, daughter of Walter Hanson. True it is that Daniel Jenifer named a son Walter Hanson, but he also named a son Warren Dent and no immediate connection with the Dent

By 1727 Robert Hanson had taken upon himself a third wife—
Violetta, daughter of Francis and Elizabeth Harrison. On May 5, 1727,
Violetta Hoskins, the widow and administratrix of William Hoskins,
filed her administration bond in the amount of £800, with Robert
Hanson and Richard Harrison as her bondsmen. By August 1727 the
widow was Mrs. Hanson and as such she waived dower when her husband Robert Hanson deeded to his son Samuel for natural love and
affections the tract "Lampton".[3]

The court on June 13, 1730, commissioned George Dent to pass the
account "on the petition and prayers of Robert Hanson who married
Violetta administratrix of William Hoskins and the said Robert Hanson
executor of Mary Lenoir, both of Charles County, deceased".[4]

The children of this union are proved absolutely, inasmuch as they
were named as the grandchildren of Madame Elizabeth Thorne who died
testate in 1756.

Violetta was a widow with two daughters—Elizabeth and Mary.
Elizabeth married Walter Hanson, while Mary married John Cunningham and Mungo Muschett.[5]

Children of Robert and Violetta (Harrison) Hanson

7. Sarah Hanson married Gerard Fowke. Issue: Gerard; Sarah;
   Catherine; Roger.
8. Violetta Hanson, died spinster 1786, naming nephew Gerrard
   Fowke; James and John sons of John and Catherine Robertson.[6]
9. Robert Hanson, *d.s.p.* 1770.

The fourth and last wife of Robert Hanson was Anne, the widow of
John Maconchie. On April 14, 1747, they signed a marriage agreement
by which Robert Hanson renounced all claims in the estate of Anne

---

family is known. Walter Hanson, Jr., distinctly willed property to his sister
Elizabeth Smoot who is identified as the wife of William Barton Smoot. (Wills,
Liber A H no. 9, folio 145.) The wife of Daniel Jenifer pre-deceased him, but
as Mary Jenifer she waived dower in 1768. (Deeds, Liber O no. 3, folio 366.)
Also in 1768. (Deeds, Liber S no. 3, folio 127.)

Furthermore, Mary Hanson by the will of her father inherited "Hanson's
Plain" and "Habber Adventure". At that time Mary was unmarried. On December
13, 1770, "Daniel Jenifer, of Charles County, Gent., conveyed to Thomas Stone
of the same county Gent. his heirs and assigns forever all that tract or parcel of
land lying and being in Charles County aforesaid called Haberdeventure and
Hanson's Plains Enlarged which was heretofore wit on 23 day of September in
the year of our Lord God 1768 by patent granted unto the said Daniel Jenifer
... with all waters, water Courses, woods, underwoods, Houses, Buildings, rails,
Hereditaments, Benifts advantages Conveniences and Appurtenances ... standing on the west side of the main road that leads from Port Tobacco to Piscataway
... for £400". Mary Jenifer wife of Daniel Jenifer waived dower, while Walter
Hanson and Josias Hawkins witnessed. (Deeds, Liber S no. 3, folio 127.) It is
thus shown that Mary married Daniel Jenifer and not John Briscoe unless the
latter was a first marriage.

Maconchie. The Rev. Theophilus Swift was a party to the prenuptial contract, while the witnesses were Matthew Stone, Jr., Mary Swift, and Margaret Chapman.[7]

Robert Hanson was most active in negotiating bonds for his neighbors and friends which indicated that he was not only a gentleman of wealth but of trust and confidence. In 1711 he and William Hoskins were sureties for Jane Sanders the administratrix of Edward Sanders. In 1713 he was bondsman for Frances Boughton the administratrix of Samuel Boughton; Catherine Thomas the executrix of Benoni Thomas; Joan Elliott the executrix of William Elliott; Thomas Dixon the administrator of Christopher Shadwell; and Mary Theobald the executrix of John Theobald.

In 1716 he was the administrator of the estate of Cornelius Kelly, at which time his brother Samuel Hanson and Thomas Dent were the bondsmen. In 1717 he was named the executor of the estate of Osmond Waple when Samuel Hanson and William Hoskins offered bond.

In 1727 and at other times he was one of the sureties for his brother Samuel Hanson, the Deputy Commissary for Charles County. In the same year he and his son Robert certified to the deposition of Bigger Head as his being the brother and one of the representatives of Kendall Head, deceased, of Prince Georges County.

In 1733 he and Anne Eburnathy were executors of John Eburnathy, at which time Matthew Barnes and Francis Ware were their bondsmen. And in November 1734, citations were issued by the court to show why they had failed to file an account. In 1736 he and John Theobald were bondsmen for Elizabeth Thorne, widow and executrix of Absolom Thorne, who was also the grandmother of his children by Violetta Harrison. The same year he and James Smallwood, Sr., were sureties for Edmund Devine, the administrator of James Proffee. During 1741 he and Benjamin Douglas were bondsmen for Elizabeth, executrix of his brother Sanuel Hanson.

His first public office of significance seems to have been as early as 1716, when he was High Sheriff of Charles County. In September 1746, he was referred to as Colonel Robert Hanson. In 1724 he was Justice of the Peace.[8]

Robert Hanson established his seat at "Betty's Delight" which he had inherited from his father. On March 1, 1717, he purchased from William Lampton, of Richmond County, Virginia, "Lampton", lying on Port Tobacco Creek, adjoining the land of Juliana Price, widow, formerly in the possession of Colonel Benjamin Rozier and called "St. Patrick". Matthew Stone acted as attorney for the grantor, with John Beale, William Wills, and Thomas Green as the witnesses.[9]

On April 28, 1717, he purchased from Juliana Price, widow, "St. Patrick's Hill", lying on the west side of Port Tobacco Creek. The witnesses were Thomas Hussey Luckett, Andrew Simpson, and Elizabeth Luckett.[9]

On November 12, 1720, he bought of William Chandler, Gent., "Chandler Hill" of 300 acres, lying at the head of Port Tobacco Creek on the west side, which had been patented to Job Chandler, the grandfather of the grantor. The witnesses were Alexander Contee and Walter Story.[9]

On March 17, 1721, Robert Hanson and Dorothy his wife deeded to Thomas Parry, son of Dorothy Hanson, for natural love and affections "Digges' Baltimore Gift" and "Digges' Addition", which had been conveyed by Thomas Turner to Dorothy Hanson, then the widow of John Parry. Thomas Stone and Charles Somerset Smith witnessed the conveyance.[9]

On June 10, 1724, Robert Hanson purchased from John Lambeth "Haber de Adventure", lying at the head of Port Tobacco Creek, adjoining the lands of John Robinson and also "Simpson's Delight" then in the possession of the heirs of Francis Wine. Sarah Lambeth, wife to John, waived dower, while the conveyance was witnessed by John Briscoe and Charles Somerset Smith.[10]

On November 15, 1744, Robert Hanson and Violetta his wife, conveyed for love and natural affections to Elizabeth Hanson and Mary Cunningham, the latter two named in the deed as the daughters of Violetta Hanson, the dower which Violetta Hanson held in the tract "Friendship" which she was entitled as the widow of William Hoskins. At the time of the conveyance, Elizabeth was the wife of Walter Hanson and Mary the wife of John Cunningham. The witnesses were Allen Davis and Richard Harrison.[11]

The will of Robert Hanson was dated April 5, 1746, and proved in Charles County on September 27, 1748, by Edmond Porteus, Samuel Hanson, Jr., and Daniel of St. Thomas Jenifer. William was devised 100 acres of "Abergane", including the tracts "Robertus Granted" and "Addition to Robertus". Robert, the youngest son, received the dwelling-plantation "Betty's Delight", of 100 acres "which was left me by my father John Hanson". Robert also received 69 acres of land purchased from William Chandler, being a portion of "Chandler's Hill", and other realty. Samuel was bequeathed his sword, pistols, and silver seal.

His daughter Dorothy, the wife of Richard Harrison, was devised "Hansonston", and Mary Hanson, a single daughter, was devised "Hanson's Plain" and "Habber Adventure". Other children named were Benjamin, Robert, Mary, Sarah, and Violetta, and his grandson Robert, son of Samuel and Mary Hanson. His nephew Walter Hanson was to be placed under the guardianship of the testator's son Robert.[12]

The inventory of his personal estate was not filed until September 9, 1749, with Joseph Hanson Harrison as the executor. The estate was appraised at £878/14, with Mary Swift and William Hanson signing as the kinsmen. William Eilbeck and Walter Hanson were the greatest creditors.

An account was rendered on September 6, 1750, by Joseph Hanson Harrison and Gerard Fowke as the administrators, and Theophilus Swift and Captain William Hanson as the sureties. The balance due the estate was £1,024/6/11. An additional account on February 6, 1752, stated that Violetta Hanson, a daughter of the deceased, was at age, that Benjamin Hanson, another heir of the deceased, had died a minor since the death of his father, and that Robert Hanson was the only minor heir of the deceased, being between the ages of 10 and 11 years. Furthermore, it stated that the "accountants" had each married daughters of the deceased.*

Another account, dated July 22, 1759, showed that all legatees were of age except Robert who was under the guardianship of Walter Hanson.

On May 28, 1751, Madam Anne Hanson and William Hutchison with his wife Jane, all of Charles County, conveyed to Samuel Middleton, planter, for a consideration of £120 "Wheeler's Purchase", that part which was then in the possession of William Eilbeck. Thomas Stone and R. Harrison witnessed the conveyance.[13] In that year it was also shown that Anne Hanson had not completed the administration on the estate of her husband John Maconchie.

Her will was dated February 2, 1758, and proved in Charles County ten days later by Theophilus Swift, Mary Stone, and Richard King. She named her sons William and Alexander Macconchie; grandchildren Anne Hutchinson and John Macconchie; and niece Mary Hodgkins.[14]

The inventory was not filed with the court until December 2, 1758, when it had an appraised value of £990/19/9½. William Macconchie was the executor, and Peter Contee and Thomas Howard were the kinsmen.

Robert Hanson, the bachelor and youngest son, died in Charles County—his will being dated April 28, 1765, and proved on February 8, 1770, by Gustavus R. Brown, Warren Dent, and Mary Clarke. He devised his sister Violetta Hanson, the dwelling-plantation "Betsy's

---

*It is proved that Gerard Fowke married a daughter of Robert Hanson, but the marriage of Joseph Hanson Harrison with a daughter can not be placed.

Delight", lying in Port Tobacco Parish and the other tracts left him by their father, and certain lands in Durham Parish to his brother-in-law Captain Gerard Fowke. Other heirs were Gerard, son of Gerard and Sarah Fowke (no relationship stated); nieces Sarah Fowke and Catherine Fowke; nephews Roger Fowke, Walter Hanson, Hoskins Hanson of Walter, William Muschet and Mung Muschet*; sister Sarah Fowke; and friend John Muschet.[15]

An account on his estate, dated April 13, 1772, showed a balance of £800/15/4, with Jesse Doyne and Theophilus Hanson the sureties for the executor.

---

[1] Adm. Accts., Liber 10, folio 5.
[2] *Ibid.*, Liber 5, folio 102.
[3] Deeds, Liber no. 3, folio 692, La Plata.
[4] Test. Pro., Liber 29, folio 21.
[5] Deeds, Liber G no. 3, folio 575, La Plata.
[6] Wills, Liber A H no. 9, folio 277.
[7] Deeds, Liber Z no. 2, folio 203, La Plata.
[8] Test. Pro., Liber 32, folio 10; Liber 27, folio 209.
[9] Deeds, Liber H no. 2, folios 129, 174, 398, 425, 442, La Plata.
[10] Deeds, Liber L no. 2, folio 147, La Plata.
[11] Deeds, Liber X no. 2, folios 96, 162, La Plata.
[12] Wills, Liber 25, folio 412.
[13] Deeds, Liber Z no. 2, folio 496, La Plata.
[14] Wills, Liber 30, folio 527.
[15] Wills, Liber 37, folio 588.

JOHN HANSON, GENT.[2]

(1681 - 1754)

John Hanson, son of John and Mary Hanson, certified in 1730 that he was 49 years of age, therefore, placing his birth year as about 1681. On November 30, 1705, he married the twice widowed Elizabeth Hussey, a Catholic matron, by whom a Catholic branch of the Hansons developed.[1]

Children of John and Elizabeth (Hussey) Hanson

1. John Hanson married Elizabeth Massey. q.v.
2. Elizabeth Hanson married Leonard Wheeler.
3. Mary Hanson married William, son of John and Elizabeth Clements. Issue: Bennett Hanson; Oswald; Clothilder; Elizabeth; Henrietta; Edward; Mary; Maryanne; William.[3]
4. Eleanor Hanson married William Hagan.

In 1730 John Hanson patented "Hanson's Enlargement", and in 1734 "Hanson's Amendement". These were followed in 1737 by "Greenland" of 755 acres.

---

*The Muschets were half-nephews.

On July 13, 1721, John Hanson and Elizabeth his wife conveyed to William Wells for 20,000 lbs. of tobacco "Newport" which was described as a portion of the land taken up by Thomas Hussey father of the said Elizabeth. The witnesses were W. Hoskins, William Theobald, and Thomas Stone.[3]

On June 15, 1727, John Hanson purchased from Henry Holland Hawkins "Hussey's Addition", at which time Joan Hawkins waived dower, and Robert Hanson and Gustavus Brown witnessed the deal.[4] On April 27, 1731, he purchased from James Maddock, Innholder, for 1200 lbs. of tobacco land which Maddock had bought at a sheriff sale. Robert Hanson and Henry Hawkins signed the deed as witnesses.[5]

John Hanson negotiated his will on June 5, 1747, at which time he devised to his wife Elizabeth his entire estate during life. After her decease it was to be divided among his daughter Elizabeth the wife of Leonard Wheeler, his daughter Eleanor the wife of William Hagan, and his son John who was to receive "Hanson's Amendment". The witnesses to the will were Henry Hawkins, Samuel Hanson, and Francis Ware.[6]

His wife, however, died soon afterwards, and John Hanson married secondly Mary, the widow of Francis Goodrick. On July 20, 1749, John Hanson and Mary his wife as the administrators of the estate of Francis Goodrick filed their bond in the Prerogative Court with Edward Goodrick and Francis Goodrick as the sureties.[7]

No changes were made to the will of John Hanson, so consequently at his death in 1754 considerable litigation occurred over the estate which was acquired by the marriage with the Widow Goodrick.

On May 1, 1754, Francis Ware, of Charles County, stated that he found the will among his father's papers after the death of his father— Francis Ware, Sr. At the same time Edward Goodrick, George Goodrick, and Henry Goodrick, step-sons of the late John Hanson, certified to the fact that they believed the will to be in the hand writing of John Hanson.

Walter Hanson likewise made the same statement as well as Dr. Gustavus Brown. Charles Courts identified the signatures of Francis Barnes and Godshall Barnes.

On September 21, 1754, Mrs. Violetta Sewell stated that she first learned of the approaching marriage of John Hanson with her mother through William Hanson about ten days before its occurrence. She became somewhat concerned, but John Hanson assured her that "he did not want anything of my mother's estate". Mrs. Anne McCoy, sister of Mary Goodrick-Hanson, also was a witness at the law suit.

The inventory was taken on August 31, 1754, and filed at court in November 1755, with John Hanson as the executor. It was appraised by John Theobald and William Neale at £903/8/5, and the greatest creditors were George Dent and John Semple. The final account was rendered on January 10, 1757, and showed a balance of £1,058. Godshall Barnes and Charles Courts were the bondsmen.

---

[1] *See, The Lucketts of Portobacco;* also Test. Pro., Liber 19c, folio 118.
[2] Test. Pro., Liber 40, folio 1; Wills, Liber 29, folio 241.
[3] Deeds, Liber H no. 2, folio 446, La Plata.
[4] Deeds, Liber L no. 2, folio 365, La Plata.
[5] Deeds, Liber M no. 2, folio 250, La Plata.
[6] Wills, Liber 29, folio 241.
[7] Test. Pro., Liber 32.

JUDGE SAMUEL HANSON, GENT.[2]

(1684 - 1740)

Samuel Hanson, son of John and Mary Hanson, was born in or about 1684 in Port Tobacco Hundred, Charles County. He married about 1706 Elizabeth, daughter of Walter Story but then the widow of Benjamin Warren. In that year a commission was issued by the Prerogative Court to Samuel Hanson and Walter Story, executors of Benjamin Warren, to exhibit an inventory of the latter's estate. On July 19, 1708, Samuel Hanson and his wife "who was the executors of Benjamin Warren, Gent., late of the Province, deceased", were deeded property by John Warren, of Charles County, Gent. The deed stated that the grantor was a brother to the deceased.[1]

Some litigation and dissatisfaction arose over the settlement of the estate and as late as 1713 John Warren, brother, forced the sheriff to issue citations against "Elizabeth Warren als Hanson now wife of Samuel Hanson and against Walter Story" to settle the estate.[2]

Children of Samuel and Elizabeth (Story) Hanson

1. Elizabeth Hanson, born Nov. 9, 1707, married Benjamin Douglas.
2. Mary Hanson, born Feb. 4, 1709.*
3. Walter Hanson married Elizabeth Hoskins. *q.v.*
4. Sarah Hanson, born July 29, 1714.*
5. Samuel Hanson married twice. *q.v.*
6. William Hanson, born Mar. 18, 1718, died 1721.
7. John Hanson married Jane Contee. *q.v.*
8. Jane Hanson, born Feb. 18, 1721/22.

---

*It is said that David Stone married a daughter of Samuel Hanson—some say Mary others Sarah—no proof has been found by this compiler. *See, The Stones of Poynton Manor*, by Newman.

9. Charity Hanson, born Aug. 15, 1724, married John Howard and
   Arthur Lee. Issue: Chloe Howard; Sarah Lee.
10. William Hanson, born Sept. 29, 1726.
11. Chloe Hanson married Philip Briscoe. Issue: John Hanson;
    Samuel Hanson; Hanson; Elizabeth Story.

In 1718 Samuel Hanson and James Cottrell were sureties for Eleanor
and John Philpott, the executors of the will of Edward Philpott. In
1719 he was High Sheriff of Charles County, an office which he relinquished the next year to become Deputy Commissary for his county.
His bondsmen at various times were Robert Hanson, John Hanson, and
William Chandler.[3] On April 7, 1719, he and Alexander Contee signed
bond for Robert Hanson, the administrator of Benjamin Hanson.

His first land patent was in 1717, when he received "Hanson's Discovery" of 150 acres, followed by "Tryall" of 300 acres in 1719, "Hanson's Plains" of 75 acres in 1725, and "Wilkinson's Throne" of 506
acres in 1736. The latter tract was patented jointly with Eleanor Wilkinson.

About 1730 Daniel Dulany, Commissary General, at the request of
Samuel Hanson issued letters of administration to him as the adminis-
trator of the estate of Richard Bell, late of Charles County, deceased.
Philip Key and John Parnham were ordered to appraise the estate, and
Col. Robert Hanson "one of his Lordship's Justices" to swear them.[4]

He died at his estate in Charles County and was buried at "Equal-
ity". His gravestone reads: "Here Lyes the body of Mr. Samuel Hanson who departed this life the 26 Day of October 1740 in the 56 year
of his age".

His will was dated October 22, 1740, and proved in Charles County
on March 5, 1740/1, by Theophilus Swift, Joseph Trines, and Sarah
Trines. His wife Elizabeth was devised the dwelling-plantation known
as "Littleworth", and 203 acres of "Wilkinson's Throne" during life,
then to son William. Samuel received a 140-portion of "Green's Inheritance", and 35 acres of "Addition to Hereford"; John was willed
"Hereford", and the residue of "Addition to Hereford". Other heirs
were his daughters: Charity, Jane, Chloe, and Elizabeth wife of Benjamin Douglas; and his granddaughter Eleanor Douglas. His son
Walter was named as overseer of the estate, and his wife and son-in-law
Benjamin Douglas were named as guardian of the minor son William.[5]

The inventory of the personal estate was filed on July 10, 1741, by
his executors, with Robert Hanson and Benjamin Douglas as the sureties. The appraisement was £1,049/1/5, with Gustavus Brown and
G. Barnes as the greatest creditors, and Samuel Hanson, Jr., and John
Hanson as the next of kin.

The will of his widow, Elizabeth Hanson, was dated March 19, 1764, and proved in Charles County, on June 15, 1764, by George Lee and Leonard Marbury, Jr. She named her daughters Jane Hanson and Elizabeth Douglas, and son Samuel.[6]

[1] Deeds, Liber C no. 2, folio 123, La Plata.
[2] Test. Pro., Liber 22, folios 359, 245.
[3] Test. Pro., Liber 23, folio 400; Liber 24, folio 307.
[4] Test. Pro., Liber 29, folio 462.
[5] Wills, Liber 22, folio 296.
[6] Wills, Liber 32, folio 162.

CAPTAIN WILLIAM HANSON[3]

(1717 - 1766)

William Hanson, son of Colonel Robert Hanson, was born about 1717 in Port Tobacco Parish, Charles County. It is assumed that he was the eldest son, inasmuch as his name appears first in his father's will, and some of his children carried the family name of Hoskins. He, however, married a kinswoman, Mary, daughter of Thomas and Martha (Hoskins) Stone.*

Children of William and Mary (Stone) Hanson

1. Theophilus Hanson. *q.v.*
2. William Hanson, *d.s.p.* 1774, naming sister Jane Hoskins Hanson, and niece Mary Harris Hanson of Theophilus.
3. Samuel Hanson married Margaret Macconchie. *q.v.*
4. Aurelia Hanson.
5. Jane (Jenney) Hoskins Hanson.

In 1735 William Hanson with David Stone was bondsman for Sarah Fowke, the executor of Gerard Fowke. In 1742 he and his father were bondsmen for Mary Maconchie, the executor of the Rev. William Maconchie. In 1745 he was bondsman for John Courts, the administrator of George Love, and in 1751, he with Alexander McPherson was surety for John Theobald, the executor of William Theobald.

On December 14, 1746, William Hanson received from his father a deed to "Robertus" which had originally been granted to James Lindsey, Jr., and escheated to Robert Hanson. S. Hanson and Robert Yates were the witnesses.[1]

*For the ancestry of Mary Stone, *see, The Stones of Poynton Manor,* by Newman.

He was active in the colonial militia and at one time commanded a Company of the Horse.* When he was bondsman for the executors of his father's estate, he was styled captain.

His wife predeceased him, but she was living as late as the year 1750 when she was named in the will of her step-mother Catherine Stone. His children—Aurelia, William, Jenny Hoskins, Samuel, and Theophilus— were heirs in the will of their maternal aunt, Anne Fowke, who died in Charles County during 1761.[2]

The will of William Hanson was dated December 16, 1765, and proved in Charles County on May 14, 1766, by William Lindsey, John Stone, and Anne Lindsey. He devised the dwelling-plantation "Aborgany" and other tracts to his three sons — Theophilus, William, and Samuel—and personalty to his two daughters—Aurelia Hanson and Jenny Hoskins Hanson.[3]

The final account was not passed by the court until November 19, 1771, when Theophilus Hanson appeared as the executor and Samuel Hanson, Jr., and Robert Hanson were his bondsmen.[4]

---

[1] Deeds, Liber Z no. 2, folio 156.
[2] Wills, Liber 28, folio 26.
[3] Wills, Liber 34, folio 129.
[4] Adm. Accts., Liber 67, folio 25.

Major Samuel Hanson[2]

(17— - 1749)

Samuel Hanson, son of Colonel Robert Hanson, is believed to be a son of the first wife Mary Hoskins. If he were of the second union, his birth would have occurred after 1720, and inasmuch as he was a major of the Colonial forces and the father of eight children at the time of his death in 1749, it is rather improbable that he could have accomplished all by his twenty-ninth year. He, however, must have been quite young at the time of his mother's death and was raised consequently by his step-mother for whose affections he manifested when he named a daughter in memory of her.

He married before 1730 Mary, daughter of John and Elizabeth (Hanson) Fendall, and the granddaughter of Randolph Hanson. On February 26, 1729/30, John Fendall, Gent., conveyed to Samuel Hanson, son of Robert, and Mary his wife and daughter of the said John Fendall for natural love which he held for his daughter and also for 5 shillings a tract of land called "St. John's" lying on the north side of Piscataway.

---

* Colonial Muster Rolls, Hall of Records.

Elizabeth Fendall, wife of John, acknowledged the gift, while the witnesses were Robert Hanson and Benjamin Fendall.[1]

Samuel Hanson and Richard Marshall in 1734 were bondsmen for Thomas Marshall, the executor of the estate of Elizabeth Fendall who is identified as the mother-in-law.

Children of Samuel and Mary (Fendall) Hanson

1. Elizabeth Hanson.
2. Benedicta Hanson, died 1790, married ———— McPherson. Issue: Samuel Hanson; Henry; Josias Hanson; Alexander; Anne; Mary Hanson.
3. Robert Hanson.
4. Samuel Hanson married Sarah Marshall. *q.v.*
5. Josias Hanson died intestate; acct. Aug. 18, 1764; balance £1019; adm. Samuel Hanson, Jr.
6. Mary Hanson.
7. Dorothy Hanson.
8. Martha Hanson, will dated June 1765; named sisters Dorothy and Mary Hanson; and Elizabeth Fendall Hanson and Mary Hanson McPherson (no stated relationship).

His father Robert Hanson for natural love and affections deeded him "Lampton", at which time Violetta Hanson, wife, waived dower rights. The transfer was witnessed by William Stone and Gustavus Brown.[2] On February 26, 1725, Samuel Hanson and Bennett Hoskins were sureties for Henry Barnes, the administrator of Henry Evins.

Major Samuel Hanson died intestate in Charles County. His personal estate was appraised on July 28, 1749, and signed by William Hanson and Sarah Fowke as the nearest of kin, with his widow Mary Hanson as the administratrix. John Stoddert and William Dent appraised the estate, while Samuel Hanson and Walter Hanson were the greatest creditors.

The bond for the administratrix was filed on June 17, 1749, by her sureties Thomas Marshall and Thomas Marshall, Jr., and the first account was passed April 6, 1750, by Walter Hanson Deputy Commissary.

The estate was settled on November 17, 1753, when £1,236 were distributed by Mary Hanson the administratrix between herself and the eight named children — Elizabeth, Beneditta, Robert, Samuel, Josias, Mary, Dorothy, and Martha.

The will of his widow Mary Hanson was dated October 22, 1758, and proved in Charles County on January 31, 1759, by W. Hanson, Richard Gambra, and Sarah Alford. She named her sons Samuel and Josias; daughters Benedicta, Mary, Dorothy, Martha; and granddaughter Mary Hanson MacPherson.[3]

The inventory of the personal effects was filed on February 19, 1759, and appraised at £1,082/16/2, by Joseph M. Semmes and William Neale. Samuel Hanson, Jr., appeared as the executor and the following signed as the next of kin: Josias Hanson and Beneditta Hanson. An account on March 26, 1760, by Samuel Hanson, Jr., showed a balance of £1210/12/1.[4]

---

[1] Deeds, Liber N no. 2, folio 192, La Plata.
[2] *Ibid.*, Liber L no. 2, folio 369.
[3] Wills, Liber 30, folio 640.
[4] Adm. Accts., Liber 44, folio 345.

JOHN HANSON, GENT.[3]

(17— - 1795)

John Hanson, son of John and Elizabeth (Hussey) Hanson, was born in Port Tobacco Parish, Charles County. He married Elizabeth, daughter to Henry and Elizabeth Massey, of Prince Georges County.[1]

Children of John and Elizabeth (Massey) Hanson

1. Elizabeth Massey Hanson.
2. Sarah Hanson, bap. Feb. 11, 1753.
3. Henry Massey Hanson. *q.v.*
4. John Hanson.
5. Walter Hanson married Sarah Maddox. *q.v.*
6. Samuel Hanson. *q.v.*

On May 11, 1747, Elizabeth Massey, of Prince Georges County, filed her bond as the administratrix of the estate of Henry Massey, her deceased husband, with her son-in-law John Hanson and William Tyler, of Prince Georges County, as her sureties. On May 20, 1749, John Hanson and Samuel Hanson were bondsmen for Charity Howard, the administratrix of John Howard.[2]

On September 5, 1754, John Hanson received from William Hagan, planter, and Eleanor his wife, by deed a clear title to a portion of "Hanson's Amendment", lying on the east side of Port Tobacco, inasmuch as some doubt had arisen to his portion.[3]

John Hanson took the Oath of Allegiance and Fidelity to the State of Maryland in Charles County during 1778. His signature appears among the returns of the "Worshipful Walter Hanson".[4] In 1783 he was seized of 546 acres of "Second Amendment" in Port Tobacco Lower Hundred, and 172 acres of "Harmonious' Hard Bargain", in Upper East Hundred of Port Tobacco Hundred. He died intestate sometime before 1795.

The will of his widow Elizabeth Hanson was dated May 31, 1795, and proved in Charles County, on November 30, 1795. She bequeathed negroes and other personalty to her daughter Elizabeth Hanson and the residue to her son Henry Massey Hanson whom she named as executor.[5]

¹ Wills, Liber 30, folio 243.
² Test. Pro., Liber 32, folio 273.
³ Deeds, Liber A no. 1½, folio 299.
⁴ Unpub. Md. Rec., vol. 5, p. 1, DAR.
⁵ Wills, Liber A K no. 11, folio 301.

JUDGE WALTER HANSON[3]

(1711 - 1794)

Walter Hanson, son of Samuel and Elizabeth (Story) Hanson, was born "Tuesday the eleventh day of March 1711 about 6 in ye morning at ye head of Portobacco Creek". He married Elizabeth, born 1721, the daughter of William Hoskins and Violetta Harrison his wife.[1]

Children of Walter and Elizabeth (Hoskins) Hanson

1. Hoskins Hanson married Catherine Thompson. *q.v.*
2. Samuel Hanson. *q.v.*
3. William Hanson married Sarah Sinnett. *q.v.*
4. Walter Hanson, *d.s.p.*; will named brothers Hoskins, William, and Samuel; sisters Elizabeth Smoot and Violetta Hanson; Elizabeth Hanson Muschett and friend John Muschett.
5. Elizabeth Hoskins Hanson married William Barton Smoot.*
6. Violetta Hanson married Henry Barnes.
7. Anne Hanson married Hugh Mitchell and Samuel Stone.**
8. Heloise Hanson, died spinster 1763; will named sister Elizabeth and father Walter.
9. Margaret Hanson married John Muschett.

Walter Hanson succeeded his father as Judge or Deputy Commissary for Charles County of the Prerogative Court of Maryland. His bond for the said office was exhibited on December 27, 1740, with Robert Hanson and David Stone as his sureties.[2] In 1744 he passed the account of the Rev. Theophilus Swift and Mary his wife who were the executors of the late Rev. William Maconchie.[3]

On February 13, 1744, Walter Hanson, Gent., and Elizabeth his wife deeded to their daughter Heloise Hanson for the consideration of natural love the tract "Lindsey" which had been granted by Archibald Wauhob to his daughter Elizabeth, the wife of Philip Hoskins, and

*See, Newman's *The Smoots of Maryland and Virginia*.
**See, Newman's *The Stones of Poynton Manor*.

grandfather to the said Elizabeth Hanson and which was to be delivered to Heloise at the age of sixteen. Robert Hanson and R. Harrison witnessed the conveyance.[4]

On November 6, 1744, Walter Hanson and Elizabeth his wife leased to George Harrie and Anne his wife for a period of 14 years 130 acres of land being a portion of a tract granted to James Lindsey and adjacent to the dwelling-plantation of William Hanson. The rental was 800 pounds of tobacco annually.[5]

On September 10, 1746, Walter Hanson and Elizabeth his wife and John Cunningham and Mary his wife for 10,000 pounds of tobacco purchased from George Geofrey land on St. Thomas Creek in Port Tobacco. Mary Geofrey, wife of George, waived dower. In the body of the deed the land was referred to as the land purchased by "George Godfrey's father Clement Theobald by deed of 8 March 1674" and also the "burying place made use of by said Godfrey's father".[6]

In the same year Walter Hanson and Elizabeth his wife "eldest daughter of William Hoskins late of Charles County" conveyed to John Cunningham and Mary his wife "the other daughter of William Hoskins" the tract known as "Friendship" lying on Mattawoman Swamp.[7]

In 1763 Walter Hanson patented "His Excellency's Gift", of 221 acres lying in Charles County.

During March 1778 as one of the magistrates of Charles County he took in his district the Oath of Allegiance and Fidelity to the State of Maryland.[8]

His wife died on May 9, 1773, in her 52 year.[9] On October 13, 1782, he entered into a marriage agreement with Elizabeth Hanson by which they agreed that whosoever died first the other was to enjoy their respective estate during life. They signed the contract and it was witnessed by Walter Hanson, Yost, and Sarah H. Hanson. It was not recorded, however, until May 26, 1791.[10] The marriage was performed by the rector of Port Tobacco Parish on April 20, 1783.

On June 24, 1780, Walter Hanson, Gent., conveyed to Margaret Muschett wife of John Muschett, Gent., for natural love which he had for his sister and also for £10 a portion of the land then in possession of Walter Hanson, Sr., father of the said grantor called "Lindsey".[11]

On the same day, Walter Hanson, Sr., Gent., deeded to Margaret Muschett wife of John Muschett, Gent., for natural love for his daughter and also for £10 land lying on the west side of the eastern-most branch of Nanjemoy Creek originally granted to James Lindsey and afterwards became the right of Archibald Wauhob and granted by the latter to Elizabeth, the wife of Philip Hoskins, grandfather to Elizabeth Hanson, late wife of Walter Hanson, and known by the name of "Lindsey". The witnesses were Richard Barnes and Hoskins Hanson.[12]

According to the tax list of 1783, Walter Hanson was seized of the following tracts all lying in Port Tobacco and Pomonkey Hundreds: "Chandler's Hills" of 100 acres, "Thomason Town" of 100 acres, "Harwood" of 633 acres, "His Excellency's Gift", "Friendship" of 733 acres, and "Improved Friendship" of 733½ acres.

The will of Walter Hanson was dated May 21, 1794, and proved in Charles County on December 1, 1794, with Henry Barnes as the executor. Hoskins was bequeathed all family and other portraits and the wearing apparel. Samuel was devised the dwelling-plantation "Harwood", being a portion of "His Excellency Gift", lying on the north side of the road leading from Port Tobacco Town to Nanjemoy. William was willed 100 acres of "Thomson Town", while his wife Elizabeth received a portion of the personal estate.

The inventory was filed on April 25, 1796, by Henry Barnes, the executor, with William Hanson and Samuel Hanson, his sons, signing as the kinsmen.

---

[1] Adm. Accts., Liber 23, p. 50.
[2] Test. Pro., Liber 31, folio 146.
[3] *Ibid.*, Liber 31, folio 497.
[4] Deeds, Liber Z no. 2, folio 8, La Plata.
[5] Deeds, Liber Z no. 2, folio 13.
[6] *Ibid.*, Liber Z no. 2, folio 120.
[7] *Ibid.*, Liber Z no. 2, folio 64.
[8] Unpub. Md. Records, DAR Library, vol. 5.
[9] Md. Hist. Mag., vol. 18, p. 279.
[10] Deeds, Liber K no. 4, folio 272, La Plata.
[11] *Ibid.*, Liber V no. 3, folio 497.
[12] *Ibid.*, Liber V no. 3, folio 497.

COLONEL SAMUEL HANSON[3]

(1716 - 1794)

Samuel Hanson, son of Samuel and Elizabeth (Story) Hanson, was born Thursday, December 20, 1716, about 2 or 3 in ye morning, perhaps at "Littleworth" in Port Tobacco Parish, Charles County. He first married Anne, daughter to Thomas and Sarah Hawkins. On March 3, 1743, he with Marmduke Semmes was bondsman for his mother-in-law when she administered on the estate of her deceased husband. About 1753, Samuel Hanson administered on her estate.[1]

Children of Samuel and Anne (Hawkins) Hanson

1. Chloe Hanson married George Lee.
2. Sarah Hawkins Hanson married William Beane.*
3. Samuel Hanson married Mary Key. *q.v.*
4. Thomas Hanson married Rebecca Dulany. *q.v.*
5. ———— Hanson married John Addison.
6. Mildred Hanson married William Baker.
7. Eleanor Hanson married Henry Hendley Chapman, Lieut. 2d Md. Regt., Rev. War; Soc. of Cincinnati.
8. Anna Hanson married Nicholas Lingan.**
9. Elizabeth Hanson married John Anderson.

He was styled colonel in official papers, and at the beginning of the Revolutionary War was chairman of the Committee of Safety for Charles County.[2] In 1778 he was one of the magistrates for Charles County and in that capacity during March 1778 he administered the oaths of allegiance and fidelity to the patriots in his district.[3]

After the death of his first wife, he married Anne Brown, kinswoman to Dr. Gustavus Brown, but the widow successively of Samuel Clagett and Robert Horner. A pre-nuptial agreement was recorded on August 12, 1774, as follows: "Samuel Hanson of Charles County Gent. of the first part and Anne Horner widow, relict of Robert Horner, of the second part, and Dr. Gustavus Brown, her brother, of the third part . . . whereas as a trustee mutually appointed by the said Samuel Hanson and Anne Horner . . . and whereas a marriage is intended by God's permission shortly to be had and celebrated between the said Samuel Hanson and the said Anne Horner . . ."[4]

According to the tax list of 1783, Samuel Hanson was seized of the following tracts of land: "Green's Inheritance" of 52 acres, lying in upper portion of East Port Tobacco Hundred; "Herefordshire" of 150 acres, with a "very good large dwelling house with fine gardens"; "Addition to Herefordshire" of 75 acres in upper portion of East Port Tobacco Hundred, "Green Forest" of 82 acres in same hundred, "Hanson's Retreat" of 54 acres, and "Hanson's Triffle" of 48 acres.

---

*The following are tombstone inscriptions: "William Beanes, son of William and Mary Beanes, was born January 24, 1749, and was married to Sarah Hawkins Hanson, November 25, 1773, died October 12, 1828, in the 80th year of his age".

"Here lies the Body of Sarah Hawkins Beanes, daughter of Samuel and Anne Hanson, born August 12, 1750, married William Beane November 25, 1773, and died July 15, 1822, in the 70th year of her age".

**Anna Hanson daughter of Samuel Hanson married October 15, 1789, at Green Hill, Charles County, Nicholas Lingan, Merchant of Georgetown. (Md. Journal, Oct. 30, 1789.) Her tombstone, very interesting, at Popular Hill, states that she was married Oct. 28: "Anna daughter of Samuel Hanson married 28 October 1789 to Nicholas Lingan, Merchant, of Georgetown died 13 January 1793, aged 27, and an infant daughter".

The will of Samuel Hanson was dated January 24, 1793, and admitted to probate in Charles County on November 25, 1794, with Henry H. Chapman as the executor.[5] Chloe Lee, his daughter and wife of George Lee, was devised a legacy and was to provide for the testator's "poor sister (unnamed) during her life". Samuel received all wearing apparel and the ring with his mother's name engraved therein. Legacies were left to his son Thomas and the latter's children; to son Samuel and his children; to John Addison and Anne Addison grandchildren of the testator; and to the children of the testator's deceased daughter Mildred Baker. Eleanor Chapman was devised the watch and ring left the testator by his daughter Anna Lingan, then to the former's daughter Anna Hanson Chapman. His granddaughter Chloe Anne Lingan was left £5. He mentioned Nicholas Lingan, but failed to state relationship.

The following bequests of portraits were interesting: Sarah Bean was bequeathed her own picture; Nancy Baker that of her mother's; Nancy Addison her mother's; Sammy and Tony their own pictures; Nelle "shall have her grandmother's mother's minature"; Chloe Lee her own picture and "poor Anna's picture", but after her death to Anna Hanson Chapman.

The inventory of his estate was filed on December 8, 1794, and appraised at £1,653/19/4, with T. Hanson and William Baker signing as the kinsmen. The first account on August 27, 1796, displayed a balance of £2,678/17/2.

The will of his widow Anne Hanson was dated April 8, 1800, and proved October 3, 1800, in Fauquier County, Virginia, where she made her home after the death of her husband.

She devised to her son Samuel Clagett the tract of land which she purchased from her son, Gustavus Brown Horner, lying in Fauquier County, and other realty because "he sustained much lost by my two marriages". To her grandson, William Edmond Horner, son of William, her house and lot in Fauquier County. She also bequeathed property to her son Gustavus Brown Horner, son of her husband Robert Horner. She also named Mary, the wife of her son William, and Frances, the wife of her son Gustavus, and her granddaughters—Frances Horner, Elizabeth Horner, Catherine Horner, and an unnamed daughter of her son Samuel Clagett.

She bequeathed £50 to Susan W. Harris, granddaughter of her late husband Samuel Hanson for her own use and "not that of her husband". Anne Hanson, daughter of Colonel Samuel Hanson, of Georgetown, was bequeathed her silver shoe buckles.

The universal Bible and a large gold ring with a stone under which "some of my sister Threlheld's hair is set" were bequeathed to her son Gustavus Brown Horner. The residue was willed to her four sons— Samuel Clagett, Gustavus Brown Horner, John Horner, and William Horner.[6]

About 1799 a case developed in the chancery court over the proceeds from the sale of land, instituted by certain heirs against Henry Henley Chapman.[7] It was shown that Samuel Hamilton, of Prince Georges County, had bought the following tracts: "Green's Inheritance" 140 acres, "Herefordshire" 150 acres, and "Addition to Herefordshire" 70 acres, "Fendell's Neglect" 46 acres, "Hanson's Retreat" 54 acres, "Hanson's Trifle" 48 acres, "Green's Forest' 183 acres, "Addition to Green's Forest" 82 acres, "Coomes Park" 100 acres, "Uncle and Nephew" 90 acres, "Smith's Chance" 11 acres, "Slater's Benefit" 100 acres, and "Poverty" 40 acres.

George Hillary Spalding, of Charles County, had bought 45 acres of "Green's Inheritance", William Penn Ford 57 acres of the same tract, and George Lee 267 acres. Henry Green, of Charles County, bought "Three Brothers" of 160 acres, "Robey's Help" of 118 acres, and "Smallwood's Gore". Thomas H. Hanson, of Prince Georges County, purchased "Robey's Range" of 100 acres, and Charles Mankin, of Charles County, purchased "Middleton's Rich Thickett" of 100 acres.

The case furthermore showed that Chloe A. Lingan, granddaughter to Colonel Samuel Hanson, had married William McKenny (also written McKenna). Also that Ann Hanson Chapman and Eleanor Chapman had died without issue, and that John Addision was the son-in-law of the deceased and the father of John and Ann Addison. At the settlement the grandson John Addison had died and his sister Ann Addision received his portion of the estate.

Dr. William Baker on June 20, 1800, certified that the children by his wife Mildred Hanson were Samuel H., born September 20, 1773; Philip T., born July 29, 1775; Nancy H., born October 6, 1777; William, born March 4, 1782; Chloe L., born January 24, 1784; and Eleanor, born October 28, 1785, and died in 1796. Samuel Hanson and Thomas H. Hanson, both sons of the deceased, also certified to the births of their children.

---

[1] Test. Proc., Liber 33 pt. 2, folio 116.
[2] Archives.
[3] Unpub. Md. Records, vol. 5, p. 1.
[4] Deeds, Liber S no. 3, folios 613, 621; G no. 3, folio 28, La Plata.
[5] Wills, Liber A K no. 11, folio 235.
[6] Wills, Warrenton, Va.
[7] Chancery Papers no. 2287.

HON. JOHN HANSON, GENT.[3]

(1721 - 1783)

John Hanson, son of Samuel and Elizabeth (Story) Hanson, was born April 3, 1721, "about 2 or 3 in ye afternoon" at Mulberry Grove, Port Tobacco Parish, Charles County. His wife was Jane, born about 1727, the daughter of Alexander and Jane Contee, of Prince Georges County.[1]

Children of John and Jane (Contee) Hanson

1. Alexander Contee Hanson married Rebecca Howard.
2. Samuel Hanson, born Aug. 25, 1756, died 1781; surgeon on staff of George Washington.
3. Peter Contee Hanson, born Dec. 9, 1758, died at Fort Washington during Revolution. Original Member of Society of Cincinnati.
4. Grace Hanson, born 1762, died 1763.
5. Catherine Contee Hanson, born Nov. 16, 1744, married Philip Alexander.
6. Jane Contee Hanson, born Feb. 23, 1747, died June 17, 1781, married Feb. 18, 1773, Dr. Philip Thomas. Issue: James; Catherine Hanson, born Oct. 15, 1775; Rebecca Bellicum, born Feb. 8, 1777; John Hanson, born May 16, 1779.
7. Elizabeth Hanson, born 1751, died 1753.
8. John Hanson, born 1753, died 1760.
9. ————.

In 1751 as the Sheriff of Charles County, he was summoned by the Prerogative Court as follows: "Attachment issued and order directed to any one of the coroners of Charles County against John Hanson, Sheriff, for his comtempt in not bringing Anne Muncaster widow of William Muncaster into court".[2]

On April 27, 1731, John Hanson purchased from James Maddock, Innholder, of Charles County, for 1200 pounds of tobacco land lying in Charles County containing 300 acres. The conveyance was witnessed by Robert Hanson and Henry Hawkins.

On February 28, 1744/45, he, styled as "the youngest son of Samuel Hanson, Gent., of Charles County", purchased from John Contee, of Prince Georges County, "Rozer's Refugee". The transfer was made in the presence of Thomas Lee and Peter Contee, while Margaret Contee, wife of John, acknowledged the conveyance.[3] On March 12, following, he transferred one-half of the tract to Jane Contee, at which time Jane Hanson, his wife, relinquished her third.[4] On April 12, 1746, he deeded to Samuel Hanson, Jr., Gent., "Herfordshire", beginning at Major Dent's Quarters on the Mattawoman to the head of Port Tobacco. Jane Hanson, wife, waived dower.[5]

In 1747 John Hanson was one of the bondsmen for his sister Elizabeth Douglas, the administratrix of her deceased husband's estate. He and his brother Samuel Hanson were also bondsmen for their sister Charity Howard, when on May 20, 1749, she filed her bond as the administratrix of John Howard, her deceased husband.

At a young age John Hanson entered public service and for nine terms was a delegate from Charles County to the Lower House of the General Assembly. In 1757 he entered the Council and served in that body until 1773 when he moved to Frederick Town. From that place he was a delegate to the General Convention of Annapolis in 1774, and a member of the Maryland Convention of 1775 which issued its famous declaration known as the "Association of Freemen of Maryland". In 1780 he was elected to the Continental Congress and was elected the president of that body on November 5, 1781, an office which sometimes gives him the distinction of being the First President of the United States. While serving in that capacity he tendered George Washington the thanks of Congress for the victory at Yorktown. He also was one of the signers of the Articles of Confederation.

Ill health forced him to retire from public life and he sought seclusion and rest at the home of his nephew at Oxon Hill, Prince Georges County, where he died on November 27, 1783. He was interred in the ancient burying ground of the Addison family at Oxon Hill.

The following obituary appeared in the Maryland Journal of December 2, 1783: "On Saturday last (15 November 1783) departed this life at Oxon Hill, the seat of Mr. Thomas Hanson, in the 63 year of his age, the Hon. John Hanson, Esq: He had long been a servant to his country in a variety of employments, the last of which was that of President of the Congress".

The will of John Hanson was dated September 20, 1781, and proved in Frederick County on April 13, 1784, by John Nelson, Jeffry Magruder, and Richard Butler. He devised his wife Jane the houses and lots in Frederick Town purchased from Adam Koon during life then to his son Alexander Contee. He named his son-in-law Dr. Philip Thomas and his grandchildren—Catherine Thomas, Rebecca Thomas, and John Hanson Thomas.[5]

The following appeared in the *American* of February 25, 1812: "Died this evening in the 85th year Mrs. Jane Hanson relict of John Hanson, esq., a delegate to the old Revolutionary Congress".

---

[1] Deeds, Liber A no. 3, folio 87, pt. 1.
[2] Test. Pro., Liber 34, folio 145.
[3,4] Deeds, Liber Z no. 2, folios 14, 34, 99.
[5] Wills, Liber G M no. 2, folio 75, Frederick.

WILLIAM HANSON, GENT.[3]

(1726 - 179-)

William Hanson, son of Samuel and Elizabeth (Story) Hanson, was born September 29, 1726, in Charles County. His wife was Rachel ——.

Children of William and Rachel Hanson

1. Mary Hanson.
2. William Horner Hanson.
3. Rachel Hanson married George Sibbald. License Pr. Geo. Co., Jan. 5, 1786.
4. Elizabeth Hanson married John Halkerstone. License Chas. Co., Nov. 4, 1779.
5. John Hanson.

According to the terms of his father's will, he was to enjoy the dwelling-plantation "Littleworth" and the tract "Wilkinson's Throne" after the decease of his mother.

Prior to September 22, 1760, he settled in Talbot County and there established a mercantile house, when, on that date as a resident of that county, he conveyed to Walter Hanson, merchant, of Charles County, for the consideration of £205 "Littleworth", where on "my" mother Elizabeth Hanson lived. Rachel Hanson his wife waived dower, while the deed was attested to by Thomas Stone and Daniel Jenifer.[1]

On November 20, 1769, still a resident of Talbot County, he purchased from John Hanson, Jr., for £1,291/10 the plantation "Rozer Refuge" where John Hanson was then living. Jane Hanson, the wife of John, acknowledged the sale. Walter Hanson and Josias Hawkins witnessed the transfer.[2]

This is the approximate time of his returning to Charles County. Two years later, on December 21, 1771, "William Hanson of Charles County Gentleman" sold to Thomas Contee, merchant, of Prince Georges County, for £1,350 "Rozer's Refugee" lying on the east side of Port Tobacco Creek adjoining the land of Jane Contee. His wife Rachel relinquished her third.[3]

Somehow William Hanson seems to have re-possessed "Rozer's Refuge" (sometimes written Roger's), because on January 16, 1776, as William Hanson, Sr., he conveyed a portion of it to Walter Pye for £5,800/8. At the same time he sold the other portion to Thomas Contee of Prince Georges County for £45. His wife Rachel gave her consent, while the conveyances were witnessed by Walter Hanson Jenifer.[4]

During March 1778, William Hanson took the oath of fidelity and allegiance to the State of Maryland in Charles County.

On September 6, 1798, the heirs of William Hanson filed action against the creditors of their father's estate which had been ordered on May 17, 1796, to be sold for the payment of the deceased's debts. The representatives were the five children—William Hanson, John Hanson, Mary Hanson, Rachel Sibbald, and Elizabeth Halkerson.[5]

William Horner Hanson and John Hanson, both of Charles County, declared that their father, of Annapolis, left a widow who never applied for letters of administration, but who was then deceased, but Mary Hanson, daughter, had been issued letters of administration. The will had provided that the entire estate descend to the widow, but at her death it was to be divided among the children. Among the many papers submitted to the chancery court, was found a note, dated September 10, 1801, from George Sibbald, of Augusta, Georgia, requesting that the share of his wife from the estate of her father be paid to "Mary Hanson my wife's sister".

---

[1] Deeds, Liber G no. 3, folio 510, La Plata.
[2] *Ibid.*, Liber O no. 3, folio 685.
[3] *Ibid.*, Liber S no. 3, folio 229.
[4] *Ibid.*, Liber V no. 3, folios 232, 250.
[5] Chancery Papers no. 2261.

THEOPHILUS HANSON[4]

(1743 - 1808)

Theophilus Hanson, son of William and Mary (Stone) Hanson, was born about 1743 in Port Tobacco Hundred, Charles County. At the probation of the will of Clement Wheeler of Charles County in 1799, Theophilus Hanson declared himself to be about 56 years of age. Research fails to disclose the family of his wife or even her given name, but the names of Harris and Love among his children are perhaps significant.

Children of Theophilus Hanson

1. Robert Hanson married Priscilla ————. *q.v.*
2. Mary Harris Hanson.
3. Pamelia Love Hanson married Philip Truman Briscoe.

During the Revolutionary War, Theophilus Hanson served as a private in the militia company of Captain Sinnett.[1] At one time he was the Deputy Surveyor of Charles County, and on July 18, 1768, he purchased from his brother, William Hanson, Gent., one-third of the land that Major William Hanson had died seized of and which his brother was entitled, that is, 130 acres. In 1772 he had recorded in the land records of Charles County his share of his father's estate including that portion which he had purchased from his brother. It lay on the easternmost branch of the Avon River, adjoining on the north the land of his other brother.[2]

According to the 1783 tax list of Charles County, Theophilus Hanson was seized of 243 acres of "Abergary Resurveyed" and 67 acres of "Hanson Green", both tracts lying in Port Tobacco and Pomonkey Hundreds.

On December 20, 1783, he purchased from Richard Barnes for £100 "Robertus" and the "Addition to Robertus", both tracts lying in Charles County. Walter Hanson and Samuel Hanson, Jr., witnessed the transfer. No wife of Barnes waived dower. On February 2, 1784, he sold to Henry Barnes 40 acres of "Abergary Resurveyed". No wife waived her third.[3]

The will of Theophilus Hanson was dated September 13, 1807, and proved in Charles County on March 26, 1808. He left his entire landed estate to his son, Robert, who was to support his two sisters. He also named his daughters, Mary Harris Hanson and Pamelia Love Briscoe; granddaughter Jane Love Briscoe; and son-in-law Philip Truman Briscoe.[4]

The final distribution of the estate of Theophilus Hanson was made in Charles County on October 18, 1820, by Thomas Burgess, when one-third of the proceeds was distributed to the children of Robert Hanson deceased, and two-thirds to the children of Pamelia Love Briscoe, deceased.

---

[1] Unpub. Md. Records, vol. 2, p. 280, DAR.
[2] Deeds, Liber O no. 3, folio 433; S no. 3, folio 311, La Plata.
[3] Deeds, Liber Z no. 3, folios 44, 47, La Plata.
[4] Wills, Liber A L no. 12, folio 512, La Plata.

MAJOR SAMUEL HANSON[4]

(17— - 1806)

Samuel Hanson, son of William and grandson of Robert and Mary Hoskins, was born in Port Tobacco Hundred, Charles County, Maryland. He married Margarey, daughter to William and Theodosia (Stone) McConchie.*

---

*For the ancestry of Theodosia Stone, *see*, *The Stones of Poynton Manor*, by Newman.

Children of Samuel and Margarey (McConchie) Hanson

1. Janney Hoskins Hanson.
2. Robert Winder Hanson married twice. *q.v.*
3. Theodosia Stone McConchie Hanson.
4. Elizabeth McConchie Hanson.

On August 1, 1779, Samuel Hanson was commissioned a lieutenant of the Maryland Line and assigned to the Fifth Regiment. He was in service as late as June 1, 1781.[1] At the conclusion of the war, he was elected a charter member of the Society of the Cincinnati.

His seat was at "Hanson Green" of 144 acres lying in Port Tobacco and Pomonkey Hundreds, of Charles County, on which he paid taxes in 1783.

On May 24, 1800, Samuel Hanson of William, planter, and his wife Margarey conveyed to Mary Harris Hanson, the daughter of Theophilus Hanson, a portion of "Poynton Manor" where Barton Stone formerly lived on the east side of Ward's Creek and recently devised by Mary Stone to Margarey Hanson.[2] On June 7, 1800, Mary Harris Hanson for a consideration of £5 conveyed the above portion of "Poynton Manor" to Samuel Hanson of William.[2]

His will was dated February 13, 1806, and proved in Charles County on June 18, 1806. He devised his wife Margarey, the dwelling-plantation during life and one-third of the personal estate, then to their only son Robert Winder Hanson. The latter was to provide a comfortable residence for his sister Jenny during her life. Personalty was bequeathed to the three daughters—Jenny, Theodosia, and Elizabeth.[3]

The inventory of the personal estate was returned by his widow and executrix on July 24, 1806.[4] Her will was proved in Charles County on November 4, 1815, with Walter McConchie and James Brawner as the executors. She devised negroes to her three unmarried daughters. The inventory of her estate was filed by James Brawner on November 6, 1815.

The final account on the estate of Samuel Hanson was not filed with the court until 1818, when Thomas Rogerson appeared as the executor.

[1] Saffell's Records, p. 237.
[2] Deeds, Liber I B no. 3, folios 265, 266, La Plata.
[3] Wills, Liber A L no. 12, folio 334, La Plata.
[4] Liber 1806, folio 311, La Plata.

SAMUEL HANSON[4]

(17— - 1817)

Samuel Hanson, son of Samuel and Mary (Fendall) Hanson, was born in Port Tobacco Parish, Charles County. He married Sarah, the widow of Basil Beall (Beale) and the daughter of Thomas Marshall.[1] She was named as an heir in the will of her father, dated January 15, 1801, and proved in Charles County on April 24, same year.

Children of Samuel Hanson

1. Margaret Beall Hanson married Apr. 10, 1787, John Fendall Beall.
2. Charity Fendall Noble Hanson.
3. Samuel Hanson married Elizabeth Marshall. *q.v.*
4. John Beall Hanson married Elizabeth Marshall. *q.v.*
5. Mary Fendall Hanson married ———— Cawood.
6. Elizabeth B. Hanson married ———— McPherson.

As Samuel Hanson, Jr., in 1783, he paid taxes on 150 acres of "Lampton" and 36 acres of "Spring Plains", both tracts lying in Port Tobacco Upper Hundred.

His will was dated September 29, 1817, and proved on October 15, 1817, in Charles County. He devised his wife Sarah and his daughters —Margaret B. Beall and Charity F. N. Hanson—during their single lives the use of the dwelling, then in fee simple to his son Samuel. He willed his son John B. Hanson a legacy of $1250. After the death of the widow, the personal property was to be divided among his four daughters—Margaret Beall, Mary Fendall Cawood, Elizabeth B. Mc-Pherson, and Charity Hanson. To his grandsons — Samuel Hanson, Thomas Marshall Hanson, and William Hanson he devised land in Nanjemoy on the Potomac. Other grandchildren mentioned were Elizabeth Fendall McConchie, Thomas James Marshall, Elizabeth Marshall, John F. Beall, Samuel Hanson Beall, John Hancock Beans, and Elizabeth B. McPherson.

The inventory of estate was filed on June 9, 1818, in Charles County, with his sons Samuel Hanson and John B. Hanson as the executors.[2]

His daughter Mrs. Mary Cawood died without issue in Charles County during 1821. By her will she referred to the property left by "father Samuel Hanson to his wife Sarah Hanson during her life."[*] Her portion of this property she devised to her three sisters—Margaret B. Beall, Elizabeth B. McPherson, and Charity Fendall Noble Hanson. Other heirs were her nephew Dr. William Marshall and his children Elizabeth Fendall Hanson Marshall, John Hancock Barnes Marshall, and the youngest child (daughter) yet unnamed; nephew John Fendall Beall; and nieces Elizabeth Margaret Hanson McPherson (daughter of sister Elizabeth McPherson), Mary Margaret Hanson (daughter of

---

[*]She does not refer to Sarah Hanson as her mother. Could she be a step-mother?

brother Samuel Hanson), and Pusy Hanson (daughter of brother John
B. Hanson). She named Dr. William Marshall and John Fendall Beall
as the executors.

¹ Chancery Papers no. 2638; Deeds, Liber I R M no. 3, folio 558, Marlborough.
² Liber H B no. 13, folio 533, La Plata.

LIEUT. HENRY MASSEY HANSON, GENT.⁴

Henry Massey Hanson, son of John and Elizabeth (Massey) Hanson, was born perhaps in Charles County. On November 14, 1767, his
father deeded him for the sum of £50 "Second Amendment" in the
presence of Joseph H. Harrison and John Dent. On April 22, 1771, his
father again transferred a portion of "Second Amendment" to him. In
neither instance did the wife of John Hanson waive dower rights.¹

On February 26, 1776, the Committee of Observation recommended
him for First Lieutenant of Captain John Hanson's Company of Charles
County militia, and his appointment was approved by the Council on
March 7, same year. During March 1778, he took the oath of allegiance
and fidelity to the State of Maryland in Charles County, his name appearing among the returns of the Worship Walter Hanson, Magistrate.²

On December 23, 1776, Henry Massey Hanson leased to James
Russell Schwester a portion of "Hanson's Second Amendment". The
event was witnessed by W. B. Smoot, Walter Morris, and Timothy
Carrington.³ On March 17, 1787, he conveyed for the sum of £22/10
a portion of "Second Amendment" to John May, cooper. On March 22,
1790, he deeded another portion of the same tract to Martha Porteus
for £33/15. On July 21, 1792, he sold for £226 another portion of
the tract to Basil Robey.⁴ No wife waived her third. On May 21, 1794,
he bought from his brother "Samuel Hanson of John of Culpeper
County, Virginia, but at present in Charles County" for a consideration
of £286 a portion of "Greenland".

¹ Deeds, Liber O no. 3, folio 294; S no. 3, folio 149, La Plata.
² Archives, vol. 11, pp. 186, 206.
³ Deeds, Liber V no. 3, folio 234, La Plata.
⁴ Deeds, Libers D no. 4, folio 43; K no. 4, folios 25, 440, La Plata.

CAPTAIN WALTER HANSON⁴
(1760 - 1792)

Walter Hanson, son of John and Elizabeth (Massey) Hanson, was
born about 1760 in Charles County. On December 25, 1781, he married
Sarah Hatch Maddox.¹

Children of Walter and Sarah (Maddox) 'Hanson

1. Elizabeth Hanson married ———— Knox.
2. Mary Anne Theobald Tyler Hanson.
3. John Maddox Hanson, born 1787, died 1838, married 1816, Margaret Sophia Hanson, born 1800, died 1891.*
4. Sarah Eleanor Hanson, died young.

During the Revolution Walter Hanson commanded a company of the 12th Battalion of Militia in Charles County. In 1778 he took the oath of allegiance and fidelity to the State of Maryland in Charles County.[2] At the tax list of 1783 he was seized of 200 acres of "Greenland", lying in Port Tobacco Hundred, which had been patented by his grandfather John Hanson in 1737.

He died intestate in Charles County in 1792, when an inventory was filed of his personal estate appraised at £328/2/8. His widow Sarah Hatch Hanson was issued letters of administration, while his brother John Hanson, Jr., signed the papers as the next of kin and the greatest creditor. At the filing of the inventory with the court his widow had become Mrs. William Morris.

The final account on the estate was rendered on December 21, 1794, by William Morris and Sarah Hatch Morris his wife, at which time the proceeds were divided among the widow and four unnamed children.

In 1795 John Maddox Hanson, Mary Anne Theobalds Tyler Hanson, and Sarah Eleanor Hanson were placed under the guardianship of their stepfather.

At a second distribution of the estate on January 6, 1802 the heirs of Walter Hanson were shown to be Mrs. Sarah H. Morris, Mrs. Elizabeth Knox, Anne T. T. Hanson, and John M. Hanson.

---

[1] Maryland Marriages 1777-1804, p. 188, Md. His. Soc.
[2] Militia Lists, Md. Hist. Soc.; Unpub. Md. Rec., vol. 5.
[3] Liber 1802, folio 79, La Plata.

JOHN HANSON[4]

John Hanson, son of John and Elizabeth (Massey) Hanson, was born in Charles County. He was generally referred to as John Hanson, Jr. In 1783 he paid taxes on 355 acres of "Greenland" and 145 acres of "Fendall's Delight". In 1792 he signed the papers as the kinsman and greatest creditor of his brother Captain Walter Hanson, deceased.

---

*DAR lineage 150,604, only authority for dates and marriage.

SAMUEL HANSON[4]

Samuel Hanson, son of John and Elizabeth (Massey) Hanson, was born perhaps at "Second Amendment" in Charles County. During March 1778, he took the oath of fidelity and allegiance to the State of Maryland in Charles County before Magistrate Walter Hanson.[1] In 1783 he as Samuel Hanson of John paid taxes on 200 acres of "Greenland". He removed to Culpeper County, Virginia, but while in Charles County on May 21, 1794, as Samuel Hanson of John he deeded to his brother Henry M. Hanson for £286 the tract "Greenland". No wife waived her third.[2]

[1] Unpub. Md. Rec., vol. 5, p. 2.
[2] Deeds, Liber N no. 4, folio 264, La Plata.

LIEUT. HOSKINS HANSON, GENT.[4]

(17— - 1796)

Hoskins Hanson, son of Walter and Elizabeth (Hoskins) Hanson, was born at "Harwood", in Port Tobacco Parish, Charles County. His wife was Catherine Queen Thompson, daughter of Richard Matthews and Sarah (Douglas) Thompson.

Children of Hoskins and Catherine (Thompson) Hanson

1. Richard Thompson Hanson married Elizabeth Ray. *q.v.*
2. Catherine Queen Hanson married 1804 Gerard Robertson. Issue: Walter Hanson; Catherine; John Richard; Alexander Hanson; and Hoskins Hanson.
3. Sarah Douglas Hanson married William Penn.

During the Revolutionary War, Hoskins Hanson served as first sergeant of the militia company of Captain Walter Hanson, later he was promoted to second lieutenant of the same company.[1]

On April 25, 1782, Hoskins Hanson received from his father for natural love and affections 189 acres of "Littleworth", originally patented in 1689, and whereon Hoskins Hanson was then seated, also 203 acres of "Wilkinson's Throne". On September 18, 1782, he purchased from Catherine Mitchell, spinster, for £262 "Cain's Purchase" of 100 acres, lying on the west side of Port Tobacco Creek which had been willed Catherine by her father Hugh Mitchell.[2]

According to the 1783 tax list, Hoskins Hanson was seized of 6 acres of "Middle's Branch", 230 acres of "Thompson's Chance", 200 acres of "Wilkinson's Throne", 187 acres of "Littleworth", and 100 acres of "Cain's Purchase".

On May 9, 1788, Hoskins Hanson purchased from William Thompson for £227 "Arelough" lying on the south side of the main fresh of St. Thomas' Creek on the Mattawoman. Those present at the conveyance were Henry Barnes and William D. Briscoe.[3]

On August 20, 1790, Hoskins Hanson sold to Edward Sanders for £262 "Cain's Purchase", at which time his wife Catherine waived dower rights. On September 27, 1791, he conveyed to John Ward for £100 "Arelough", and his wife Catherine likewise waived dower. On March 12, 1795, he deeded to Samuel Hanson, of Charles County, "Harwood", of 1266 acres.[4]

Hoskins Hanson died intestate. Letters of administration upon the estate were issued to his widow, Catherine Hanson, at which time Mungo Muschett and Samuel Hanson of William offered bond. The inventory, appraised at £530/4/0, was filed at court in September 1796, by his widow, with Sarah D. Hanson and William H. Hanson signing as the kinsmen, and Humphrey Barnes and Henry Barnes as the creditors.[5]

On June 10, 1800, Sarah Douglas Penn, Richard Thompson Hanson, and Catherine Hanson, the children of Hoskins Hanson, purchased from Samuel Hanson of Walter, for the sum of £1,000 "Harwood" which had been conveyed by Hoskins Hanson to Samuel Hanson on March 12, 1795. Mary Hanson, wife of Samuel, waived her third, and the conveyance was witnessed by Richard Harrison and Daniel Jenifer.[6]

On the next day William Penn and Sarah his wife sold to Catherine Queen Hanson their interest in "Harwood" for £500. The witnesses were Samuel Hanson of Walter and Daniel Jenifer.[6]

On July 21, 1800, Catherine Hanson sold to Sarah Douglas Penn for £1,000 "Thompson's Chance" lying on road leading from Port Tobacco to Pickawaxon. Witnessed by Samuel Hanson of Walter.[6]

The will of his widow, Catherine Hanson, was proved in Charles County February 14, 1815, by Henry H. Chapman and Gerard Robertson. She named only her granddaughter, Catherine Robertson, whom she placed under the guardianship of her nephew, Dr. Walter Hanson.[7] The final account upon her estate was rendered on August 21, 1816, by her administrator Josias H. Hanson.

[1] Unpub. Md. Rec., vol. 2, pp. 291, 296, DAR.
[2] Deeds, Libers Z no. 3, folio 1; V no. 3, folio 616.
[3] Deeds, Liber D no. 4, folio 290.
[4] Deeds, Liber K no. 4, folios 138, 371; N no. 4, folio 381.
[5] Inventories, Liber 1791-98, folio 401.
[6] Deeds, Liber I B no. 3, folios 212, 247, 345.
[7] Wills, Liber H B no. 13, folio 353.

SAMUEL HANSON[4]

(17— - 1810)

Samuel Hanson, son of Walter and Elizabeth (Hoskins) Hanson, was born in Charles County. During the Revolutionary War he served as a private in Capt. Sinnett's Company of Charles County militia.[1] During 1778 he took the oath of allegiance and fidelity to the State, his name appearing among the returns of His Worshipful Walter Hanson.[2] He died intestate in Charles County, where an inventory of his personal estate was filed at court on February 13, 1810, by Thomas Rogerson as the administrator. The estate was appraised at $1468. An additional inventory was filed on April 12, same year, but the final account was not filed until December 15, 1818, by Thomas Rogerson, showing no distribution of the balance. All accounts referred to "Samuel Hanson of Walter".[3]

---

[1] Unpub. Md. Rec., vol. 2, p. 280, DAR.
[2] *Ibid.*, vol. 5, p. 2.
[3] Liber 1808-12, folios 197, 275.

WILLIAM HANSON[4]

(17— - 1797)

William Hanson, son of Walter and Elizabeth (Hoskins) Hanson, was born in Charles County. It is assumed that Sarah, his wife, was born a Sinnett. His will was dated January 21, 1796, and proved in Charles County on February 5, 1796, by Godfrey Bell, George X Cato, and John Muschett, Jr. He bequeathed his sisters-in-law, Hannah Sinnett and Elizabeth Sinnett, each £25. His wife received one-third of the realty during life and one-third of the personal estate, with the residue going to an unborn child.[1] The inventory of his personalty was taken on January 26, 1797, with his widow Sarah Hanson as the administratrix and Gerard Briscoe and James Franklin as her sureties.[2] During the Revolutionary War he took the oath of allegiance under Magistrate Walter Hanson.[3]

---

[1] Wills, Liber A K no. 11, folio 322, La Plata.
[2] Inventory, Liber 1791-98, folio 423.
[3] Unpub. Md. Records, vol. 5, p. 1, DAR.

COLONEL SAMUEL HANSON[4]

(1752 - 1830)

Samuel Hanson, son of Samuel and Anne (Hawkins) Hanson, was born about 1752 in Port Tobacco Parish, Charles County. On November 20, 1777, he joined the Continental Army of General Washington with the rank of captain. It was in this capacity and at Philadelphia that he married Mary Key, sometimes spelled Kay, at the Church of Christ and St. Peter's on April 29, 1777, by the Rev. Jacob Duckle. He severed his relations with the Continental Establishment in May 1778, and returned to his father's seat in Maryland. Within a short time he was commissioned a lieutenant-colonel of the militia and served in that capacity for a considerable period.

Children of Samuel and Mary (Key) Hanson

1. Maria Hanson, born Dec. 30, 1781.
2. Samuel Hanson, born May 14, 1786, married Matilda Calloway Hickman.
3. Isaac Kay Hanson, born Jan. 14, 1790, married Maria H. Jones. License D. C. Aug. 22, 1815.
4. Thomas Hanson, born Aug. 10, 1792.
5. Ann Hanson, born Dec. 9, 1793, died spinster D. C. Will proved D. C. 1872, naming niece Serena L. Weightman.
6. John Hanson, born 1795, died 1796.
7. Louisa Serena Hanson, born Feb. 25, 1799, died May 23, 1840, married Roger Chew Weightman. License D. C. May 5, 1812.

After the war Sanuel Hanson settled in Alexandria, Virginia, when on August 11, 1787, he conveyed property. A portion of the deed reads as follows: "Samuel Hanson son of Samuel Hanson late of Charles County but at present of Alexandria, Virginia, and Mary his wife of the first part and Henry Rozer of Prince Georges County, Maryland, of the second part" . . . conveyed for 9300 pounds of tobacco "Jockey's Discovery" containing 15 acres "granted by Lord Baltimore to Samuel Hanson father of the said Samuel" and also land in Mattawoman Creek called "Acquinick". The witnesses were Richard Barnes and Hoskins.[1]

Later he settled in the National Capital, where he died in 1830 aged 78 years. One reference stated that he died on December 16, 1830, another on December 30, same year.

His widow Mary Hanson, aged 75, of Washington, applied on November 28, 1836, for a pension by rights of her deceased husband's Revolutionary services under the Act of 1836. She stated that her husband commanded a militia regiment at the time the *H. M. S. Roebuck* and other ships were in the Potomac River and when the dwelling of Colonel Lyles was burned by the marauders. As evidence of his services, she submitted a copy of a ledger showing the accounts of Lieutenant-Colonel Samuel Hanson with the militia of Charles County.[2]

At this time William Horner, aged 71, of Fauquier County, Virginia, certified that the applicant Mary Hanson was the widow of Colonel Samuel Hanson and that he (Horner) was the son of Anne

Hanson who married Samuel Hanson, Sr., of Charles County, the father of Lieutenant-Colonel Hanson. That he lived in the home of Colonel Samuel Hanson, Sr., for sometime, particularly from August 1774 to June 1782, and that about March 1778 Lieutenant Colonel Samuel Hanson, Jr., married Mary Key and brought her to the home of his father in Charles County. He furthermore stated that he remembered when Samuel Hanson left home about 1778 to join the army. In 1837 Horner made an additional deposition in which he certified that Samuel Hanson commanded a militia regiment in Charles County, when the British were in the Potomac above Mt. Vernon, and remembered seeing Hanson paying off the officers who had served with him in the militia.

R. C. Weightman, of Washington, certified that he lived in the home of Colonel Samuel Hanson and that since his death he had continued to remain in the same house which was now the home of his widow.

---

[1] Deeds, Liber D no. 4, folio 122.
[2] Pension Claim, U. S. Archives Bldg.

Thomas Hawkins Hanson[4]

(1750 - 1810)

Thomas Hawkins Hanson, son of Samuel and Anne (Hawkins) Hanson, was born about 1750 in Port Tobacco Hundred, Charles County. At the beginning of the Revolutionary War, he commanded a company of the Flying Camp composed of men from Charles County and saw active service in the early campaign around New York.[1]

On March 2, 1778, he married Rebecca, daughter of Walter and Mary (Grafton) Dulany, of Annapolis, but more recently the wealthy widow of Thomas Addison, of Oxon Hill Manor, Prince Georges County.

Children of Thomas and Rebecca (Dulany) Hanson

1. Grafton Dulany Hanson, born Sept. 17, 1783. *q.v.*
2. Rebecca Hanson, born Nov. 25, 1784.
3. Samuel H. Hanson, born Aug. 4, 1786, married Eleanor Bayly. License D. C., Mar. 13, 1817. *q.v.*
4. Thomas H. Hanson, born Mar. 4, 1792, married Elizabeth Beall. *q.v.*

Thomas Hawkins Hanson died intestate, when letters of administration were issued to his step-son Thomas Grafton Addison on November 10, 1810.

---

[1] Revolutionary Pension Claim 16783.

ROBERT HANSON[5]

(17— - 1810)

Robert Hanson, son to Theophilus, was born in Charles County. He married Priscilla B. ————.

Children of Robert and Priscilla Hanson

1. William Hanson. Account on his estate filed Jan. 14, 1830, by Joseph Young and Francis R. Hanson, showing a balance of $1657.32. (Liber 1829-33, folio 56.)
2. Chloe Anne Hanson married Henry A. Moore.
3. Jane Love Hanson married Joseph Young.
4. Francis Robert Hanson.

Robert Hanson died intestate in Charles County. The inventory of his personal estate was filed on February 13, 1810, by Priscilla B. Hanson, his widow and administratrix. She shortly afterwards married Hezekiah Haislep. The final distribution of the estate was made on June 14, 1817, by Hezekiah Haislep to the widow and four named children.[1]

On January 29, 1839, Chloe Anne Hanson, Joseph Young and Jane L. his wife, and Francis Robert Hanson, all of Charles County, conveyed to John Barnes, same county, for $250 the following tracts: "Discovery", "Friendship", "Manning's Discovery", adjacent to "White Haven Dock", and "McConchie Deal". On the same day, Joseph Young and Jane L. his wife deeded to Francis R. Hanson for $620 a portion of the land formerly laid out for James Lindsey which Jane L. Young inherited from her father, Robert Hanson, and a portion of "McConchie's Deal" purchased by the heirs of Robert Hanson from Captain John Barnes. Also on the same day Chloe Anne Hanson, Joseph Young and Jane his wife, and Francis Robert Hanson, of Charles County, conveyed to Walter Alexander Haislip and Emeline Haislip for love and affection which they bore to them and also for their better support all their interest in tenements of which Priscilla B. Haislip died seized. The conveyance was delivered in the presence of Henry C. Bruce and Charles McCann.[2]

On April 2, 1829, it was recorded in Charles County, the conveyance of "McConchie's Deal" for $250 from John Barnes to Henry A. Moore and Chloe A. his wife, Joseph Young and Jane L. his wife, and Francis Robert Hanson. No wife of Barnes waived dower.

---

[1] Liber 1817, folio 366, La Plata.
[2] Deeds, Liber I B no. 18, folios 223, 224, 340, 344.

Robert Winder Hanson[5]

(1797 - 1853)

Robert Winder Hanson, son of Samuel and Margarey (McConchie) Hanson, was born about 1797 at "Hanson Green", Charles County. On January 21, 1836, at his father's seat he married Mary H. Ford, of the same county.[1] On April 14, 1840, he took as his second wife Frances Speake, the ceremony being performed at "Woodland Plains".[2]

The following children composed his household at the 1850 census: Ernest, aged 9; Francis, aged 6; and Mary M., aged 1.

He maintained his seat on a portion of "Poynton Manor" which had come to him through his mother. In 1824 he sold to John Williams for $515.50 a portion of the manor described as "between the land of the late Gerard Fowke, David Stone, and the said Robert W. Hanson then with the head line of the said David Stone to John Taylor's portion".[3] In 1826 he conveyed another portion to Alexander Matthews.[4] It is said that he died in Charles County during 1853.

---

[1] Nat. Intelligence, Jan. 29, 1836.
[2] Somerset Herald, May 5, 1840.
[3] Deeds, Liber I B no. 15, folio 555.
[4] Deeds, Liber I B no. 16, folio 451.

Samuel Hanson[5]

(17— - 1824)

Samuel Hanson, son of Samuel, was born in Charles County, where on August 10, 1788, he was married to Elizabeth Fendall Marshall. A daughter Mary Margaret was named in the will of her aunt Mary Cawood.

He died intestate. An inventory of his personalty was filed in Charles County on April 14, 1824, by his widow Elizabeth C. Hanson, with an appraisement of $2835. An account was rendered by Elizabeth C. Hanson on October 13, 1824, showing a balance of $1009. The third account was filed on May 18, 1825, by Elizabeth C. Nalley and her husband Uzziel Nalley 'administrators of Samuel Hanson Jr." They claimed an overpayment of $379.75.[1] Noble Barnes, however, administrator *ad colligendum bononum,* rendered an account on May 17, 1825, upon the estate of Dr. Samuel Hanson, Sr., and displayed an inventory valued at $4704.50.[2]

---

[1][2] Liber W D N no. 15, folios 3, 8.

JOHN BEALL HANSON[6]

John Beall Hanson, son of Samuel, was born in Charles County. His wife was Elizabeth, daughter to Philip and Priscilla (Marshall) Marshall. Philip Marshall by his will proved in Charles County on May 1, 1815, referred to his daughter Elizabeth Hanson and her children (unnamed). A daughter Pusy Hanson was an heir in the will of her aunt Mary Cawood.

In July 1817, John B. Hanson and his wife Elizabeth, of Charles County, received certain property by deed from Richard Marshall Scott, of Bush Hill, Virginia. The deed specifically stated that Elizabeth Hanson was the daughter of Philip Marshall, deceased, and that James Elgin Marshall, late of Charles County, had died testate and appointed Richard Marshall Scott the guardian of the three children—Anne Douglas, Robert, and Eleanor Douglas. Other grantees in the same deed were Priscilla Price Marshall, widow of Philip Marshall; John Marshall, son of the said Philip; and Druscilla Price Marshall.[1]

[1] Deeds, Liber I B no. 12, folio 125, La Plata.

RICHARD THOMPSON HANSON[5]

Richard Thompson Hanson, son of Hoskins and Catherine (Thompson) Hanson, was born at "Littleworth" in Port Tobacco Parish. On April 9, 1808, he conveyed to Catherine Queen Hanson for $2,000 "Harwood" with all improvements, lying near Port Tobacco Town on the west side of Port Tobacco Creek. Raphael Saxton and David Stone witnessed the transaction, but no wife waived dower.[1]

It is said that he married Elizabeth Ray. He migrated to Oglethorpe County, Georgia, where he is found as the head of a family at the 1820 census, with the following schedule: he and his wife were both between the ages of 26 and 45, and in his household were 3 girls and 2 boys all under 10 years of age, 1 girl between 10 and 16, 1 boy between 16 and 18, and 19 slaves.

[1] Deeds, Liber I B no. 8, folio 83.

SAMUEL H. HANSON[5]
(1786 - 1863)

Samuel H. Hanson, son of Thomas and Rebecca (Dulany) Hanson, was born August 4, 1786, at Oxon Hill Manor, Prince Georges County. On March 13, 1817, he secured license in the District of Columbia to marry Eleanor Bayly.

Children of Samuel and Eleanor (Bayly) Hanson

1. Montjoy Hanson, born D. C. 1819.
2. Grafton Hanson, born D. C. 1821.
3. Richard Hanson, born D. C. 1824.
4. Rebecca Hanson, born Md. 1827.

At the 1850 census for Washington City, Samuel Hanson and his wife stated that they were born in Maryland. In addition to the above four children at home in 1850, there were in his household B. Grey (female) aged 44 and born in Maryland; F. E. Hasler (male), aged 32, born in New Jersey; and Betty Hasler, aged 27, born in Washington.

Samuel Hanson and his wife are both buried in Congressional Cemetery, Washington. The head stones read: "Eleanor Hanson, wife of Samuel died July 27, 1864, aged 72"; "Samuel Hanson died April 26, 1863, in the 77th year".

THOMAS HAWKINS HANSON[5]

(1792 - 18—)

Thomas Hawkins Hanson, son of Thomas Hawkins and Rebecca (Dulany) Hanson, was born March 4, 1792, at Oxon Hill Manor, Prince Georges County. On February 10, 1802, he obtained license in Washington to marry Elizabeth Beall. She was the daughter of Captain William Dent Beall, a distinguished officer of the Revolutionary Army and member of the Society of the Cincinnati.

On May 16, 1831, Thomas H. Hanson and Elizabeth his wife, Issac B. Beall, and Mary Beall, the heirs of William Dent Beall, deceased, of Prince Georges County, received from Clement Smith and Daniel Kurtz, of Georgetown, and Richard Smith, of Washington, the tract "Independence", lying partly in Prince Georges and Charles Counties which the late William Dent Beall had conveyed to Clement Smith.[1]

It is said that Thomas Hawkins Hanson ultimately settled in Fredericksburg, Virginia, where he died leaving a large issue.

[1] Deeds, Liber I B no. 19, folio 425.

GRAFTON HANSON[5]

Grafton Dulany Hanson, son of Thomas and Rebecca (Dulany) Hanson, was born September 17, 1783, in Maryland. The census of 1850 shows that in that year he was living in the Fifth Ward of Washington, aged 62, his wife Anna, aged 50, born in Maryland, and the following members of his household: Samuel Hanson, aged 23, born D. C.; John McLean, aged 20, born in D. C.; E. Brown, aged 60, born in Maryland; and A. Brown, aged 40, born in D. C.

MISCELLANEOUS

Mary Hanson, wife of Samuel Hanson of Samuel, died Sept. 1818 in her 92 year. (Congressional Cemetery, D. C.)

Margaret Hanson. "Died at Georgetown on May 5, 1792, aged about 59 years Margaret Hanson the wife of Major Samuel Hanson of Charles County, Maryland". (Maryland Journal, May 29, 1792.)

Samuel Hanson of Charles County, married Emily M. Barron, of Prince William County, Va., July 25, 1837. (Balto. *Sun.*)

Walter Warren Hanson. "Died in Charles County, Md., 29 August 1838, Walter Warren Hanson, Sr., long a respectable citizen of that county". (*American,* 8 Sept. 1838.)

Walter Hanson, Jr., killed September 15, 1791, in the city of Washington by falling of a tree in opening one of the streets. (Maryland Journal, Sept. 23, 1791.)

Sarah Hanson, of Harrison County, Kentucky, dated her will February 5, 1827, it being proved during May, same year, by Benjamin Hodges, Devall Hodges, and A. S. H. Hawkins. She named: brother John Hanson; sister Jane Hawkins; niece Polly Ship; and the following of no expressed relationship: Polly H. Taylor, Fanny Taylor, and Albert Hanson. Thomas Hawkins was appointed executor.

Margaret Hanson was the head of a family in Wilkes County, Georgia, at the 1850 census. She was born about 1795 in Maryland and had realty appraised at $2,000. In her household were: Walter Hanson, aged 29; John Hanson, aged 27; William Hanson, aged 22; Anne Hanson, aged 19; Mary Hanson, aged 17; Kitty Hanson, aged 14; Henry Hanson, aged 12; and Eugenia Adams, aged 2. All except the head of the house were born in Georgia.

Pickawaxon Hundred
Wicomico River
Charles County, Maryland
circa 1670

NEWMAN FAMILY

George Newman, planter, the progenitor of the Newman family of the Western Shore of Maryland, stated in court during October 1654, that he was "twenty years of age or thereabouts". The latter statement leaves a little latitude in reckoning his age, but it is self evident that his birth occurred either before or after 1634. In view of the fact that he frequently appeared in business transactions about this year, it is believed that it happened sometime before. To some it would be difficult to consider a latitude of three or four years to his age and that in 1654 he was nearing twenty-four, but such discrepancies are not unusual in genealogical research.

If such be the case, it is not unlikely that he was the George Newman who was born on September 1, 1629, the son of Roger Newman, of Kensington Parish, London, and other circumstances lead in this direction. It is noted that Roger Newman, of Kensington, was a merchant. Contemporary with George Newman of Charles County was a Roger Newman who was a merchant of Anne Arundel County, but exhaustive research fails to prove by documents any relationship between the two of Maryland—yet nothing has been found to disprove such a relationship. Roger Newman of Anne Arundel County died without issue in 1704 and his tombstone in the churchyard of St. Anne's in Annapolis displays emblazonments. He mentioned in his will no kinsmen in Charles County.

George Newman in his early days was identified with Captain William Battin, merchant, under whom he was indentured for a brief period. It is possible that George Newman as a boy had acquired considerable experience in the merchandise establishment of his father in Kensington and this experience attracted the attention of William Battin whom we place in London before his settlement in Maryland and for this reason Battin induced him to accompany him to America. George Newman was educated for his handwriting is now extant on numerous documents, whereas Battin always made his X mark. And the fact that George was schooled made him of particular value to an illiterate merchant.

These conditions give more than slender threads to the conclusion that George Newman of Charles County was the younger son of Roger Newman, of Kensington. The following pedigree is thus established by the parish register of Kensington Parish, London:

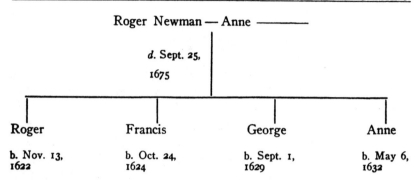

Roger Newman — Anne ———

d. Sept. 25,
1675

Roger	Francis	George	Anne
b. Nov. 13,	b. Oct. 24,	b. Sept. 1,	b. May 6,
1622	1624	1629	1632

Whether George Newman was a son of Roger is at present an opened question, but by 1651 he had indentured himself to William Battin and was domiciled in the Province of Maryland. The following proves these facts:[1]

> "1 January 1652/3. Demandeth 650 acres of land for transporting himself (Battin) Margarey his wife, and Lydia Ashcomb his wife's Daughter, and Thomas Joyce a servant which he bought of Robert Brooke Esq. for whom he is to have 50 acres and Richard and Susannah his servants in the year 1651 and George Newman his servant in the same year".

The residence of Captain Battin was at first on the Patuxent in what is now St. Mary's County, but after 1656 he and George Newman settled at Pickawaxon—the oldest settlement in Charles County on the Wicomico River.

The period of indenture with Battin was of brief duration, because George Newman testified in court in 1654 which is the occasion for his approximate age:[2]

> "16 October 1654. George Newman aged twentie years of there-abouts Sworne Saith that he this Deponent heard Mrs. Brookes relate that she heard that Mrs. Goulson had beaten her maid two hours by the hour by the clock and that there were that would take their oathes that it was an hour and a halfe by the Clock".

On January 9, 1655/6, George Newman purchased from Mary Smith, widow, the dwelling-plantation on which she was then residing, it being 100 acres of land granted to her deceased husband Captain John Smith by Richard Preston. She signed the deed which was witnessed by Thomas Semar and Ffrancis X Abramson.[3]

It was about this time that he married Lydia Achcomb, the step-daughter of his benefactor Captain William Battin.

Children of George and Lydia (Ashcomb) Newman

1. George Newman, born 1659. Issue: William; John; George; Elizabeth.
2. William Newman married Mary Fowke. *q.v.*
3. Margaret Newman.
4. Lydia Newman married John Gee, Edward Smoot, and Gerard O'Cane.*
5. Mary Newman.
6. Elizabeth Newman.

In 1656 George Newman and Henry Keene witnessed a note of William Battin and the next year he served on the jury at a court held in St. Mary's County. In 1658 the Sheriff of Charles County subpenaed him to testify in a lawsuit between William Battin and Edward Goodman. The same year he witnessed a note of Arthur Turner. In 1660 he demanded that a warrent be issued for Robert Hundley and that John Hatch, Thomas Smoote, John Gouldsmith, and William Bowles be subpenaed.

Captain William Battin dated his will May 29, 1662, it being proved at court a short time afterwards. He bequeathed his wife Margarey one half of the estate and appointed her executrix. Personalty was bequeathed to Charity Adams, William Love, daughter Ledia Newman, son George Newman, and their children George, William, and Margaret Newman, sister Jane Smute, and William Smute the son of his sister Jane Smute. The overseers so named were Josias Fendall, Robert Henley, and his brother-in-law Thomas Smute.[4]

On November 4, 1662, George Newman was a witness to the papers by which his mother-in-law Margarey Batten "relict of Captain William Battin deceased of Charles County Merchant" appointed Josias Fendall, Gent., her attorney to collect all sums due the estate in Maryland and Virginia.[5]

At the settlement of the estate it was shown that George Newman gave receipt to William Sanford for "the use and on behalf of my father in law Captain William Batten in nayles and too axes amounting to the sum of 275 pounds of tobacco". The receipt was witnessed by Robert Gerrard and Christopher Hatton.

In February 1662/3, Humphrey Warren demanded a warrant be issued for George Newman, and James Walker, aged 44, swore that he demanded of George Newman 1,167 pounds of tobacco for the use of Humphrey Warren and Newman stated that he would "if Nicholas Guyther would go his security".

---

*For descendants, see, The Smoots of Maryland and Virginia, by Newman.

In 1663 he was sued for debt by William Sanford, and in 1664 by John Bateman. At court on July 12, 1664, he presented a servant Hamlet Baker to have his age judged which was 14 years, and on March 14, 1664/5, another servant Catherine Cumber who was 17 years old.[6] From these facts it is concluded that George Newman was not only a landed proprietor but maintained a staff of servants—typical of the gentleman planters of that day. His dwelling-plantation was located in what later became William and Mary Parish on or near the confluence of Wicomico and Potomac Rivers in Charles County.

On September 22, 1665, he purchased 100 acres of land. The deed reads: "Captain Nicholas Gwyther, of St. Mary's County, Gent., to George Newman, of Charles County, Planter, for 3,200 pounds of tobacco . . . land in Charles County on the north side of the Potomac River near Mr. Neale's Back Creek". It was witnessed by Francis Pope, John Bowles, and John Morris.[7]

A few months later George Newman conveyed this tract to Francis Pope for 3,800 pounds of tobacco. The deed was signed by George Newman, but his wife Lydia made her X mark.[8]

In 1665 and 1666 George Newman served on the jury. And on August 15, 1678, George Newman, Sr., witnessed the will of Thomas King of Charles County. In 1679 he was a juryman of the chancery court in the lawsuit over 1,000 acres of land which Bridget Heard died seized. The court decided that John Douglas, Jr., aged 15, was the rightful owner, he being the son and heir of John Douglas, Sr., who was named executor in the will of Mistress Heard.[9]

On September 21, 1680, Peter Carr a neighbor of George Newman on the Wicomico negotiated his will and among his legatees were the unnamed children of George Newman.[10]

He died intestate in Charles County during the summer of 1683, being about fifty years of age. The inventory of his personal effects was filed at court on August 20, 1683, with an appraised value of £103/7/5½. At an account rendered on July 9, 1686, by George Newman, II, the administrator, disbursements were made to William Newman (1000 pounds of tobacco), to Edward Smoot (2,362 pounds), and to John Monough "in right of his wife being one-third of the said estate".[11]

From the latter statement it is concluded that the widow remarried. An additional account was rendered by George Newman, II, on August 2, 1687.

Prior to the death of George Newman, Sr., John Bowles who had married the widow of William Battin and the mother of Mistress Newman negotiated his will, April 8, 1675, and devised his nephew James

Tyre (Tyler) 550 acres of "Bowles' Purchase", 700 acres of "Oneal's Desert" and 500 acres of "Bowleston", but in the event that James Tyre died without issue then to George Newman, Jr., the son of George.[12]

James Tyre, however, married Rebecca ————, and left issue. His widow married Robert Yates and administrated upon his estate. On April 3, 1689, Robert Yates and Rebecca his wife who were executors of the last will of James Tyre who was executor of Peter Carr rendered an account upon the estate of the said Carr and showed a legacy paid to "Edward Smoot who intermarried with Lydia Newman".[13] During the same year Robert Yates and Rebecca his wife filed an additional account and showed the payment of a legacy to Mary Newman and Elizabeth Newman.[14]

[1] Liber ABH, folio 202, Land Office.
[2] Archives, vol. 10, p. 401.
[3] Archives, vol. 10, p. 444.
[4] Wills, Liber 1, folio 162.
[5] Archives, vol. 53, p. 269.
[6] Archives, vol. 53, pp. 327, 398, 485, 564.
[7] Archives, vol. 53, p. 611.
[8] Deeds, Liber B no. 1, folio 254.
[9] Archives, vol. 51, p. 297.
[10] Wills, Liber 4, folio 12.
[11] Inv. & Accts., Liber 6, folio 139.
[12] Test., Proc., Liber 15c, folio 77½; Wills, Liber 5, folio 39.
[13] Inv. & Accts., Liber 10, folio 227.
[14] Inv. & Accts., Liber 10, folio 324.

WILLIAM NEWMAN[2]

(1660 - 1714)

William Newman, son of George and Lydia (Ashcomb) Newman, was born about 1660 in Charles County. Being the second son of a father who died intestate he was deprived of the realty, therefore his landed estate was acquired through his own initiative. He settled in Nanjemoy Hundred of Charles County, and there after 1686 he married Mary, the youngest daughter of Gerard and Anne (Thoroughgood) Fowke.* Colonel Gerard Fowke prior to his removal to Maryland represented Westmoreland County in the Virginia House of Burgesses in 1663. Within two years he was in Maryland and represented Charles County at the General Assembly in 1665 and 1666.[1]

*It has been erroneously stated that Mary Fowke married George Mason of Virginia. Dates and circumstances disprove this connection. A descendant has stated that it was Mary daughter to Chandler Fowke who married the Mason. It has also been stated, though without proof, that Gerard Fowke came to Virginia with his kinsman George Mason. Gerard Fowke was transported into Virginia by his brother Thomas Fowke before 1652. (Patent Book no. 3, folio 301, Richmond.) Capt. George Mason in 1656 claimed headrights for his own emigration and transportation of 18 persons into Virginia. (Pat. Bk. no. 4, folio 37.)

Only one issue has been proved for this marriage, but that there were daughters is highly probable.

Children of William and Mary (Fowke) Newman

1. William Newman married Elizabeth Stonestreet. *q.v.*

On August 5, 1684, William Newman received from William Smoot and Anne his wife land which "was recorded" by Captain Randolph Brandt in September 1683, lying in Pickawaxon then a part of a tract granted to William Smoot by patent.[2]

On March 26, 1689, John Courts of Charles County reported to Captain Lawrence Washington of Virginia that William Newman informed him that Mr. Hutchinson told him (Newman) that about 9,000 Indians had landed at the mouth of the Patuxent.[3] In 1697 William Newman signed as one of the civil officers of Charles County.[4]

About 1703 William Newman petitioned the Land Office to have the land lying in St. Mary's County originally surveyed on July 14, 1663, for Jane Clark containing 300 acres patented to him in view of the fact that the land had become escheat for want of heirs.[5] The warrant was issued on July 14, 1704, to him by a survey made on May 3, 1704, by Luke Gardiner, Jr., under the name of "St. Nicholas".[6] A Rent Roll of an unknown date shows that "St. Nicholas" was surveyed on July 14, 1663, for Mrs. Jane Clark in the name of Ignatius Causeen lying on the west side of the fresh run of Port Tobacco Creek for 400 acres, and that 300 acres was then possessed by William Newman.[7]

On November 13, 1705, William Newman and Mary his wife of Charles County deeded to "Elizabeth Dent the natural daughter of Major William Dent[8] deceased of the same county said William Newman and Mary his wife as well as for consideration of the entire love and affection which they have bear towards the said Elizabeth Dent as for divers other good causes" the tract known as "St. Nicholas".*

The will of William Newman was dated February 31, 1710/11, and devised the entire estate to his wife Mary whom he named as executrix. It was witnessed by Mary Contee, Judith Warren, and Daniel Dulaney. At its probation in Charles County on August 14, 1714, Mary Contee had become Mary Hemsley.[9]

---

*The late Mrs. Hodges, well known and beloved Maryland genealogist, interpreted this deed as Mary Dent married William Newman. As it has been now proved, it was Mary Fowke, sister to Elizabeth Fowke the mother of Elizabeth Dent, who married William Newman, and the natural love was that of aunt for a niece.

The inventory of the estate was appraised at £197/7/0, by Robert Hanson and Benjamin Hanson on August 4, 1714.

---

[1] Proceedings of Virginia House of Burgesses; Archives of Maryland, vol. 5, pp. 8, 63.
[2] Deeds, Liber N, folio 213, La Plata.
[3] Archives, vol. 8, folio 93.
[4] Archives, vol. 20, folio 543.
[5] Patents, Liber W D, folio 404.
[6] Liber D D no. 5, folio 181.
[7] Rent Roll, Chas. Co., p. 97.
[8] Deeds, Liber Z no. 1, folio 217, La Plata.
[9] Wills, Liber 13, folio 736.

WILLIAM NEWMAN[3]

William Newman, son of William and Mary (Fowke) Newman, was born in Port Tobacco Hundred, of Charles County. He was not named in his father's will of 1711, but deeds show that he inherited eventually land once held by William Newman, Sr. He married Elizabeth, the daughter of Edward Stonestreet by his first wife. Edward Stonestreet died testate in Charles County during 1749 and named his daughter Elizabeth Newman.[1]

Children of William and Elizabeth (Stonestreet) Newman

1. Butler Newman married Verlinda Stonestreet. *q.v.*
2. Edward Newman.

On May 19, 1726, William Newman, planter, mortgaged to Peter Montgomery the tract "Monmouth Beginning". The transaction was witnessed by Thomas Thompson and Mary Jameson.[2] On August 10, 1730, William conveyed this tract to Peter Montgomery for 4,000 pounds of tobacco "Monmouth formerly taken up by my father William Newman containing 87 acres more or less". The assignment was witnessed by Robert Hanson and Robert Yates, and at the same time Elizabeth Newman, wife, relinquished her dower.[3]

The conveyance of his land, first by mortgage and then by assignment and other circumstances, indicates that William Newman sustained financial reverses from this period on. In 1741 by his petition the court of Charles County allowed him 800 pounds of tobacco for support.[4]

He died before the Revolution and his estate being small it was privately settled among his heirs.

[1] Wills, Liber 27, folio 170.
[2] Deeds, Liber L no. 2, folio 280.
[3] Deeds, Liber M no. 2, folio 233.
[4] Chas. Co. Crt. Proc., folio 280.

BUTLER NEWMAN[4]

(1735 - 179–)

Butler Newman, son of William and Elizabeth (Stonestreet) Newman, was born near Port Tobacco in Charles County about 1735. He
married his kinswoman Verlinda, the eldest daughter of Butler Stonestreet by his second wife Jane Edelen. Butler Newman settled in St.
John's Parish of Prince Georges County and there the births of his
five children are registered.

Children of Butler and Verlinda (Stonestreet) Newman

1. George Newman, born Oct. 23, 1760. *q.v.*
2. Butler Newman, born Mar. 29, 1763.
3. Mary Eleanor Newman, bap. May 19, 1765.
4. Elizabeth Newman, born Nov. 1767.
5. Jane Newman, born Apr. 28, 1773.

In December 1771, Butler Newman and Jonathan Burk were bonds-
men for John Stonestreet, the executor of Thomas Stonestreet, and in
the same month he with Elisha Lanham went bondsmen for Eleanor
Stonestreet, the executor of Edward Stonestreet.[1] In 1773 he and Robert
Wade were bondsmen for John Dawson, the administrator of Dines
(Doyne) Dawson.[2]

On March 20, 1778, Butler Newman took the oath of allegiance and
fidelity to the State of Maryland in Prince Georges County.[3] No active
military service has been found.

He died before 1790. According to the census for that year his
widow Verlinda Newman was the head of a family with one male over
16, two males under 16, six females, and three slaves. On the adjoining
plantation lived her eldest son, George, with one male (himself) over
16, four females, and ten slaves. Verlinda Newman died after 1820, the
last census in which she appeared as the head of a household.

The eldest son and heir, George, at the age of 16, on July 15, 1776,
enlisted in the Flying Camp and saw active service in the early campaign
around New York. He was enrolled by Ensign Horatio Clagett and
passed by Colonel John Addison, who commanded the regiment from
Prince Georges County. He married about 1782, and died after 1810
leaving a young family, with many descendants living today.[4]

---

[1] Test. Pro., Liber 44, folio 302.
[2] Test. Pro., Liber 45, folio 325.
[3] Brumbaugh's Md. Records, vol. 2, p. 307.
[4] Archives, vol. 18, p. 35.

Warren

THE HOUSE OF WARREN

The house of Warren, according to the best recognized authority, is traced to Hugh of Normandy, born 990, later to be ordained Bishop of Contances.* He married, name unknown, a sister of Gunnora, the wife of Richard I, Duke of Normandy. He died in 1020, leaving among his sons Rodulf (Ralph) de Warenne.

Rodulf, son to Hugh, and nephew to Richard, was a benefactor to the Abbey of La Trinite du Mont, and died *circa* 1050. He married first Beatrix and secondly Emma. The latter became the mother of his son William who was created Count de Warenne of Normandy and later the first Earl of Surrey.**

The following pedigree appears in the 1896 edition of Complete Peerage:***

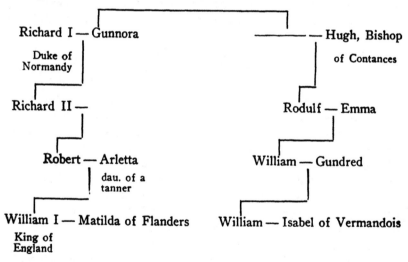

WILLIAM DE WARENNE

(*d.* 1088)

William de Warenne, son of Rodulf, was born in Normandy and accompanied William the Conqueror to England in 1066. At the battle

Complete Peerage, edited by George Edward Cokayne, 1896 edition.

**L. C. Loyd writing in the Yorkshire Archaeological Journal (vol. 31, 1932-34), states that the relationship of the Warennes with the Dukes of Normandy was through Beatrix who was the niece of Duchess Gunnora, wife to Richard, and furthermore that William de Warenne was a son of Beatrix and not Emma.

***Complete Peerage* is being revised and to date the first 8 volumes have appeared in print. It will be several years before the volume containing the ancestry of the Earls of Surrey will be ready for publication, but it will be interesting to see if any corrections are made in the above pedigree.

of Hastings he commanded one of the detachments and after the conquest he remained in England and received by the grace of William many estates and manors in Norfolk as well as other parts of the realm. He was ultimately created the first Earl of Surrey.

Before 1070 William de Warenne married Gundred, a lady whose parentage has been the cause of probably greater controversy than any other person. Her tomb with *stirps ducum* shows definitely that she was of ducal birth, but the statement that she was a daughter of William the Conqueror is now questioned by several scholars. The belief that she was a daughter of William by his Queen Matilda of Flanders was current for a number of years and that the *duces* in her epitaph referred to the dukes of Normandy, her paternal ancestors. At St. John's Church, Southover, Lewes, appears the following inscription: "Within this Pew stands the Tomb-Stone of Gundrad, Daughter of William the Conqueror, and Wife of William, the First Earl of Warren, which having been deposited over her remains in the Chapter-House of Lewes Priory and lately discovered in Iffield Church was removed to this Place at the expence of William Burrell Esqr A.D. 1775".

The known facts regarding the consanguinity of Gundred are that Matilda was her mother, that she was a daughter to William the Conqueror, and that she was a sister to Gherbod, the first Earl of Chester. These facts, however, have been difficult for the antiquarian to reconcile.

After 1085 William de Warenne made a grant for the soul of Gundred his deceased wife and for that of Queen Matilda *matris uxoris mee*. This proves definitely that his wife was a daughter of Matilda, but it does not necessarily imply that William was her father. William, however, in his charter to the monks of Walton names Gundred as his daughter *uxoris suae Gondradae filioe meoe*. It is argued by some genealogists that the relationship was that of foster-father.

Then there is documentary evidence that she was a sister to Gherbod, a Fleming, son to Gherbod who was advocate of St. Bertin and Abbey at St. Omer. Gherbod, the son, received on the dismemberment of Mercia, early in 1070, a large portion of that district, together with the city of Chester, whereby he was created Earl of Chester by William the Conqueror. Gherbod returned shortly afterwards to Flanders where he remained.

The antiquarian, Freeman, declares that Matilda was a mature woman upon her marriage to William the Conqueror and that some of the children credited to her could not be the issue of William. He puts forth the theory that Matilda married first Gherbod, Sr., and that Gundred and Gherbod, Earl of Chester, were issue of this union. And the *duces* of her epitaph were from the counts of Flanders.

The paternal parent of Gundred is therefore in doubt, but the best authorities agree that she was a daughter of Queen Matilda, and thus her Flemish ancestry is as follows showing direct descent from Charlemagne and Alfred the Great:

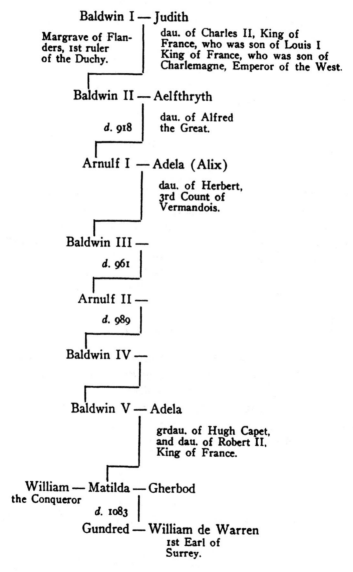

Baldwin I — Judith

Margrave of Flanders, 1st ruler of the Duchy.

dau. of Charles II, King of France, who was son of Louis I King of France, who was son of Charlemagne, Emperor of the West.

Baldwin II — Aelfthryth

d. 918

dau. of Alfred the Great.

Arnulf I — Adela (Alix)

dau. of Herbert, 3rd Count of Vermandois.

Baldwin III —

d. 961

Arnulf II —

d. 989

Baldwin IV —

Baldwin V — Adela

grdau. of Hugh Capet, and dau. of Robert II, King of France.

William — Matilda — Gherbod
the Conqueror

d. 1083

Gundred — William de Warren
1st Earl of Surrey.

Gundred died in childbirth at Castle Acre May 27, 1085, and was buried in the chapter house of the Priory of Lewes in County Sussex.

Four of her children matured—William son and heir, Reginald, Gundred, and Edith.

William, now Earl of Surrey, rebuilt, enlarged, and strengthened Lewes Castle which is now used as the museum of the Sussex Archaeological Society. He founded Cluniac Priory in 1078, now in ruins, and endowed the chapter house of the Priory. He married secondly a daughter of William, sister to Richard Goet (Guet), of Montmirail. He died on June 24, 1088, from the effects of a wound at the seige of Pevensey, and was buried near the remains of his first wife. His widow sent 100 shillings to the monks of Ely to pray for his soul. She was living as late as 1098.

WILLIAM, 2D EARL OF SURREY

(*died* 1138)

William, son and heir, of the first earl, married Isabel, the third daughter of Hugh the Great, Earl of Vermandoise, and widow of Robert de Beaumont, Earl of Mellent in Normandy, later of Leicester. By her he had: William; Reginald (*q.v.*) ; Ralph; Gundred; and Ada. Isabel, Countess of Surrey, died February 13, 1131. The earl died May 11, 1138, and was buried at the feet of his father in the chapter house at Lewes. He was succeeded by William, his son and heir.

REGINALD DE WARREN

Reginald, the second son of William II, was recognized as a brother to the Third Earl by extracts from the register book of Castle Acre, wherein are mentioned charters of William, Earl Warren, to his brother Reginald (Harleian M S 1967). Before October 1160 he was the keeper of Norwich Castle, and in 16 Henry II (1170) was one of the barons of the exchequer. He married Aldelia, daughter to Roger de Mowbray, and had

WILLIAM DE WARREN

Like his father, William was one-time keeper of Norwich Castle. He married Isabel, daughter of Sir William de Haydon, Knt, and by her he had

SIR JOHN DE WARREN, KNT.

He married Alice, daughter to Roger de Townsend, of County Norfolk. By her he had

John de Warren

He married Joan, daughter of Sir Hugh de Port, of Etwall, Derbysire, and by her had

Sir Edward de Warren, Knt.

He married Matild (Maud) de Nerford, daughter of Sir Richard de Skegeton, County Norfolk, and by her had

Sir Edward de Warren, Knt.

Third but only surviving son of Sir Edward, he married Cecily, daughter and heiress of Sir Nicholas de Eton, by Joan de Stockport his wife, the daughter of Sir Richard Stockport. At that time, she was the divorced wife of Sir John Ardene. This marriage brought 'Sir Edward a large estate in Cheshire which added to his prominence and affluence. The MS *Baronagium Cestrie* states definitely that he was lineally descended from the Earls of Warren and Surrey. By his wife he had

Sir John de Warren, Knt.
(*died* 1386)

He was aged 26 at the death of his father, Sir Edward. He married Margaret, daughter and heir of Sir John Stafford, of Wickham, Knt. His will was dated 8 Richard II (1384) and proved 10 Richard II (1386). He was buried at Boton. His widow *circa* 13 Richard II was married to John Mainwaring of Over Pever in Cheshire and died 6 Henry V (1428). By his wife, Sir John had

Nicholas de Warren
(*died* 1413)

He was born 1371, being aged 14 at the death of his father. In 15 Richard II (1390) he married Agnes, the daughter of Sir Richard de Wynnington, Knt. His death occurred *circa* 1413; his wife survived. By her he had

Sir Laurence de Warren, Knt.
(*died* 1444)

He was born *circa* 1394, and married Margarey (Isabel), daughter of Hugh Bulkeley of Oure Com Salop; was knighted soon after the

accession of Henry VI; and died 22 Henry VI (1444), aged 50. His
seat was at Poynton. His son and heir was

JOHN DE WARREN
(*born* 1414)

He was born about 1414, being aged 30 at the death of his father.
He married 10 Henry V (1422) Isabel, the daughter of Sir John Stanley of Latham, Knight of the Garter and Steward of the household to
King Henry IV. At the time of the marriage, his father was in France
and as he was only about 8 years of age, Sir John Stanley secured a dis-
pensation from the Pope. By his wife he had

SIR LAURENCE DE WARREN, KNT.

He married Isabel, daughter of Robert Legh, of Adlington, Cheshire,
before 1458, and received the orders of knighthood soon after the accession of Edward IV. He was Lord of the Manors of Stockport, Poynton, Wode Plumpton, Fornely, Rotteley, Boton, and Skegeton. He died
in the lifetime of his father, and his widow married 1475 Sir George
Holford, Knt. By his wife he had

SIR JOHN WARREN, KNT.
(1461 - 1518)

He was born *circa* 1461 and was knighted at Rippon, Yorkshire, by
King Henry VII on St. Bartholomew's Day 1487. He was first married
about 1480 to Eleanor, daughter of Sir Thomas Gerard of Bryn Com,
Lancashire, Knt., and secondly to Joan, daughter of Ralph Arderne of
Harden, and widow of Thurston Holland of Denton, and ———— Done
of Utkinson. Sir John died January 11, 1518, seized of the Manors of
Wode Plumpton, Stockport, Poynton, and others. His wife survived
and married as her fourth husband John Davenport of Davenport. By
his first wife he had

LAURENCE DE WARREN
(*died* 1531)

The eldest son and heir of his father, he married first Margaret,
daughter of Sir Piers Legh of Lyme, Cheshire, Knt., the marriage settlement being made July 1494. He took for a second wife Sibil, widow of

William Honford of Honford. His will was dated November 18, 1529, and proved 22 Henry VIII (1531). By his first wife he had

SIR EDWARD WARREN, KNT.

(*died* 1558)

The third issue but first son of his father, he was knighted May 11, 1554, at Leith in Scotland by the Earl of Hertford while fighting the Scots under the Cardinal of St. Andrews. He married 1516 Dorothy, daughter of Sir William Booth of Dunham-Massey, Knt. His first son Francis was disinherited, so the estates fell to the second son John. He died on October 12, 1558, and was buried in the chancel of the church at Prestbury. His widow was buried on March 14, 1584, at Prestbury.

JOHN WARREN

(*died* 1587)

The second son but heir of his father, he married Margaret, daughter of Sir Richard Molineux of Sefton, Lancashire, Knt. He frequently used the title of Baron of Stockport, an inheritance from his ancestress Joan de Stockport, the sole heiress of her father Baron of Stockport. In 19 Elizabeth (1577) he was High Sheriff of Cheshire. He died December 7, 1587; his wife survived him and was buried June 21, 1617, at Stockport.

The register of Stockport Parish contains the following entry upon the death of his widow:

> "Margaret Warren of Lostock, widow, of John Warren, late of Pointon, Esq., was buried the 21st (1617). Margaret Warren lived at Lostock near Poynton, and was the daughter of Sir Richard Moly-neux, of Sefton, Knt. She married c 1558 John Warren of Poynton, 2d son of Sir Edward Warren who was knighted at Leith in 1544. Her husband John Warren was High Sheriff of Cheshire in 1577. He died December 1587, and was buried at Stockport, December 14, leaving issue seven sons and six daughters, his eldest son Edward being Knighted in Ireland in 1599".

SIR EDWARD WARREN, KNT.

(1563 - 1609)

He was baptized April 9, 1563, was knighted 1599 during the Irish Wars of Elizabeth, and was High Sheriff of Cheshire 40 Elizabeth (1598). He married first a daughter of Sir Edward Fitton of Gaws-

worth, Knt., but no issue resulted. He married secondly *circa* 1581
Ann, the daughter of Sir William Davenport of Bramhall, Knt., and by
her had: John, died young; John; Ralph; Humphrey; William; Margaret, died young;·Margaret, died young; Ann; Francis; Margaret;
Catherine; and Anne. His wife died 1597. He married thirdly Susan,
sixth daughter of Sir William Booth, of Dunham-Massey, Knt., and by
her had: George; Edward; Lawrence; Thomas;* Elizabeth; Radcliffe;** Ralph; and Posthumous. The register of Wood Plumpton,
Lancashire reads: "Edward Warren of Poynton, knyght, and baron of
Stockporte, deceased, died at Poynton the 13th daye of November
1609".

JOHN WARREN

(*died* 1621)

Son and heir of Sir Edward Warren, he married on October 28,
1594, Anne, the daughter of George Ognell of Bilsley, Warwickshire.
He died June 20, 1621; his widow survived him many years dying in
1652.

EDWARD WARREN, ESQ.

(1605 - 1687)

Son and heir of John, he was born May 10, 1605, and baptized May
19, following, according to the register of Wood Plumpton Parish. He
was placed under the guardianship of Sir John Radcliffe of Ordall,
Lancashire, Knt., and Humphrey Davenport, Esq. He married first
Margaret, second daughter of Henry Arderne of Harden, near Stockport.

Children

1. Anne Warren, bap. Jan. 21, 1626, married 1650 Edward, son and
   heir of Richard Holland of Denton, Lancashire.
2. John Warren, son and heir.
3. Humphrey Warren, born June 7, 1632, later of Maryland. *q.v.*
4. Henry Warren, born Dec. 18, 1635, rector of Stockport, buried
   May 6, 1674, married Catherine Clayton.
5. Charles Warren, born 1637, died 1645.
6. Edward Warren, born 1639, died 1676.
7. Radcliffe Warren ⎫ Twins, born 1644.
8. Posthumous Warren ⎭

---

*Said to have been killed on Isle of Kent, Md., in 1635, in one of Claiborne's
raids.
**Settled it is said in Charles City County, Va., and later of Surry Co.

The mother died at the birth of her twins and was buried April 20, 1644, at Stockport. He married secondly Anne Hough, widow of Humphrey Booth of Salford, Gent. No issue resulted. She was buried May 31, 1662, at Stockport. By his will dated January 26, 1663, he founded the almshouses at the east side of the old church yard at Stockport and was buried under the arch on the left side of the communion rails in the parish church on September 10, 1687.

BIBLIOGRAPHY

Visitations of Cheshire 1580, 1612, 1663.

Ancient Earls of Warren and Surrey and their Descendants, by Rev. John Watson, pub. 1782.

Manuscripts, British Museum, London.

Parish Registers of Lancashire and Cheshire.

Ormerod's, History of Cheshire.

HUMPHREY WARREN, GENT., OF MARYLAND
(1632 - 1671)

The most difficult task in proving the European background of the American emigrants is documentary evidence for proof of the immediate parentage. And on this point lies the weakness of many assumptions by genealogical researchers as well as genealogists. In establishing facts and circumstances to prove that Humphrey Warren, Merchant, of London and Maryland, was the son of Edward Warren, Gent., of Stockport, Cheshire, apparently only one snag presents itself.

The Rev. John Watson in his excellent discourse stated that "Humphry, born June 7, 1632, brought up a merchant, went into the West Indies, where he married and died *s. p.* about 1680".[1]

Knowing the agnosticism which exists among a limited group of negative genealogists, especially those who wish to denounce the work of others in order to glorify their own importance, this group will contend or hold strictly to the statement made by the Rev. Mr. Watson, disregarding other facts and circumstantial evidence, and will state dogmatically as well as arbitrarily that Humphrey Warren of Maryland was not the son of Edward of Stockport.

It must be remembered that the Rev. Mr. Watson wrote his book more than 100 years after the death of Humphrey of Maryland, and it is known that very few if any of the American descendants of early colonists kept up with their English kinsmen for any great length of time. It may have been an assumption on the part of Mr. Watson or it may have come from the statement of the surviving members of the family in England through ignorance. One can not always accept statements, even though some are official, as absolutely correct.*

Although Humphrey Warren had an uncle by the name of Humphrey, he was more probably named from his father's guardian Humphrey Davenport as it is seen that another son carried the name of Radcliffe, family name of the other guardian. It is possible that he was in the West Indies before his settlement in Maryland, but it is known that Britishers often referred to the West Indies or Virginia, when they meant any part of North America.

---

*Contributory to this point, the compiler of this history was reported killed in action in France during the First World War and it was published in the papers of his home town. While he was injured during the war, he never received a scratch from the enemy's lead. Consequently, it is possible as well as probable that 100 years from now, if he happens to have any surviving heirs, their patrimony may be questioned by some "negative" individual, if the printed statements of his death in 1918 are taken as absolute truth.

Being the second son, he could not inherit the ancestral estates of his parents, so it was only natural that he sought an opportunity to create an estate for himself and heirs. At that time the settlements in America had offered wonderful advantages to mercantile establishments in the seaport towns of Great Britain and it is seen that at a young age Humphrey Warren had established himself at London.

He was in Maryland by 1657, inasmuch as on April 20, 1659, in court he stated that two years ago he saw a "mare of Mr. Starkeys with two stone colts following her".[2] On April 14, 1658, he demanded that the goods of Robert Hill be attached to the value of £25.[3] It is believed that his residence in Maryland was more or less of a temporary nature, inasmuch as until 1662 he referred to himself as "Humphery Warren, of London, Merchant". Later he established his domicile permanently in the Province.

On May 12, 1658, upon a contemplated trip to England he appointed Matthew Stone his attorney to act in his behalf during his absence.[4] He was back in Maryland by 1659, and in that year served on the jury of the Provincial Court.

On January 14, 1660/1, while in Maryland he signed the following statement: "Know all men that by these present that I Humphrey Warren Citizen of London doe Constitute and ordain Captain Nicholas Gwyther my lawful Attorney for me and in my name to arrest William Head, cooper, in action for debt".[5]

On January 27, 1661/2, as "Humpherie Warring London Merchant" he was granted power of attorney for James Walker. It was also shown at the same court in which he proved power of attorney that he had sold several white indentured servants, and on April 22, 1662, he appeared with power of attorney for Edward Walker, London, Merchant, to prosecute claims for the non-payment of debts.[6]

It was not until October 12, 1662, that Humphrey Warren applied for land, and by it we have proof of his transporting his son Humphrey, Jr.[7]

> "Lay out for Humphrey Warren, Merchant, 1000 acres of land, demanded for himself and his son Humphrey and Francis Jenkins and Anne Lane his servants transported in this prest year for which he demands 200 acres".

On December 18, 1662, Humphrey Warren caused a warrant to be issued against George Newman. At court on February 10, 1662/3, George Newman stated that the 1,167 pounds of tobacco demanded by James Walker for the use of Humphrey Warren was due to him (Newman) and not Warren, and requested that Nicholas Gwyther give security.[8]

On May 12, 1663, he registered his cattle and hog marks at the county court. Later in that year he was granted a pass to "depart this Province this yeare for England".

On November 8, 1664, Humphrey Warren accused his servant Richard Lamb of selling his clothing and absenting himself for periods without permission. At the same time he sued James Fox for debt. Also on the same day, Robert Hatton and Thomas Hatton acknowledged a debt of 20,000 pounds of tobacco due to Humphrey Warren, Merchant, and in payment thereof conveyed 250 acres of land beginning at Hatton's Point and extending to Hatton's Creek on the west side of the Wicomico.[9]

In 1664 as the executor of the will of Bridget Heard, he was described as of the Wicomico River which indicates his domicile in that area—the oldest settlement in present Charles County. In the same year "Humphrey Warren Gent." and Francis Pope were ordered to appraise the estate of Walter Story, and also that of Thomas Smoot.

In 1665 he again served on the jury and was referred to as merchant. On December 13, 1667, he was appointed a Commissioner of Peace for Charles County.[10] By an act of the Assembly in 1668 it was ordered that a port be erected "nigh Humphrey Warrens plantacon in Wiccocomoc River".[10]

On September 4, 1669, the Assembly passed an act by which 10,000 pounds of tobacco were to be raised and granted to Capt. Coode, Col. Jowles, and Col. Warren "as a gratuity from this House to the soldiers late in Armes under their command". A careful search fails to disclose any other personage who could be addressed as Colonel Warren, thus it is shown that he was active in military affairs.[11]

He served as a delegate from Charles County to the General Assembly which convened on January 18, 1670/1, but died before the adjournment in March.[12]

It was stated that Humphrey Warren married while in the West Indies. This may be correct. A search through the British records for his marriage has so far proved futile, but it is known that he was married before his settlement in Maryland and was the father of more than one progeny. He brought his son and namesake to Maryland in 1662, but there is no record of his transporting a wife, yet one finds a Mary Warren contemporary with him during his earlier years in the Province. In 1661 Mary Warren was subpoenaed in a case involving James Walker. It is recalled that Humphrey Warren had at one time been attorney for Walker. And in 1663 Humphrey Warren and Mary Warren were subpoenaed at the same time by the Sheriff of Charles County.

One or more of his children remained in England or elsewhere, inasmuch as Humphrey, Jr., referred to a brother who had not settled or come to Maryland.

It is established, however, that he did marry Eleanor ———, who survived him. It is claimed by some that she was the daughter of Thomas Smoot, which is highly probable—though proof is lacking. The dwelling-plantation of Thomas Smoot was also on the Wicomico near to that of Humphrey Warren, but inasmuch as he died intestate in 1668, a complete list of his heirs has not been proved. Two sons have been established, but it is difficult to prove female issue at that date from an intestate.*

The only land patent negotiated by Humphrey Warren was "Frailty" of 300 acrees in 1664, lying on the west side of the Wicomico. Frequently, the Maryland proprietors named their estates after their ancestral homes in the British Isles, but the place-name "Frailty" can not be located, in sofar as this research was carried out.

Before his death, as Humphrey Warren of Hatton's Point, he conveyed to Josias Fendall in trust for his wife Ellen Warren and son Thomas the tract known as "Ffrailty", lying upon the west side of the Wicomico River, for the love which he bore his wife Ellen and for the proper maintainance and education of his youngest son Thomas. The witnesses were Thomas Notley and Thomas Lomax.[13]

At the session of the Assembly on March 27, 1671, it was reported that Humphrey Warren, Sr., a delegate from Charles County, was deceased. He died intestate, and accordingly letters of administration were issued to the widow, as follows:[14]

> "24 April 1671. Administration of all the Singular Goods Chattels Rights and Debts were of Humphrey Warren the Elder late of Charles County intestate deceased was unto Ellinor Warren his widdow (comitted). The Eldest sonne of the said deceased refusing the same. Commission then issued to Henry Adams of Charles County, Gent., to take bond of the said Ellinor, James Walker and Richard Smoot in the sum of 100,000 pounds of tobacco for her administration and according to the form therewith and also to administer ye . . . oath of Administration to the said Administratrix to make Returne of ye bond . . ."

Warrants were issued to Captain Josias Ffendall and Robert Henly to appraise the estate, and to Henry Adams for the administering of their oaths.

---

*See, *The Smoots of Maryland and Virginia*, by Newman.

The widow soon afterwards married Thomas Howell, of Charles County. Apparently the administration of the estate was neglected, as the following appears on the court books:[15]

> "9 May 1673. Came Thomas Howell who married Ellinor the Relict of Humphrey Warren late of Hatton's Point in Charles County intestate deceased and in right of his said wife demanded letters of administration upon the estate of the deceased . . . who was (represented) by Captain William Wheatley the Attorney of William Barret of London Mercht that no administration had been made . . . Thomas Howell of your County Planter who married Ellinor the relict of Humphrey Warren Sr. late of Hatton's Point in Charles County deceased hath in right of his said Wife and prayed letters of administration upon the estate . . . authorize you to take bond of Thomas Howell in the amount of 10,000 pounds of tobacco with James Walker and ———— Tompkinson his sureties . . ."

The inventory of his personal estate was exhibited at court on March 24, 1674/5, and manifested an appraisement of 8,150 pounds of tobacco. Thomas Howell died before the estate was settled, and consequently, Humphrey Warren, II, on April 19, 1677, appeared in court and stated that Thomas Howell had died intestate and left three orphans and requested letters of administration upon the estate. The bond was placed at 15,000 pounds of tobacco, with Major Benjamin Rozer as his surety.

The estate of Thomas Howell was appraised by Colonel John Douglas and Captain Robert Henley and was valued at 11,984 pounds of tobacco. Several white servants appeared among the inventory, but no mention was made of a seal or coat-of-arms.[16]

At the chancery Court in 1679, it was stated that Humphrey Warren, deceased, had assigned several warrants to William Heard.[17]

There is a very colorful case in Maryland regarding Susan Warren, widow of Humphrey Warren, who became the paramour of William Mitchell, one-time member of Lord Baltimore's Council, but inasmuch as this Humphrey Warren was deceased by 1651, and it is known that Humphrey, the Emigrant to Maryland, was alive in 1658, the two can not be the one and the same. He was no doubt a kinsman of the Maryland emigrant, because all parties concerned in this colorful affair were members of the English Gentry, Susan being a daughter of William Smith, Gent.[18]

---

[1] Watson's, vol. 2, p. 147.
[2] Archives, vol. 41, p. 277.
[3] *Ibid.*, vol. 41, p. 52.
[4] *Ibid.*, vol. 41, p. 151.
[5] *Ibid.*, vol. 41, p. 437.
[6] *Ibid.*, vol. 53, pp. 178, 201-3.

⁷ Liber 5, folio 235, Land Office.
⁸ Archives, vol. 53, pp. 318, 327, 353.
⁹ *Ibid.*, vol. 53, pp. 538-9; vol. 49, p. 333.
¹⁰ *Ibid.*, vol. 5, pp. 21, 31.
¹¹ *Ibid.*, vol. 13, p. 247.
¹² *Ibid.*, vol. 51, p. 362.
¹³ Deeds, Liber H no. 2, folio 431.
¹⁴ Test. Pro., Liber 5, folio 43.
¹⁵ *Ibid.*, Liber 5, folio 439.
¹⁶ Inv. & Accts., Liber 4, folio 191.
¹⁷ Archives, vol. 51, p. 297.
¹⁸ *Ibid.*, vol. 10.

COL. HUMPHREY WARREN, GENT[2]

(16— - 1695)

Humphrey Warren, son and heir of Humphrey, was born about 1655, and thus was under age when he was brought to Maryland. In 1674 William Barrett, Jr., of London, merchant, conveyed property to him, the deed of which referred to "judgement against Humphrey Warren Elder father of the said Humphrey Warren".[1]

On March 2, 1675/6, he received his first public office under the Calverts as Gentleman Justice of Charles County.[2] At this time it is evident that he had attained at least his majority. In the same year he received 525 pounds of tobacco for public services.[3]

As early as 1677 he was styled Captain Humphrey Warren, and on July 18, of that year, he exhibited the bond of Walter Davies, the administrator of the estate of Richard Smoot. In the same year he stated before the Prerogative Court that Thomas Howell had died intestate leaving three orphans under age and requested letters of administration on the estate.

On June 8, 1678, he was appointed a coroner of Charles County, and in 1679 he was ordered to make a thorough search for Captain Josias Fendall who was wanted for treason. In 1680 he was again a Gentleman Justice of Charles County as well as the next year.[4] In 1681 he received 360 pounds of tobacco for public services, and in 1683 he was on the commission for the advancement of trade in the Province.[5] In 1689 he signed as one of the loyal protestant subjects of Their Majesties, was on the commission to regulate civil affairs in the county, and succeeded Colonel Edward Pye as the Colonel of Foote in Charles County.[6]

The following letter throws a sidelight on the military events of the day. It was signed by John Courts, dated September 16, 1690, and addressed to Captain Blackistone.[7]

"This day I received a letter from Major Smallwood directed to Coll. Warren and myself where he desires our speedy assistance to

advise with him concerning a late Information given him by the
Emperor of Piscattua last night . . . this day I will goe to Coll.
Warren, Capt. Barton, and Capt. Hoskins".

In 1692 he accounted for 4,914 pounds of tobacco as pay to a captain,
lieutenant, ensign, two sergeants, a drummer, and 10 files of men. The
next year he was High Sheriff of Charles County, when Sir Thomas
Lawrence, Baronet, stated that he was "forceably detained by Coll Warren Sheriff".[8] In 1694 Coll Humphrey Warren was ordered to deliver
Captain John Addison 100 pounds of shot and bullets for use of the
rangers of Charles County.[9]

In 1683 he negotiated his first land patent, when he received a warrant for 280 acres of land which he called "Warren's Discovery". In
1684 he patented "The Cabbin" of 280 acres, and in 1689, "The Tanyard" of 79 acres.

About 1688 John Gooch conveyed to Humphrey Warren a tract of
land lately in the possession of Bridget Legate but then in the possession
of John Gooch her son for the consideration that Warren allow the said
John Gooch "sufficient meat Drink washing lodging and aparrell in
every respect . . . and to provide for his niece Bridget Fafendall until
the age of 16 years or day of marriage". The land adjoined the estates
of John Hatch and John Courts.[10]

It is stated that Humphrey Warren, like his father, had more than
one wife. The only one proved, however, is Margarey, the daughter of
John Cage, and the widow of Robert Rowland. The will of her father
in 1676 named her as Margarey Rowland.[11]

The inventory of the estate of Robert Rowland (Roeland) was appraised on May 12, 1679, by John Ffaning and Thomas Clipsham at a
value of 51,186 pounds of tobacco. Among the assets were servants
Johannah Noble, William Harbot, and John Wray (a boy).[12]

Before July 27, 1680, Humphrey Warren had married the widow as
shown by the following from the proceedings of the court:[13]

> "Humphrey Warren who Married the Relict and admx of Robert
> Rowlants immediately after his death and was . . . to all payment
> proved this account in her behalfe by his oath . . ."

Children of Humphrey Warren

1. Notley Warren, *d.s.p.*
2. Benjamin Warren married Elizabeth Story. *q.v.*
3. Charles Warren, *d.s.p.*
4. John Warren married Judith Townley. *q.v.*
5. Humphrey Warren, *d.s.p.*
6. Mary Warren married Col. John Contee, Philemon Hemsley, and
   William Rogers.

Humphrey Warren held the rank of Colonel of the Foote until his death early in 1695, when he was succeeded by John Addison.[14] He made his will on August 14, 1689, but it was not probated until February 24, 1694/5, by Thomas Burford, John Wilder, John Gooch, and Elizabeth Dutton.[15]

He devised his wife Margarey during life "Hatton's Point" of 500 acres, then to his son Notley. He willed Benjamin a 190-acre portion of "The Hills", lying on the west side of the Wicomico, and 280 acres of "Warren's Discovery", and to Charles he willed 50-acre portion of "The Hills", "Smoot's Purchase", of 100 acres, that had been sold by Edward Smoot, 100-acre portion of "Wicomico's Fields", and a portion of a tract purchased from William Smoot. To John he devised 400 acres of land lying on the west side of the Wicomico, formerly belonging to John Gooch. He provided for an unborn child, leaving it two tracts including "The Town House" of 170 acres. He also referred to the possibility of a brother coming into the Province.

By codicil dated January 21, 1694/5, he named Humphrey as the unborn child mentioned in the main body of the will, and appointed his wife and son Notley as the executors.

On October 15, 1695, "Came Mrs. Margarey Warren, relict of Coll. Humphrey Warren late of Charles County deceased, and petitioned the Honorable Commissary that according to law and custome of this Province shee may have her Palapharnilia allowed unto her she having renounced ye relinquisht her interest to the administration of her deceased husbands estate. That which was granted unto her and ordered that forthwith the executor of the said deceased delivered unto her her bed and furniture, six chairs, and also Ring glass belongin to her roome". She soon afterwards married the widower Thomas Burford.[16]

The inventory of the personal estate of Humphrey Warren was taken on July 18, 1695, and appraised at £552/4. The executor Notley Warren rendered an account on October 7, 1696, and showed a disbursement to Richard Morris "due him from the decease in right of his wife the daughter of Robert Rowland". Thus it was shown that Humphrey Warren had not closed the estate of Robert Rowland.[17]

The third matrimonial adventure of the widow was brief, for the will of Thomas Burford was proved at court on March 1, 1697/8, by John Gooch, Notley Warren, and Richard Morris.[18] Although he failed to mention his wife, during the law suit over his will a Madame Burford is mentioned. He named no heirs of his body, but bequeathed property to his "sons" Benjamin Warren and Charles Warren, "godson" Humphrey Warren, and Notley Warren (no relationship mentioned). Other heirs were his sisters Elizabeth Cattle (Cottrell) and Jane Dodd, and brothers-in-law James Cattle and Richard Dodd.

Letters of administration were issued to Walter Story, with John Theobald as his bondsman. The inventory was exhibited at court on June 28, 1698.

The records of the court show that Richard Boughton summoned the following: James Cottrill and Elizabeth his wife, Richard Dodd and Jane his wife, and George Plater and Ann his wife, with the following notation: "I have command from the Honorable Commissary General to examine the Evidence subscribed to Mr. Burford's Will and request evidence to be brought on 10 March at my house at Nanjemoy".[19]

Notley Warren, namesake and godson of Governor Thomas Notley, was made the administrator of his father's estate in 1695. If he were a son of Margarey, he was therefore not more than 14 years of age, a fact which indicates that Humphrey Warren had contracted an earlier marriage before his union with the relict of Robert Rowlands in 1680. In 1698 Thomas Burford did not refer to him like the other children of Humphrey Warren as "son", but merely Notley Warren.

Notley Warren died intestate without issue. His estate was much involved, and as a consequence letters of administration were granted to John Beane (Bayne) the greatest creditor. On April 23, 1700, the inventory of the personalty was filed at court and showed a value of £219/11/4.

On May 27, 1712, Walter Bayne petitioned the court and "showeth that Notley Warren of Charles County died in 1698 and your petitioner father (as nearest of Kin to witt John Bean) of Charles County and greatest creditor obtained administration". The estate at that time was still unsettled, thereupon Walter Bayne requested that he might close the accounts.[20]

NOTE: Governor John Seymour, supposedly a descendant of the ancient Dukes of Somerset, named Mary Contee as his cousin, by his will of 1708. Mary was the daughter of Humphrey Warren, II, and the second wife of Colonel John Contee.

[1] Deeds, Liber F no. 1, folio 169.
[2] Archives, vol. 15, p. 71.
[3] *Ibid.*, vol. 2, p. 553.
[4] *Ibid.*, vol. 115, pp. 327, 406.
[5] *Ibid.*, vol. 7, pp. 251, 611.
[6] *Ibid.*, vol. 13, pp. 242-3.
[7] *Ibid.*, vol. 8, p. 206.
[8] *Ibid.*, vol. 8, pp. 391, 404, 495.
[9] *Ibid.*, vol. 20, p. 74.
[10] Deeds, Liber P, folio 16.
[11] Wills, Liber 5, folio 289.
[12] Inv. & Accts., Liber 6, folio 665.
[13] Test. Pro., Liber 7a, folio 166.

[14] Archives, vol. 20, p. 109, 130.
[15] Wills, Liber 7, folio 65.
[16] Test. Pro., Liber 16, folio 113.
[17] Adm. Accts., Liber 14, folio 74.
[18] Wills, Liber 6, folio 93.
[19] Test. Pro., Liber 17, folios 138, 150.
[20] Ibid., vol. 22, folio 111.

THOMAS WARREN, GENT.[2]

(16— - 1710)

Thomas Warren, son of Humphrey Warren and Eleanor his wife, was born in Charles County. As a minor he was deeded "Frailty" by his father in 1674, but by 1688 he had attained majority and had married Mary Barton. On May 13, 1688, William Barton, Gent., conveyed to Thomas Warren, planter, and Mary his wife "the natural borne daughter of the said William Barton and for fatherly affections" land near Zachia Swamp adjoining the estates of Nathan Barton and Thomas Smoot, formerly taken up by Daniel Johnson. William Barton signed the deed, while his wife Mary X Barton made her mark. The witnesses were Randolph X Hinson and John Addision.[1]

In the seventeenth century "natural" child implied legitimate blood relationship to distinguish from step-children. The deed furthermore stipulated that in the event that his daughter Mary Warren died without issue, then the land was to revert to the heirs of his daughter Elizabeth Smoot, the wife of Thomas Smoot. Apparently, only one issue resulted from this union, inasmuch as Barton Warren was the only recognized Warren grandchild named in the will of William Barton in 1717.[2]

Thomas Warren married secondly Jane ————, who survived him and who became the mother of at least one of his children.

On June 17, 1689, Richard Ffowke, of Maryland, conveyed to Thomas Warren for five shillings and for the consideration of maintenance the tract "Haggotts Perry" lying on the north side of Piscataway Creek and originally laid out for David Thomas, providing that the tract was delivered to his brother Hallolujah Ffowke upon his 21st birthday. He signed the deed which was witnessed by William Hutchison, Cleborne Lomax, and Edward Tyson.[3]

On January 12, 1690, Thomas Warren deeded to William Harbert for 6,000 pounds of tobacco "Little Ease" which adjoined "Thomas His Choice" and the lands of Edward Price. Robert Middleton and Thomas Whichaley witnessed the sale, but no wife waived dower.[4]

Children of Thomas Warren

1. Barton Warren. q.v.
2. Elizabeth Warren.

3. Sarah Warren.
4. Thomas Warren.
5. ———— Warren.

The Rent Roll of Wicomico Hundred for an unknown date states that Thomas Warren was seized of "Frailty" of 300 acres surveyed June 22, 1663, for Humphrey Warren.

The will of Thomas Warren was dated January 6, 1708, and proved in Charles County on November 23, 1710, by John Lofte, Joseph Bowells, and John Harris, with his widow Jane Warren as the executrix. His widow was devised 50 acres of the dwelling-plantation and a 300-acre portion of "Frailty". Thomas was to receive the dwelling-plantation at the decease of the widow, but in the event that Thomas died without issue then to an unborn child if it were a male, if not, then to Barton. The latter with his sisters, Elizabeth and Sarah, were bequeathed personalty. The sons were to be of age at eighteen years.[5]

The personal estate was small, inasmuch as the bond of the widow and executrix was placed at only £40. John Vinson and John Loffton were the sureties.

---

[1] Deeds, Liber P, folio 6.
[2] Wills, Liber 14, folio 658.
[3] Deeds, Liber P, folio 196.
[4] *Ibid.*, Liber R, folio 142.
[5] Wills, Liber 14, folios 65, 658.

BENJAMIN WARREN[3]

(16— - 1706)

Benjamin Warren, son of Humphrey and Margarey (Cage) Warren, was born in Charles County. His wife was Elizabeth, daughter to Walter and Anne Story. His widow, living as late as 1763, stated that one son, Humphrey, was born to the union, but died the day after that of his father.

The will of Benjamin Warren was dated February 3, 1705/6, and proved in Charles County on February 11, 1705/6, by Richard Morris, John Haly, and Matthew Murphy.

He bequeathed his son, Humphrey, one-half of the personal estate, and the residue to his wife, Elizabeth. In the event of the death of his son, Humphrey, and his widow, then two-thirds to "father" Walter Story, and one-third to his brother, John Warren.[1]

The inventory papers of his personal estate was filed on June 18, 1706. His widow soon married Samuel Hanson and with him filed an account on October 1707.

His widow on May 2, 1763, as Elizabeth Hanson made a long deposition in which she stated to be about 75 years of age, and that Mary the wife of Stephen Compton and Mrs. Anne Dent were sisters and the daughters of John Warren by his wife, Judith Townley. She furthermore stated that she married Benjamin, the brother of John Warren, and that they both were the sons of Humphrey and Margarey Warren. She lived in Picawaxen from 16 to 20 years after she was married to Benjamin Warren.[2]

---

[1] Wills, Liber 3, folio 743.
[2] Pro. Crt., Liber D D no. 2, folio 409.

JOHN WARREN, GENT.[3]

(1687 - 1714)

John Warren, son of Humphrey and Margarey (Cage) Warren, was born about 1687 in Charles County. In 1708 at the probation of the will of Colonel John Contee, he declared himself to be 21 years of age. His wife was Judith Townley.

Children of John and Judith (Townley) Warren

1. Mary Warren married Notley Maddox* and Stephen Compton.
2. Anne Warren married William Dent. *q.v.*

On November 19, 1708, John Warren, Gent., by recorded deed granted to Samuel Hanson and Elizabeth his wife, executrix of Benjamin Warren, all claims to the estate of his deceased brother Benjamin. The witnesses were William Harbert, Robert Yates, and Thomas Court.[1]

In 1710 John Warren administered upon the estates of his brothers, Charles and Humphrey, both of whom had died without issue and intestate. Daniel Dulaney was his bondsman on both occasions. In 1711 Thomas Dent, Sheriff of Charles County, summoned Philemon Hemsley and Mary his wife and John Warren to appear in court regarding the

---

*NOTE: The fact that Mary married first Notley Maddox is proved by one of the most interesting deeds on record, showing ownership of land for five generations. On May 28, 1800, John Maddox, of William and Mary Parish, conveyed to Thomas Harris, of the same parish, Charles County, for £2,250 "all that tract of land which on 26 May 1658 was laid out for William Smoot called the Hills or Smootwood which John Maddox held as heir at law of John Maddox who was eldest son and heir at law of his mother Mary who intermarried with Notley Maddox and said Mary was one of the daughters of John Warren, surviving son of Humphrey Warren and to whom the said tract descended, and also Wicomico Fields which descended to said John Maddox as descendant of Humphrey Warren". "Hanson's Discovery" was also conveyed at the same time to Thomas Harris. (Ref.: Deeds, Liber I B no. 3, folio 215, La Plata.)

unsettled estate of John Courts, and at the same time he summoned Philemon Hemsley in regards to the executorship of the will of Colonel John Contee.[2]

On December 28, 1711, a bond in the amount of £500 was executed by Philemon Hemsley in right of his wife Mary, administratrix *d.b.n.* of Colonel John Courts, deceased. John Warren and Michael Martin were the sureties.[3]

The Rent Roll of an unknown date shows that "John Warren son of Humphrey" was seized of "Smoothly" of 100 acres surveyed January 25, 1652/3, for William Smoot; "West Hatton", of 500 acres surveyed June 22, 1663, for Thomas Hatton; 100-acre portion of "Wicomico Fields", surveyed April 7, 1666, for Thomas Smoot; "Free Booty", surveyed April 7, 1666, for Richard Smoot, all lying in Wicomico Hundred; and "Warren's Discovery", of 280 acres, surveyed July 31, 1683, for Humphrey Warren in Pickawaxen.

The will of John Warren was dated August 12, 1713, and proved in Charles County on February 13, 1713/4, by John Maddox, Alexander Contee, and Thomas Lewis. He devised his wife Judith the dwelling-plantation and the tract "Hatton's Point". Mary received "Rich Thicketts", with the tract of 500 acres adjoining called "The Hills" and "Warren's Discovery". Anne was devised "The Tanyard" and "Smoot's Purchase".[4]

The bond of his widow and executrix was dated February 13, 1713/4, with Philemon Hemsley and William Foster as the sureties. The inventory was filed on February 22, same year. On January 30, 1716/7, John Bruce who had married the widow petitioned the court to pass their account upon the estate of John Warren. Another account was filed by them on May 6, 1720.[5]

Issue resulted from the marriage of the Widow Warren with John Bruce. In 1722 Mary Hemsley, widow of Anne Arundel County, for the love which "I bear to my sister Mrs. Judith Bruce, of Charles County, deceased, do bequeath to her four children"—Charles Bruce the eldest son, Townely Bruce the youngest son, Francis Bruce the eldest daughter, and Elizabeth Bruce the youngest daughter—certain negroes. Madame Hemsley refers to Judith Bruce as "sister", when actually she was a sister-in-law.[6]

[1] Deeds, Liber C no. 2, folio 123.
[2] Test. Pro., Liber 22, folio 82.
[3] *Ibid.*, Liber 22, folio 71.
[4] Wills, Liber 13, folio 627.
[5] Test. Pro., Liber 23, folio 83; Adm. Acts., Liber 2, folio 16.
[6] Deeds, Liber L no. 2, folio 84.

Captain Barton Warren[3]

(16— - 1757)

Barton Warren, son of Thomas and Mary (Barton) Warren, was born in Charles County. He is proved as an issue of the first marriage, inasmuch as he not only carried the maiden name of his mother but was named as grandson in the will of Captain William Barton in 1717.[1] He married twice, but the name of his first wife is unknown. His second wife by whom no issue resulted was the Catholic lady Elizabeth, widow of John Boarman and daughter of Richard and Ann Maria (Neale) Edelen.[2]

Children of Barton Warren

1. Notley Warren married Sarah ————. *q.v.*
2. John Warren married Jane ————. *q.v.*
3. William Barton Warren. *q.v.*
4. Susannah Warren.
5. Edward Warren. *q.v.*
6. Robert Warren.
7. Jane Warren married Barton Hungerford. Issue: Thomas Taylor; Mary; Elizabeth; Jane; Susan; and Sarah.
8. Mary Warren married Harrison Musgrove and John Stone.*

He was active in the colonial militia and an old muster roll dated 1748 shows him to have commanded a Company of Foote.**

Barton Warren dated his will February 3, 1757/8, in the presence of Charles Bruce, John Ford, and William Brown, all three of whom proved it on March 9, 1757/8. Elizabeth Warren his widow was granted dower in the landed estate and one-third of the dwelling-plantation "Frailty" during life and one-third of the personal estate. Notley and John were devised the dwelling-plantation equally, John having the land next to Robert Yates. William Barton was willed "Stripe" at Port Tobacco. Susannah, Edward, and Robert were left personalty. Thomas Warren, his brother, was left wearing apparel. The residue of the estate was to be divided among the eight named children—Jane Hungerford, Mary Musgrove, Notley Warren, John Warren, William Barton Warren, Susannah Warren, Edward Warren, and Robert Warren.[3]

The bond of Notley Warren and John Warren was dated March 15, 1757/8, with Robert Yates and Thomas Dutton as the sureties. The inventory was returned on March 20, 1757/8, at which time William Barton Warren signed as the next of kin. At an additional

---

*For the ancestry and descendants of Mary (Warren) Stone, *see,* Newman's *The Stones of Poynton Manor.*

**Box 1, folder 4a, Hall of Records.

inventory in 1758, William Warren and Mary Musgrove signed as the kinsmen. The final account was rendered on June 6, 1758, and showed a balance of £941/11/7, distributed to the widow, Thomas Warren, Susannah Warren, Edward Warren, Robert Warren, Jane Hungerford, Mary Musgrove, John Warren, and William Barton Warren.[4]

The will of his widow, Elizabeth Warren, was dated July 3, 1769, and admitted to probate in Charles County on March 4, 1771, by Edward Edelen, John Smoot, and Charles Bradley. She bequeathed her son, Richard Boarman, "Widow's Discovery", and named the following heirs: Sons Joseph Boarman and Raphael Boarman; daughter Henrietta Thompson; and grandchildren Elizabeth Thompson, Jane Thompson, Baltis Thompson, and greatgranddaughter Anne Bradford, the daughter of Eleanor Bradford.[5]

The bond of her executor, Raphael Boarman, was dated March 20, 1771, and placed at £1,500, with William Barton Smoot of William and William Cooksey as his sureties. The inventory was filed five days later, when Joseph Boarman, Sr., and Richard Boarman signed as the next of kin.

---

[1] Wills, Liber 14, folio 568.
[2] Crt. Rec., Liber B no. 2, folio 340, La Plata.
[3] Wills, Liber 30, folio 275.
[4] Balance Book, Liber 2, folio 92.
[5] Wills, Liber 38, folio 231.

NOTLEY WARREN[4]
(1736 - 1768)

Notley Warren, son to Barton, was born in William and Mary Parish, in or about 1736, inasmuch as he declared himself to be 32 years of age in January 1768. His wife was Sarah ————.

Children of Notley and Sarah Warren

1. Sarah Warren married Robert Massey, May 3, 1783, Wm. and Mary Par., Chas. Co.
2. Charity Warren, born Nov. 1765, married John Briscoe.
3. Joanna Warren married Robert Rogers. *q.v.*

Notley Warren was made the executor of the estate of his brother-in-law, Barton Hungerford, and the guardian of his orphan children.

On March 15, 1758, Notley Warren and Thomas Dutton were sureties for Mary Maddox, the executrix of Notley Maddox, late of Charles County. On April 29, 1760, he and John Warren were sureties for Mary Musgrove, the administrator of Harrison Musgrove. The bond was placed at £350. In 1765 he administered upon the estate of Barton Hungerford, with Stephan Compton and Richard Smith as his sureties.[1]

The will of Notley Warren was dated July 19, 1768, and proved in Charles County on October 29, 1768, by John MacPherson, Jon Yates, and John Scott. He bequeathed his wife Sarah the estate in its entirety, but in the event that she remarried then only her third. The daughters all unnamed were to have their share at marriage. He appointed his brother John Warren and friends Stephen Compton and Joseph Joy as the trustees. His widow and friend Major Zachariah Bond, of St. Mary's County, were named as executors.[2]

The bond of his executrix, Sarah Warren, was dated October 29, 1768, at which time John Warren, Stephen Compton, and William Maddox were the bondsmen. The inventory was filed on January 28, 1769, with John Warren and Edward Warren as the kinsmen. By 1770 the widow had married James Maddox. On March 20, 1771, they both filed an account with the court. The final distribution of £708/0/4 was made by James Maddox.[3]

The court on June 27, 1768, placed Charity Warren, the daughter of Notley Warren "aged 13 9 November next" under the guardianship of Robert Rogers.[4]

On June 24, 1784, Robert Rogers, of Charles County, and Joana his wife, conveyed lands to Thomas Hungerford. At the same time Thomas Hungerford and Jane Hungerford conveyed "Batchelor's Delight" to Robert Rogers and Joana his wife. The deed stated that Jane Hungerford was the mother of Thomas Hungerford and had a dower interest in the tract. Violetta Hungerford, wife of Thomas, waived dower rights.[5] On the same day Robert Massey, of King George County, Virginia, and Sarah his wife "one of the coheirs of Notley Warren" deeded to Thomas Hungerford one-quarter portion of the 280-tract "Frailty", of which Notley Warren died seized.[6]

On September 27, 1785, John Briscoe, of Pittsylvania County, Virginia, and Charity his wife "one of the coheirs of Notley Warren" conveyed to Thomas Hungerford one-quarter portion of "Frailty".[7]

---

[1] Test. Pro., Liber 27, folios 29, 377.
[2] Wills, Liber 36, folio 646.
[3] Test. Pro., Liber 44, folios 91, 219.
[4] Deeds, Liber A F no. 7, folio 178.
[5] *Ibid.*, Liber Z no. 3, folios 105, 107.
[6] *Ibid.*, Liber Z no. 3, folio 89.
[7] *Ibid.*, Liber Z no. 3, folio 174.

JOHN WARREN[4]

(17— - 1773)

John Warren, son of Captain Barton Warren, was born at the ancestral plantation "Frailty" on the Wicomico. His wife was Jane ————, who was bequeathed property in the will of Sarah Maddox probated in 1761.

Children of John and Jane Warren

1. Anne Warren married Burford Cotterel.
2. John Warren married Elizabeth Shaw, Sept. 20, 1786, Wm. and Mary Parish.
3. Elizabeth Warren married Dec. 23, 1781, Henry Smoot.*
4. Eleanor Warren married Nov. 21, 1786, Clement Billingsley, Wm. and Mary Parish.

On November 12, 1760, John Warren with John Marshall was surety for Robert Yates, the administrator of Charles Yates. On April 26, 1766, he and Notley Warren were the executors of John Hungerford at which time William Warren and Charles Brandt were their sureties. On March 29, 1770, he and John Marshall signed the bond of Jane Hungerford, the executrix of Barton Hungerford.[1]

The will of John Warren was dated December 21, 1771, and proved in Charles County on November 10, 1773. He named his eldest daughter, Anne Warren, the executrix of his estate and appointed Samuel Love and Stephen Compton as trustees. Anne was bequeathed various negroes and 30 pounds of tobacco "due from my brother William Barton Warren of Virginia". Personalty was bequeathed to the three children—John, Elizabeth, and Eleanor, with the residue of the estate being divided among the four children. Mrs. Small was given the privilege of living at the plantation with the children if she desired.[2]

The bond of Anne Warren, the executrix, was dated November 11, 1773, and placed at £1,000. Samuel Love and Stephen Compton were the sureties. Her account in September 1775, as Anne Warren was passed by the Deputy Commissary of the court.[3]

On May 9, 1778, the inventory and final account upon the estate was rendered by Anne Cotterel, formerly Anne Warren and wife of Burford Cotterel as the executrix. Edward Warren and Robert Warren signed the inventory as the next of kin, while Samuel Love and Stephen Compton were the bondsmen. The balance due to heirs was £696/3/7.[4]

---

*For ancestry of Henry Smoot, *see,* Newman's *The Smoots of Maryland and Virginia.*

A case before the Chancery Court of Maryland, filed on July 24, 1798, by Zereal Penn and Burford Cotterel, showed that in 1764 John Warren and William Penn, both of Charles County, since deceased, became the sureties for Robert Yates, the administrator of Jonathan Yates, to the value of £1,200. Zereal Penn was the only brother and representative of William Penn who at his death left no issue, and Burford Cotterel was the husband of Anne, the daughter of executor of John Warren, deceased. Robert Yates died without settling the estate of Jonathan Yates, and the said Robert Yates left an only daughter Anne, unmarried, aged 40, deaf, dumb, and *non compos mentis*.[5]

---

[1] Test. Pro., Libers 41, folio 377; 43, folio 535.
[2] Wills, Liber 39, folio 431.
[3] Test. Pro., Liber 45, folio 234.
[4] Liber A F no. 7, folios 147.
[5] Chancery Papers no. 3935.

WILLIAM BARTON WARREN[4]

William Barton Warren, son of Barton and his first wife, was born in Charles County. By the terms of his father's will, he received "Strife", which on April 6, 1761, he sold to Jacob B. Morris for a consideration of £183. John Winter and George Dent witnessed the deed, but no wife waived dower.[1] On April 26, 1766, he and Notley Warren signed the administration bond of John Gwynn, administrator of Susannah Gwynn.[2] He was subsequently appointed the administrator of John Gwynn, when on August 12, 1768, Charles Brandt and Edward Warren signed his bond in the value of £500.[3] On September 26, 1768, "William Warren" conveyed to Philip Richard Fendall for £160 "Batton's Clifts" and "Three Brothers". Jane Warren, his wife, waived dower, and Daniel of St. Thomas Jenifer and Samuel Jones witnessed.[4] On May 26, 1769, as the administrator *d.b.n.* of John Gwynn, he filed an account with the court.[5]

He later settled in the State of Virginia. An undocumented source stated that he was born 1738, married 1773 Mary Jane Yates, and died 1818. Another source states that he died at Georgetown, Kentucky, in 1809.

---

[1] Deeds, Liber G no. 3, folio 530.
[2] Test. Pro., Liber 41, folio 378.
[3] *Ibid.*, Liber 43, folio 103.
[4] Deeds, Liber O no. 3, folio 500.
[5] Test. Pro., Liber 43, folio 271.

ENSIGN EDWARD WARREN[4]

Edward Warren, son to Barton, was born in William and Mary Parish, Charles County. During March 1774 the court issued citations against him as the administrator of Susan Gwynn. In 1775 he signed the petition to the Maryland Convention asking clemency for Patrick Graham of Port Tobacco. On September 12, 1775, he signed the bond of his sister Mary Stone as the executrix of her deceased husband's estate. In March 1778 he took the oath of fidelity and allegiance to the State of Maryland in Charles County before the Worshipful John Lancaster of William and Mary Parish.[1] On May 28, 1779, he was commissioned an ensign in the militia company of Captain Jonathan Yates, of Charles County.

---

[1] Unpub. Md. Rec., vol. 5, DAR.

JOHN WARREN[5]

(1759 - ——)

John Warren, only son of John and Jane his wife, was born October 21, 1759, at "Frailty" on the Wicomico. On June 17, 1778, at the age of 18 years, he made choice of his brother-in-law Burford Cotterel as guardian.[1] In March 1778, he subscribed to the patriot's oath in Charles County before Magistrate George Dent.[2] On January 17, 1786, he conveyed to Burford Cotterll for £800 "Frailty" which had been "originally granted unto a certain Barton Warren grandfather of the said John Warren for 496 acres". No wife waived dower, while the witnesses were Walter Winter and B. Ferndall.[3] On September 20, 1786, he was married by the rector of William and Mary Parish to Elizabeth Shaw.

---

[1] Deeds, Liber A F no. 7, folio 134.
[2] Unpub. Md. Rec., vol. 5, DAR.
[3] Deeds, Liber Z no. 3, folio 216.

JOANNA WARREN[5]

Joanna Warren, daughter to Notley Warren and Sarah his wife, was born in Charles County, Maryland. Prior to 1784 she married Robert Rogers of the same county.

In 1768 Robert Rogers was appointed the guardian of Charity Warren who was then the sister of his future wife. The census of 1775-76 shows him domiciled in Port Tobacco East Hundred of Charles County. During March 1778, he subscribed to the patriot's oath of fidelity before Magistrate George Dent.*

In 1790 Robert Rogers was the head of a family in Charles County with two males under 16, eight females, and eleven slaves completing his immediate household. Sometime after this year he and his family removed to Fauquier County, Virginia, where he spent the remaining years of his life.

The following list of children may or may not be complete:

1. Notley Warren Rogers married Eleanor Walters. Issue: Mary Jane, born Dec. 17, 1814; Robert Richard, born Jan. 9, 1817; William Warren, born Apr. 8, 1819; Rachel Ann, born Oct. 29, 1821; Thomas Notley, born Apr. 13, 1824; Sarah Catherine, born Nov. 13, 1826; Elizabeth Frances, born Dec. 29, 1829; Louisa Ellen, born Apr. 8, 1831; Virginia, born July 20, 1832; Henry Clay, born Apr. 10, 1835.
2. Elizabeth Rogers.
3. Polly Rogers.

---

*Unpub. Md. Records, DAR Library. A Robert Rogers enlisted as a private May 1, 1777, in 5th Md. Regt. (Archives, vol. 18, p. 240.) He was probably not the one of Charles County, inasmuch as the 5th Regt. was of the Maryland Line and the enlistment was for 3 years.

INDEX OF PERSONS AND LAND TRACTS

CPSIA information can be obtained at www.ICGtesting.com
Printed in the USA
BVOW041934210812

298477BV00005B/111/P